by Elizabeth Castro

XML for the World Wide Web:
Visual QuickStart Guide
by Elizabeth Castro

Peachpit Press
1249 Eighth Street
Berkeley, CA 94710
(510) 524-2178
(510) 524-2221 (fax)

Find us on the World Wide Web at: http://www.peachpit.com
Or check out Liz's Web site at http://www.cookwood.com/
Or contact Liz directly at xml@cookwood.com

Peachpit Press is a division of Addison Wesley Longman

Cover design: The Visual Group

ISBN: 0-201-71098-6

0 9 8 7 6 5 4 3 2 1

Printed in the United States of America

This book about 21st century technology
is dedicated
to all those people
who are working to conserve our earth
and its amazingly diverse population
for centuries to come.

We can only save the tiger from extinction
if we try.

Special thanks to:

Nancy Davis, *at Peachpit Press, who I'm happy to report is not only my awesome editor, but also my friend. This book would not exist without her.*

Kate Reber, *at Peachpit Press, for her careful eye and skillful hand, who made sure that the final book looked really sharp.*

Noah Mendelsohn, *of Lotus Development Corporation and the W3C's XML Schema Working Group, whose generous, precise, and detailed answers to my queries immeasurably improved the schema and namespaces chapters.*

Andreu Cabré, *for his feedback, for his work on the new XML Web site (http://www.cookwood.com/xml), for keeping the rest of my life going as I worked on this book, and for sharing his life with me.*

TABLE OF CONTENTS

Part 3: XML Schema and Namespaces

Part 4: XSLT and XPath

Part 5: Cascading Style Sheets

Part 6: XLink and XPointer

Appendices

Index, Colophon, and Note

INTRODUCTION

Clearly, the Internet is changing the world. In the last ten years, since Tim Berners-Lee designed the World Wide Web (1991) and Marc Andreesen and company developed Netscape—née Mosaic (1993)—to display it on any PC or Mac, the Internet has gone from interesting to essential, from ancillary to completely central. Web sites are now a required part of a business' infrastructure, and often part of one's personal life as well. The amount of information available through the Internet has become practically uncountable. No one knows exactly how many Web pages are out there, although the number is probably close to two billion, give or take a few.

Almost all of those pages are written in HTML—HyperText Markup Language—a simple but elegant way of formatting data with special tags in a text file that can be viewed on virtually any computer platform. While HTML's simplicity has helped fuel the popularity of the Web—*anyone* can create a Web page—it also presents real limitations when faced with the Web's huge and growing quantity of information.

XML, or Extensible Markup Language, while based on the same parent technology as HTML, is designed to better handle the task of managing information that the growth of the Internet now requires. While XML demands a bit more attention at the start, it returns a much larger dividend in the end. In short, HTML lets everyone do some things, but XML let's some people do practically anything. This book will show you how to begin.

The Problem with HTML

HTML's success is due to its simplicity, ease of use, and tolerance. HTML is easy-going: it doesn't care about upper- and lowercase letters, it's flexible about quotation marks, it doesn't worry excessively about closing tags. Its tolerance makes it accessible to everyone.

But HTML's simplicity limits its power. Since HTML's tags are mostly formatting-oriented, they do not give information about the content of a Web page, and thus make it hard for that information to be reused in another context. Since HTML is not obsessive about case and punctuation, browsers have to work twice as hard to display HTML content properly.

And because HTML is limited with respect to formatting and dynamic content, numerous extensions have been tacked on, usually in a hurry, in order to add power. Unfortunately, these extensions usually only work in some browsers, and thus the pages that use them are limited to visitors who use those particular browsers.

```
code.html
<BODY bgcolor=#ffcc99 text=red leftmargin=5>

<center><img src=tiger.jpg></center>

Animal species are disappearing from the earth at
a frightening speed.

<P>According to the World Wildlife Federation, at
present rates of extinction, as much as a third of the
world's species could be gone in the next 20 years.

<hr width=50% size=5 noshade>
```

Figure i.1 *Here is a bit of perfectly reasonable HTML code. Notice how there are no opening* HTML *or* HEAD *tags (and no* TITLE*). Some of the tags are uppercase and some are lowercase. One is not even part of the standard HTML specifications (*leftmargin*). None of the values are enclosed in quotation marks (not even the URL). The* P *tag has no matching closing* </P> *tag, and there is an attribute with no value at all (or a value with no attribute, depending on how you look at it):* noshade *(in the* hr *tag).*

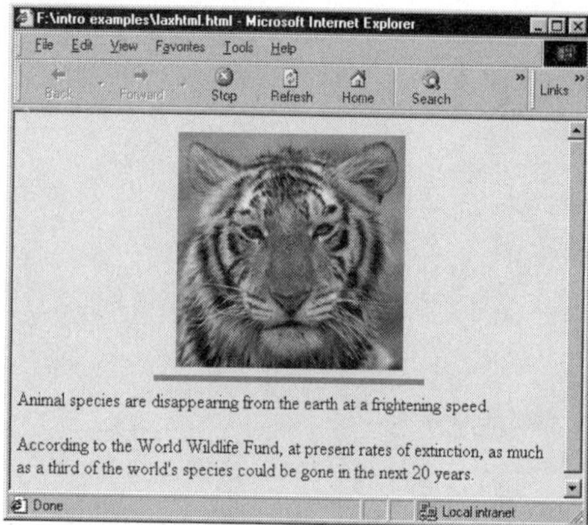

Figure i.2 *Despite the looseness of the HTML, the page is displayed quite correctly.*

```
code.xml
<?xml version="1.0" encoding="UTF-8"?>
<endangered_species>
<animal>
<name language="English">Tiger</name>
<name language="Latin">panthera tigris</name>
<threats>
<threat>poachers</threat>
<threat>habitat destruction</threat>
<threat>trade in tiger bones for traditional Chinese
    medicine (TCM)</threat>
</threats>
<weight>500 pounds</weight>
<length>3 yards from nose to tail</length>
<source sectionid="101" newspaperid="21"/>
<picture filename="tiger.jpg" x="200" y="197"/>
<subspecies>
<name language="English">Amur or
    Siberian</name>
<name language="Latin">P.t. altaica</name>
<region>Far East Russia</region>
<population year="1999">445</population>
</subspecies>
...
</endangered_species>
```

Figure i.3 *At first glance, XML doesn't look so different from HTML: it is populated with tags, attributes, and values. Notice in particular how the tags describe the contents that they enclose. XML is, however, written much more strictly, the rules of which we'll discuss in Chapter 1, Writing XML.*

The Power of XML

The answer to the lenient but limited HTML is XML, Extensible Markup Language. From the outside, XML looks a lot like HTML, complete with tags, attributes, and values **(Figure i.3)**. But rather than serving as a language just for creating Web pages, XML is a language for *creating other languages*. You use XML to design your own custom markup language and then you use that language to format your documents. Your custom markup language, officially called an *XML application*, will contain tags that actually describe the data that they contain.

And herein lies XML's power: If a tag identifies data, that data becomes available for other tasks. A software program can be designed to extract just the information that it needs, perhaps join it with data from another source, and finally output the resulting combination in another form for another purpose. Instead of being lost on an HTML-based Web page, labeled information can be reused as often as necessary.

But, as always, power comes with a price. XML is not nearly as lenient as HTML. To make it easy for XML *parsers*—software that reads and interprets XML data, either independently or within a browser—XML demands careful attention to upper- and lowercase letters, quotation marks, closing tags and other minutiae happily ignored by HTML authors. And while I think this persnickety character of XML may keep it from becoming a tool for creating personal Web pages, XML certainly gives Web designers the power to manage information on a grand scale.

XML's Helpers

XML in and of itself is quite simple. It is XML's sister technologies that harness its power.

A *schema* defines the custom markup language that you create with XML. Either written as a DTD or with the XML Schema language, a schema specifies which tags you can use in your documents, and which tags and attributes those tags can contain. You'll learn about DTDs in Part 2 *(see page 33)* and XML Schema in Part 3 *(see page 67)*.

Perhaps the most powerful tools for working with XML documents are XSLT, or *Extensible Stylesheet Language - Transformation*, and XPath. XSLT lets you extract and transform the information into any shape you need. For example, you can use XSLT to create summary and full versions of the same document. And perhaps most importantly, you can use XSLT to convert XML into HTML. XPath is a system for identifying the different parts of the document. XSLT and XPath are described in detail in Part 4 *(see page 133)*.

Since you create your XML tags from scratch, it shouldn't come as a surprise to hear that those tags have no inherent formatting: How can a browser know how to format the `<animal>` tag? The answer is it can't. It is your job to specify how a given tag should be displayed. While there are two main systems for formatting XML documents, XSL-FO and CSS, only CSS *(Cascading Style Sheets)* has strong, albeit incomplete, support by browsers. You'll learn about CSS in Part 5 *(see page 175)*.

Finally, XLink and XPointer add links and embedded images to XML. While the specifications for both are considered final, neither has been incorporated into any major browser. In other words, they don't work yet. Still, since they are an integral part of XML, you can begin to get a taste of them in Part 6 *(see page 223)*.

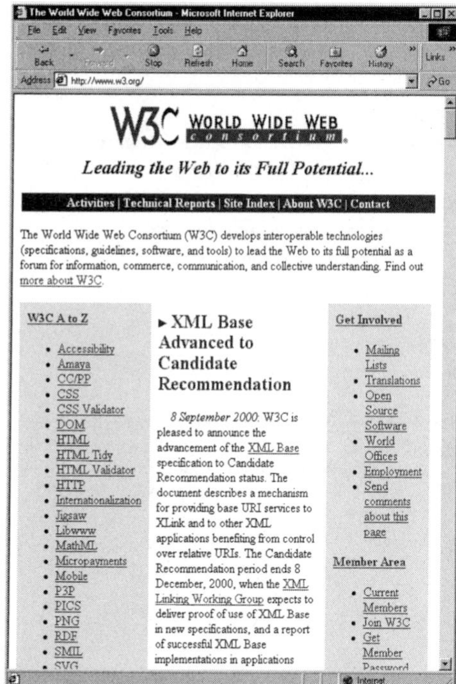

Figure i.4 *The World Wide Web Consortium (http://www.w3.org) is the main standards body for the Web. You can find the official specifications there for all of the languages discussed in this book, including XML (and DTDs), XML Schema and Namespaces, XSLT and XPath, CSS, XLink and XPointer, and of course HTML and XHTML.*

XML in the Real World

Unfortunately, the reality of using XML is still not quite up to the vision. While a few browsers can view XML documents right now—namely Internet Explorer 5 (for both Macintosh and Windows) and the beta versions of Netscape 6 (also called Mozilla)—older browsers simply treat XML files as strange bits of text.

The biggest impediment to serving XML pages, however, is that no browser supports XLink or XPointer. And that means, no browser can show links or images on an XML page. Until this is solved, nobody will be serving XML pages directly.

The temporary solution is to use XML to manage and organize information and then to use XSLT to convert those XML documents into the already widely accepted HTML for viewing on a browser. In this way, you benefit from XML's power at the same time that you take advantage of HTML's universality.

The World Wide Web Consortium (W3C), recommends using *XHTML*—a system of writing HTML tags with XML's strict rules—as an intermediary step between HTML and XML. I find XHTML problematic: you lose HTML's easy going nature but don't gain XML's information-labeling power. Still, I'll discuss how to write and use XHTML in Appendix A, *XHTML*.

Theoretically, you could use Explorer 5 for Windows' supposed support for XSLT to serve XML pages and transform them on the fly, in the visitor's browser. Unfortunately, Explorer does not support the standard version of XSLT (sound familiar?) but instead supports a combination of an older version along with some extensions that Microsoft decided would be neat. I therefore recommend that, at least for the time being, you use an external XSLT processor for transforming XML documents into HTML, as described in Chapter 10, *XSLT* and on page 246.

About This Book

This book is divided into six major parts: Writing XML, DTDs, XML Schema, XSLT and XPath, CSS, and XLink and XPointer. Each part contains one or more chapters with step-by-step instructions that explain how to perform specific XML-related tasks. Wherever possible, I display the code under discussion together with a representation of what that code will look like in a browser.

I often talk about two or more different documents on the same page, perhaps an XSLT document and the XML file that it will transform. You can tell what kind of document is in question by looking at the header above it **(Figure i.5)**. Also pay careful attention to text and images highlighted in red; they're generally the focus of the discussion for that page.

I also recommend that you download the example files from the Web site *(see page 18)* and have them handy as you work through the different parts. In many cases, it's impossible to show an entire document on each page, and yet it's helpful to see it. Having a paper printout could prove very useful.

Most of the browser shots in this book were taken with Internet Explorer 5 for Windows for the simple reason that it is the browser that best supports the features being talked about. Be aware, however, that your visitors may use some other browser and some other platform. It is extremely important to keep in mind who you're designing the site for and what browsers that audience is likely to use. Then test your pages on all of those browsers to make sure they display acceptably.

You should be at least somewhat familiar with HTML, although you don't need to be an expert coder, by any stretch. No other previous knowledge is required.

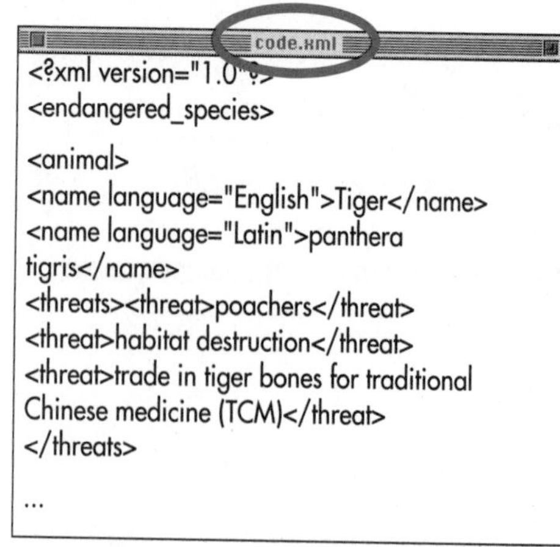

Figure i.5 *You can tell this is an example of XML code because of the title bar. (You'll usually be able to tell pretty easily anyway, but just in case you're in doubt, here's an extra clue.)*

What This Book is Not

XML is an incredibly powerful system for managing information. You can use it in combination with many, many other technologies. You should know that this book is not—nor does it try to be—an exhaustive guide to XML. Instead, it is a beginner's guide to using XML for creating Web pages.

This book won't teach you about the DOM, SAX, SOAP, or XML-RPC. Nor will it teach you JavaScript, Java, or ASP, also commonly used with XML. Many of these topics deserve their own books (and have them). While there are numerous ancillary technologies that can work with XML documents, this book focuses on the core elements of XML: XML itself, schemas, transformations, styling, and links. These are the basic topics you need to cover in order to start creating your own XML-based Web sites.

Sometimes, especially when you're starting out, it's more helpful to have clear, specific, easy-to-grasp information about a smaller set of topics, rather than general wide-ranging data about everything under the sun. My hope is that this book will give you a solid foundation in XML and its core technologies which will enable you to move on to the other pieces of the puzzle, once you're ready.

The XML VQS Web Site

On the *XML for the World Wide Web: Visual QuickStart Guide* Web site *(http://www.cookwood.com/xml/)*, you'll be able to find and download all of the examples from this book. You'll also find links to all of the various tools that I use, including XML parsers, XSLT processors, and Schema validators.

The *XML for the World Wide Web: Visual QuickStart Guide* Web site will also contain additional support material, including an online table of contents and index, a question and answer section, updates, and more.

Peachpit's companion site

Peachpit Press, the publisher of this book, also offers a companion Web site with the full table of contents, all of the example files, an excerpt from the book, and a list (hopefully short) of errata. You can find it at *http://www.peachpit.com/vqs/xml/*.

Questions?

I welcome your questions and comments on my special XML Question and Answer board *(http://www.cookwood.com/xml/qanda/)*. Answering questions publicly lets me help more people at the same time (and gives readers the opportunity to help each other). You will also find instructions on my site for contacting me personally, should that be necessary.

Part 1: XML

Writing XML

XML is a grammatical system for constructing custom markup languages. For example, you might want to use XML to create a language for describing genealogical, mathematical, chemical, or business data.

Since every custom language created with XML depends on XML's underlying grammar, that is where we will begin. In this chapter, you will learn the basics rules for writing documents in XML, and thus, in any custom language created with XML.

I have to admit here that custom markup languages created with XML are officially called *XML applications.* The word application has the sense of "use" as in "an application of XML". But for me, an application is a full-blown software program, like Photoshop. I find the term so imprecise, that I usually try to avoid it.

Tools for Writing XML

XML, like HTML, can be written with any text editor or word processor, including the very basic TeachText or SimpleText on the Macintosh and Notepad or Wordpad for Windows. There are some specialized text editors that can test your XML as you write it. And finally, there are several mainstream programs that have filters that can convert other kinds of documents (from layout programs, spreadsheets, databases, and others) into XML.

I'll assume that you know how to create new documents, open old ones for editing, and save them. Be sure and save all your XML documents with the .xml extension.

Elements, Attributes, and Values

XML uses the same building blocks that HTML does: elements, attributes, and values. An XML *element* is the most basic unit of your document. It can contain practically anything else, including other elements and text. An element has an opening tag with a name—written between less than (<) and greater than (>) signs—and sometimes attributes **(Figure 1.1)**. The name, which you invent yourself, should describe the element's purpose and in particular its contents, if any, which immediately follow the opening tag. An element is generally concluded with a closing tag, comprised of the same name preceded with a forward slash, enclosed in the familiar less than and greater than signs.

Attributes, which are contained within an element's opening tag, have quotation-mark delimited values that further describe the purpose and content (if any) of the particular element **(Figure 1.2)**. Information contained in an attribute is generally considered metadata, that is, they contain information *about the data* in the XML document, as opposed to being that data itself. An element can have as many attributes as necessary, as long as each has a unique name.

The rest of this chapter is devoted to writing elements, attributes, and values.

White Space

You can add extra white space around the elements in your XML code to make it easier to edit and view **(Figure 1.3)**. While extra white space is passed to the parser, both IE5 and Mozilla (Netscape 6's beta version) ignore it—as they do with HTML.

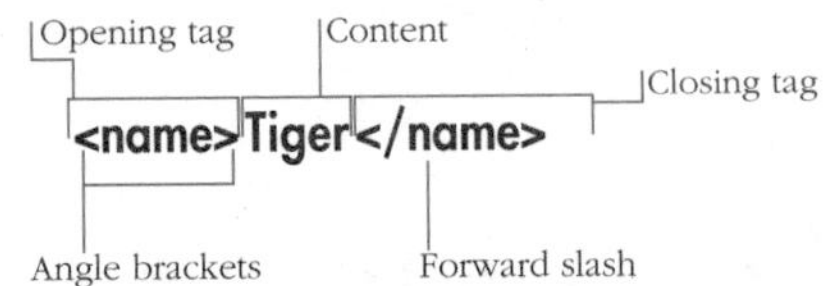

Figure 1.1 *A typical element is comprised of an opening tag, content, and a closing tag. This* `name` *element contains text.*

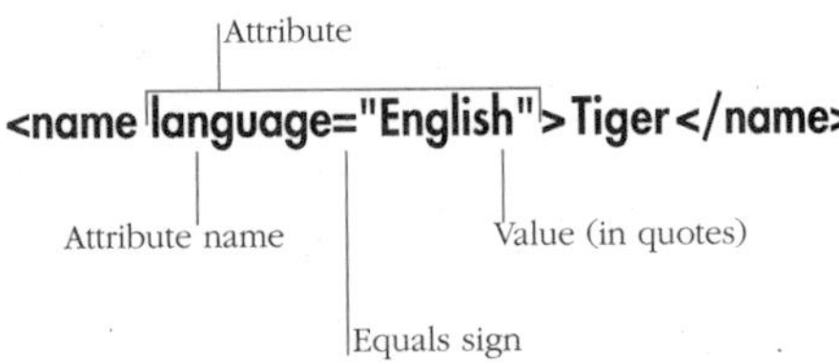

Figure 1.2 *The* `name` *element now has an attribute called* `language` *whose value is* English. *Notice that the word* English *isn't part of the* `name` *element's content. The name isn't* English, *or even* English Tiger. *Rather, the attribute* describes *that content.*

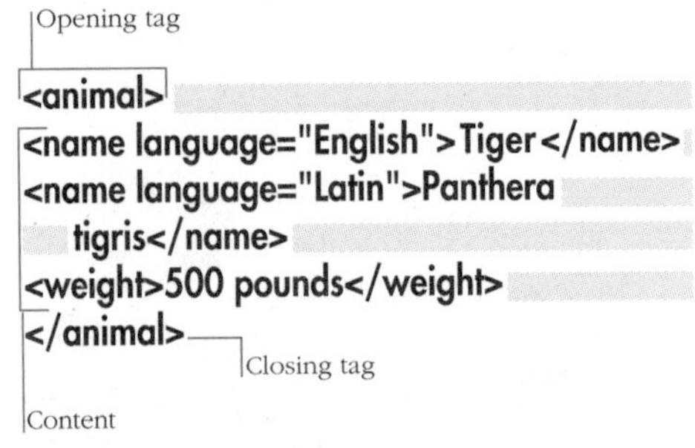

Figure 1.3 *The* `animal` *element shown here contains three other elements (two* `name` *elements and a* `weight` *element) but no text. The* `name` *and* `weight` *elements contain text, but no other elements. Notice also that I've added extra white space (pink, in this illustration), to make the code easier to read.*

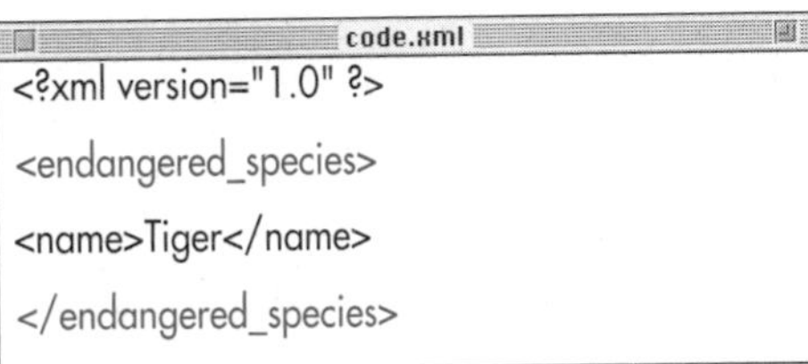

```
<?xml version="1.0" ?>
<endangered_species>
<name>Tiger</name>
</endangered_species>
```

Figure 1.4 *In a well-formed document, there must be one element (*`endangered_species`*) that contains all other elements. The first line is a processing instruction and is allowed outside of the root.*

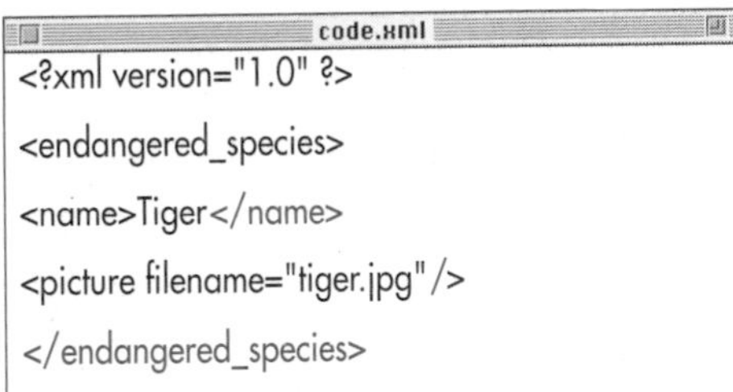

```
<?xml version="1.0" ?>
<endangered_species>
<name>Tiger</name>
<picture filename="tiger.jpg" />
</endangered_species>
```

Figure 1.5 *Every element must be enclosed. Empty elements can have an all-in-one opening and closing tag with a final slash. Notice that they are properly* nested, *that is, there are no overlapping elements.*

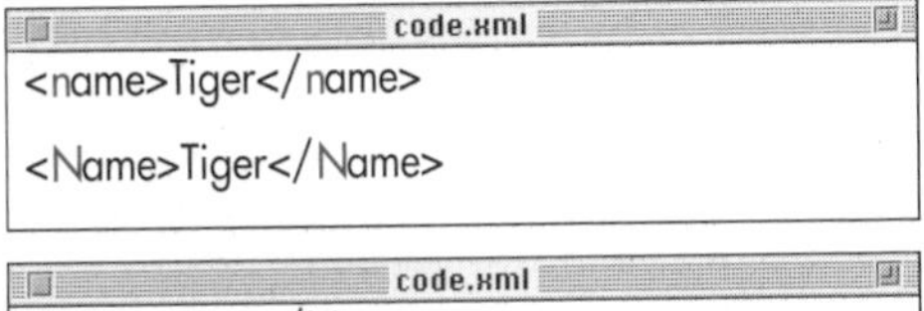

```
<name>Tiger</name>
<Name>Tiger</Name>
```

```
<name>Tiger</Name>
```

Figure 1.6 *The top example is legal, if confusing. The two elements are considered completely independent. The bottom example is incorrect since the opening and closing tags do not match.*

```
<picture filename="tiger.jpg"/>
```

Figure 1.7 *Those quotation marks are required. They can be single or double, as long as they match.*

Rules for Writing XML

In order to be as flexible—and powerful—as possible, XML has a structure that is extremely regular and predictable, defined by a set of rules, the most important of which are described below. If your document satisfies these rules, it is considered *well-formed.* Once a document passes the "well-formed threshold", it can be displayed in a browser.

A Root element is required

Every XML document must contain one root element that contains all of the other elements in the document. The only pieces of XML allowed outside (preceding) the root element are comments and processing instructions **(Figure 1.4)**.

Closing tags are required

Every element must have a closing tag. Empty tags can either use an all-in-one opening and closing tag with a slash before the final > **(Figure 1.5)** or a separate closing tag.

Elements must be properly nested

If you start element A, then start element B, you must first close element B before closing element A **(Figure 1.5)**.

Case matters

XML is case sensitive. The `animal`, `ANIMAL`, and `Animal` elements are considered completely separate and unrelated **(Figure 1.6)**.

Values must be enclosed in quotation marks

An attribute's value must always be enclosed in either single or double quotation marks **(Figure 1.7)**.

Entity references must be declared

Unlike HTML, any entity reference used in XML, except the five built-in ones *(see page 31)*, must be declared in a DTD before being used.

Declaring the XML Version

In general, you should begin each XML document with a declaration that notes what version of XML you're using. This line is called the *XML declaration.*

To declare the version of XML that you're using:

1. At the very beginning of your document, before anything else, type **<?xml**.
2. Type **version="1.0"** (which is the only version there is so far).
3. Type **?>** to complete the declaration.

✔ Tips

- Tags that begin with **<?** and end with **?>** are called *processing instructions.* In addition to declaring the version of XML, processing instructions are also used to specify the stylesheet that should be used, among other things. Style sheets are discussed in detail in Part 5, beginning on page 175.
- Be sure to enclose the version number in double or single quotation marks. (It doesn't matter which.)
- The XML declaration is optional. If it is included, however, it must be the very first line in your document.
- You may also indicate whether your document is dependent on any other document *(see pages 39–40).*
- You may also need to use this initial XML processing instruction to designate the character encoding that you're using for the document, if it is something other than UTF-8 or UTF-16.

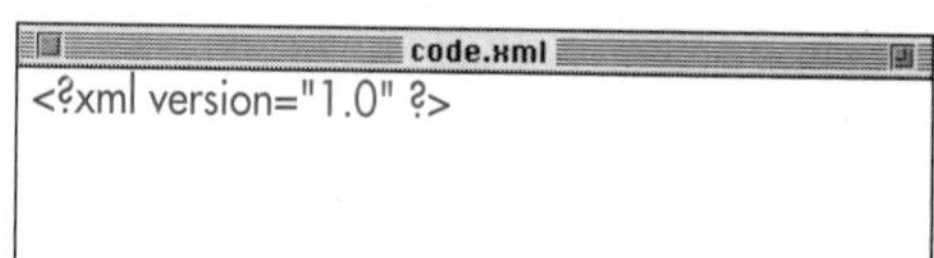

Figure 1.8 *Because the XML declaration is a processing instruction and not an element, there is no closing tag.*

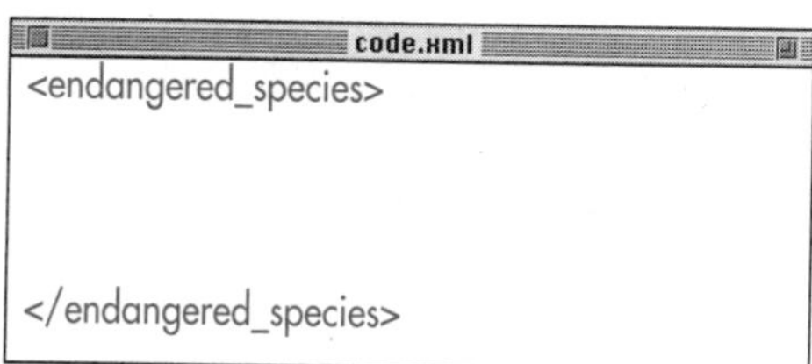
```
<endangered_species>



</endangered_species>
```

Figure 1.9 *In HTML, the root element is always* `HTML`*. In XML, you can use any valid name for your root element, including* `endangered_species`*, as shown here. No content or other elements are allowed before or after the opening and closing root tags, respectively.*

Creating the Root Element

Every XML document must have one element that completely contains all the other elements. This all-encompassing element is called the *root* element.

To create the root element:

1. At the beginning of your XML document, type **<root>**, where *root* is the name of the element that will contain the rest of the elements in the document.
2. Leave a few empty lines for creating the rest of your document (using the rest of this book).
3. Type **</root>**, where *root* exactly matches the name you chose in step 1.

✔ Tips

- Case matters. `<NAME>` is not the same as `<Name>` or `<name>`.
- Valid element (and attribute) names begin with a letter, an underscore (_), or a colon (:) and can be followed by any number of additional letters, digits, underscores, hyphens, periods, and colons.
- Note that colons are usually restricted to specifying namespaces *(see page 113)*, and names that begin with the letters *x*, *m*, and *l* (in any combination of upper- and lowercase) are reserved by the W3C.
- The root element's closing tag is required.
- No other elements are allowed outside the opening and closing root tags. The only things that are allowed before the opening root element are processing instructions *(see page 24)* and schemas *(see page 67)*.

Writing Non-Empty Elements

You can create any elements you like in an XML document. The idea is that you can use names that identify content so that it's easier to process the information at a later date.

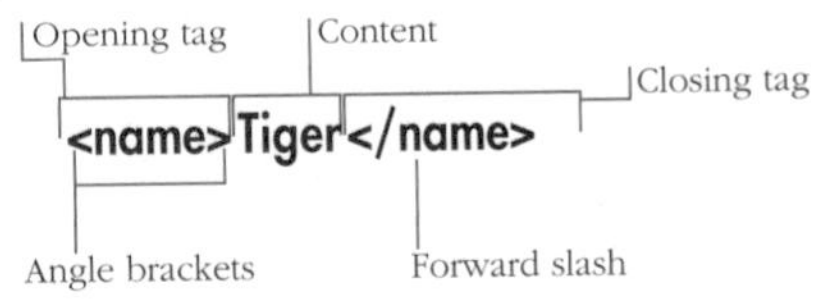

Figure 1.10 *A simple XML element comprises an opening tag, content (which might include text, other elements, or be empty), and a closing tag whose only difference with the opening tag is an initial forward slash.*

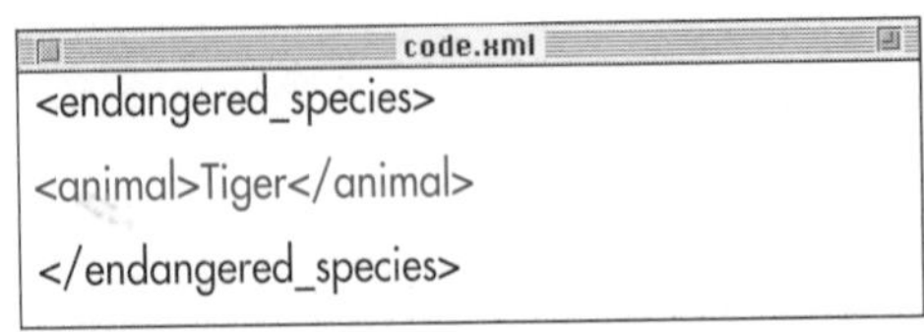

Figure 1.11 *Every element in the XML document must be contained within the opening and closing tags of the root element.*

To write a non-empty element:

1. Type **<name>**, where *name* is the word that identifies the content that is about to appear.
2. Create the content.
3. Type **</name>**, where *name* corresponds to the word you chose in step 1.

✓ Tips

- The closing tag is never optional (as it sometimes is in HTML).
- The rules for naming regular elements are the same as those for root elements: case matters; names must begin with a letter, underscore or colon; names may contain letters, digits, underscores, hyphens, periods, and colons; colons are generally only used for specifying namespaces; and names that begin with the letters *x, m,* and *l* (in any combination of upper- and lowercase) are reserved by the W3C.
- Names need not be in English or even the Latin alphabet.
- Information for writing attributes and their values is described on page 28.
- You define which tags are allowed in an XML document by using a schema. For more details about schemas, consult Part 3, beginning on page 67.
- If you use descriptive names for your elements, your data will be easier to leverage for other uses.

Correct (no overlapping lines)

<name>Tiger <baby>cub</baby></name>

<name>Tiger <baby>cub</name></baby>

Incorrect (the sets of tags cross over each other)

Figure 1.12 *To make sure your tags are correctly nested, connect each set with a line. None of your sets of tags should overlap any other set; each interior set should be completely enclosed within the next larger set.*

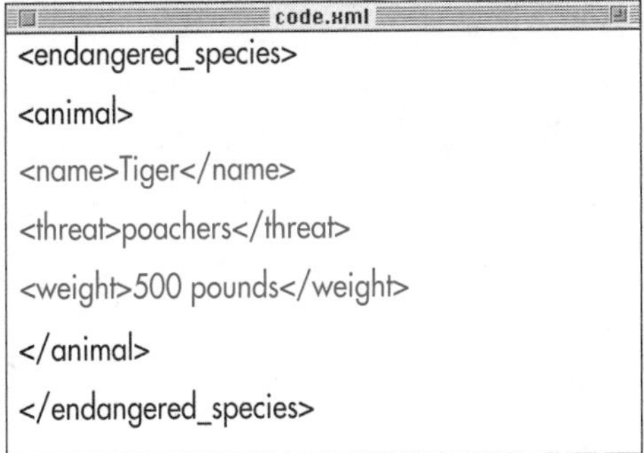

```
code.xml
<endangered_species>
<animal>
<name>Tiger</name>
<threat>poachers</threat>
<weight>500 pounds</weight>
</animal>
</endangered_species>
```

Figure 1.13 *Now the* `animal` *element contains three other elements which each contain a labeled piece of information that we can access and use.*

Nesting Elements

Sometimes you'll want to break down a chunk of data into smaller pieces so that you can identify and work with each of the individual parts.

To nest elements:

1. Create the opening tag of the outer element as described in step 1 on page 26.
2. Type **<inner>**, where *inner* is the name of the first individual chunk of data.
3. Create the content of the <inner> tag, if any.
4. Type **</inner>**, where *inner* matches the name chosen in step 2.
5. Repeat steps 2–4 as desired.
6. Create the closing tag of the outer element as described in step 3 on page 26.

✔ Tips

- It is essential that each element be completely enclosed in another. In other words, you may not write the closing tag for the outer element until the inner element is closed. Otherwise, the document will not be considered well formed.
- You can nest as many levels of elements as you like.
- An element nested within another is often referred to as the *child* element of the outer, or *parent* element.

Adding Attributes

An attribute creates additional information without adding text to the element.

To add an attribute:

1. Before the closing > of the opening tag, type **attribute=**, where *attribute* is the word that identifies the additional data.
2. Then type **"value"**, where *value* is that additional data. The quotes are required.

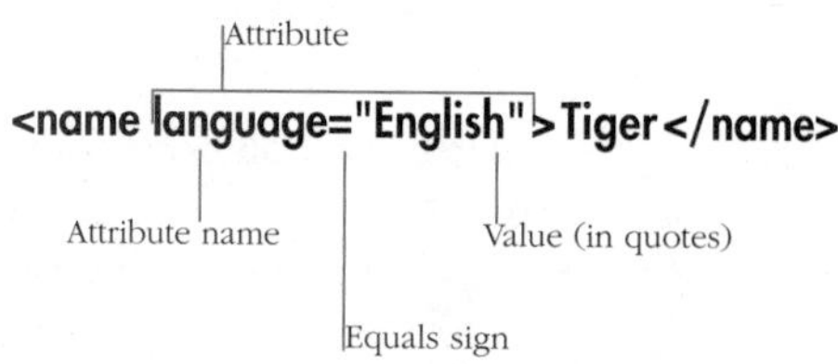

Figure 1.14 *Attributes are name-value pairs enclosed within the opening tag of an element. The value must be contained in quotation marks (either single or double).*

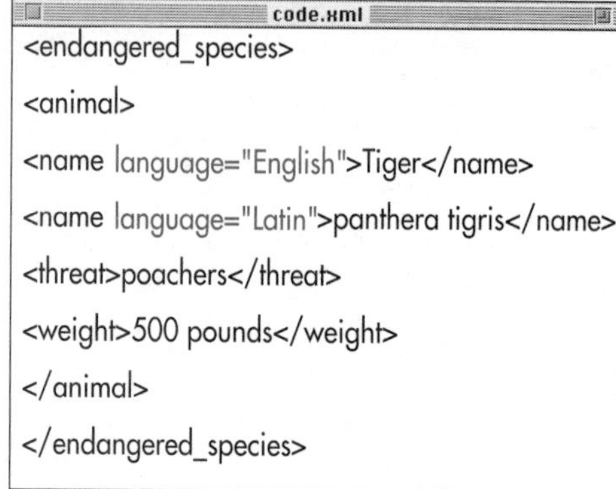

```
code.xml
<endangered_species>
<animal>
<name language="English">Tiger</name>
<name language="Latin">panthera tigris</name>
<threat>poachers</threat>
<weight>500 pounds</weight>
</animal>
</endangered_species>
```

Figure 1.15 *Attributes let you add information about the contents of an element.*

✔ Tips

- Attribute names must follow the same rules as for valid element names *(see page 26).*
- Unlike in HTML, attribute values must, must, **must** be in quotes. You can use either single or double quotes, as long as they match within a single attribute.
- If a value contains double quotes, use single quotes to contain the value (and vice versa). For example, **comments= 'She said, "The tigers are almost gone!"'**.
- No two attributes in a given element may have the same name.
- An attribute may not contain a reference to an external entity *(see page 58)*, and it may not contain the symbol <. If the value needs to contain that symbol, use **<** to represent it.
- Typically, the information contained in attributes is considered less central to the data than the element's content. It often is *meta-information*, that is, information *about* the content.
- An additional way to mark and identify distinct information is with nested elements *(see page 27).*

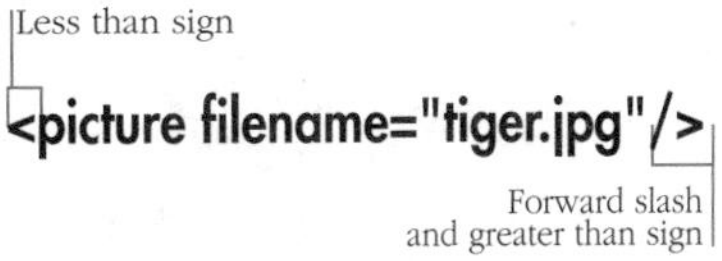

Less than sign

```
<picture filename="tiger.jpg"/>
```

Forward slash and greater than sign

Figure 1.16 *Empty elements can combine the opening and closing tags in one, as shown here, or can consist of an opening tag followed immediately by an independent closing tag.*

code.xml

```
<endangered_species>
<animal>
<name language="English">Tiger</name>
<name language="Latin">panthera tigris</name>
<threat>poachers</threat>
<weight>500 pounds</weight>
<source sectionid="120"
newspaperid="21"></source>
<picture filename="tiger.jpg" x="200" y="197"/>
</animal>
</endangered_species>
```

Figure 1.17 *Typical empty elements are those like* `source` *that contain data only in their attributes, and like* `picture` *that point to external binary data (not text).*

Using Empty Elements

Some elements do not have content that you can write out with text. For example, you might have a `picture` element that references the source of an image with an attribute, but which has no text content at all.

To write an empty element with a single opening/closing tag:

1. Type **<name**, where *name* is the word that identifies the empty element.
2. Create any attributes as necessary, following the instructions on page 28.
3. Type **/>** to complete the element.

To write an empty element with separate opening and closing tags:

1. Type **<name**, where *name* is the word that identifies the empty element.
2. Create any attributes as necessary, following the instructions on page 28.
3. Type **>** to complete the opening tag.
4. Type **</name>** to complete the element, where *name* matches the word in step 1.

✓ Tips

- In XML, both methods are equivalent.
- Unlike in HTML, you are not allowed to use an opening tag with no corresponding closing tag. A document that contains such a tag is not considered well formed and will generate an error in the XML parser.

Writing Comments

It's often useful to annotate your XML documents so that you know why you used a particular element or when a piece of information needs to be updated. You can insert comments into your document that are all but invisible to the visitor.

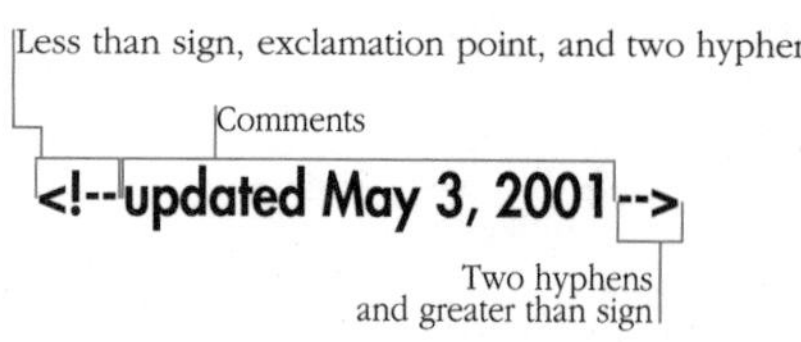

Figure 1.18 *XML comments have the same syntax as HTML comments.*

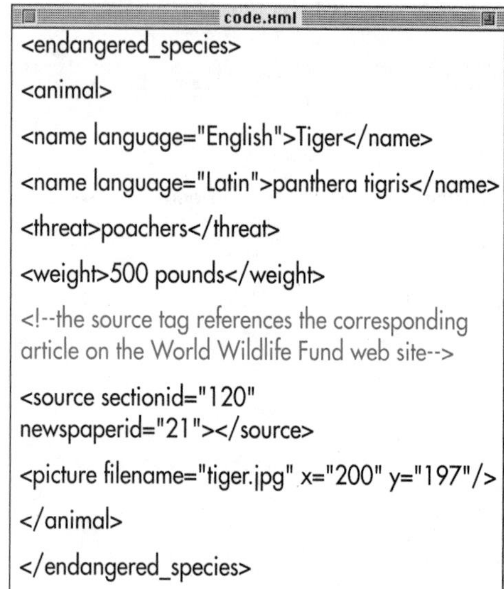

```
code.xml
<endangered_species>
<animal>
<name language="English">Tiger</name>
<name language="Latin">panthera tigris</name>
<threat>poachers</threat>
<weight>500 pounds</weight>
<!--the source tag references the corresponding
article on the World Wildlife Fund web site-->
<source sectionid="120"
newspaperid="21"></source>
<picture filename="tiger.jpg" x="200" y="197"/>
</animal>
</endangered_species>
```

Figure 1.19 *Comments let you add information about your code. They can be incredibly useful when you (or someone else) needs to go back to a document and understand how it's constructed.*

To write comments:

1. Type **<!--**.
2. Write the desired comments.
3. Type **-->**.

✔ Tips

- No spaces are required between the double hyphens and the content of the comments itself. In other words **<!--this is a comment-->** is perfectly fine.
- You may not use a double hyphen within comments and thus you may not nest comments within other comments.
- You may use comments to hide a piece of your XML code during development or debugging. This is called "commenting out" a section. The elements within a commented out section are no longer visible to the parser, and thus any errors that they may contain will be temporarily taken out of the picture.
- Comments are also useful for documenting the structure of an XML document (including style sheets) in order to facilitate changes and updates in the future.
- Comments are not displayed by a browser. However, they remain visible in the XML code itself.

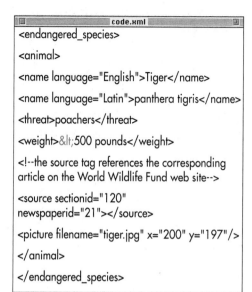

```
code.xml
<endangered_species>
<animal>
<name language="English">Tiger</name>
<name language="Latin">panthera tigris</name>
<threat>poachers</threat>
<weight>&lt;500 pounds</weight>
<!--the source tag references the corresponding
article on the World Wildlife Fund web site-->
<source sectionid="120"
newspaperid="21"></source>
<picture filename="tiger.jpg" x="200" y="197"/>
</animal>
</endangered_species>
```

Figure 1.20 *When this document is parsed, the < entity will be displayed as <.*

Writing Five Special Symbols

There are a whole slew of special symbols that can be inserted into HTML documents by using name entities: basically an ampersand followed by a name, followed by a semi-colon. In XML, only five entities are allowed by default. Other entities must be pre-defined in a DTD before they can be legally used.

To write the five special symbols:

- Type **&** to create an ampersand character (&).
- Type **<** to create a less than sign (<).
- Type **>** to create a greater than sign (>).
- Type **"** to create a double quotation mark (").
- Type **'** to create a single quotation mark or apostrophe (').

✔ Tips

- You may not use any other entities until they have been pre-defined in a DTD *(see page 55)*.
- You may not write a < or & in your XML document except to begin a tag or an entity, respectively. If you are not writing a tag or entity, you must use the special entity as described in the steps above.
- You may write ", ', or > directly into your document unless they'd be misconstrued (see tip below and last tip on page 32).
- One good (but obscure) reason to write **"** or **'** instead of " or ' is when you have an attribute value that contains both single and double quotes. You must use one or the other to contain the value and can use the entity to represent the other within the value.

Displaying Elements as Text

If you want to write about elements and attributes in your XML documents, you will want to keep the parser from interpreting them and instead just display them as regular text. To do this, you must enclose such information in a CDATA section.

To display tags into text:

1. Type **<![CDATA[**.
2. Create the elements, attributes, and content that you would like to display but not parse.
3. Type **]]>**.

✔ Tips

- One good use for the CDATA section (apart from creating XML documents about XML itself) is for enclosing Cascading Style Sheets *(see page 187)*.
- You may not nest CDATA sections.
- Since the whole point of a CDATA section is to strip the special meaning from symbols, you write less than symbols and ampersands as < and &. You need not and, in fact, may not write **<** and **&**.
- CDATA sections can appear anywhere after the opening tag of the root element until just before the closing tag of the root element.
- If, for some reason, you want to write **]]>** and you are *not* closing a CDATA section, the > must be written as **>**. See page 31 and Appendix C, *Special Symbols* for more information on writing special symbols.

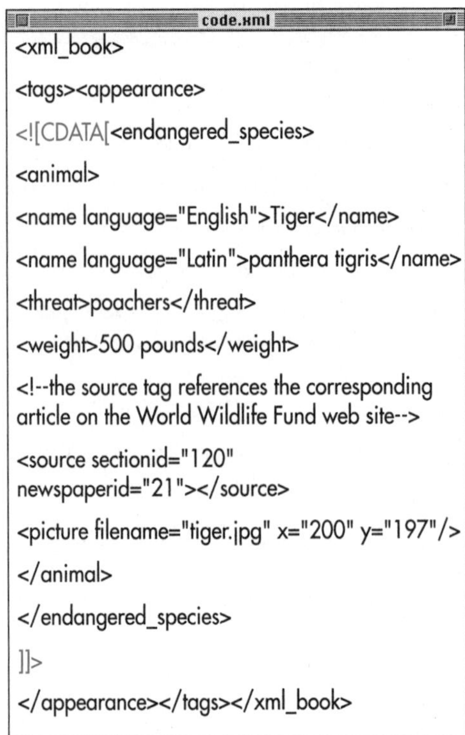

```
code.xml
<xml_book>
<tags><appearance>
<![CDATA[<endangered_species>
<animal>
<name language="English">Tiger</name>
<name language="Latin">panthera tigris</name>
<threat>poachers</threat>
<weight>500 pounds</weight>
<!--the source tag references the corresponding
article on the World Wildlife Fund web site-->
<source sectionid="120"
newspaperid="21"></source>
<picture filename="tiger.jpg" x="200" y="197"/>
</animal>
</endangered_species>
]]>
</appearance></tags></xml_book>
```

Figure 1.21 *In this example about an example, we use CDATA to display the actual code, without parsing it first.*

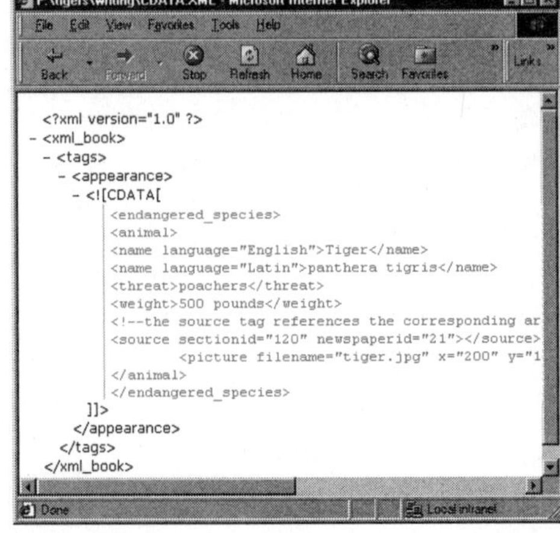

Figure 1.22 *Shown here using Internet Explorer 5 for Windows' parser, you can see how the tags within the CDATA section are treated as text—in contrast with the* `xml_book`, `tags`, *and* `appearance` *tags, which are parsed.*

Part 2: DTDs

2

Creating a DTD

As I've mentioned, you don't really write documents in XML. Instead, you use XML to create your own specific custom markup languages (officially called *XML applications*), and then write documents in those languages.

You define such a language by specifying which elements and attributes are allowed or required in a complying document. This set of rules is called a *schema*. For example, a wildlife conservationist might want to create EndML, the (fictitious) Endangered Species Markup Language, as a system for cataloging data about endangered species. EndML might have elements like `animal`, `subspecies`, `population`, and `threats`.

Schemas, while not required, are important tools for keeping documents consistent. You can compare a particular document to the corresponding schema in a process known as *validation (see pages 244–245)*. If a document conforms to all of the rules specified in the schema, it is considered *valid*—which means you can be sure that its data is in the desired form.

There are two principal systems for writing schemas: DTDs and XML Schema. A DTD, or Document Type Definition, is an old-fashioned, but widely used system of rules with a peculiar, rather limited syntax. The next three chapters are devoted to writing DTD-style schemas. The new-fangled system, XML Schema—developed by the W3C—is described in great detail in Part 3 beginning on page 67.

Declaring an Internal DTD

For individual XML documents, it is simplest to create the DTD within the XML document itself.

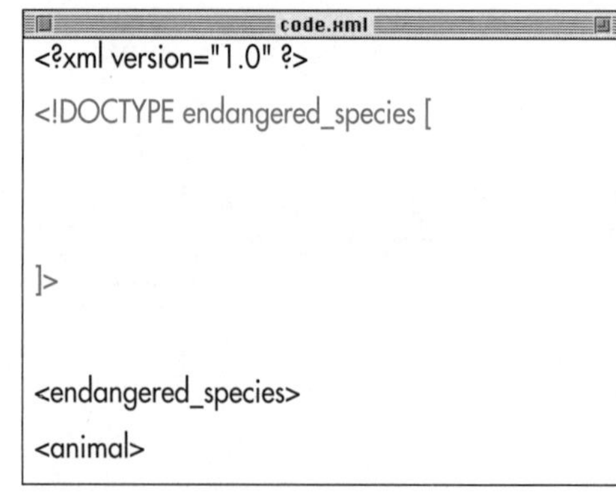

Figure 2.1 *Here are the beginnings of an internal DTD. It goes right after the XML declaration and before the actual tags in the body of the XML document.*

To declare an internal DTD:

1. At the top of your XML document, after the XML declaration *(see page 24)*, type **<!DOCTYPE root [**, where *root* corresponds to the name of the root element in the XML document that this DTD will be applied to.
2. Leave some space for the contents of the document type definition (which you will create using the information in Chapter 3, *Defining Elements and Attributes in a DTD* and Chapter 4, *Entities and Notations in DTDs*).
3. Type **]>** to complete the DTD.

✔ Tips

- Here's some terminology fun. The lines of code that spell out or refer to the DTD are called a *document type declaration*. Of course, the collection of rules themselves is called a DTD, or *document type **definition***. To distinguish them, think of the document type declaration as the thing that starts with <!DOCTYPE and ends with >. The DTD is the set of rules that goes between the brackets [ ]. (The DTD could also be in a separate (or *external*) file, but we'll get to that on page 37.)
- For a document to be *valid*, it must conform to the rules of the corresponding DTD (whether it be internal or external).

```
code.dtd
<!ELEMENT endangered_species (animal*)>

<!ELEMENT animal (name+, threats, weight?,
length?, source, picture, subspecies+)>

<!ELEMENT name (#PCDATA)>
<!ATTLIST name language (English | Latin)>

...
```

Figure 2.2 *Don't worry about how to write the specific declarations yet. We'll get there in the next two chapters. For now, it's important to know that the rules in an external DTD start right up at the top of an empty text document, and that they form an independent file that is not part of the XML document. You should save an external DTD with the* .dtd *extension.*

Writing an External DTD

If you have a set of related documents, you may want them to all use the same DTD. Instead of copying the DTD into each document, you can create an external file that contains the DTD and simply reference its URL from each of the XML documents that needs it.

To write an external DTD:

1. Create a new text file with any text editor.
2. Define the rules for the DTD as described in Chapter 3, *Defining Elements and Attributes in a DTD* and Chapter 4, *Entities and Notations in DTDs.*
3. Save the file as text only with the .dtd extension.

✔ Tip

- You can find more information about naming and using external DTDs on pages 38–40.

Naming an External DTD

If your DTD will be used by others, you should name your DTDs in a standard way: using a formal public identifier, or FPI. The idea is that an XML parser could use the FPI to find the latest version of the external DTD on a public server out on the Web.

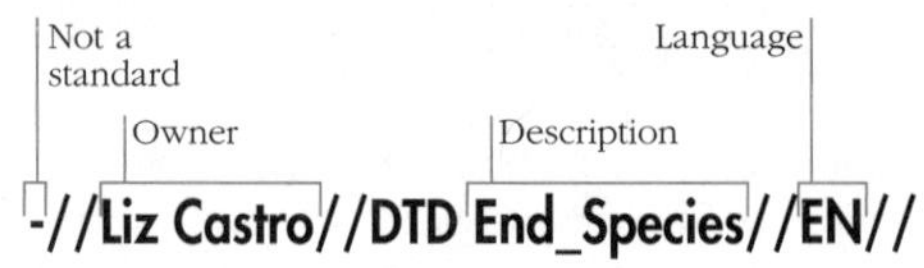

Figure 2.3 *Here is the official name for the DTD that will describe my Endangered Species XML documents.*

To name an external DTD:

1. Type

   + if your DTD has been approved by a standards body like the ISO.

   - if your DTD is not a recognized standard.
2. Type **//Owner//DTD**, where *Owner* identifies the person or organization that wrote and maintains the DTD.
3. Type a space followed by **label**, where *label* gives a description of the DTD.
4. Type **//XX//**, where *XX* is the two-letter abbreviation for the language of the XML documents the DTD applies to. Use *EN* for English (and see tip for more on other languages).

✔ Tips

- You can find the complete, official list of two-letter language abbreviations in ISO 639 online at *(http://www.unicode.org/unicode/onlinedat/languages.html).*
- DTD names let you identify a DTD by a label instead of a specific, static URL. That means an application looking for the DTD might be referred to the latest, or most conveniently located version (or both), instead of to a particular, perhaps outdated file on a given server.

```
code.xml
<?xml version="1.0" standalone="no"?>
<!DOCTYPE endangered_species SYSTEM
    "http://www.cookwood.com/xml/examples
    /dtd_creating/end_species.dtd">


<endangered_species>
<animal>
```

Figure 2.4 *In this example, I will use the external DTD found at the given URL for defining the XML document.*

```
code.xml
<?xml version="1.0" standalone="no"?>
<!DOCTYPE endangered_species SYSTEM
"http://www.cookwood.com/xml/examples
/dtd_creating/end_species.dtd"
[
<!ELEMENT continent (Asia | Europe | Africa)>
]
>


<endangered_species>
<animal>
```

Figure 2.5 *If desired, you can use additional internal DTD declarations at the end of the DOCTYPE declaration. Be sure to enclose the additional rules in brackets. Any rules defined locally override those brought in from an external file.*

Declaring a Personal External DTD

If you've created a personal DTD for your own purposes, the only way to refer to it from your XML document is with a URL.

1. In the XML declaration at the top of the document, add **standalone="no"**.
2. Type **<!DOCTYPE root**, where *root* corresponds to the name of the root element in the XML document that this DTD will be applied to.
3. Type **SYSTEM** to indicate that the external DTD is a personal, non-standardized DTD (e.g., one that *you've* written).
4. Type **"file.dtd"**, where *file.dtd* is the URL (absolute or relative) that indicates the location of the DTD.
5. Type **>** to complete the document type declaration.

✔ Tip

- If necessary, you can use both an internal and external DTD by adding the extra internal DTD declarations after linking to the external DTD (that is, after step 4). They must be enclosed by brackets. For more information about internal DTDs, consult *Declaring an Internal DTD* on page 36. The rules in an internal DTD override those that you bring in from an external DTD.

Declaring a Public External DTD

If my Endangered Species DTD becomes very popular and there are copies of it distributed wide and far, there may come a time when it is possible to refer to it with its formal public identifier, the name I created for it on page 38. When an XML parser sees a public identifier, it can try to get a copy of the DTD from the best possible source, perhaps one that's closer or has the latest version of the DTD. If it can't find the DTD by using the public identifier, it can then resort to using the URL.

To refer to a public external DTD:

1. In the XML declaration at the top of the document, add **standalone="no"**.
2. Type **<!DOCTYPE root**, where *root* is the name of the root element in the XML document to which the DTD will apply.
3. Type **PUBLIC** to indicate that the DTD is a standardized, publicly available set of rules for writing XML documents about the topic at hand.
4. Type **"DTD_name"**, where *DTD_name* is the official name of the DTD that you're referencing *(see page 38)*.
5. Type **"file.dtd"**, where *file.dtd* is the URL for the public DTD and indicates its location on the (presumably) remote server.
6. Type **>** to complete the document type declaration.

✔ Tip

- Again, you can override an external DTD with an internal DTD. See the tip on page 39 for more details.

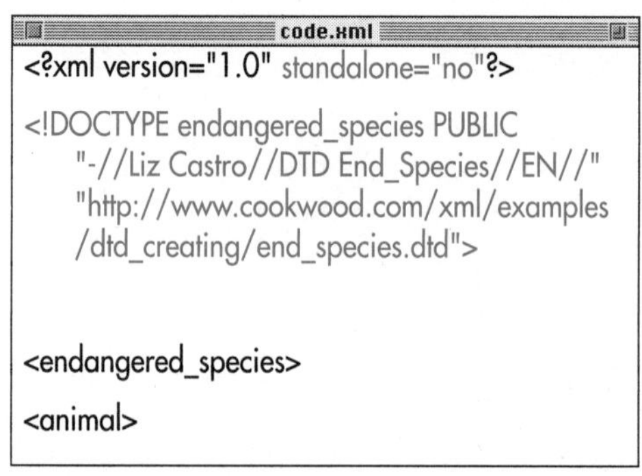

```
code.xml
<?xml version="1.0" standalone="no"?>

<!DOCTYPE endangered_species PUBLIC
    "-//Liz Castro//DTD End_Species//EN//"
    "http://www.cookwood.com/xml/examples
    /dtd_creating/end_species.dtd">


<endangered_species>

<animal>
```

Figure 2.6 *This time, the XML parser will use the public identifier to try and find the DTD, perhaps in a public repository. If that proves unsuccessful, it will use the DTD referenced by the given URL.*

3 Defining Elements and Attributes in a DTD

In Chapter 2, *Creating a DTD*, you learned how to set up a DTD. In this chapter, you'll learn how to create its contents. Whether you're writing an internal or external DTD, you write the rules that determine what elements and attributes are allowed in your XML documents in the same way.

A DTD must define rules for each and every element and attribute that will appear in the XML document. Otherwise, the XML document will not be considered valid. If at some point you need to add elements to the XML document, you will also have to add their definitions to the corresponding DTD (or create a new DTD, if you prefer).

Defining Elements

In order to limit your XML documents to a certain content and structure, you define the content and structure of each element contained within the XML document.

To define an element:

1. Type **<!ELEMENT *tag***, where *tag* is the name of the element you wish to define.
2. Next type **EMPTY** if the element will contain nothing.

   Or type **(contents)**, where *contents* describes the elements and/or text that the element will contain. Don't forget the parentheses. The possible options for this variable are discussed on pages 44–48.

   Or type **ANY** to allow the element to contain any combination of unspecified elements and text.
3. Finally, type **>** to complete the element declaration.

✔ Tips

- Attributes are not considered content. Even empty elements may have attributes associated with them *(see page 49)*.
- You should be judicious with your use of ANY. The whole point of a DTD is to set up rules for what an element can and cannot contain. If you're going to allow each element to contain *anything*, you might as well skip the DTD altogether. DTDs aren't required; they simply help keep data consistent.
- ANY does not allow an element to contain elements that are not defined in the DTD.

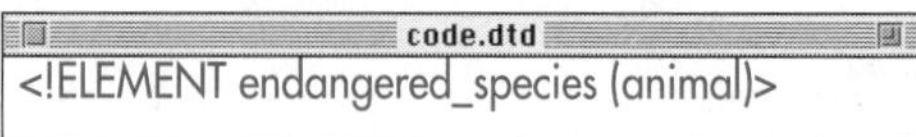

Figure 3.1 *You must define each and every element that is to appear in the XML document. Here, the* `endangered_species` *element is defined as containing just one other element,* `animal`*, and nothing else.*

Figure 3.2 *Elements that will reference binary data are generally declared as EMPTY—since they will contain no XML data. More often than not, they have attributes associated with them as well (see page 49).*

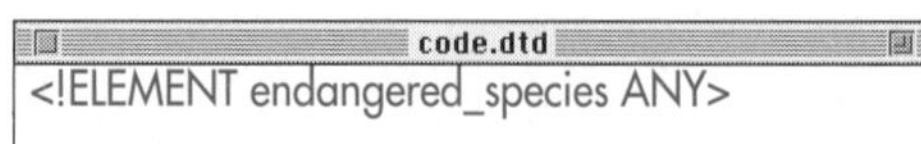

Figure 3.3 *The* `ANY` *value is so vague that it's practically useless. If you'd rather not limit your XML document, you might as well skip the DTD altogether. This* `endangered_species` *element can contain anything including text and/or other elements (these other elements must still be defined in the DTD).*

- An element may be contained in as many other elements as desired. Nevertheless, every element must be defined exactly once. No elements may appear in a valid XML document that have not been defined in the DTD.
- You can control how many of a particular element are allowed in a particular location *(see page 48)*.
- The order in which you declare elements doesn't matter in the least. For example, you can declare an element before the element declaration in which it is contained without causing any havoc.
- You can control the order in which elements must appear in an XML document by using a sequence *(see page 46)*.
- Everything is case sensitive in XML. The word **<!ELEMENT** must be typed just so. **<!Element** just doesn't cut it. And don't forget the exclamation point. You can choose a mixed-case *name* for the element, as long as you always refer to it and use it in exactly the same way. Sometimes it's just easier to use all lowercase. Then you don't have to spend time remembering what case it should be.
- DTD declarations are not XML elements and thus require no closing slash before the final >.

Defining an Element to Contain Only Text

Some elements in your XML document will probably contain just text. While an `Address` may contain `Street`, `City`, `State`, and `Zip` elements, the `State` element itself will probably just contain two letters of text.

To define an element:

1. Type **<!ELEMENT tag**, where *tag* is the name of the element you wish to define.
2. Next type **(#PCDATA)** (*with* parentheses!). This defines the element as one that should only allow text content.
3. Finally, type **>** to complete the element type declaration.

✔ Tips

- PCDATA stands for *parsed character data* and refers to everything except markup text, including numbers, letters, symbols, and entities *(see page 55)*.
- An element that is defined to contain PCDATA can't contain any other element.
- You may also include #PCDATA as one of a series of choices *(see page 47)*. It may not be used in a sequence.
- One of the major limitations of DTDs is that you can't specify that the data entered be a number, date, text, or whatever. In other words, an XML document with **<YEAR>dragon</YEAR>** is just as valid as one with **<YEAR>2005</YEAR>**. This so called *data typing* is available with XML Schema *(see page 67)*.

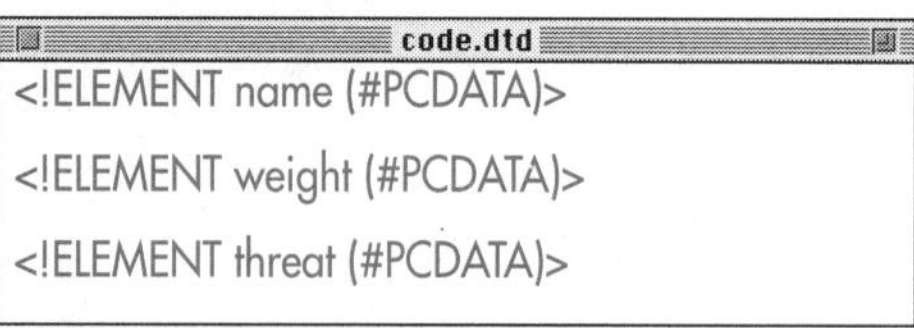

code.dtd

```
<!ELEMENT name (#PCDATA)>
<!ELEMENT weight (#PCDATA)>
<!ELEMENT threat (#PCDATA)>
```

Figure 3.4 *Almost every DTD contains elements defined as text only.*

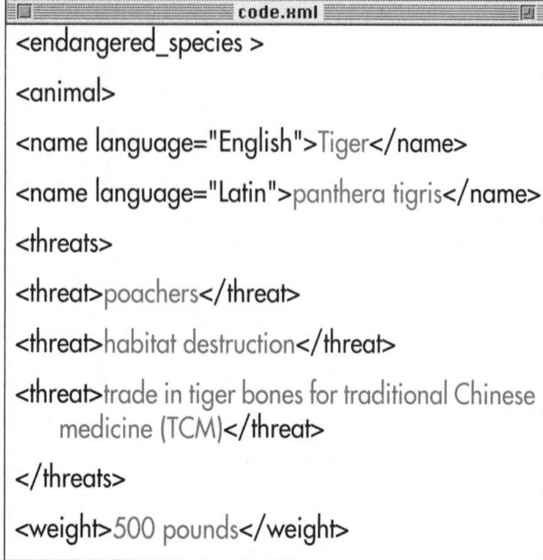

code.xml

```
<endangered_species >
<animal>
<name language="English">Tiger</name>
<name language="Latin">panthera tigris</name>
<threats>
<threat>poachers</threat>
<threat>habitat destruction</threat>
<threat>trade in tiger bones for traditional Chinese
    medicine (TCM)</threat>
</threats>
<weight>500 pounds</weight>
```

Figure 3.5 *Notice in this excerpt of a valid XML document that the* `name` *element is text only, despite its attribute (which we'll define on page 50). The individual* `threat` *elements are also text only while* `threats` *is not (it contains* `threat` *elements but no text).*

```
code.dtd
<!ELEMENT endangered_species (animal)>
```

Figure 3.6 *With this definition, the* `endangered_species` *element can contain a single* `animal` *element.*

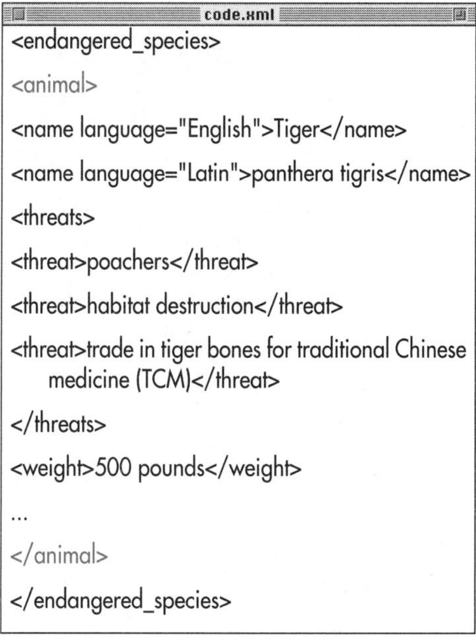

```
code.xml
<endangered_species>
<animal>
<name language="English">Tiger</name>
<name language="Latin">panthera tigris</name>
<threats>
<threat>poachers</threat>
<threat>habitat destruction</threat>
<threat>trade in tiger bones for traditional Chinese
    medicine (TCM)</threat>
</threats>
<weight>500 pounds</weight>
...
</animal>
</endangered_species>
```

Figure 3.7 *While the* `endangered_species` *element can only contain the* `animal` *element, the* `animal` *element's contents depend strictly on its declaration (and are not affected by the* `endangered_species` *element declaration in the least).*

Defining an Element to Contain One Child

When you divide up your information into smaller chunks, you will probably have elements that contain other elements.

To define an element to contain one child element:

1. Type **<!ELEMENT tag**, where *tag* is the name of the element you wish to define.
2. Type **(child)**, where *child* is the name of the element that will be contained in the element you're defining.
3. Type **>** to complete the declaration.

✔ Tips

- Once you say that an element must contain some other element, that means that it must contain that element in every single XML document that your DTD is applied to. Otherwise, the document will not be considered *valid*.
- A tag that is defined to contain one other element may not contain anything except that element. For example, it may not contain any other element, nor may it contain text.
- You can make a child element optional, or have it appear multiple times. For more details, consult *Defining How Many Units* on page 48.
- A child element can be contained in as many different parent elements as desired. Regardless, each child (and parent) element should only be defined once.

Defining an Element to Contain a Sequence

Often, an element needs to contain a series of other elements, in order. You can define a sequence of child elements that should be contained in the parent element.

To define an element with a sequence:

1. Type **<!ELEMENT tag**, where *tag* is the name of the element you wish to define.
2. Type **(child1**, where *child1* is the first element that should appear in the parent element.
3. Type **, child2**, where *child2* is the next element that should appear in the parent element. Separate each child element from the next with a comma and space.
4. Repeat step 3 for each child element that should appear in the parent element.
5. Type **)** to complete the sequence.

✓ Tips

- The most important thing in a sequence is the comma. The comma is the character that separates elements (or groups of elements) in a sequence.
- You may not use #PCDATA in any part of a sequence.
- The elements contained in a sequence may of course contain other elements. In Figure 3.9, the `threats` element contains individual `threat` elements.
- You can also create a sequence of *units*, where each unit is either an element, a (parenthesized) choice of elements, or a (parenthesized) sequence of elements.
- Each unit in a sequence can be defined to appear any number of times *(see page 48)*.

```
code.dtd
<!ELEMENT animal (name, threats, weight, length,
    source, picture, subspecies)>
```

Figure 3.8 *The* `animal` *element must contain one of each listed element, in order. It may not contain anything else.*

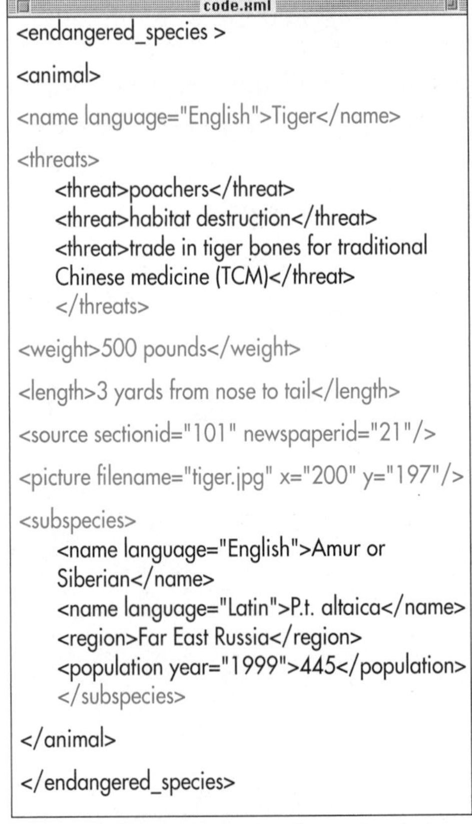

```
code.xml
<endangered_species >

<animal>

<name language="English">Tiger</name>

<threats>
    <threat>poachers</threat>
    <threat>habitat destruction</threat>
    <threat>trade in tiger bones for traditional
    Chinese medicine (TCM)</threat>
    </threats>

<weight>500 pounds</weight>

<length>3 yards from nose to tail</length>

<source sectionid="101" newspaperid="21"/>

<picture filename="tiger.jpg" x="200" y="197"/>

<subspecies>
    <name language="English">Amur or
    Siberian</name>
    <name language="Latin">P.t. altaica</name>
    <region>Far East Russia</region>
    <population year="1999">445</population>
    </subspecies>

</animal>

</endangered_species>
```

Figure 3.9 *Notice that there is only one of each element in this valid instance of the XML document. The* `name` *element can not (yet) appear twice, nor can we have more than one* `subspecies` *element (yet). We'll get there* *(see page 48)*.

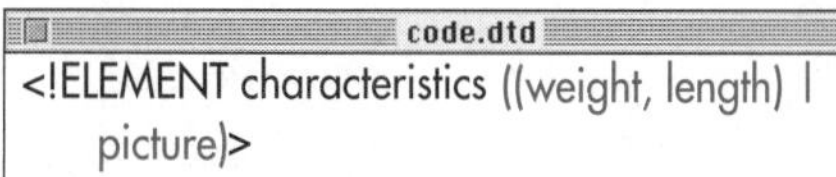

```
<!ELEMENT characteristics ((weight, length) |
    picture)>
```

Figure 3.10 *In this example, the* `characteristics` *element can contain either the sequence of elements* `weight` *followed by* `length`*, or it can contain the* `picture` *element.*

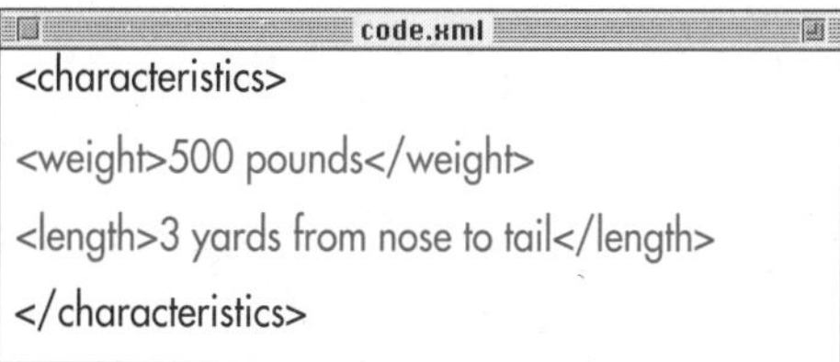

```
<characteristics>
<weight>500 pounds</weight>
<length>3 yards from nose to tail</length>
</characteristics>
```

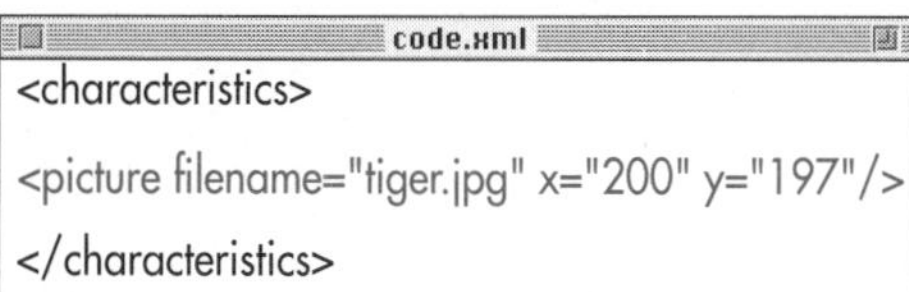

```
<characteristics>
<picture filename="tiger.jpg" x="200" y="197"/>
</characteristics>
```

Figure 3.11 *Both of these XML instances are perfectly valid.*

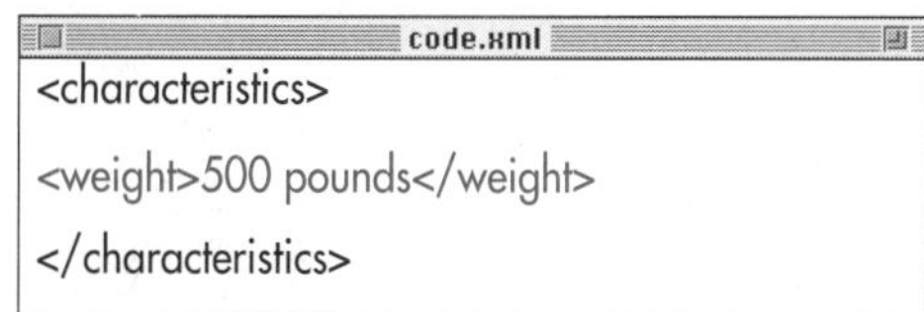

```
<characteristics>
<weight>500 pounds</weight>
</characteristics>
```

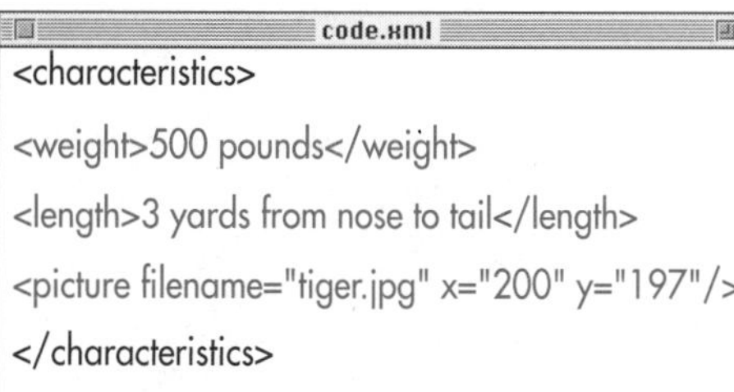

```
<characteristics>
<weight>500 pounds</weight>
<length>3 yards from nose to tail</length>
<picture filename="tiger.jpg" x="200" y="197"/>
</characteristics>
```

Figure 3.12 *Neither of these XML instances is valid. The first is wrong because the first choice is the sequence of* `weight` *followed by* `length` *(not just the* `weight` *element). The second is invalid because only one of the choices may be used (not both).*

Defining Choices

It's not unusual to want one element to be able to contain *either* one thing *or* another.

To define choices for the content of an element:

1. Type **<!ELEMENT tag**, where *tag* is the name of the element you wish to define.
2. Type **(child1**, where *child1* is the first child element that may appear (if the other does not).
3. Type **|** to indicate that if the first element appears, the following one may not (and vice versa).
4. Type **child2**, where *child2* is the second child element that may appear (if the other does not).
5. Repeat steps 3–4 for each additional choice.
6. Type **)** to complete the list of choices.
7. Type **>** to complete the element declaration.

✔ Tips

- You can add a * after step 6 to allow the element to have any number of any of the choices. This is one way to define an unordered list of contained elements in the parent element. (Also see page 48.)
- The first choice may be #PCDATA—in effect creating an element with mixed content, but you are required to add the asterisk as described in the previous tip.
- You may also define choices between *units*, where units are either elements, (parenthesized) choices between elements, or (parenthesized) sequences of elements.

Defining How Many Units

There are three special symbols in DTDs that can be used to specify how many units can appear in an element. A unit is either a single element, a (parenthesized) choice between two or more elements, or a (parenthesized) sequence of elements.

To define how many units:

1. In the contents portion of the element declaration, type **unit**, where *unit* is a single element, a parenthesized choice between two or more elements, or a parenthesized sequence of elements.
2. Type **?** to indicate that the unit can appear at most once, if at all, in the element being defined.

   Or type **+** to indicate that the unit must appear at least once, and as many times as desired, in the element being defined.

   Or type ***** to indicate that the unit can appear as many times as necessary, or not at all, in the element being defined.

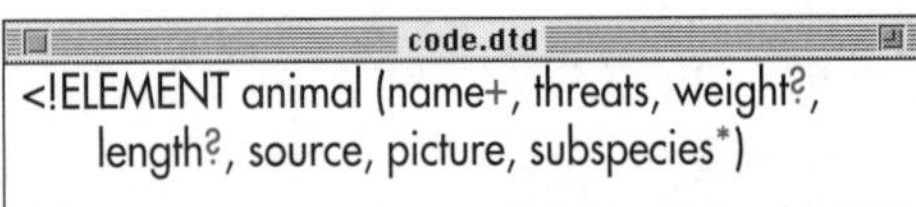

```
<!ELEMENT animal (name+, threats, weight?,
    length?, source, picture, subspecies*)
```

Figure 3.13 *The quantifiers make the declaration much more flexible. Now, the* `animal` *element must contain at least one (and an unlimited number) of* `name` *elements, the* `weight` *and* `length` *elements may be omitted (or may appear at most once), and there may be any number of* `subspecies` *elements (including none). The* `threats`, `source`, *and* `picture` *elements must all appear exactly once (which is the default).*

```
<!ELEMENT threats (threat, threat, threat+)>
```

Figure 3.14 *The* `threats` *element must contain at least three* `threat` *elements (and may contain an unlimited number).*

✔ Tips

- There's no good way to define a specific quantity of a given unit (like, say *3*). One rather clumsy workaround is to use **(unit, unit, unit+)** which requires at least three units, and allows for more.
- An asterisk applied to a list of choices contained in parentheses means that the element can contain any number of any of the individual choices, in any order.

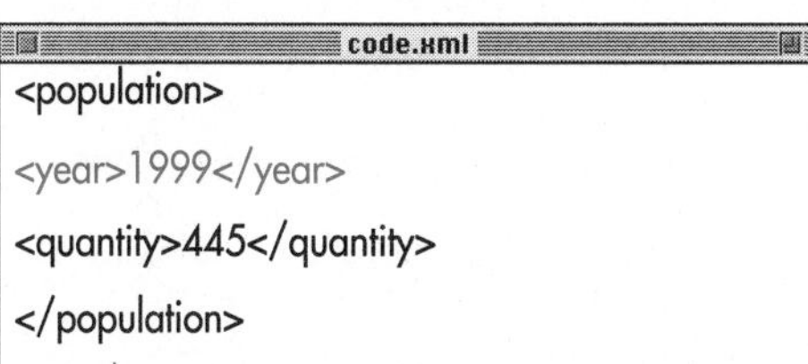

Figure 3.15 *Both of these bits of XML code contain the same information: as of 1999 there were 445 Siberian tigers left in the wild. The difference lies in how the information is organized. In the top example,* 1999 *is an attribute's value. In the bottom example, both* 1999 *and* 445 *are content, enclosed in individual elements. Both ways are fine; the choice is yours. There is no "right" way.*

About Attributes

While you can break down an element into smaller and smaller chunks of information, sometimes it's more useful to add supplementary data to the element itself instead of to the element's contents. An attribute does just that.

Information contained in attributes tends to be *about* the content of the XML page, as opposed to a *part* of that content. For example, in our Endangered Species database, the `name` element contains a `language` attribute which *describes* the language that the content of the `name` element is in.

You could conceivably contain the same information in individual elements. The `name` element could contain a `language` element and a `local_name` element. Either way is fine. Elements are perhaps better for information you want to display; attributes for information about information.

Attributes are very common with empty elements since they often point to the content of the element.

Defining Simple Attributes

An attribute may not appear in an XML document unless it has been declared (exactly once) in the DTD.

To define an attribute:

1. Type **<!ATTLIST tag**, where *tag* is the name of the element in which the attribute will appear.

2. Type **attribute**, where *attribute* is the name that identifies the extra information you want to add to the tag.

3. Type **CDATA** (with no parentheses or *#P*!) if the attribute's value will be composed of any combination of characters (but no tags).

   Or type **(choice_1 | choice_2)**, where *choice_n* represents each possible value for the attribute, only one of which may be used in the XML document. Each choice should be separated from the last with a vertical bar, and the full set should be enclosed in parentheses.

4. Next, type **"default"**, where *default* will be the value for the attribute if none is explicitly set.

   Or type **#FIXED "default"**, where *default* is the default value *and* you want to insist that the attribute be set to this value.

   Or type **#REQUIRED** to specify that the attribute must contain some (not pre-specified) value.

   Or type **#IMPLIED** if the attribute has no default value and in addition, may be completely omitted if desired.

5. Repeat steps 2–4 for each attribute that the element should contain.

6. Type **>** to complete the attribute declaration.

```
code.dtd
<!ELEMENT population (#PCDATA)>
<!ATTLIST population year CDATA #IMPLIED>
```

Figure 3.16 *This attribute definition says that the* `population` *element shall contain an optional (because of #IMPLIED)* `year` *attribute that contains any combination of characters (because of CDATA).*

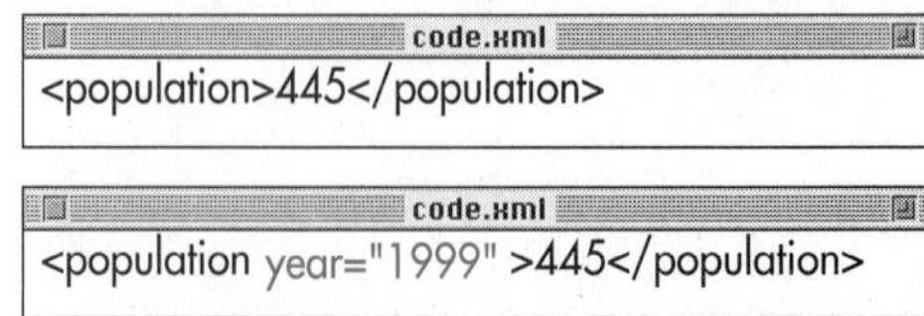

```
code.xml
<population>445</population>
```

```
code.xml
<population year="1999" >445</population>
```

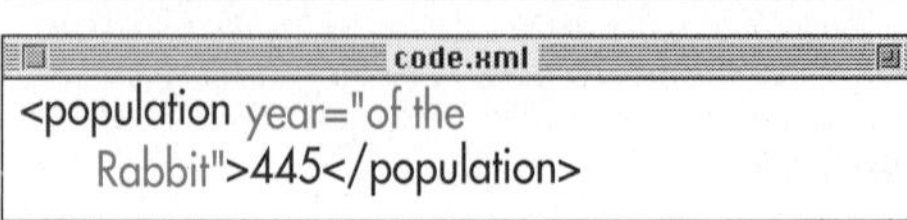

```
code.xml
<population year="of the
   Rabbit">445</population>
```

Figure 3.17 *According to the DTD in Figure 3.16, all three of these XML documents are valid, since the* `year` *attribute is optional (#IMPLIED) and its contents may be any combination of characters. Note that there is no way to ensure that the value of an attribute will be an actual year. You need XML Schema for that (see page 69).*

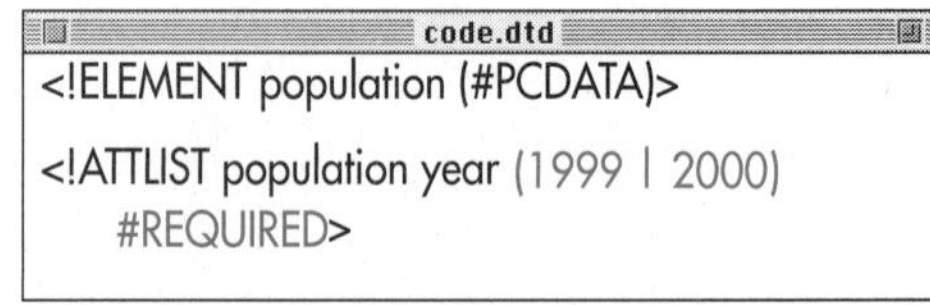

```
code.dtd
<!ELEMENT population (#PCDATA)>
<!ATTLIST population year (1999 | 2000)
   #REQUIRED>
```

Figure 3.18 *In this example, I only want to allow there to be two possibilities for the value of the* `population` *attribute in the* `year` *element: 1999 or 2000. The list of choices appears between parentheses, separated by vertical bars. Note that the attribute must be set (because of the #REQUIRED value).*

```
code.xml
<population year="1999">445</population>
```

```
code.xml
<population>445</population>
```

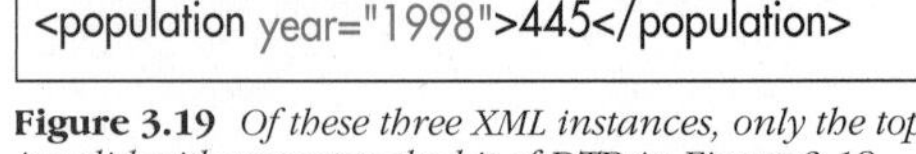

```
code.xml
<population year="1998">445</population>
```

Figure 3.19 *Of these three XML instances, only the top is valid with respect to the bit of DTD in Figure 3.18. The middle example is invalid because the* `year` *attribute is missing despite being #REQUIRED. The bottom example is invalid because 1998 is not one of the allowed choices for the content of the attribute.*

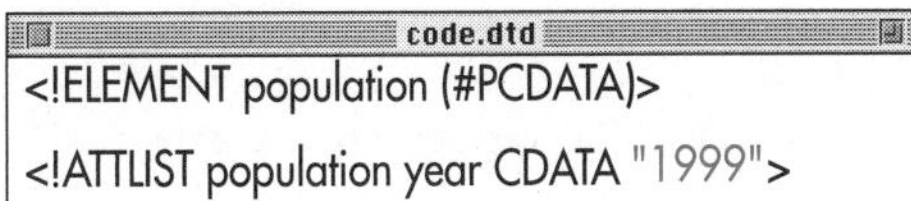

```
code.dtd
<!ELEMENT population (#PCDATA)>
<!ATTLIST population year CDATA "1999">
```

Figure 3.20 *This time, we add a default value of* 1999 *for the* `year` *attribute.*

```
code.xml
<population year="1999">445</population>
```

```
code.xml
<population year="1998">445</population>
```

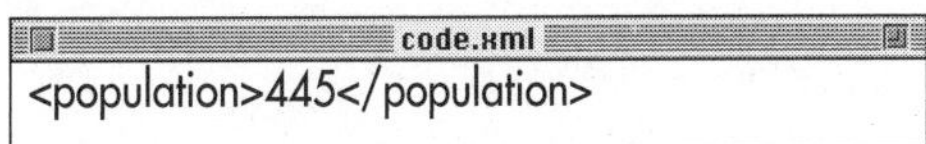

```
code.xml
<population>445</population>
```

Figure 3.21 *All three of these XML instances are valid. The* `year` *can be set to any value and may even be omitted. The interesting part is that if the value is omitted, as in the third example, the parser will act as if the* `year` *attribute is present and that its value is set to* 1999.

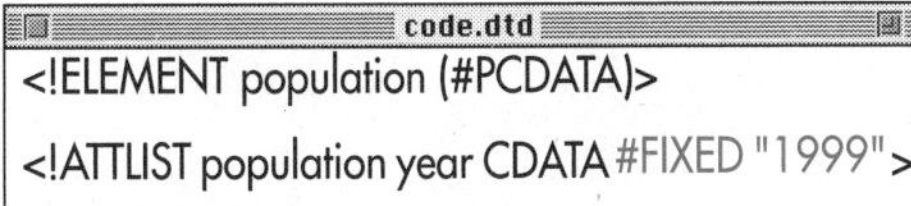

```
code.dtd
<!ELEMENT population (#PCDATA)>
<!ATTLIST population year CDATA #FIXED "1999">
```

Figure 3.22 *A fixed value can be useful for ensuring that an attribute has a given value, whether or not it actually appears in the XML document.*

```
code.xml
<population year="1999">445</population>
```

```
code.xml
<population year="1998">445</population>
```

```
code.xml
<population>445</population>
```

Figure 3.23 *These examples are the same as those shown in Figure 3.21 above. When validated against the DTD in Figure 3.22, however, the middle example is no longer valid: if the attribute is set, it must contain a value of* 1999 *(and not* 1998 *or any other characters). Note that in the bottom example, the parser acts as if the* `year` *attribute was set to 1999.*

✔ Tips

- Each choice in a list must follow the rules for valid XML names *(see page 26)*.
- You can either declare all the attributes in a single attribute declaration (as described in step 5), or create individual attribute declarations for each attribute.
- There are several special kinds of attributes: ID, IDREF, and IDREFS are explained on pages 52–53; NMTOKEN and NMTOKENS attributes are described on page 54. I don't detail the ins and outs of ENTITY attributes until Chapter 4, *Entities and Notations in DTDs*.
- If you define an attribute with a default value, the XML parser will automatically add the default value if the attribute is not explicitly set in the XML document **(Figure 3.21)**.
- If you define an attribute with **#FIXED "default"**, the value of the attribute in the XML document *must* be set to the *default* value, if set at all. If the attribute is not set at all, the parser automatically sets it to the value of the default **(Figure 3.23)**.
- A properly functioning parser will return an error if the DTD contains an attribute defined as **#REQUIRED** but whose corresponding XML document contains no value for the attribute.
- A parser is also supposed to return information about attributes defined as **#IMPLIED** that are not actually set in the XML document.
- Note that all of the parts of an attribute definition are case sensitive. Type them as I have them here. Something like **#Required** doesn't mean a thing in a DTD.
- You may not combine a default value with either **#REQUIRED** or **#IMPLIED**.

Defining Attributes with Unique Values

There are a few special kinds of attributes. ID attributes are defined to have a value that is unique (that is, not repeatable) throughout the XML document. An ID attribute is ideal for keys and other identifying information (product codes, customer identification codes, etc).

To define ID attributes:

1. Follow steps 1–2 on page 50 to begin the attribute definition.
2. Type **ID** if you want the value to be unique and non-repeatable throughout the XML document. In other words, no other element may have an attribute with the same value.
3. Complete the attribute definition as described in steps 4–6 on page 50.

✔ Tips

- A document will not be considered valid if two elements with ID type attributes have the same values for those attributes.
- The value of an ID attribute must follow the same rules as valid XML names: that is, it must begin with a letter or underscore and be followed by additional letters, numbers, underscores, periods, or hyphens. (That means, an ID attribute may not contain purely numerical values like Social Security numbers or telephone numbers, unless you prefix them with a letter or underscore.)
- Using ID as the attribute type is like using NMTOKENs that must be unique *(see page 54)*.

code.dtd

```
<!ELEMENT animal (name+, threats, weight?,
    length?, source, picture, subspecies+)>

<!ATTLIST animal code ID #REQUIRED>
```

Figure 3.24 *If you're going to create an ID type attribute in order to identify particular elements within your XML document, it's a good idea to require it.*

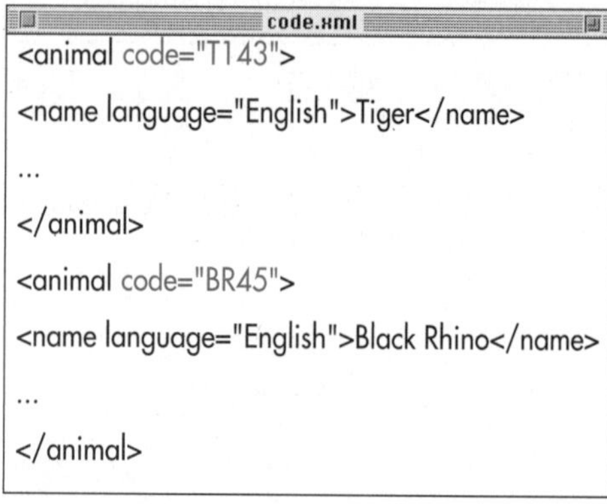

code.xml

```
<animal code="T143">
<name language="English">Tiger</name>
...
</animal>
<animal code="BR45">
<name language="English">Black Rhino</name>
...
</animal>
```

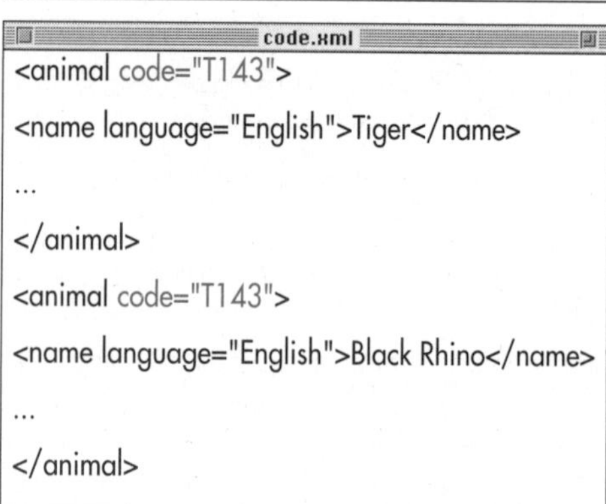

code.xml

```
<animal code="T143">
<name language="English">Tiger</name>
...
</animal>
<animal code="T143">
<name language="English">Black Rhino</name>
...
</animal>
```

Figure 3.25 *Since, according to the DTD shown in Figure 3.24, the* `code` *attribute must contain a unique value throughout the XML document, the first example is valid but the second is not.*

```
code.dtd
<!ELEMENT specialized_website (title, url)>

<!ATTLIST specialized_website animal_focus IDREF
    #REQUIRED>
```

Figure 3.26 *Imagine an element in the XML document that keeps track of web sites dedicated to one particular animal. I'll use IDREF to relate the web sites to the code of the animal that they focus on.*

```
code.xml
<resources>
<specialized_website animal_focus="T143">
    <title>Tigers in Crisis</title>
    <url>http://www.tigersincrisis.com/</url>
</specialized_website>
<specialized_website animal_focus="T143">
    <title>Tigers!</title>
    <url>http://www.geocities.com/RainForest/6
    612/</url>
</specialized_website>
<specialized_website animal_focus="O735">
    <title>International Otter Survival Fund</title>
    <url>http://www.otter.org/</url>
</specialized_website>
```

Figure 3.27 *An IDREF type attribute must contain a value which is contained in an ID type attribute somewhere in the document (for example, see the top example in Figure 3.25 on page 52). Notice that more than one* `specialized_website` *element may have the same value for the* `animal_focus` *attribute.*

```
code.dtd
<!ELEMENT general_website (title, url)>

<!ATTLIST general_website contents IDREFS
    #REQUIRED>
```

Figure 3.28 *Use IDREFS type attributes to contain a series of ID values.*

```
code.xml
<general_website contents="T143 O735 BR45">
<title>World Wildlife Fund</title>
<url>http://www.worldwildlife.org/</url>
</general_website>
```

Figure 3.29 *An IDREFS type attribute must contain one or more white-space-separated values, each of which is contained in ID type attributes somewhere in the same document.*

Referencing Attributes with Unique Values

An attribute whose value *refers* to one of the ID attributes we defined on page 52 is called an IDREF. An IDREF<u>S</u> attribute contains a white-space-separated list of values found in the document's ID attributes.

To reference attributes with unique values:

1. Follow steps 1–2 on page 50 to begin the attribute definition.
2. Type **IDREF** to define an attribute that will contain a value that matches another attribute's ID value (that you defined following the instructions on page 52).

   Or type **IDREFS** (with an *s*) for attributes that can contain several white-space-separated ID values.
3. Complete the attribute definition as described in steps 4–6 on page 50.

✔ Tips

- It only makes sense to define IDREF type attributes if the DTD also contains definitions for the ID type attributes that will be referred to *(see page 52)*.
- Note that there may be several IDREF type attributes that refer to the same ID **(Figure 3.27)**. That's fine. It's just the ID itself that must be unique to one element.
- There's nothing that keeps repeated items out of an IDREFS type attribute. Something like **contents="T143 T143 T143"** is perfectly valid for the parser, whether or not it's what you want. For more control over element and attribute contents, you have to abandon DTDs in favor of XML Schema *(see page 67)*.

Referencing Attributes with Unique Values

Restricting Attributes to Valid XML Names

DTDs don't allow for much data typing, but there is one restriction that you can apply to attributes: that the value be a valid XML name. That is, that it begin with a letter or an underscore and contain only letters, numbers, underscores, hyphens, and periods.

To ensure attribute values follow the rules for valid XML names:

1. Follow steps 1–2 on page 50 to begin the attribute definition.
2. Type **NMTOKEN** if you want the value to be an XML name as defined on page 26.

   Or type **NMTOKENS** if you want the value of the attribute to be a white-space-separated list of XML names.
3. Complete the attribute definition as described in steps 4–6 on page 50.

✔ Tips

- NMTOKEN type attributes may not contain any white space—which may be a good reason to use this particular type.
- If you want the value of an attribute to not only be a valid XML name but also to be unique throughout the XML document, use ID instead of NMTOKEN *(see page 52)*.

code.dtd

```
<!ELEMENT appearance (#PCDATA)>
<!ATTLIST appearance most_prominent_color
    NMTOKEN #IMPLIED>
```

Figure 3.30 *In this rather contrived example, I want concise, simple descriptions of my animals, including a one word value for* `most_prominent_color`. *To keep the value of the* `most_prominent_color` *attribute to just one word (with no white space), I can assign it the NMTOKEN type.*

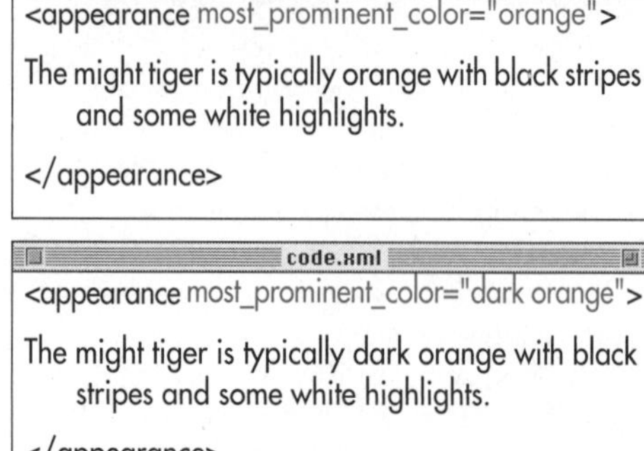

code.xml

```
<appearance most_prominent_color="orange">
The might tiger is typically orange with black stripes
    and some white highlights.
</appearance>
```

code.xml

```
<appearance most_prominent_color="dark orange">
The might tiger is typically dark orange with black
    stripes and some white highlights.
</appearance>
```

Figure 3.31 *Only the first instance would be considered valid since in the second, the* `most_prominent_color` *attribute has a space in its value. Spaces are not allowed in an NMTOKEN type attribute.*

Entities and Notations in DTDs

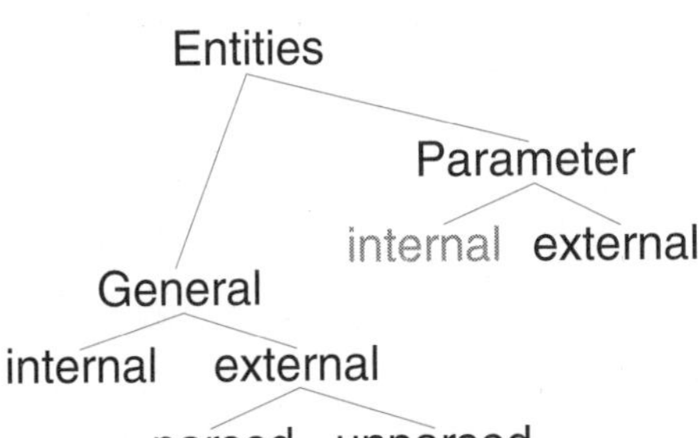

Figure 4.1 *There are five different kinds of entities used in DTDs. General entities are used in the body of an XML document. Parameter entities are only used within a DTD. (Internal parameter entities are so limited that I wouldn't recommend using them.)*

Entities are like those tiny flat sponges that expand to regular size when you add water. With an entity, you define an abbreviation (the entity reference) and the data that it should expand into when it is called in your XML document. When you type the entity reference in a DTD or XML document, you get the whole sponge.

There are several kinds of entities, but they all work in the same way. The differences lie in where the entity is defined and what kind of information it contains.

Entities can be divided into two main groups: general entities and parameter entities. General entities load data into the XML document itself; parameter entities reference data that becomes part of a DTD.

General entities can be further subdivided into internal and external, depending on whether they're defined within the DTD or in an external file, respectively. Finally, external entities can be either parsed or unparsed. Parsed entities are analyzed by the XML parser as it goes through the XML document. Unparsed entities—that generally point to binary, non-text data—are not.

Parameter entities are always parsed. While there are both internal and external types, the internal ones are pretty limited and thus I focus on the external ones here *(see page 60)*.

Creating Shortcuts for Text

code.dtd
<!ENTITY hwi "Hornocker Wildlife Institute">

Figure 4.2 *You can use internal general entities for quickly typing long, arduous phrases.*

The simplest kind of entities are defined within the DTD and represent text. Officially, they are called *internal general entities*. I call them *shortcuts for text*.

To create shortcuts for text:

1. In the DTD, type **<!ENTITY**.
2. Type **abbreviation**, where *abbreviation* will be the text part of the entity reference (that is, the code you'll type to use the entity).
3. Type **"content"**, where *content* is the text that should appear when you use the entity in your XML document.
4. Type **>** to complete the entity definition.

✔ Tips

- For details on using these shortcuts, see *Using Shortcuts for Text* on page 57.
- The entity reference (the abbreviation in step 2 above) must follow the rules for valid XML names *(see page 26)*.
- There are five built-in internal general entities: **&**, **<**, **>**, **"**, **&apost;** *(see page 31)*. All other entities must be declared in the DTD before being used.
- An entity may contain another entity as long as there is no circular reference.
- While character references—used for adding special symbols to a document—look rather similar, they are not entities, and do not need to be declared in the DTD *(see page 247)*.
- Many common entities have already been defined. For more details, see pages 60–61.

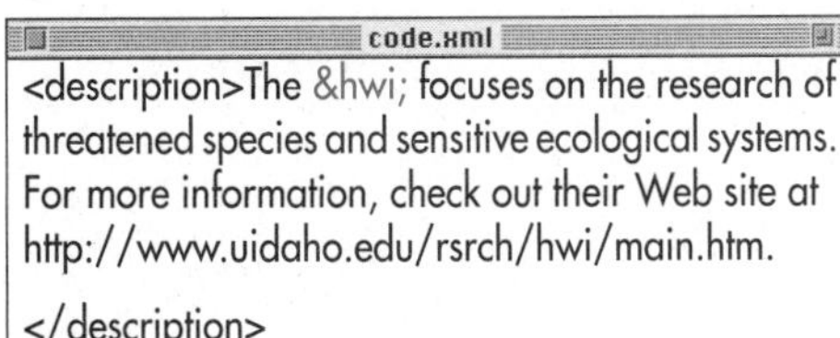

```
code.xml
<description>The &hwi; focuses on the research of threatened species and sensitive ecological systems. For more information, check out their Web site at http://www.uidaho.edu/rsrch/hwi/main.htm.
</description>
```

Figure 4.3 *It's much easier to type* `&hwi;` *than* `Hornocker Wildlife Institute`.

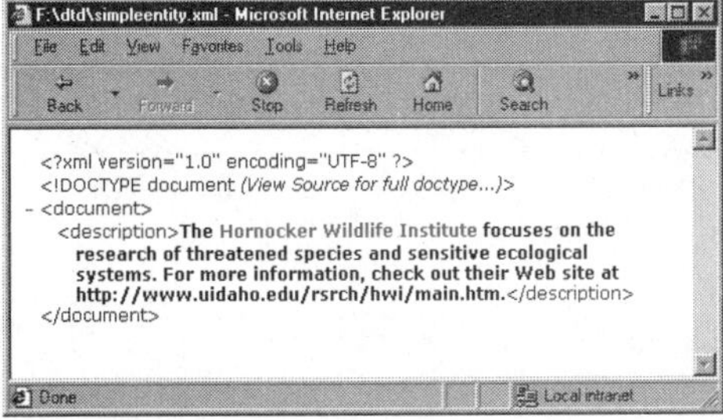

Figure 4.4 *The entity "expands" when it is viewed with the parser (in this case, Internet Explorer 5 for Windows). Note that we can't "properly" view a page with a browser until we apply some sort of styles, which we'll get to in Part 5, beginning on page 175.*

Using Shortcuts for Text

Once you have defined an entity, you can then use it throughout any XML document that references the given DTD.

To use text shortcuts:

1. In the XML document, type **&** (that's an ampersand).
2. Type **abbreviation**, where *abbreviation* is the identifying name of your entity and matches the one you used in step 2 on page 56 or step 4 on page 58.
3. Type **;** (that's a semicolon).

✓ Tips

- You may use an entity within another entity's definition as long as there is no circular reference.
- You may not use an entity until and unless it has been defined in the document's DTD. Otherwise, the parser will give you an error.
- A general entity (like those described on pages 56 and 58) may be used in a DTD as long as the content is eventually used *in the body* of the XML document. Entities that are exclusively used to expand and add to the DTD itself are called *parameter entities* and have a slightly different syntax *(see page 60)*.

Shortcuts for Text in External Files

If you have a larger entity, it is sometimes more convenient to save it in a separate, external document. This system also lets you share your entities with others, as well as borrow entities from others.

To create a shortcut in an external document:

1. Create the content for the entity in an external file. Save the file as text only. The extension is not important.
2. In the XML document itself, add **standalone="no"** to the initial XML declaration *(see page 24)* since the document must rely on the external file that contains the entity definition.
3. In the DTD for the XML document that will use the entity, type **<!ENTITY** to begin the entity definition.
4. Type **abbreviation**, where *abbreviation* is the identifying name for the external entity.
5. Type **SYSTEM** to indicate that the abbreviation is defined in another document.
6. Type **"entity.url"**, where *entity.url* is the location of the file created in step 1.
7. Type **>**.

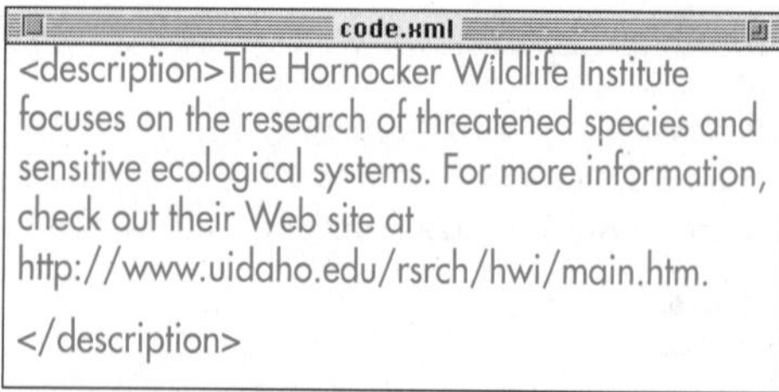

code.xml

```
<description>The Hornocker Wildlife Institute
focuses on the research of threatened species and
sensitive ecological systems. For more information,
check out their Web site at
http://www.uidaho.edu/rsrch/hwi/main.htm.
</description>
```

Figure 4.5 *This time, this entire chunk of XML code is the content of the entity I'm about to define. I'll save it as a text file called* hwi.ent.

code.dtd

```
<!ENTITY hwi_descrip SYSTEM "hwi.ent">
```

Figure 4.6 *The* `hwi_descrip` *entity points to the URL of the file that contains the entity's contents (Figure 4.5).*

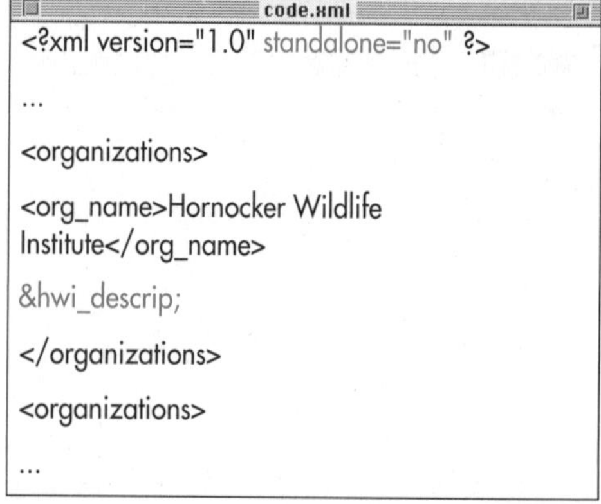

code.xml

```
<?xml version="1.0" standalone="no" ?>
...
<organizations>
<org_name>Hornocker Wildlife
Institute</org_name>
&hwi_descrip;
</organizations>
<organizations>
...
```

Figure 4.7 *Be sure to add* `standalone="no"` *to the XML declaration. Then you can use the external general entity in the document, as* `&hwi_descrip;` *is used here.*

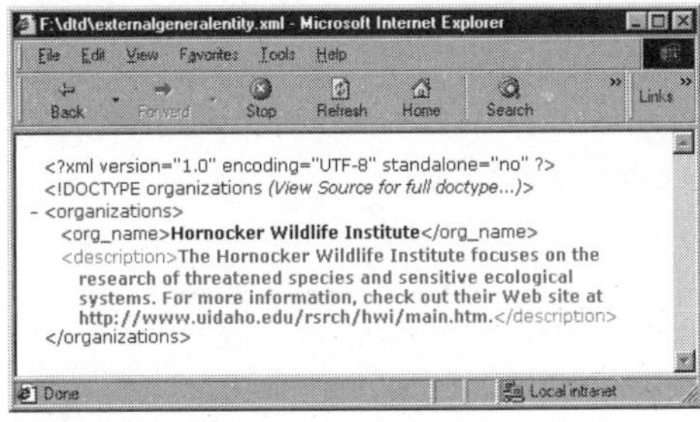

Figure 4.8 *This time, the external entity contained elements as well as text. Still, the idea is the same: you type something short, and the parser replaces it with the referenced content. Note that any elements that come from an external entity must still be defined in the DTD for the document to be valid.*

✔ Tips

- For details on using your new entity, consult *Using Shortcuts for Text* on page 57.
- This is one way to create a single document from several others.
- Entities whose content is XML or text but that are defined outside of the XML document's DTD are officially called *external general entities.*

Creating and Using Shortcuts for DTDs

The entities that we've talked about so far all reference text that will be used in the content of the XML document. You can also create shortcuts for chunks of the DTD itself. These kinds of abbreviations are called *external parameter entities.*

To create shortcuts for DTDs:

1. Create the content for the entity in an external file. Save the file as text only. The extension is not important.
2. In the XML document itself, add **standalone="no"** to the initial XML processing instruction *(see page 24)* since the document must rely on the external file that contains the entity definition.
3. In the DTD for the XML document that will use the entity, type **<!ENTITY** to begin the entity definition.
4. Type **%** to note that the abbreviation is for a DTD.
5. Type a space.
6. Type **abbreviation**, where *abbreviation* is the name for the external entity.
7. Type **SYSTEM** to indicate that the abbreviation is defined in another document.

   Or type **PUBLIC "name"**, where *name* is the official name for an official listing of publicly available, standardized entities.
8. Type **"entity.url"**, where *entity.url* is the location of the file created in step 1.
9. Type **>**.

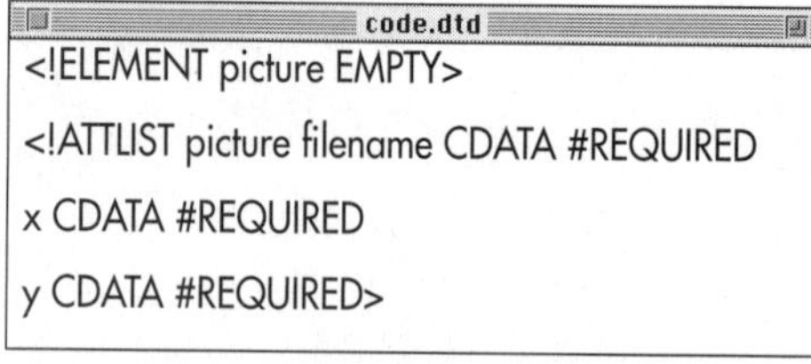

```
code.dtd
<!ELEMENT picture EMPTY>
<!ATTLIST picture filename CDATA #REQUIRED
x CDATA #REQUIRED
y CDATA #REQUIRED>
```

Figure 4.9 *Here is the chunk of DTD that I want to use in several other DTDs. It contains the declarations for the* `picture` *element and its attributes and is saved in a separate file called* pic.dtd.

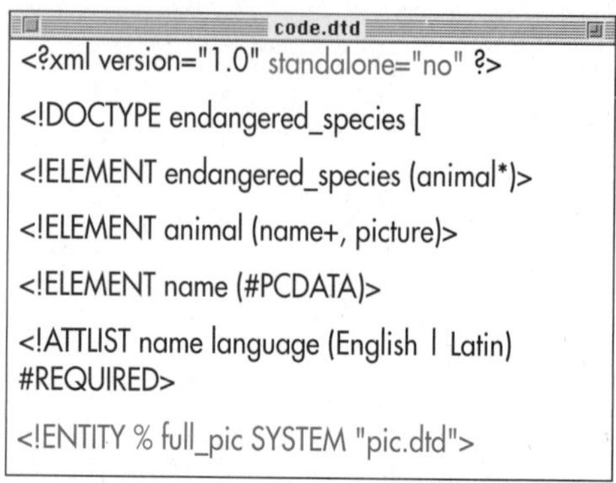

```
code.dtd
<?xml version="1.0" standalone="no" ?>
<!DOCTYPE endangered_species [
<!ELEMENT endangered_species (animal*)>
<!ELEMENT animal (name+, picture)>
<!ELEMENT name (#PCDATA)>
<!ATTLIST name language (English | Latin)
#REQUIRED>
<!ENTITY % full_pic SYSTEM "pic.dtd">
```

Figure 4.10 *In each DTD in which I want to declare the* `picture` *element and its attributes, I have to define the entity (as shown here).*

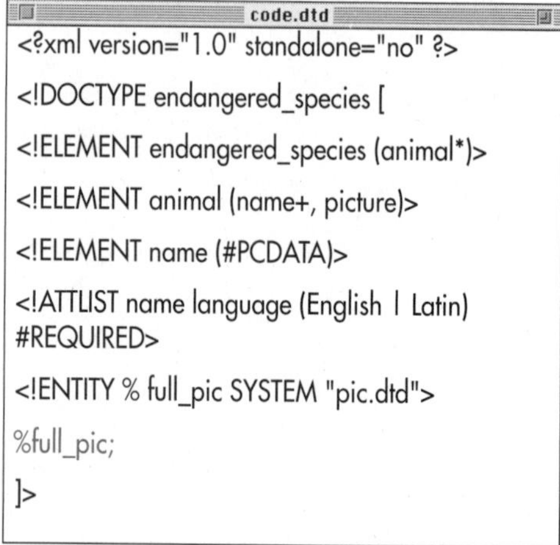

```
code.dtd
<?xml version="1.0" standalone="no" ?>
<!DOCTYPE endangered_species [
<!ELEMENT endangered_species (animal*)>
<!ELEMENT animal (name+, picture)>
<!ELEMENT name (#PCDATA)>
<!ATTLIST name language (English | Latin)
#REQUIRED>
<!ENTITY % full_pic SYSTEM "pic.dtd">
%full_pic;
]>
```

Figure 4.11 *Once the entity is defined, you can use it by typing its reference, in this case* `%full_pic;`.

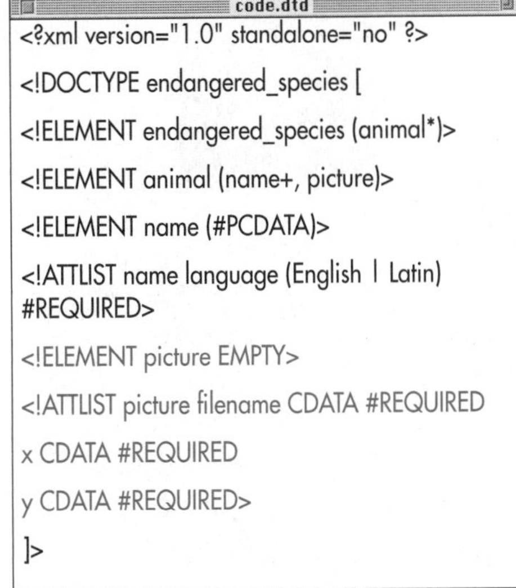

```
code.dtd
<?xml version="1.0" standalone="no" ?>
<!DOCTYPE endangered_species [
<!ELEMENT endangered_species (animal*)>
<!ELEMENT animal (name+, picture)>
<!ELEMENT name (#PCDATA)>
<!ATTLIST name language (English | Latin)
#REQUIRED>
<!ELEMENT picture EMPTY>
<!ATTLIST picture filename CDATA #REQUIRED
x CDATA #REQUIRED
y CDATA #REQUIRED>
]>
```

Figure 4.12 *The XML parser replaces the entity reference with the contents of the associated file. (The DTD shown above is a sort of "dramatization" of what happens when you use a parameter entity reference. The DTD itself doesn't physically change.)*

Once you've defined the parameter entity, you can use it.

To use a shortcut for a DTD:

Type **%abbreviation;**, where *abbreviation* is the name you used when defining the entity in step 6 on page 60 **(Figure 4.11)**.

✔ Tips

- Parameter entities must be defined before they're used in the DTD. In this case, the order does matter.
- You can also create internal parameter entities (within an internal DTD), but they are restricted to containing complete declarations—and not just pieces of them—and thus are really not much use.
- Be extra vigilant about punctuation. There are so many double quotes, greater than and less than signs, and brackets!
- You can use this technique to use someone else's standard DTD in addition to your own. For example, you can reference the XHTML DTD so that you can use the defined elements (which look and act much like familiar HTML elements) without going to the trouble of defining them yourself.
- Or you could link to a standardized list of entities, like the ones available at *http://www.schema.net*. This would let you use the easy-to-remember entity references for accented characters to your pages without having to manually define the entities for each one.
- Remember that you can use as many DTDs as you like.

Creating Entities for Unparsed Content

So far, we've only talked about entities whose content is text. Entities that contain text are called *parsed entities* because the XML parser looks at them and analyzes them in the course of going through the XML document. *Unparsed entities*, which we'll describe in this section, don't necessarily contain text (but can), but most importantly are completely bypassed by the XML parser. They can be used to embed non-text or non-XML content into an XML document.

To create unparsed content:

Create the data that you want to embed in the XML document. It may contain virtually anything, including plain text, an image file, a movie, a pdf file, or anything else.

To define an entity for the unparsed content:

1. In the DTD of the document in which you want to embed the data, type **<!ENTITY** to begin the definition of the unparsed entity.
2. Type **abbreviation**, where *abbreviation* is the name for the external entity.
3. Type **SYSTEM** to indicate that the entity is defined in another document.
4. Type **"entity.url"**, where *entity.url* is the location of the file with the unparsed content.
5. Type **NDATA id**, where *id* is the word that identifies the notation that will describe the unparsed data. (We'll create that notation in just a moment.)
6. Type **>** to complete the entity declaration.

Figure 4.13 *Here is a typical chunk of unparsed data: a JPEG image. It's called* tiger.jpg.

code.dtd

```
<?xml version="1.0" encoding="UTF-8"
standalone="no"?>
<!DOCTYPE endangered_species [
<!ELEMENT endangered_species (animal*)>
<!ELEMENT animal (name+, photo)>
<!ELEMENT name (#PCDATA) >
<!ATTLIST name language (English | Latin)
#REQUIRED>
<!ENTITY tiger_pic SYSTEM "tiger.jpg" NDATA jpg>
```

Figure 4.14 *The entity has a name,* `tiger_pic`*, references an external* `SYSTEM` *file called* tiger.jpg, *and we can get more information about the file by looking at the* `NOTATION` *declaration called* `jpg`.

Creating Entities for Unparsed Content

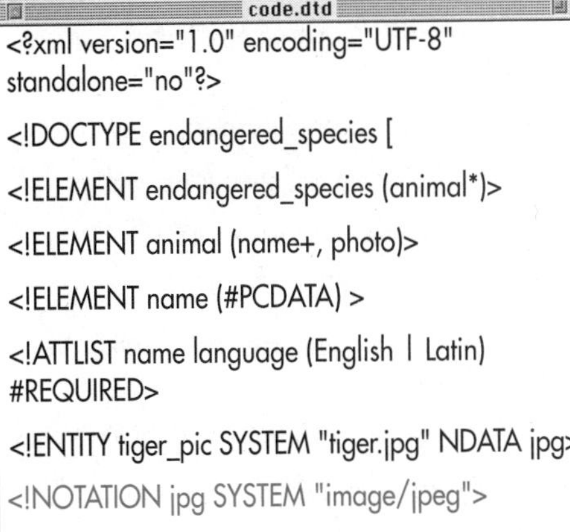

```
code.dtd
<?xml version="1.0" encoding="UTF-8"
standalone="no"?>
<!DOCTYPE endangered_species [
<!ELEMENT endangered_species (animal*)>
<!ELEMENT animal (name+, photo)>
<!ELEMENT name (#PCDATA) >
<!ATTLIST name language (English | Latin)
#REQUIRED>
<!ENTITY tiger_pic SYSTEM "tiger.jpg" NDATA jpg>
<!NOTATION jpg SYSTEM "image/jpeg">
```

Figure 4.15 *The name of the notation element must match the value after NDATA in the entity declaration.*

To add information about the type of content:

1. On a new line in the DTD, after the corresponding entity declaration, type **<!NOTATION id**, where *id* is the name of the notation and is the same identifying word that you used in step 5 on page 62.
2. Type **SYSTEM**.
3. Type **"content_information"**, where *content_information* identifies the data you are going to embed. There is no official format for this information!
4. Finally type **>** to complete the notation declaration.

✔ Tips

- The contents of an unparsed entity can be just about anything. Often, it's an image, sound, movie, or other kind of multimedia file. It could also be plain text. It doesn't matter what it is because the XML parser won't look at it.
- Unparsed entities can only become part of the body of the XML document. They cannot become part of the DTD. In other words, all unparsed entities are general entities, not parameter entities.
- The contents of a notation declaration can be a MIME type, a URL indicating an external application that can handle the unparsed data, or practically anything else. There is no official format. Each XML application can use the notation declaration in its own way.

Embedding Unparsed Content

Once you've defined an entity for your unparsed content, as described on page 62, you can then embed it in your XML document. Unparsed entities do not have entity references (like the parsed entities we described earlier). Instead, you call them through specially declared attributes.

To declare the attribute that will contain the reference to the unparsed content:

1. In the DTD, define the element that will contain the attribute that will reference the unparsed data *(see page 42).*
2. Type **<!ATTLIST element_name**, where *element_name* describes the element you declared in step 1.
3. Type **att_name**, where *att_name* is the name of the attribute that will contain the reference to the unparsed data.
4. Type **ENTITY** to identify this attribute as one that can contain references to unparsed data.

   Or type **ENTITIES** if you want the attribute to be able to contain multiple white-space-separated references to unparsed data files.
5. Type the default value for the attribute. For more details, consult *Defining Simple Attributes* on page 50.
6. Type **>** to complete the attribute declaration.

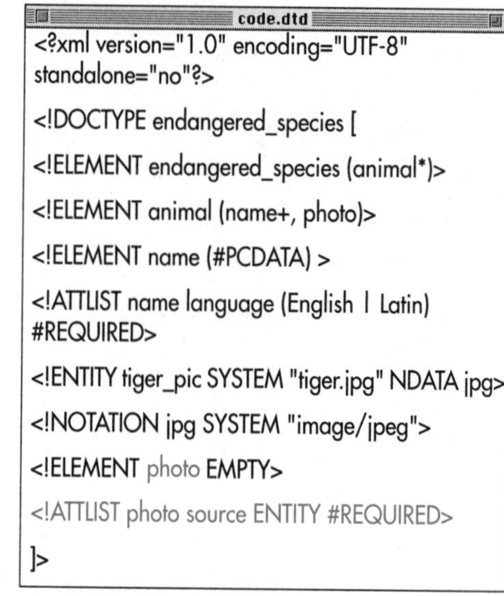

```
code.dtd
<?xml version="1.0" encoding="UTF-8"
standalone="no"?>
<!DOCTYPE endangered_species [
<!ELEMENT endangered_species (animal*)>
<!ELEMENT animal (name+, photo)>
<!ELEMENT name (#PCDATA) >
<!ATTLIST name language (English | Latin)
#REQUIRED>
<!ENTITY tiger_pic SYSTEM "tiger.jpg" NDATA jpg>
<!NOTATION jpg SYSTEM "image/jpeg">
<!ELEMENT photo EMPTY>
<!ATTLIST photo source ENTITY #REQUIRED>
]>
```

Figure 4.16 *First we define the* `photo` *element that will contain the attribute that will reference the unparsed data. Then we define the entity attribute itself, called* `source`.

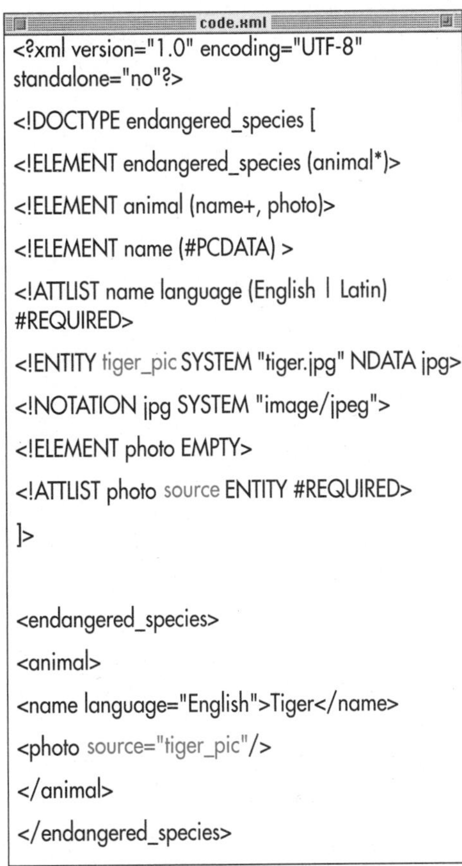

```
<?xml version="1.0" encoding="UTF-8"
standalone="no"?>
<!DOCTYPE endangered_species [
<!ELEMENT endangered_species (animal*)>
<!ELEMENT animal (name+, photo)>
<!ELEMENT name (#PCDATA) >
<!ATTLIST name language (English | Latin)
#REQUIRED>
<!ENTITY tiger_pic SYSTEM "tiger.jpg" NDATA jpg>
<!NOTATION jpg SYSTEM "image/jpeg">
<!ELEMENT photo EMPTY>
<!ATTLIST photo source ENTITY #REQUIRED>
]>

<endangered_species>
<animal>
<name language="English">Tiger</name>
<photo source="tiger_pic"/>
</animal>
</endangered_species>
```

Figure 4.17 *The value of the* `source` *attribute corresponds to the name of the entity that references the unparsed data.*

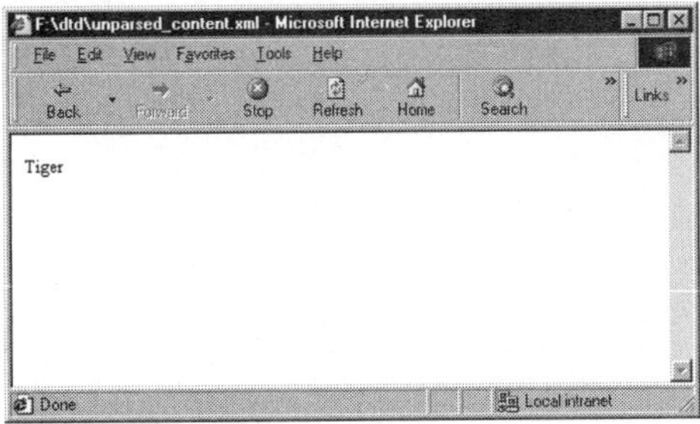

Figure 4.18 *The results are depressing in both Explorer (shown here) and Mozilla (the beta version of Netscape 6), the only browsers that can read XML files so far. While the system is set up to allow for embedding binary files, the browsers don't actually know how to take advantage of the system—yet.*

To embed unparsed content in an XML document:

In the body of the XML document, when you get to the attribute, type **att_name="value"**, where *att_name* identifies the attribute that you've declared with an entity type (on the preceding page) and *value* is the abbreviation for the entity that you created to contain the unparsed data way back in step 2 on page 62.

✔ Tips

- While XML parsers are supposed to be able to use the information in the notation to enable them to view the unparsed data referenced by the entity (with the attribute), neither Explorer nor the beta version of Netscape 6 (the only browsers that can currently read XML files) are set up to use the notation information effectively. In short, they won't show the embedded data **(Figure 4.18)**.
- You can also create attributes of type NOTATION in order to directly reference the data specified in a notation declaration *(see page 63)*. The syntax is **<!ATTLIST element_name att_name NOTATION default_value>**.

Part 3: XML Schema and Namespaces

5

XML Schema

> **Important Note!**
>
> XML Schema was still a *working draft*, albeit in "Last Call", at press time. That means that it's possible (though unlikely) that the W3C could still make changes to the syntax. If the specifications are changed, I'll post updates to my Web site *(see page 18)*. In addition, you can always find the latest specifications for XML Schema at *http://www.w3.org/XML/Schema*.

A *schema*, like a DTD, defines what a given set of one or more XML documents can look like: what elements they contain and in what order, what their content might be, and what attributes these might contain. (In fact, DTDs are a kind of schema, in the general sense of the word. In this chapter however, *schema* refers only to those schemas written in XML Schema language.)

DTDs have several disadvantages with respect to schemas written with XML Schema. First, DTDs are written in a syntax that has little to do with XML, and which thus cannot be parsed with an XML parser. Second, all the declarations in a DTD are global, which means you can't define two different elements with the same name, even if they appear in separate contexts.

Finally, and perhaps most importantly, DTDs cannot control what *kind* of information a given element or attribute can contain.

The XML Schema language, developed by the W3C, attempts to remedy each of these problems. XML Schema, written in XML itself, lets you define both global elements (that must be used in the same way throughout the XML document) and local elements (that can have a particular meaning in a particular context). In addition, XML Schema contains a system of *datatypes* that let you specify that a given element should, say, contain an integer, that another should contain a period of time, and that the last should contain a string. In short, XML Schema gives you much more control over the contents of an XML document.

Simple and Complex Types

In a schema, a document is divided into two types of content: simple and complex. Elements that can contain only text are considered to be of *simple type*. Elements that contain other elements or that contain attributes have a *complex type*. (Attributes—since they contain only text—are considered to be of simple type.)

Let's take a closer look at simple types. In a DTD, you can describe an element as containing only text by specifying its contents as #PCDATA. That PCDATA might be a name, a number, a date, or practically anything. In XML Schema, you specify exactly what kind of text you want an element to contain by assigning it a particular simple type definition. There are several built-in simple types, like *date*, *integer*, and *string*, that you can use without further modifications. Or you can build custom simple types in order to have more control over how an element's content should look. You'll find information about defining and using simple types in Chapter 6, *Defining Simple Types*.

Elements of complex type tend to describe the structure of a document, rather than its content. There are four basic kinds of complex types: elements that contain just other elements, elements that contain both elements and text, elements that contain only text, and elements that are empty. Each of these may contain attributes as well. You define the particular complex types necessary for your XML document. You'll find complete details in Chapter 7, *Defining Complex Types*.

Both simple and custom types may be either *named*, in which case they can be reused in other places throughout the schema, or *anonymous*, in which case they are used only within the element in which the definition appears.

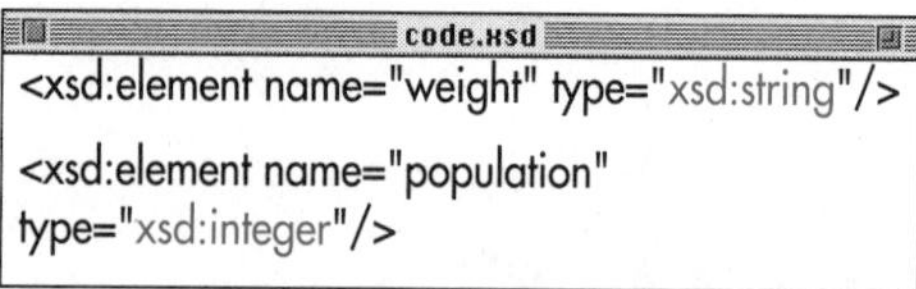

```
code.xsd
<xsd:element name="weight" type="xsd:string"/>
<xsd:element name="population"
type="xsd:integer"/>
```

Figure 5.1 *These two elements are defined with built-in simple types. The* `weight` *will be limited to a string, while the* `population` *must be an integer.*

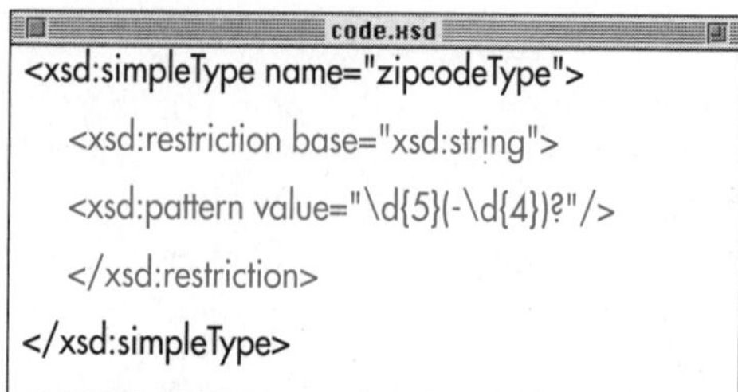

```
code.xsd
<xsd:simpleType name="zipcodeType">
    <xsd:restriction base="xsd:string">
    <xsd:pattern value="\d{5}(-\d{4})?"/>
    </xsd:restriction>
</xsd:simpleType>
```

Figure 5.2 *This custom simple type limits the content of elements defined with the* `zipcodeType` *to a string with a pattern of five digits, followed by an optional hyphen and four additional digits.*

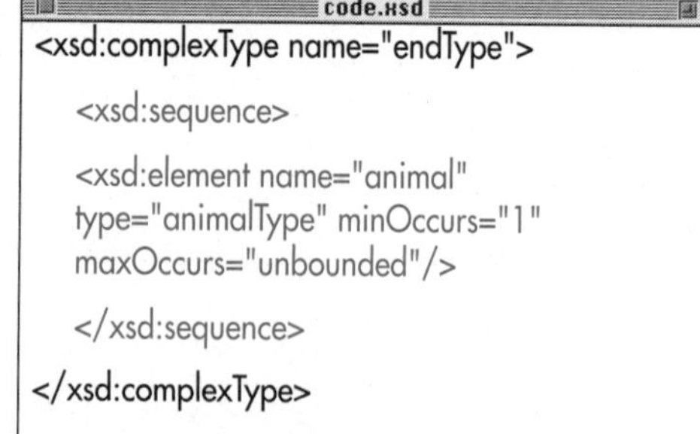

```
code.xsd
<xsd:complexType name="endType">
    <xsd:sequence>
    <xsd:element name="animal"
    type="animalType" minOccurs="1"
    maxOccurs="unbounded"/>
    </xsd:sequence>
</xsd:complexType>
```

Figure 5.3 *This complex type definition defines the* `endType` *as containing one other element (called* `animal`, *which is defined with another complex type called* `animalType`*). You can use the* `endType` *complex type to define a particular element (that will contain the* `animal` *element).*

```
code.xsd
<?xml version="1.0" ?>

<xsd:schema xmlns:xsd="http://www.w3.org
    /2000/10/XMLSchema">

<xsd:element name="endangered_species"
    type="endType"/>

<xsd:element name="name" type="xsd:string"/>

<xsd:complexType name="endType">
    <xsd:sequence>
    <xsd:element name="animal">
       <xsd:complexType>
           <xsd:sequence>
           <xsd:element ref="name"
           minOccurs="2"/>
           <xsd:element name="source"
               type="sourceType"/>
    ...
    </xsd:complexType>

<xsd:complexType name="habitatType">
    <xsd:sequence>
    <xsd:element name="river">
       <xsd:complexType>
           <xsd:sequence>
           <xsd:element ref="name"
           minOccurs="1"
           maxOccurs="unbounded"/>
           <xsd:element name="source"
           type="xsd:string"/>
    ...
    </xsd:complexType>
...
```

Figure 5.4 *There are four globally declared components in this schema excerpt, evident because they appear on the first level below the* `xsd:schema` *element. The root element (*`endangered_species`*) is automatically referenced, but the* `name` *element (since it is not a root), must be manually referenced, as shown.*

The boldly highlighted components show that you can have two locally *declared elements with the same name but different definitions. Their context keeps them distinct. Global element declarations, on the other hand, must have unique names.*

Local and Global Declarations

In a DTD, every element is declared globally. That means that each and every element has a unique name and is defined exactly once. An element can be referenced by any number of other elements, and thus might have to appear in more than one place in an XML document, but, no matter where it appears, it will always have the exact same definition.

In XML Schema, context is very important. Schema components, including elements, attributes, and named simple and complex types (as well as groups and attribute groups which we'll get to later), that are declared at the top level of a schema—just under the `xsd:schema` element—are considered *globally declared*, and are available to be used throughout the rest of the schema. Note carefully, however, that global element declarations do not determine where an element can appear in the XML document—they only determine what that element will look like. You must explicitly *reference* a global element declaration in order to actually have it appear in a corresponding XML document.

The only exception to this rule is for the root element which is automatically referenced wherever it is (globally) declared.

When you define a complex type, you can either reference existing globally declared elements, or you can declare and define new elements on the spot. These new *locally declared* elements are limited to the complex type definition in which they are declared and may not be used elsewhere in the schema. In addition, their names need only be unique within the context in which they appear. Such locally declared elements are automatically referenced—that is, the position in which they are defined also determines where the element must appear in the XML document.

Beginning a Simple Schema

A schema is an XML document, in text-only format, with the .xsd extension. It begins with a standard XML declaration, followed by a declaration of the XML Schema namespace.

To begin a schema:

1. At the top of your schema document, if desired, type **<?xml version="1.0" ?>**. For more information on the XML declaration, consult *Declaring the XML Version* on page 24.
2. Type **<xsd:schema**.
3. Type **xmlns:xsd="http://www.w3.org/2000/10/XMLSchema"** to declare the namespace for the "schema of schemas". Henceforth, any element or type that is prefixed with *xsd:* will be recognized as coming from this namespace.
4. Type **>** to complete the opening schema element.
5. Leave a few lines that will contain the schema's rules, which you'll learn to define in Chapter 6, *Defining Simple Types*, and in Chapter 7, *Defining Complex Types*.
6. Finally, type **</xsd:schema>** to complete your schema document.
7. Save your schema as text only with the .xsd extension.

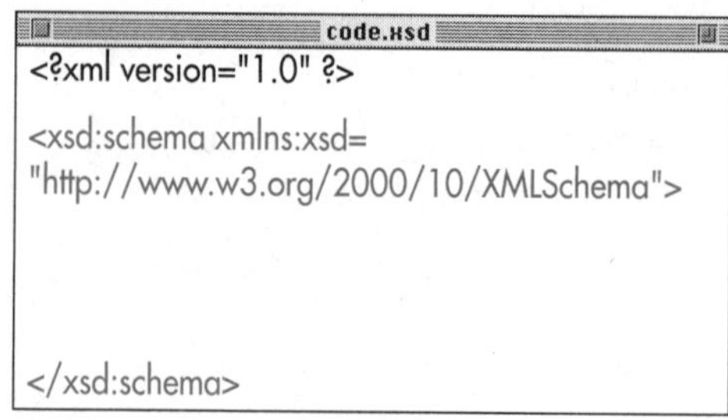
```
<?xml version="1.0" ?>

<xsd:schema xmlns:xsd=
"http://www.w3.org/2000/10/XMLSchema">



</xsd:schema>
```

Figure 5.5 *In the root element of the schema, declare the namespace for the Schema of Schemas.*

✔ Tip

- While you can declare additional namespaces and/or declare the XML Schema as the default namespace, we're not going to get into that until a bit later *(see pages 126–128)*. We'll keep it simple here in order to focus on how to create the schema itself.

```
code.xml
<?xml version="1.0" ?>

<endangered_species
xmlns:xsi="http://www.w3.org/2000/10/
XMLSchema-instance"

xsi:noNamespaceSchemaLocation=
"http://www.cookwood.com/ns/end_species/
end_species.xsd">
```

Figure 5.6 *You can point processors to the schema file that defines your document by using the* `xsi:schemaLocation` *attribute in the root element of your XML document.*

Indicating a Simple Schema's Location

Depending on the validator you use to compare an XML document to a schema, it may be necessary to indicate in the XML document where the corresponding schema can be found.

To declare and indicate a schema's location:

1. In the root element of your XML document, type **xmlns:xsi="http://www.w3.org/2000/10/XMLSchema-instance"** to make the elements available with which you'll indicate the schema location. (This is called *declaring a namespace* and we'll cover it in more detail on page 116.)
2. Type **xsi:noNamespaceSchemaLocation=**.
3. And finally, type **"file.xsd"**, where *file.xsd* is the URL of the actual schema file (that you created in step 7 on page 72) that you want to use to validate this XML file.

✔ Tips

- There are several programs available for validating documents against a schema. The most reliable I've found is XML Schema Validator *(see page 245)*. Or you can also try XML Spy, an XML editor, that you can find at *http://www.xmlspy.com.*
- The `xsi:noNamespaceSchemaLocation` attribute only works when there is no target namespace declared in the schema. And no, we haven't gotten to target namespaces yet, but just in case you're skipping around... (We get to them in Chapter 9, *Namespaces, Schemas, and Validation.*)

Annotating Schemas

You can add information about your schema or its elements to make it easier for others (or a future you) to work with your schemas.

To annotate schemas:

1. Type **<xsd:annotation>**.
2. Next type **<xsd:documentation>** to begin a note designed for people to read (as opposed to machines).
3. Type the note.
4. Type **</xsd:documentation>** to complete the note.
5. And finally type **</xsd:annotation>** to complete the annotation.

✔ Tip

- You can create annotations right after the `xsd:schema` element (to document the entire schema) or after individual element declarations (to give more information about them), or both.

```
code.xsd
<xsd:schema xmlns:xsd="http://www.w3.org/
2000/10/XMLSchema">

<xsd:annotation>

<xsd:documentation>

This schema will be used to validate the set of XML
documents for the Endangered Species
project.</xsd:documentation>

</xsd:annotation>
```

Figure 5.7 *An annotation helps you document the schema itself. It can facilitate future revisions.*

6

An element with a simple type can contain only text. It may not contain other elements and it may not have attributes. Still, "text" is a pretty general term. Instead of just limiting an element's content to "text", you can demand that it have a particular kind of text. You create that limit by using a pre-defined simple type definition, or by deriving your own custom one.

XML Schema includes a collection of built-in simple types for the most common kinds of text. These include strings, booleans, URLs, various date formats, and numbers of all kinds. You can also apply restrictions, or *facets*, to a built-in simple type in order to limit it further, thereby creating your own custom simple type. For example, you might want to require that an element contain a string that matches a certain pattern (like a telephone number or product code). Or you might want to have an element that can only contain one of a specific set of dates.

Declaring an Element with a Simple Type

An element has a simple type if it's only allowed to contain other elements or attributes. There are many different built-in simple types, or you can create your own, based on one of the built-in types.

To declare an element of simple type:

1. Type **<xsd:element** to begin the declaration.
2. Type **name="label"**, where *label* is the name of the element that you're declaring, that is, in your XML document it will look something like: <label>.
3. Type **type="**.

   Then type **xsd:string** if this element should contain a string of characters.

   Or type **xsd:decimal** if the element will contain a decimal number. For other possible number types, see page 80.

   Or type **xsd:boolean** if the element will contain the values *true* or *false* (or *1* or *0*).

   Or type **xsd:date** if the element will be a date. For other date types, see page 78.

   Or type **xsd:time** if the element will be a time of day. For other possible time types, see page 78.

   Or type **xsd:uri-reference** (it is *uri* and not *url*) if the element will contain a URL.

   Or type **xsd:language**, if the element will contain one of the two-letter language abbreviations listed in ISO639.

   Or type **custom**, where *custom* is the name of a custom simple type *(see page 81)*.
4. Then type **"** to complete the type.
5. Finally, type **/>** to complete the tag.

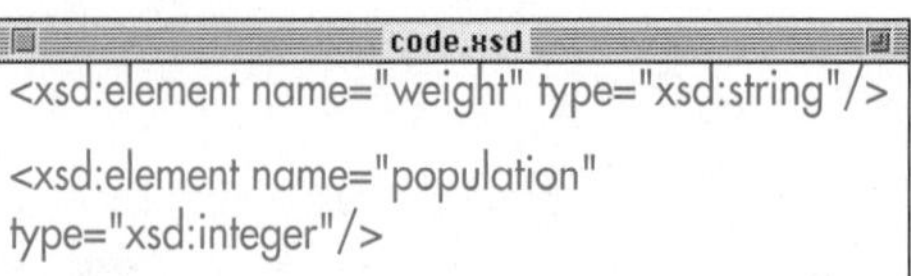

```
code.xsd
<xsd:element name="weight" type="xsd:string"/>

<xsd:element name="population"
type="xsd:integer"/>
```

Figure 6.1 *When declaring an element, you choose its name and what kind of content it should contain.*

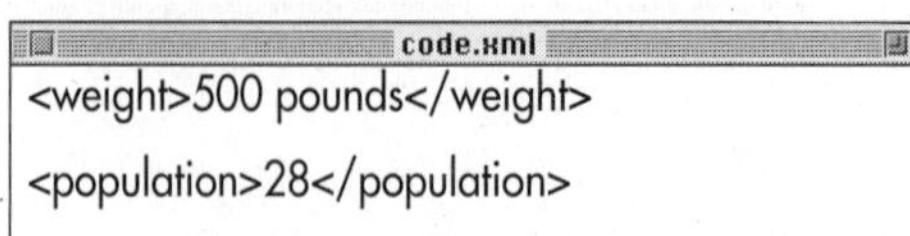

```
code.xml
<weight>500 pounds</weight>

<population>28</population>
```

Figure 6.2 *A string is a series of letters, numbers, and/or symbols. An integer is any whole number. Therefore, both the* `weight` *and* `population` *elements are valid when compared against the declarations in Figure 6.1.*

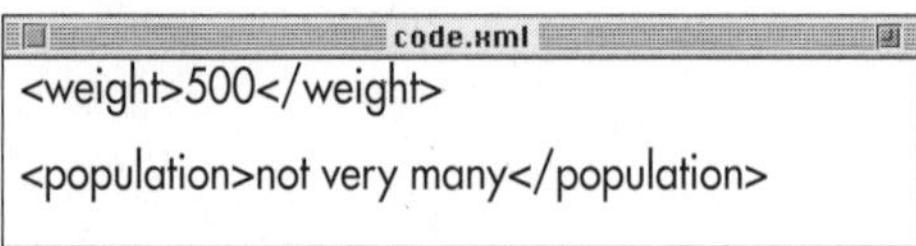

```
code.xml
<weight>500</weight>

<population>not very many</population>
```

Figure 6.3 *In this instance, the* `weight` *element looks at first glance like it might not be right, but in fact, it is valid since a number is a kind of a string (though, conversely, not all strings are numbers). The* `population` *element, of course, is invalid. The phrase "not very many" is not an integer.*

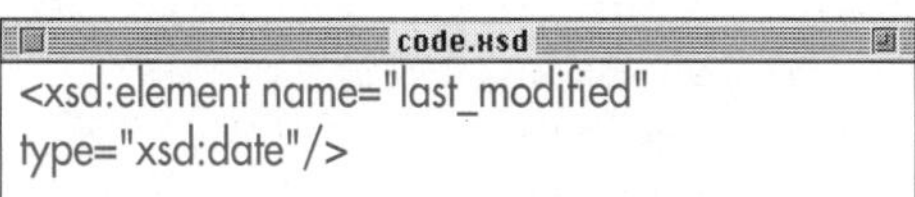

```
code.xsd
<xsd:element name="last_modified"
type="xsd:date"/>
```

Figure 6.4 *In this example, we want the* `last_modified` *element to contain a date.*

```
code.xml
<last_modified>1999-05-16</last_modified>
```

Figure 6.5 *The element must contain a date in the form CCYY-MM-DD in order to be valid, that is, a four-digit year, followed by a dash, two digits representing the month, another dash, and then two digits representing the day. There are many other built-in date formats available (see page 78).*

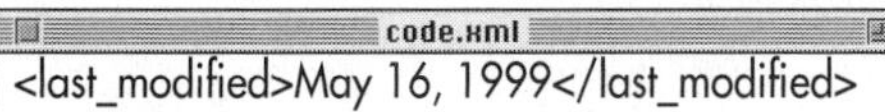

```
code.xml
<last_modified>May 16, 1999</last_modified>
```

Figure 6.6 *This* `last_modified` *element is not valid because the date is not in the proper format.*

✔ Tips

- There are many other built-in simple types. You can find the entire list at *http://www.w3.org/TR/xmlschema-2/#built-in-datatypes.*
- You can also create *custom* simple types by building on the built-in simple types. For more details, consult *Deriving Custom Simple Types* on page 81.
- Built-in simple types generally begin with *xsd:*. (For an exception, see page 128.) This makes them easy to distinguish from custom simple types *(see page 81).*
- Attributes themselves are always simple types (since they cannot contain content nor have attributes of their own) and they are declared in much the same way as elements of simple type. But, it doesn't make sense to declare them until we can declare them within an element, which we'll do in the next chapter *(see page 108).*
- If an element is allowed to contain attributes or other elements, it is said to have a complex type. For more details, see Chapter 7, *Defining Complex Types.*
- A valid element name must begin with a letter or underscore, followed by any number of additional letters, numbers, underscores, hyphens, and periods. For more details, see *Writing Non-Empty Elements* on page 26.
- Elements of simple type can either be declared globally (at the first level below the `xsd:schema` element), in which case they need to be called (or *referenced*) in a complex type definition, or they can be declared locally within a complex type definition, in which case they're considered automatically referenced. You'll find complete details in Chapter 7, *Defining Complex Types.*

Using Date and Time Types

XML Schema has several built-in data types for dates. Use (in step 3 on page 76) the one that suits your purposes or derive your own type from one of these *(see page 81)*.

To use date and time types:

1. Choose **xsd:timeDuration** when you want the content to represent a certain amount of time, like 2 hours, 12 minutes, and 45.3 seconds.

   The time duration should be formatted as **PnYnMnDTnHnMnS**, where *P* is always required (it stands for Period), the *T* begins the optional time section, and each *n* (always a non-negative integer) indicates how many of the following units there are (Years, Months, Days, Hours, Minutes, Seconds). Add an optional leading hyphen to indicate the duration goes back in time (not forward).

2. Choose **xsd:time** when you want the content to represent a particular time of day, that recurs every day, like 4:15pm. It should be formatted as **hh:mm:ss.sss** with optional time zone indicator (**Z** for UTC or one of **-hh:mm** or **+hh:mm** to indicate the difference from UTC).

3. Choose **xsd:timeInstant** when you want the content to refer to a specific moment in time, like 4:15pm on the 6th of May, 1935. It should be formatted as **CCYY-MM-DDThh:mm:ss.sss** with an optional time zone indicator.

4. Choose **xsd:date** when you want the content to represent a certain day in time, like May 6, 1935. It should in the form of **CCYY-MM-DD**.

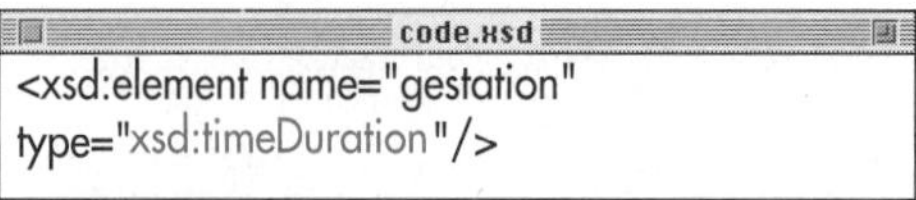


```
<xsd:element name="gestation"
type="xsd:timeDuration"/>
```

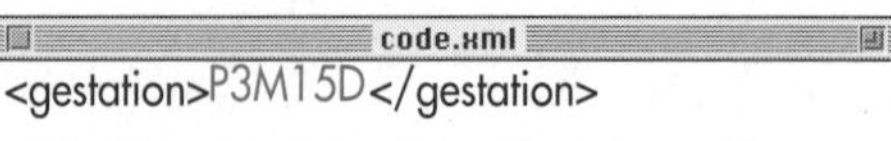


```
<gestation>P3M15D</gestation>
```

Figure 6.7 *The tiger has a gestation period of about three and a half months. Notice that you don't have to specify all of the units. Only the initial P is always required. If the* `period` *contains time data, you must also add the T.*

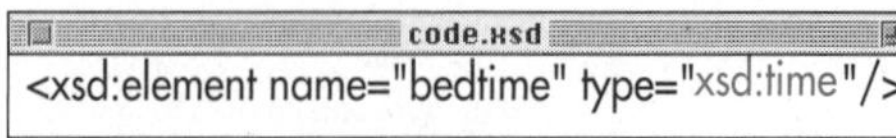


```
<xsd:element name="bedtime" type="xsd:time"/>
```

```
<bedtime>20:15-05-05:00</bedtime>
```

Figure 6.8 *Notice that the time is in "military" or universal format. The contents of this* `bedtime` *element represents 8:15pm EST (not daylight savings time).*

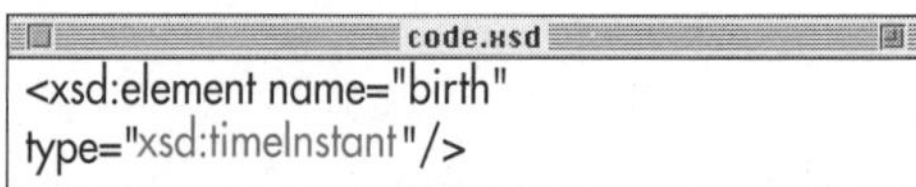


```
<xsd:element name="birth"
type="xsd:timeInstant"/>
```

```
<birth>1999-03-14T18:27:46.2398Z</birth>
```

Figure 6.9 *The contents of this element note the birth of a tiger at precisely 6:27pm and 46.2398 seconds on March 14, 1999, in universal time).*

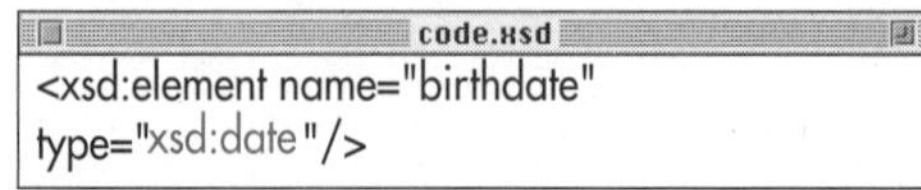


```
<xsd:element name="birthdate"
type="xsd:date"/>
```

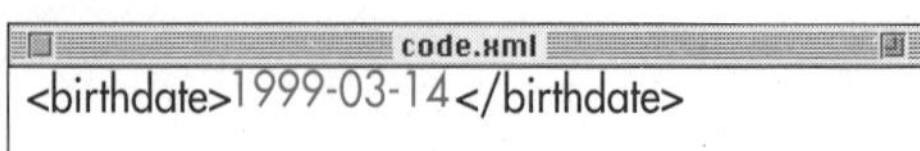


```
<birthdate>1999-03-14</birthdate>
```

Figure 6.10 *An* `xsd:date` *type element looks much like* `xsd:timeInstant`*, without the time data.*

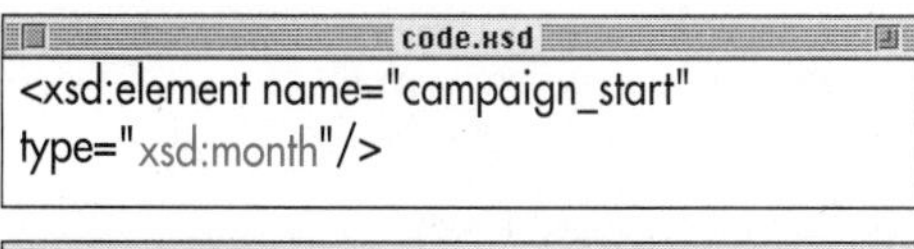

```
<xsd:element name="campaign_start"
type="xsd:month"/>
```

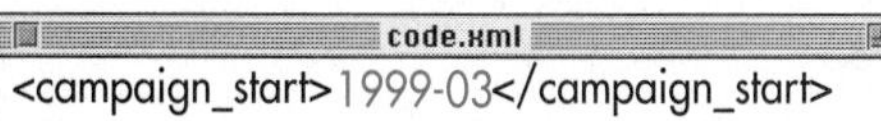

```
<campaign_start>1999-03</campaign_start>
```

Figure 6.11 *If the day is irrelevant, you can specify just the year and month in an element of type* `xsd:month`.

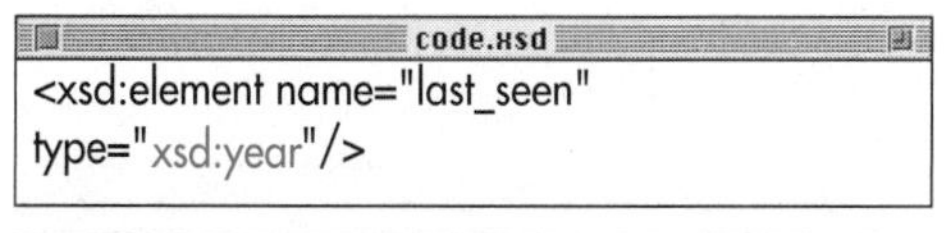

```
<xsd:element name="last_seen"
type="xsd:year"/>
```

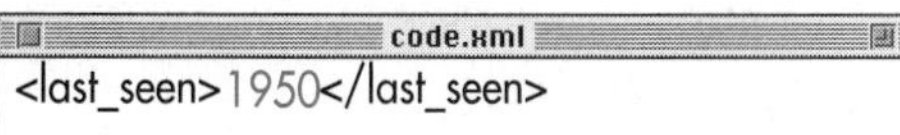

```
<last_seen>1950</last_seen>
```

Figure 6.12 *The last Caspian tiger was seen in 1950. The day and month are not known, and so it makes sense to have an element that only requires the year.*

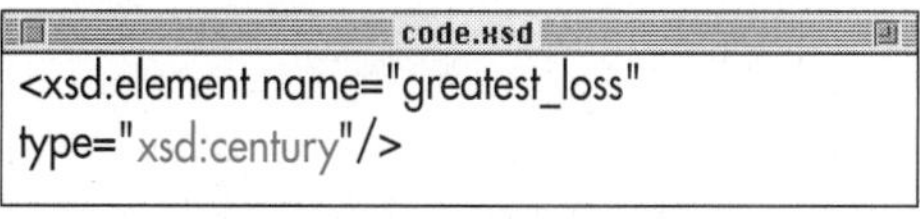

```
<xsd:element name="greatest_loss"
type="xsd:century"/>
```

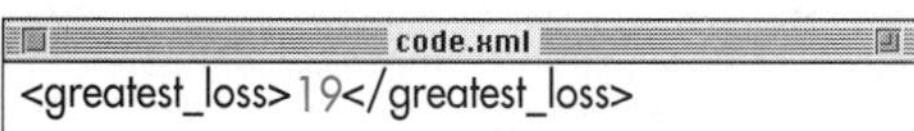

```
<greatest_loss>19</greatest_loss>
```

Figure 6.13 *Remember that 19 refers to the 20th century, that is, the years from 1900–1999 (during which 96% of the tigers of the world disappeared).*

```
<xsd:element name="birthday"
type="xsd:recurringDate"/>
```

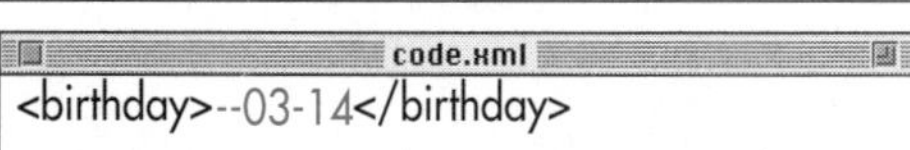

```
<birthday>--03-14</birthday>
```

Figure 6.14 *When the year doesn't matter, but the month and day do, use* `xsd:recurringDate`.

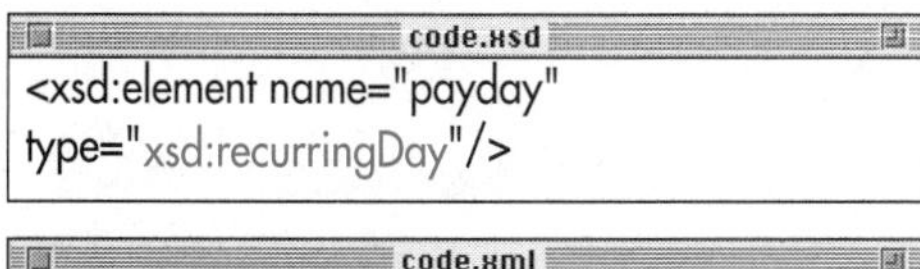

```
<xsd:element name="payday"
type="xsd:recurringDay"/>
```

code.xml

```
<payday>---30</payday>
```

Figure 6.15 *For an event that occurs on the same day of each month, use* `xsd:recurringDay`.

5. Choose **xsd:month** when you want the content to represent a certain month in time, like May, 1935. It should be in the form of **CCYY-MM**.

6. Choose **xsd:year** when you want the content to represent a certain year in time, like 1935. It should be in the form of **CCYY**.

7. Choose **xsd:century** when you want the content to contain a certain century, like the 1900's. It should be formatted as **CC** (which means the 20th century is represented by *19*).

8. Choose **xsd:recurringDate** when you want the content to represent a particular day of a particular month without regard for the year, like January 1st. It should be formatted as **--MM-DD.** (That's two initial dashes: one to represent the "missing" year, one to act as a separator.)

9. Choose **xsd:recurringDay** when you want the content to represent a particular day of the month, without regard to the month or year, like the 6th of every month. It should be formatted as **---DD**. (Three initial dashes here: one for each "missing" piece, and one as separator.)

✔ Tip

- UTC (Coordinated Universal Time) is set by the International Time Bureau (Bureau International de l'Heure) and is the same time as Greenwich Mean Time, which happens to be the local time in London, England (and Greenwich, too!). Eastern Standard Time (EST) in the U.S. is UTC -5. Pacific Standard Time (PST) is UTC - 8. Most of Western Europe is UTC+1. Russia is UTC+3. Japan is UTC+9. Australia is UTC+10. You can find a table of world times at my web site *(see page 18)*.

Using Number Types

XML Schema has several built-in number types that you can use (in step 3 on page 76) to limit the content of your elements and attributes. You can also use these types as the foundation on which to build your own number types *(see page 81)*.

To use number types:

1. Choose **xsd:decimal** for content that will contain either positive or negative numbers that have a finite number of digits on either side of the optional decimal point, like 4.26, -100, or 0.
2. Choose **xsd:integer** to limit the content to positive or negative whole numbers, that is, those that have no fractional part, like 542 or -7.
3. Use **xsd:positiveInteger** (1, 2, etc.), **xsd:negativeInteger** (-1, -2, etc.), **xsd:nonPositiveInteger** (0, -1, -2, etc.), and **xsd:nonNegativeInteger** (0, 1, 2, etc.) to limit the content to those kinds of numbers.
4. Use **xsd:float** to allow the content to contain single precision 32-bit floating point numbers like 43e-2, including positive and negative (0 and -0), positive and negative infinity (INF and -INF), and `not a number` (NaN).
5. Use **xsd:double** to allow the content to contain double precision 64-bit floating point numbers.

✔ Tip

■ You can find a couple more (obscure in my opinion) number types explained at *http://www.w3.org/TR/xmlschema-2/*, as well as more detailed explanations of the ones I've mentioned here.

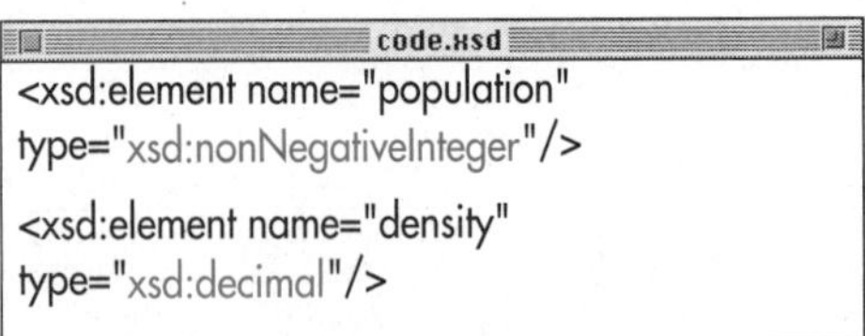

```
code.xsd
<xsd:element name="population"
type="xsd:nonNegativeInteger"/>
<xsd:element name="density"
type="xsd:decimal"/>
```

Figure 6.16 *It's more precise to require a non-negative integer for the* `population`*. (A positive integer would not be appropriate, because unfortunately, the value might be zero, which* `xsd:positiveInteger` *doesn't allow.) The* `density` *element (which tracks how many animals there are per square kilometer of habitat) needs the precision of a decimal number.*

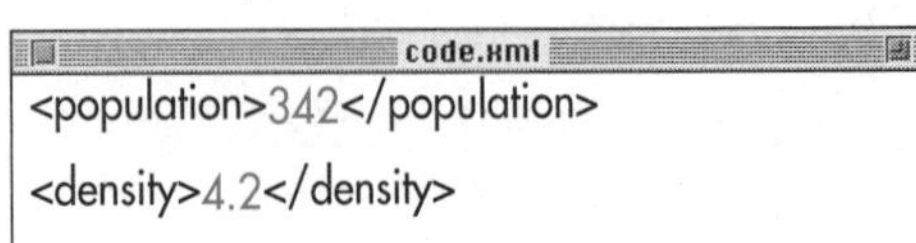

```
code.xml
<population>342</population>
<density>4.2</density>
```

Figure 6.17 *As long as the* `population` *is 0 or higher, the element is valid. The* `density` *may have both a fractional and a whole part.*

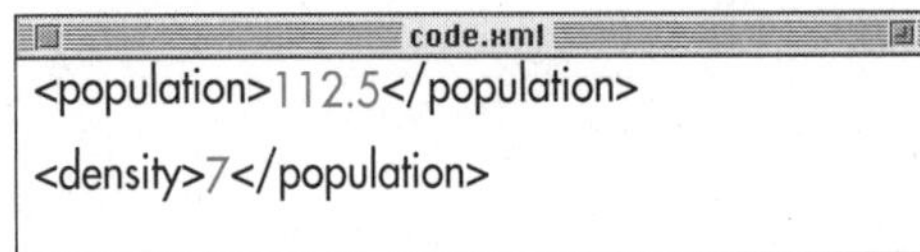

```
code.xml
<population>112.5</population>
<density>7</population>
```

Figure 6.18 *The* `population` *element is invalid since an integer cannot have a decimal part, as does the content of the* `population` *element shown here. The* `density` *element is still valid, since a decimal number may have a fractional portion, but is* not *required to have one.*

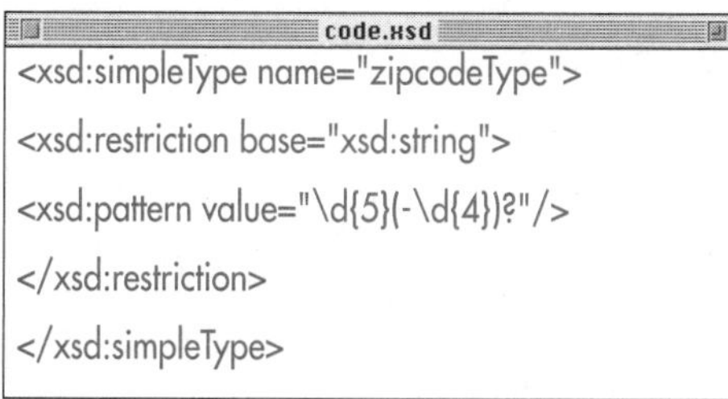

```
code.xsd
<xsd:simpleType name="zipcodeType">
<xsd:restriction base="xsd:string">
<xsd:pattern value="\d{5}(-\d{4})?"/>
</xsd:restriction>
</xsd:simpleType>
```

Figure 6.19 *Here I've created a new type called* `zipcodeType` *which is based on the* `xsd:string` *type, but includes a pattern that limits the content of elements of this type to five digits followed by an optional hyphen and four additional digits.*

```
code.xsd
<xsd:element name="zipcode"
type="zipcodeType"/ minOccurs="1">
```

Figure 6.20 *You can use the new* `zipcodeType` *in element declarations (see page 76). I'll explain the* `minOccurs` *attribute (for determining how many times an element appears) on page 101.*

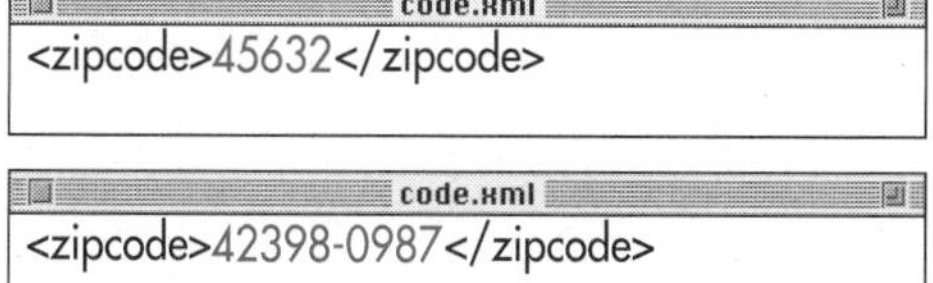

```
code.xml
<zipcode>45632</zipcode>
```

```
code.xml
<zipcode>42398-0987</zipcode>
```

Figure 6.21 *Both of these* `zipcode` *elements are valid.*

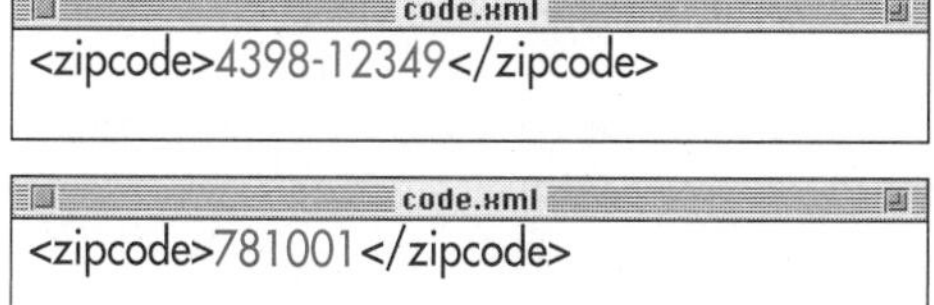

```
code.xml
<zipcode>4398-12349</zipcode>
```

```
code.xml
<zipcode>781001</zipcode>
```

Figure 6.22 *Both of these* `zipcode` *elements are invalid. The first because it contains four digits followed by a hyphen and five digits (instead of the other way around). The second element is invalid because it does not follow the pattern at all, despite being a real postal code in Guwahati, India, near the Manas Tiger Reserve. It may be necessary to create a new element to accommodate non-U.S. postal codes.*

Deriving Custom Simple Types

While the XML Schema language contains many built-in simple types, you can expand on these types for your particular needs.

To derive a custom simple type:

1. Type **<xsd:simpleType** to begin the definition of the custom simple type.
2. Type **name="label">**, where *label* will identify the new custom simple type (but is not the name of the element, since the type can be used for more than one element).
3. Type **<xsd:restriction base="foundation">**, where *foundation* is the simple type upon which you're basing the custom type.
4. Specify as many restrictions (or *facets*) as necessary to define your new custom type *(see pages 84–90)*.
5. Type **</xsd:restriction>**.
6. Type **</xsd:simpleType>** to complete the custom simple type definition.

✔ Tips

- Once you've defined your named custom simple type, you can use it as described in the last paragraph under step 3 on page 76. Notice that you don't refer to it as `xsd:label`, but rather just `label` **(Figure 6.20)**.
- You can also create *anonymous* simple types for use in a single element declaration *(see page 82)*.
- You can also create *list* simple types. For more information consult *Creating List Types* on page 90.

Using Anonymous Custom Types

You don't have to name every custom type that you create. If you're just going to use a type once to set a particular element, you can omit the cross reference between the element and the type.

To define and use an anonymous custom type:

1. Begin the declaration of your element by typing **<xsd:element name="label">**, where *label* is the name of the element that you're declaring, that is, in your XML document it will look something like: <label>.
2. Type **<xsd:simpleType>**.
3. Type **<xsd:restriction base="foundation">** where *foundation* is the simple type upon which you are building the custom type.
4. Specify as many restrictions (or *facets*) as necessary to define your new custom type *(see pages 84–90)*.
5. Type **</xsd:restriction>**.
6. Type **</xsd:simpleType>** to complete the definition of the new simple type.
7. Finally, type **</xsd:element>** to complete the declaration of the element with the anonymous simple type.

✔ Tips

- Of course, this only makes sense for custom types. For built-in types, just reference the type with the `type` attribute.
- The only difference between an anonymous type and a named type is that a named type can be used more than once (just by setting the `type` attribute to the name), whereas the anonymous type can only be used for the element in which it is contained.

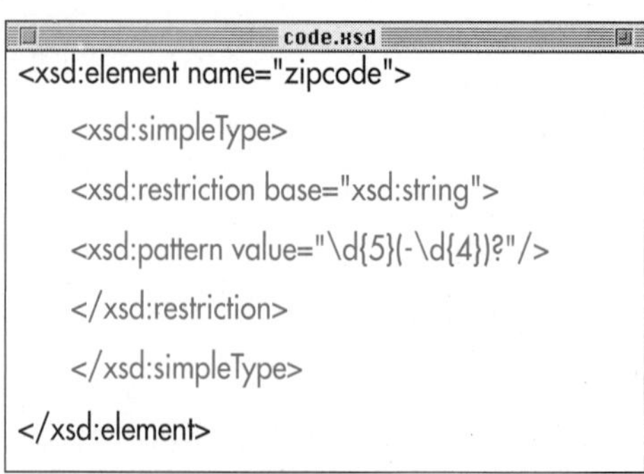

```
code.xsd
<xsd:element name="zipcode">
    <xsd:simpleType>
    <xsd:restriction base="xsd:string">
    <xsd:pattern value="\d{5}(-\d{4})?"/>
    </xsd:restriction>
    </xsd:simpleType>
</xsd:element>
```

Figure 6.23 *Compare this element declaration with the combination custom type definition and element declaration in Figure 6.19 and Figure 6.20 on page 81. The definition of the* `zipcode` *element in both examples is identical. The principal difference is that the custom type shown above cannot be reused for any other element (notice how the* `xsd:simpleType` *element has no name with which to reference it).*

```
code.xsd
<xsd:element name="continent">
<xsd:simpleType>
    <xsd:restriction base="xsd:string">
    <xsd:enumeration value="Asia"/>
    <xsd:enumeration value="Africa"/>
    <xsd:enumeration value="Australia"/>
    <xsd:enumeration value="Europe"/>
    <xsd:enumeration value="North America"/>
    <xsd:enumeration value="South America"/>
    <xsd:enumeration value="Antartica"/>
    </xsd:restriction>
</xsd:simpleType>
</xsd:element>
```

Figure 6.24 *The* `continent` *element can now contain any* single *one of these values.*

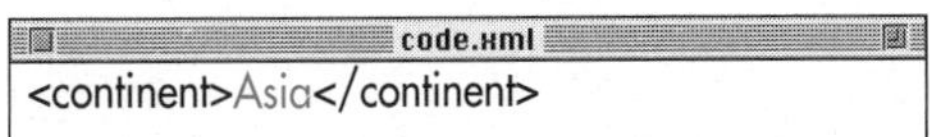

Figure 6.25 *This* `continent` *element is perfectly valid, since it matches one of the enumerated choices.*

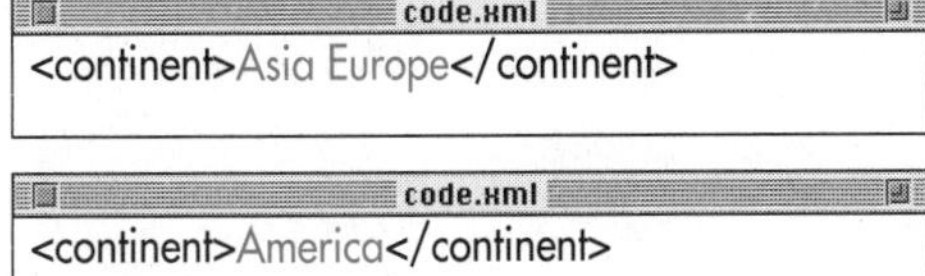

Figure 6.26 *Neither of these* `continent` *elements is valid. The first one contains two choices, when only one is allowed. The second one contains only a part of a choice. (While it's true that in many parts of the world, "America" is considered a single continent, in our list of enumerations, it only appears as a part of two enumerated values and is thus not valid on its own.)*

Specifying a Set of Acceptable Values

To keep your XML documents consistent, you may want to limit the contents of an element or attribute to a set of acceptable values.

To specify a set of acceptable values:

1. Within the custom type declaration, (that is, for step 4 on page 81), type **<xsd:enumeration.**
2. Type **value="choice"**, where *choice* is one acceptable value for the content of the element or attribute.
3. Type **/>** to complete the `xsd:enumeration` element.
4. Repeat steps 1–3 for each additional value that the element or attribute can have.

✓ Tips

- You can use the `xsd:enumeration` facet with all simple types except *boolean.*
- Each enumeration value must be unique.
- Enumeration values may contain white space.

Specifying a Pattern for a Simple Type

You can use a special regular expression *(regex)* language to construct a pattern which the content must match in order to be valid. The regex language in XML Schema is based on Perl's regular expression language, and could fill a whole chapter on its own. I'll give you a brief taste here.

To specify a pattern for a simple type:

1. Within the custom type declaration, (that is, for step 4 on page 81), type **<xsd:pattern.**
2. Next type **value="regex"**, where *regex* is a regular expression that matches what the content should look like, and is made up of the following:

   Specific letters, numbers, and symbols, in the order in which those letters, numbers, and symbols should appear in the content.

   . (the period) for any character at all

   \d for any digit; **\D** for any non-digit

   \s for any white space (including space, tab, newline, and return); **\S** for any character that is not white space

   x* to have *zero or more x*'s; **(xy)*** to have zero or more *xy*'s

   x? to have *one or zero x*'s; **(xy)?** to have one or no *xy*'s

   x+ to have *one or more x*'s; **(xy)+** to have one or more *xy*'s

   [abc] to include one of a group of values (*a*, *b*, or *c*)

   [0-9] to include the *range of values* from 0 to 9

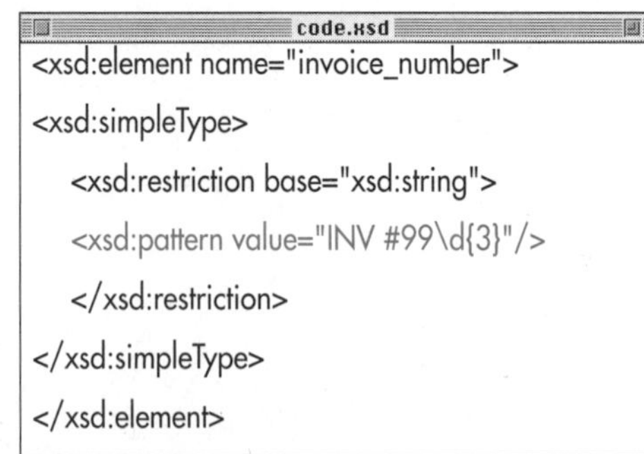

```
<xsd:element name="invoice_number">
<xsd:simpleType>
   <xsd:restriction base="xsd:string">
   <xsd:pattern value="INV #99\d{3}"/>
   </xsd:restriction>
</xsd:simpleType>
</xsd:element>
```

Figure 6.27 *This pattern limits the content of the* `invoice_number` *element to strings that begin with* INV #99 *and that have three additional digits. Any character that appears in the regex must appear in that same position in the content for the element to be valid.*

```
<invoice_number>INV #99426</invoice_number>
```

Figure 6.28 *Here is a valid instance for the bit of schema shown in Figure 6.27. We simply need the characters "INV #99" followed by any three digits.*

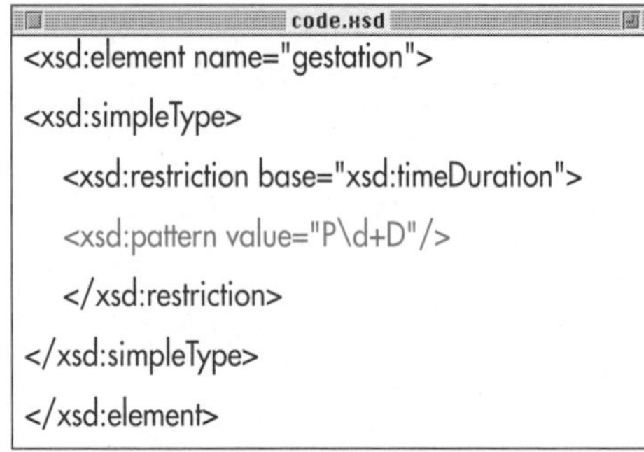

```
<xsd:element name="gestation">
<xsd:simpleType>
   <xsd:restriction base="xsd:timeDuration">
   <xsd:pattern value="P\d+D"/>
   </xsd:restriction>
</xsd:simpleType>
</xsd:element>
```

Figure 6.29 *You can also use patterns to control the contents of elements based on other types. For example, if you want the* `gestation` *element to contain a tiger's gestation period in days (and not weeks or months), you might set the pattern as shown here. Notice that this pattern doesn't "understand" what the type needs. It simply requires that the content include a capital letter* P, *followed by one or more digits, followed by a capital letter* D.

```
<gestation>P108D</gestation>
```

Figure 6.30 *Here is a valid example for the bit of schema shown in Figure 6.29.*

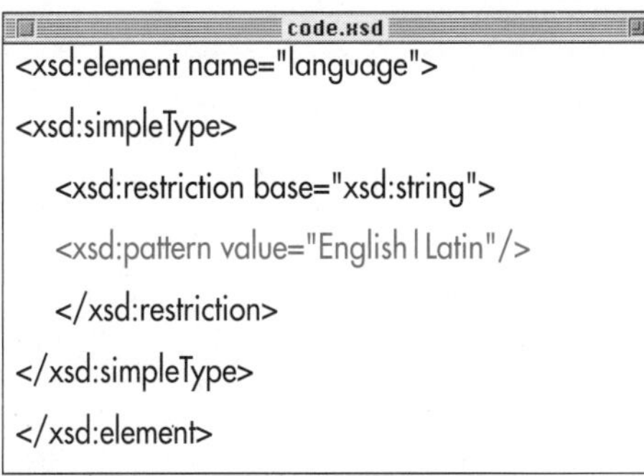

```
code.xsd
<xsd:element name="language">
<xsd:simpleType>
   <xsd:restriction base="xsd:string">
   <xsd:pattern value="English|Latin"/>
   </xsd:restriction>
</xsd:simpleType>
</xsd:element>
```

Figure 6.31 *You can use patterns to offer choices for an element's content. A more standard way to offer choices is by enumerating them (see page 83).*

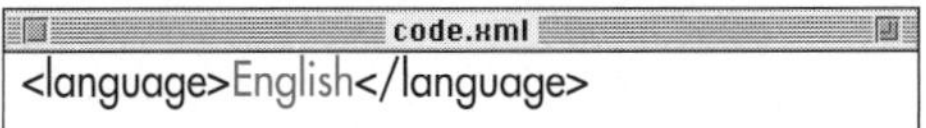

```
code.xml
<language>English</language>
```

Figure 6.32 *And here is a valid instance for the bit of schema shown in Figure 6.31.*

this | that to have *this* or *that* in the content. Separate additional choices with additional vertical bars.

x{5} to have *exactly* 5 *x*'s (in a row)

x{5,} to have *at least* 5 *x*'s (in a row)

x{5,8} to have *at least* 5 and *at most* 8 *x*'s (in a row)

(xyz){2} to have *exactly* two *xyz*'s (in a row). Parentheses control what the curly brackets and other modifiers (?, +, and *) affect.

3. Type **/>** to complete the `xsd:pattern` element.

✔ Tips

- One important difference between regular expressions in XML Schema and Perl regular expressions is that the comparison is always made between the regular expression and the entire contents of the element. There are no ^ or $ characters to limit a match to the beginning or end of a line (as there are in Perl).

- It seemed a bit of overkill to cover regular expressions in excruciating detail in this already bulging chapter. Instead, let me refer you to one of my other books, *Perl and CGI for the World Wide Web: Visual QuickStart Guide*, published by Peachpit Press. It has quite a few more examples and background information. You can also find information about Perl regular expressions at *http://www.perl.com/pub/doc/manual/html/pod/perlre.html.*

Specifying a Range of Acceptable Values

Another way to limit the content of an attribute or element is to specify the highest or lowest value (or both) that it can have.

To specify the highest possible value:

1. Within the custom type declaration, (that is, for step 4 on page 81), type **<xsd:maxInclusive** (notice the capital *I* that begins the word *Inclusive*).
2. Type **value="n"**, where the content must be less than or equal to *n* in order to be valid.
3. Type **/>** to complete the `xsd:maxInclusive` element.

Another way to specify the highest possible value:

1. Within the custom type declaration, (that is, for step 4 on page 81), type **<xsd:maxExclusive** (notice the capital *E* that begins the word *Exclusive*).
2. Type **value="n"**, where the content must be less than (but not equal to) *n* in order to be valid.
3. Type **/>** to complete the `xsd:maxExclusive` element.

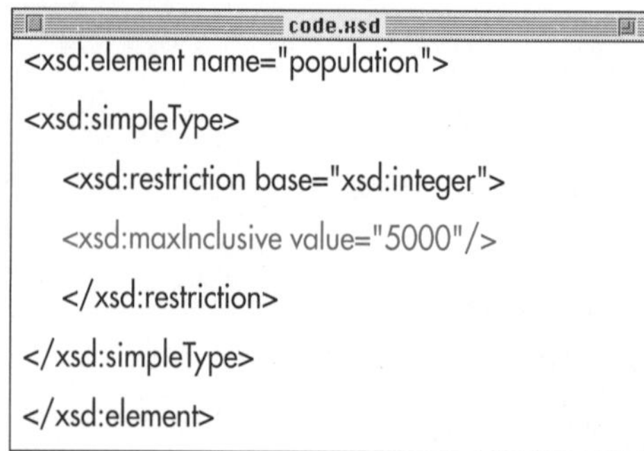

Figure 6.33 *The* `xsd:maxInclusive` *facet specifies the highest possible value for an element.*

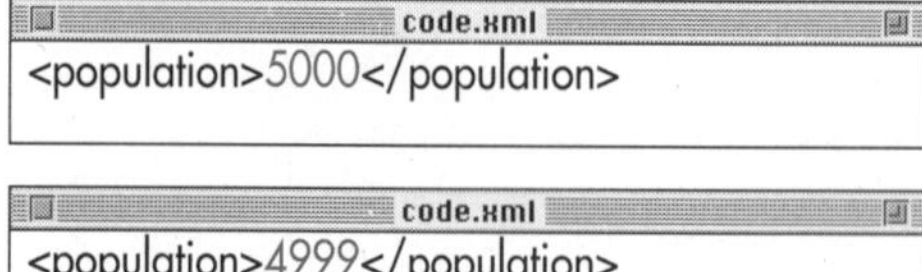

Figure 6.34 *These* `population` *elements are valid since the first is equal to and the second is less than the* `xsd:maxInclusive` *value.*

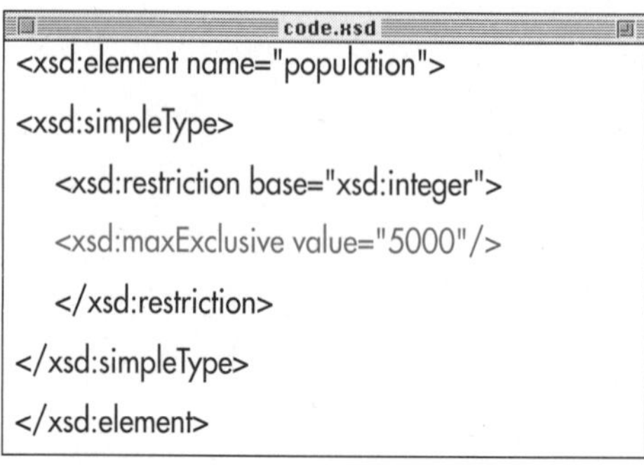

Figure 6.35 *The* `xsd:maxExclusive` *facet specifies the lowest unacceptable value, that is, the element's content must be lower than (and not equal to) the* `xsd:maxExclusive` *value.*

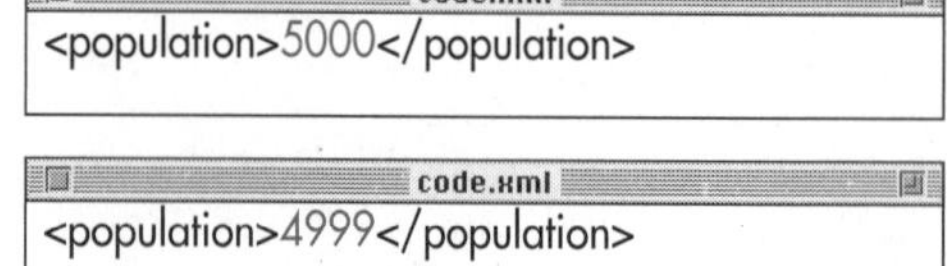

Figure 6.36 *Now the first* `population` *element is invalid, while the second is still valid.*

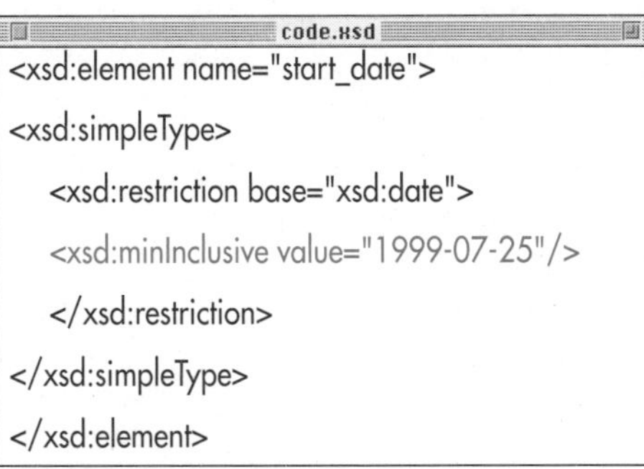

```
<xsd:element name="start_date">
<xsd:simpleType>
  <xsd:restriction base="xsd:date">
  <xsd:minInclusive value="1999-07-25"/>
  </xsd:restriction>
</xsd:simpleType>
</xsd:element>
```

Figure 6.37 *The* `xsd:minInclusive` *facet specifies the highest possible value for an element, that is, the* `start_date` *must be on July 25, 1999, or later.*

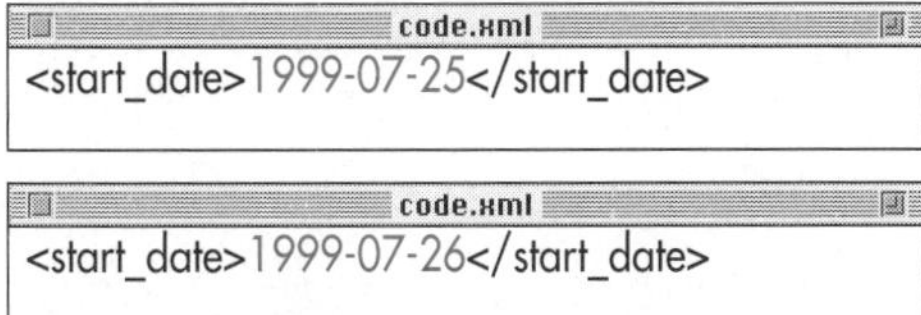

```
<start_date>1999-07-25</start_date>
```

```
<start_date>1999-07-26</start_date>
```

Figure 6.38 *These* `start_date` *elements are valid since the first is equal to and the second is greater (later) than the* `xsd:minInclusive` *value.*

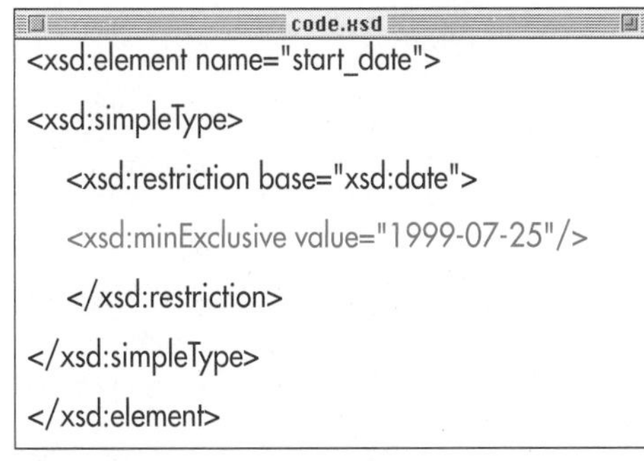

```
<xsd:element name="start_date">
<xsd:simpleType>
  <xsd:restriction base="xsd:date">
  <xsd:minExclusive value="1999-07-25"/>
  </xsd:restriction>
</xsd:simpleType>
</xsd:element>
```

Figure 6.39 *The* `xsd:minExclusive` *facet specifies the highest unacceptable value, that is, the element's content must be greater than (and not equal to) the* `xsd:minExclusive` *value.*

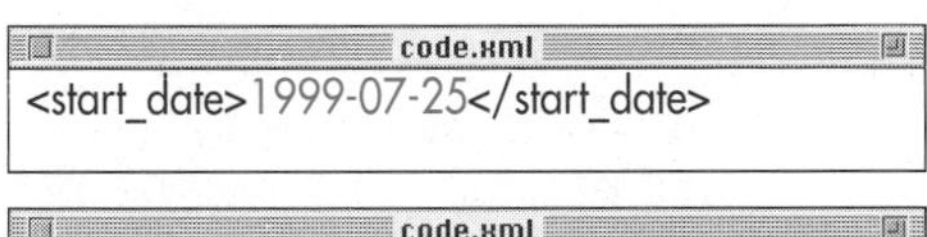

```
<start_date>1999-07-25</start_date>
```

```
<start_date>1999-07-26</start_date>
```

Figure 6.40 *Now the first* `start_date` *element is invalid (it cannot be equal to the value of* `xsd:minExclusive`*), while the second remains valid, since it's still greater (later).*

To specify the lowest possible value:

1. Within the custom type declaration, (that is, for step 4 on page 81), type **<xsd:minInclusive** (notice the capital *I* that begins the word *Inclusive*).
2. Type **value="n"**, where *n* is less than or equal to the content for it to be allowed.
3. Type **/>** to complete the `xsd:minInclusive` element.

Another way to specify the lowest possible value:

1. Within the custom type declaration, (that is, for step 4 on page 81), type **<xsd:minExclusive** (notice the capital *E* that begins the word *Exclusive*).
2. Type **value="n"**, where *n* is less than (but not equal to) the content for it to be valid.
3. Type **/>** to complete the `xsd:minExclusive` element.

✔ Tips

- While you can't use the two min limits (or the two max limits) simultaneously for the same type (it wouldn't make sense), you can mix and match the mins and maxes, as needed. You can also use just one.
- What it means for a number to be greater or less than another is pretty obvious. For a date or time to be greater, it must represent a later date or time. For a date to be less, it should represent an earlier time.

Limiting the Length of a Simple Type

One of the ways you can further define an element that is derived from a string or URL simple type is to either specify or limit its length.

To specify the exact length of an element:

Within the custom type declaration, (that is, for step 4 on page 81), type **<xsd:length value="x"/>**, where *x* is the number of characters that the element must have.

To specify the minimum length of an element:

Within the custom type declaration, (that is, for step 4 on page 81), type **<xsd:minLength value="m"/>**, where *m* is the minimum length in characters of the element.

To specify the maximum length of an element:

Within the custom type declaration, (that is, for step 4 on page 81), type **<xsd:maxLength value="n"/>**, where *n* is the maximum length in characters of the element.

✔ Tips

- If you specify the length, you cannot specify the maximum or minimum (or vice versa). Besides being incorrect, it wouldn't make sense.
- The values for `xsd:length`, `xsd:minLength`, and `xsd:maxLength` must all be non-negative integers.
- If the element is based on a binary type, the length limits the number of octets of binary data. If the element is derived by list *(see page 90)*, the length determines the number of list items.

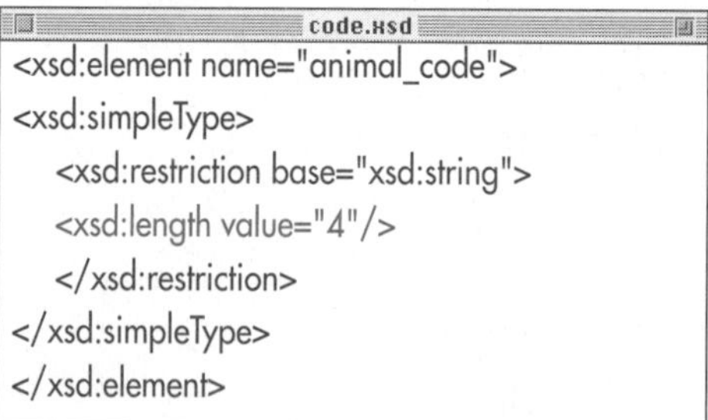

```
code.xsd
<xsd:element name="animal_code">
<xsd:simpleType>
   <xsd:restriction base="xsd:string">
   <xsd:length value="4"/>
   </xsd:restriction>
</xsd:simpleType>
</xsd:element>
```

Figure 6.41 *You can set the length of a* `string`, *although perhaps this is better left to a pattern.*

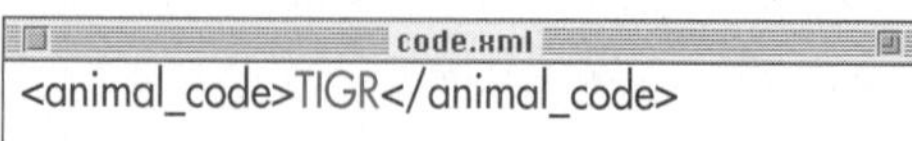

```
code.xml
<animal_code>TIGR</animal_code>
```

Figure 6.42 *This* `animal_code` *element is valid since it contains 4 characters (cf Figure 6.41).*

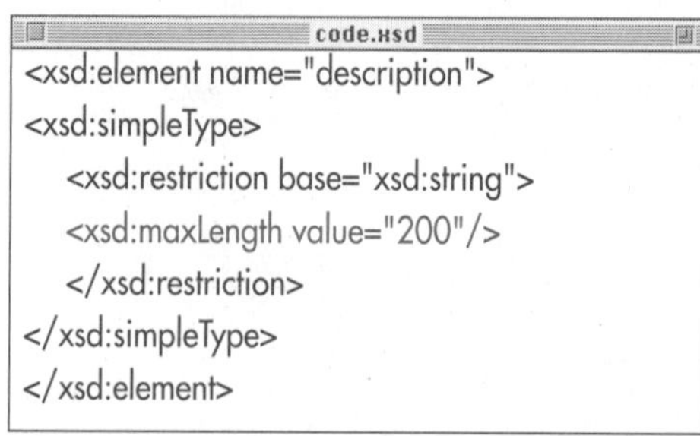

```
code.xsd
<xsd:element name="description">
<xsd:simpleType>
   <xsd:restriction base="xsd:string">
   <xsd:maxLength value="200"/>
   </xsd:restriction>
</xsd:simpleType>
</xsd:element>
```

Figure 6.43 *You can limit the length of a* `string` *element to keep it from getting out of hand.*

```
code.xml
<description> The tiger (panthera tigris), largest of all cats, is one of the biggest and most fearsome predators in the world.</description>
```

Figure 6.44 *This* `description` *element is valid because its content is comprised of 113 characters, well within the 200 character limit.*

```
code.xml
<description> The tiger (panthera tigris), largest of all cats, is one of the biggest and most fearsome predators in the world.Powerfully built with fierce retractile claws (they can be pulled into the paw, like a house cat's), the tiger's distinctive gold coloring with black stripes allows it to melt unseen into its environment. </description>
```

Figure 6.45 *This* `description` *element is invalid because it contains 317 characters.*

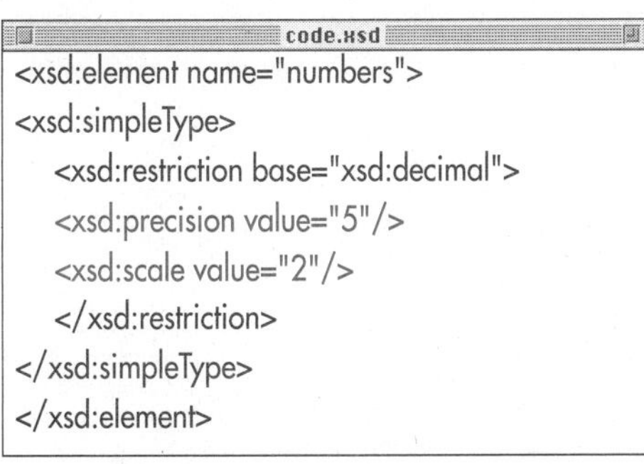

```
code.xsd
<xsd:element name="numbers">
<xsd:simpleType>
   <xsd:restriction base="xsd:decimal">
   <xsd:precision value="5"/>
   <xsd:scale value="2"/>
   </xsd:restriction>
</xsd:simpleType>
</xsd:element>
```

Figure 6.46 *The* `precision` *value determines the total number of digits.* `Scale` *specifies how many digits must appear in the fractional part of the number, to the right of the decimal point.*

```
code.xml
<numbers>564.59</numbers>
```

```
code.xml
<numbers>34.5</numbers>
```

Figure 6.47 *Both of these elements are valid, since they contain a maximum of five digits (and sometimes less), and a maximum of two fractional digits, and sometimes less.*

```
code.xml
<numbers>1476.32</numbers>
```

```
code.xml
<numbers>4.3987</numbers>
```

Figure 6.48 *These two numbers elements are invalid, the first because there are too many total digits (6), the second because while there are the proper number of total digits (5), there are too many fractional digits (4 instead of 2).*

Limiting a Number's Digits

You can limit the number of digits to the right or left of the decimal point of a number.

To specify the number of digits in a number:

1. Within the custom type declaration, (that is, for step 4 on page 81), type **<xsd:precision**.
2. Type **value="n"**, where *n* is the maximum number of digits that can appear in the number.
3. Type **/>** to complete the tag.

To specify the number of digits to the right of the decimal point:

1. Within the custom type declaration, (that is, for step 4 on page 81), type **<xsd:scale**.
2. Type **value="n"**, where *n* is the maximum number of digits that can appear to the right of the decimal in the number.
3. Type **/>** to complete the tag.

✔ Tips

- The `xsd:precision` facet must be a positive number (1, 2, 3, or higher). It may not be equal to zero. And it may not be less than the `xsd:scale` value.
- The `xsd:scale` facet must be a non-negative integer (0, 1, 2, or higher).
- Both the `xsd:precision` and `xsd:scale` facets specify the maximum values allowed. The number is still considered valid if fewer digits are present.
- You may set a `xsd:precision` and `xsd:scale` for any numerical type (but not for any string, date, or other types).

Creating List Types

So far, our elements can only contain one unit each. If you define an element as a date, it can contain just one date. But if you need an element to contain an entire list of dates, then you could derive a list type from your date type to accommodate the situation.

To create a list type:

1. Type **<xsd:simpleType** to begin the definition of the list type.
2. Type **name="label">**, where *label* is the name of the element that you're declaring, that is, in your XML document it will look something like: <label>.
3. Type **<xsd:list base="individual">**, where *individual* is the name of the simple type that defines each individual value of your list.
4. If desired, you can restrain your lists with the `xsd:length`, `xsd:minlength`, `xsd:maxLength` *(see page 88)*, and `xsd:enumeration` *(see page 83)* facets.
5. Type **</xsd:list>** to complete the list definition.
6. Finally, type **</xsd:simpleType>** to complete the simple type definition.

✔ Tips

- If you don't need to restrict your list further, you can skip steps 4–5 and type **/>** to complete the `xsd:list` element **(Figure 6.49)**.
- You can only base a list type on a simple type (not a complex one, which we'll get to in the next chapter).
- Since white space determines the number of items in a list, you have to be careful when specifying the length of a string-based list.

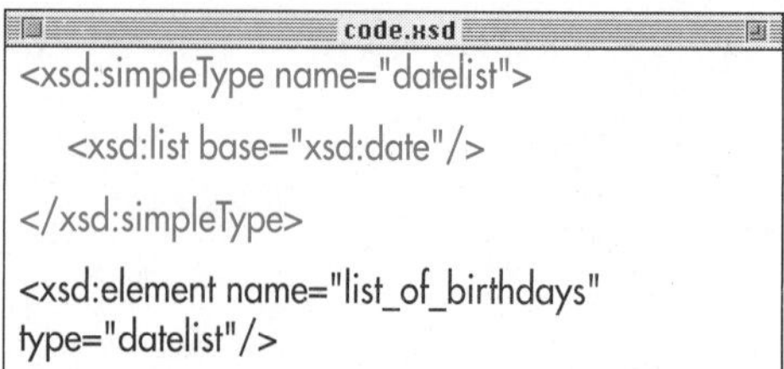

```
code.xsd
<xsd:simpleType name="datelist">
   <xsd:list base="xsd:date"/>
</xsd:simpleType>
<xsd:element name="list_of_birthdays"
type="datelist"/>
```

Figure 6.49 *A list must be based on an existing built-in or custom simpleType. The* `datelist` *list type is based on the* `xsd:date` *type. Notice that I use the new custom simple type when I declare the* `list_of_birthdays` *element.*

```
code.xml
<list_of_birthdays>1893-04-20 1904-05-11
</list_of_birthdays>
```

Figure 6.50 *A list should contain zero or more values of the type specified by the base attribute, separated by white space, as shown in this valid example.*

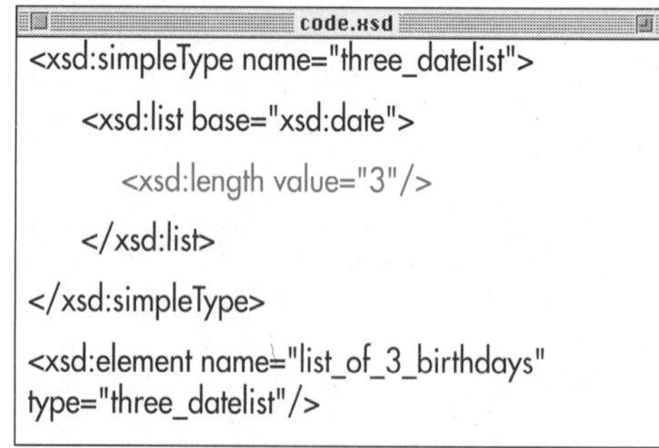

```
code.xsd
<xsd:simpleType name="three_datelist">
   <xsd:list base="xsd:date">
      <xsd:length value="3"/>
   </xsd:list>
</xsd:simpleType>
<xsd:element name="list_of_3_birthdays"
type="three_datelist"/>
```

Figure 6.51 *You can further restrict a list type with the* `xsd:length`, `xsd:maxLength`, `xsd:minLength`, *and* `xsd:enumeration` *facets.*

```
code.xml
<list_of_3_birthdays>1893-04-20 1904-05-11
1852-06-25</list_of_3_birthdays>
```

Figure 6.52 *The* `list_of_3_birthdays` *must now contain three dates in order to be valid.*

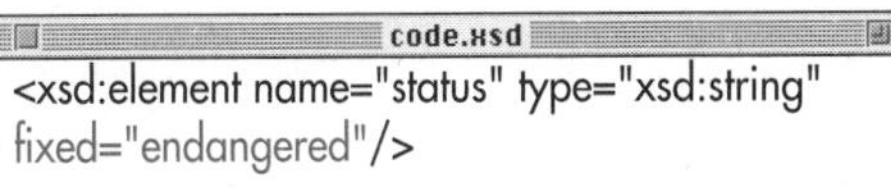

Figure 6.53 *The* `status` *element, as long as it appears in the XML document, must contain the string "endangered" (or be empty, in which case it is considered to have the string "endangered").*

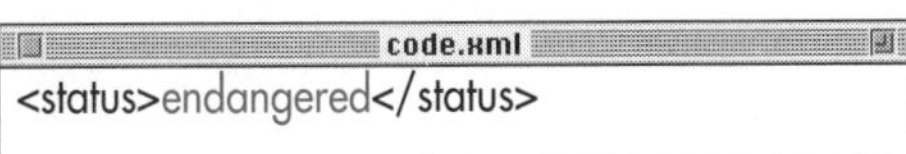

Figure 6.54 *This* `status` *element is valid, when compared with the schema data in Figure 6.53. It would also be fine if there were no* `status` *element at all.*

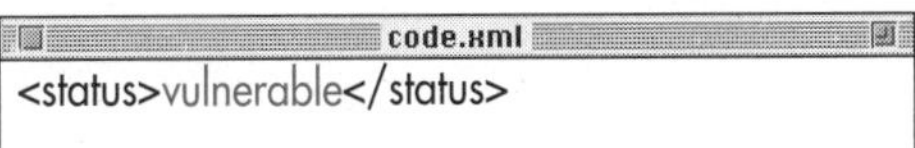

Figure 6.55 *This is not a valid* `status` *element given the declaration in Figure 6.53.*

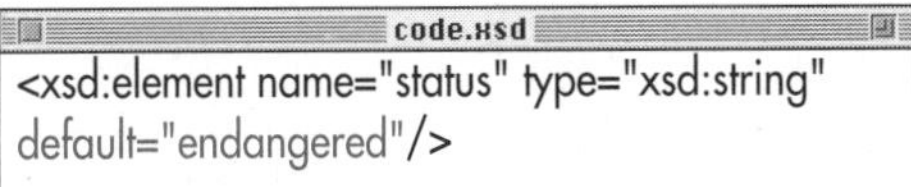

Figure 6.56 *If we define the* `status` *element with a default value, that value will be set as the initial content whether or not the* `status` *element explicitly appears in the XML document.*

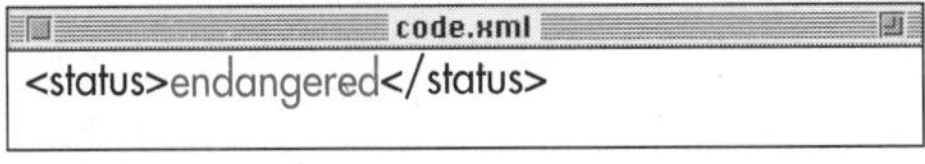

Figure 6.57 *Both of these* `status` *elements are valid. The default attribute only sets an* initial *value, and any other value is also acceptable.*

Predefining an Element's Content

There are two ways to use a schema to predefine what an element's content should be. You can either dictate the element's content or you can set a value for the element in the case in which the element appears empty in the XML. The former is called a *fixed* value; the latter is a *default* value.

To dictate an element's content:

1. Within the element tag, type **fixed=**.
2. Then type **"value"**, where *value* determines what the content of the element should be (unless it is empty).

To set an initial value for an element:

1. In the element tag, type **default=**.
2. Then type **"value"**, where *value* determines what the content of the element should be automatically set to if the element is omitted or empty.

✓ Tips

- The `fixed` attribute only sets the content if the element actually appears in the XML. If it is omitted, no content is set.
- If the `fixed` attribute is set and the element is empty, the element's value is automatically set to the fixed value.
- If the `default` attribute is set but the element is omitted from the XML, then the element's value is automatically set to the default value.
- If the `default` attribute is set and the element does appear in the XML, its content is unrestricted (depending on the `fixed` attribute).
- You may not set both the `default` and `fixed` attributes at the same time.

7

Defining Complex Types

```
code.xml
<subspecies>
<name language="English">Amur</name>
<name language="Latin">P.t. altaica</name>
<region>Far East Russia</region>
<population year="1999">445</population>
</subspecies>
```

Figure 7.1 *The* `subspecies` *element contains other elements but no loose text. Although this particular element has no attributes, it could. This kind of element is called "element only".*

```
code.xml
<source sectionid="101" newpaperid="21"/>
<picture filename="tiger.jpg" x="200" y="197"/>
```

Figure 7.2 *Both the* `source` *and* `picture` *elements are "empty" elements—they have no content. These particular empty elements have attributes (but not all do).*

```
code.xml
<description length="short">The <name
language="English">tiger</name> (panthera
tigris), largest of all cats, is one of the biggest and
most fearsome predators in the
world.</description>
```

Figure 7.3 *This* `description` *element contains text and a* `name` *element (as well as an attribute). It is considered to have "mixed" content.*

```
code.xml
<name language="Latin">panthera tigris</name>
```

Figure 7.4 *The* `name` *element contains only text (and an attribute) and is thus considered "text only".*

An element that can contain other elements or that is allowed to contain attributes is considered to have a *complex type.* Since many XML documents have elements that contain other elements, it is pretty likely that you will have to create complex types in your schema.

There are four kinds of elements of complex type: "element only" elements, that contain just other elements or attributes—but no text **(Figure 7.1)**, "empty" elements that possibly contain attributes—but never elements or text **(Figure 7.2)**, "mixed content" elements, that contain a combination of elements, attributes, and/or text—especially elements and text **(Figure 7.3)**, and "text only" elements, that contain only text—and possibly attributes **(Figure 7.4)**. We'll discuss each of these in turn.

Defining Elements to Contain Only Elements

An element with the most basic of complex types can contain other elements, and possibly attributes as well—but not text. Its content is described (despite the attributes) as "element only".

To create a complex type containing only elements:

1. Type **<xsd:complexType**.
2. Then type **name="label"**, where *label* identifies the complex type. (This is not the name of the element since you might use this complex type definition in the declarations of more than one element.)
3. Type **>** to complete the opening tag.
4. Declare a sequence *(see page 95)*, choice *(see page 96)*, or unordered group *(see page 97)* or reference a named group—which might contain any of the former three—*(see page 99)*, in order to specify which elements the complex type will be able to contain.
5. Then declare or reference the attributes *(see page 108)* or attribute groups *(see page 111)* that should appear in elements of this type, if any.
6. Then type **</xsd:complexType>**.

✔ Tips

- Once you've created a complex type, you must declare the element(s) that are defined by it. For more details, consult *Declaring an Element of Complex Type* on page 106.
- The elements contained within a complex type must be part of a sequence, choice, unordered group, or named group.

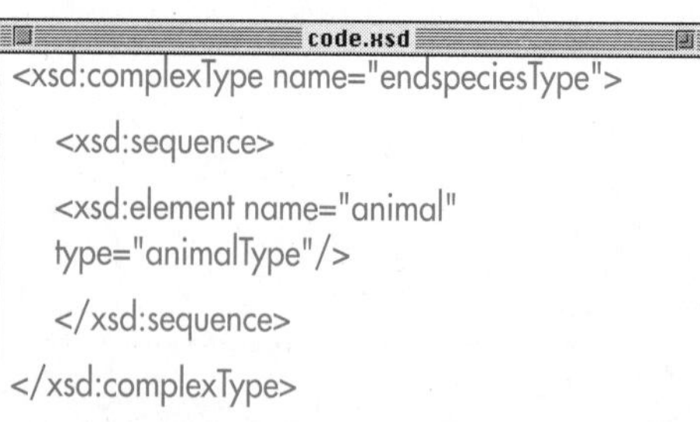

```
code.xsd
<xsd:complexType name="endspeciesType">
   <xsd:sequence>
   <xsd:element name="animal"
   type="animalType"/>
   </xsd:sequence>
</xsd:complexType>
```

Figure 7.5 *Here is a complexType definition (that we'll use to define the* `endangered_species` *element, in case you're wondering). It will contain one* `animal` *element that is defined with the* `animalType` *type. It is not at all uncommon for one complex type to contain other elements of complex type.*

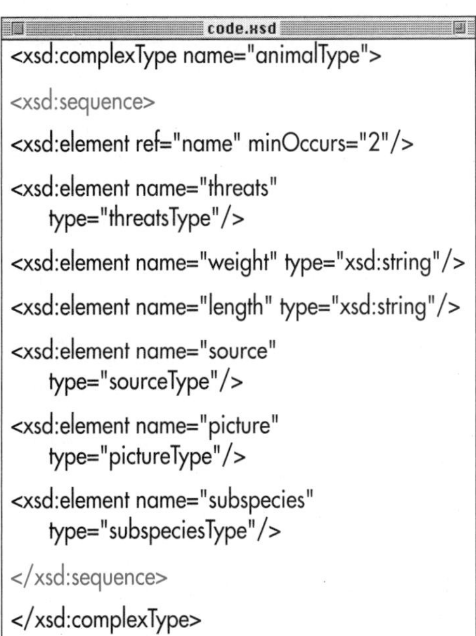

```
code.xsd
<xsd:complexType name="animalType">
<xsd:sequence>
<xsd:element ref="name" minOccurs="2"/>
<xsd:element name="threats"
   type="threatsType"/>
<xsd:element name="weight" type="xsd:string"/>
<xsd:element name="length" type="xsd:string"/>
<xsd:element name="source"
   type="sourceType"/>
<xsd:element name="picture"
   type="pictureType"/>
<xsd:element name="subspecies"
   type="subspeciesType"/>
</xsd:sequence>
</xsd:complexType>
```

Figure 7.6 *Any element defined with the* `animalType` *type will have to contain the* `name`, `threats`, `weight`, `length`, `source`, `picture`, *and* `subspecies` *elements, in order.*

Requiring Elements to Appear in Sequence

If you want an element of complex type to contain one or more other elements, *in order*, you have to define a sequence of those elements.

To require elements to appear in sequence:

1. Type **<xsd:sequence**
2. If desired, specify how many times the sequence of elements itself can appear by setting the `minOccurs` and `maxOccurs` attributes, as described on page 101.
3. Type **>** to complete the opening tag.
4. Declare *(see pages 76 and 106)* or reference *(see page 100)* each of the components that should appear in the sequence, in the order in which they should appear.
5. Type **</xsd:sequence>**.

✔ Tips

- A sequence determines the order in which its contained elements may appear in an XML document.
- A sequence can also contain other sequences, choices *(see page 96)*, or references to named groups *(see page 99)*.
- A sequence may be contained in a complex type definition *(see page 94)*, in other sequences, or in a set of choices *(see page 96)* or in named group definitions *(see page 98)*.
- The `xsd:sequence` element is roughly equivalent to the comma (,) in DTDs.
- It's perfectly legitimate for a sequence to contain only one element.

Creating a Set of Choices

It's sometimes useful to declare an element so that it can contain one element (or group of elements) or another. You do that by creating a choice.

To offer a choice:

1. Type **<xsd:choice**.
2. If desired, specify how many times the set of choices itself can appear by setting the `minOccurs` and `maxOccurs` attributes, as described on page 101.
3. Type **>** to complete the opening tag.
4. Declare *(see pages 76 and 106)* or reference *(see page 100)* each of the elements that will make up the choices in the set.
5. Type **</xsd:choice>**.

✔ Tips

- With the default `minOccurs` and `maxOccurs` attribute values (both equal to 1), only one of the elements in a set of choices can appear in the XML for the document to be valid. However, if the value of the `maxOccurs` attribute is greater than 1, that value determines how many of the choices may appear. Using `maxOccurs="unbounded"` is equivalent to adding an asterisk (*) to a set of choices in a DTD *(see page 47)*.
- A set of choices can also contain nested sequences, additional choice sets, or references to named groups *(see page 99)*.
- A set of choices may be contained in a complex type definition *(see page 94)*, in sequences, in other sets of choices, or in named group definitions *(see page 98)*.
- The `xsd:choice` element is equivalent to the vertical bar in DTDs *(see page 47)*.

code.xsd

```
<xsd:complexType name="animalType">
   ...
<xsd:choice>
    <xsd:element name="subspecies"
    type="subspeciesType"/>

    <xsd:sequence>
    <xsd:element name="region"
    type="xsd:string"/>
    <xsd:element name="population"
    type="popType"/></xsd:sequence>
</xsd:choice> ...
```

Figure 7.7 *Some endangered species have no subspecies. It would be useful to be able to list the subspecies, if there are any, or simply list the region and population of the entire species, if there are not. (While it's not shown, the* `no_subspecies` *group lists just the* `region` *and* `population` *elements.)*

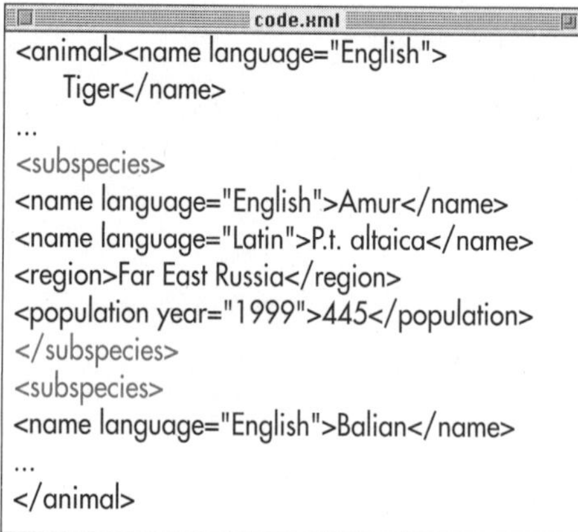

code.xml

```
<animal><name language="English">
    Tiger</name>
...
<subspecies>
<name language="English">Amur</name>
<name language="Latin">P.t. altaica</name>
<region>Far East Russia</region>
<population year="1999">445</population>
</subspecies>
<subspecies>
<name language="English">Balian</name>
...
</animal>
```

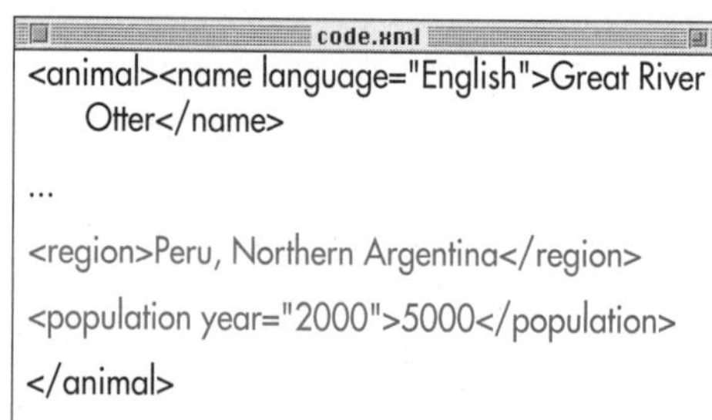

code.xml

```
<animal><name language="English">Great River
    Otter</name>

...

<region>Peru, Northern Argentina</region>

<population year="2000">5000</population>

</animal>
```

Figure 7.8 *Both these* `animal` *elements are valid. In the top* `animal`*, any number of* `subspecies` *elements appear. In the bottom* `animal`*, instead of* `subspecies`*, we have a nested sequence consisting of the* `region` *and* `population` *elements.*

```
code.xsd
<xsd:complexType name="subspeciesType">

<xsd:all>

<xsd:element ref="name"/>

<xsd:element name="region"
type="xsd:string" minOccurs="0"/>

<xsd:element name="population">
    <xsd:complexType base="xsd:integer"
    derivedBy="extension">
    <xsd:attribute name="year"
    type="xsd:year"/>
    </xsd:complexType></xsd:element>

</xsd:all>

</xsd:complexType>
```

Figure 7.9 *The* `all` *group allows the* `name`, `region`, *and* `population` *elements to appear in any order within the elements of* `subspeciesType`. *In addition, the* `region` *element is optional because its* `minOccurs` *attribute is set to 0 (see page 101). It can be omitted without problem.*

```
code.xml
<subspecies>
<name language="English">Bengal</name>
<population year="1999">3159</population>
<region>India</region>
</subspecies>

<subspecies>
<population year="1998">1227</population>
<name language="English">Amoy</region>
</subspecies>
```

Figure 7.10 *Both of these* `subspecies` *elements are valid since the* `region` *is optional and the order is unimportant.*

Allowing Elements to Appear in Any Order

If you want an element to be able to contain other elements in any order, you can group those inner elements with an `all` group.

To allow elements to appear in any order:

1. Type **<xsd:all>** to begin the unordered group of elements.
2. If desired, specify how many times the unordered group itself can appear by setting the `minOccurs` and `maxOccurs` attributes, as described on page 101.
3. Type **>** to complete the opening tag.
4. Declare *(see pages 76 and 106)* or reference *(see page 100)* each of the elements in the unordered group.
5. Type **</xsd:all>** to complete the group.

✔ Tips

- The members of an `all` group (despite its name) may appear once or not at all (depending on their individual `minOccurs` and `maxOccurs` attributes), in any order.
- The `minOccurs` and `maxOccurs` attributes may only be set to *0* or *1*.
- An `all` group can only contain individual element declarations or references, not other groups. In addition, no element may appear more than once.
- An `all` group can only be contained—and must be the sole child—of either a complex type definition *(see page 94)* or a named group definition *(see page 98)*.

Defining Named Groups

If a collection of elements appears together in several places in your XML document, you can group the elements together in order to make it easier to refer to them all at once.

To define a named group:

1. Type **<xsd:group**.
2. Type **name="label"**, where *label* is the word that will identify this particular group.
3. Type **>** to complete the opening group tag.
4. Declare the sequences *(see page 95)*, sets of choices *(see page 96)*, or the unordered group *(see page 97)* that will make up the named group.
5. Type **</xsd:group>** to complete the definition of the group.

```
code.xsd
<xsd:schema>
<xsd:group name="physical_traits">
   <xsd:sequence>
   <xsd:element name="weight"
   type="xsd:string"/>
   <xsd:element name="length"
   type="xsd:string"/>
   <xsd:element name="gestation"
   type="xsd:timeDuration"/>
   <xsd:element name="distinguishing"
   type="xsd:string"/>
   </xsd:sequence>
</xsd:group>
...
```

Figure 7.11 *A group defines a list of related elements that will all be used together in one or more other elements.*

✓ Tips

- A group is analogous to a parameter entity in DTDs *(see page 60)*.
- While a group may only be *defined* at the top-level of a schema (just under `xsd:schema`), it may be *referenced* in many situations *(see page 99)*.
- In the XML Schema specifications, they use the word "groups" and sometimes "model groups" to refer to sequences, sets of choices, unordered groups, *and* named groups. I use "named groups" to refer only to those collections of components that are defined with the `xsd:group` element (and thus, that have a name).

```
code.xsd
<xsd:element name="animal">
<xsd:complexType>
  <xsd:sequence>
  <xsd:element ref="name"/>
  <xsd:group ref="physical_traits"/>
  <xsd:element name="subspecies"
  type="subspeciesType"/>
  </xsd:sequence>
</xsd:complexType>
</xsd:element>

<xsd:element name="individual">
<xsd:complexType>
  <xsd:group ref="physical_traits"/>
  <xsd:attribute name="birthdate"
  type="xsd:date"/>
  <xsd:attribute name="nickname"
  type="xsd:string"/>
</xsd:complexType>
</xsd:element>
```

Figure 7.12 *Both the* `animal` *and* `individual` *elements will have to contain the elements listed in the* `physical_traits` *group (defined in Figure 7.11 on page 98). They also have additional, individual elements and attributes.*

```
code.xml
<animal><name language="English">Tiger
   </name><weight>500
   pounds</weight><length>3 yards from nose
   to tail</length>...<subspecies>...</animal>
<individual birthdate="1999-06-10"
   nickname="Zoe"><weight>268
   pounds</weight><length>2.5
   yards</length>...</individual>
```

Figure 7.13 *The same elements can be used in different ways within different containing elements.*

Referencing a Named Group

Once you've created a group, you can reference it in other groups or in complex type definitions.

To reference a group:

1. In the part of your schema where you want the elements in the group to appear, type **<xsd:group**.
2. Then type **ref="label"**, where *label* is the word you used to identify the group when you created it in step 2 on the preceding page.
3. Type **/>** to complete the reference.

✓ Tip

- You can reference a group in a complex type definition *(see page 94)*, a sequence *(see page 95)*, a set of choices *(see page 96)*, an unordered group *(see page 97)*, or in other named groups *(see page 98)*.

Referencing Already Defined Elements

Elements of both simple and complex type that are declared globally (that is, just inside the `xsd:schema` element) must be called or *referenced* in order to appear in the XML document.

To reference a globally declared element:

1. In the sequence *(see page 95)*, set of choices *(see page 96)*, unordered group *(see page 97)*, or named group definition *(see page 98)* in which the element should appear, type **<xsd:element**.
2. Type **ref="label"**, where *label* is the name of the globally declared element.
3. If desired, specify how many times the element can appear at this point *(see page 101)*.
4. Type **/>** to complete the element reference.

✔ Tips

- You can only reference element declarations within sequences, sets of choices, unordered groups, and named group definitions.
- You can reference a globally declared element in as many locations as necessary. Each reference may contain distinct values for `minOccurs` and `maxOccurs`.
- *Locally declared* elements are automatically referenced in the component definition in which they appear. You cannot reference them anywhere else.
- For more information about local and global declarations, consult *Local and Global Declarations* on page 71.

code.xsd

```
<xsd:element name="name" type="nameType"/>

<xsd:complexType name="animalType">
    <xsd:sequence>
    <xsd:element ref="name" minOccurs="2"/>
    <xsd:element name="threats"
    type="threatsType"/>
    ...
    </xsd:complexType>

<xsd:complexType name="subspeciesType"/>
    <xsd:sequence>
    <xsd:element ref="name" minOccurs="1"/>
    <xsd:element name="region"
    type="xsd:string"/>
    ...
    </xsd:complexType>
```

Figure 7.14 *The* `name` *element was declared globally (first line) and so can be referenced within any complex type definition.*

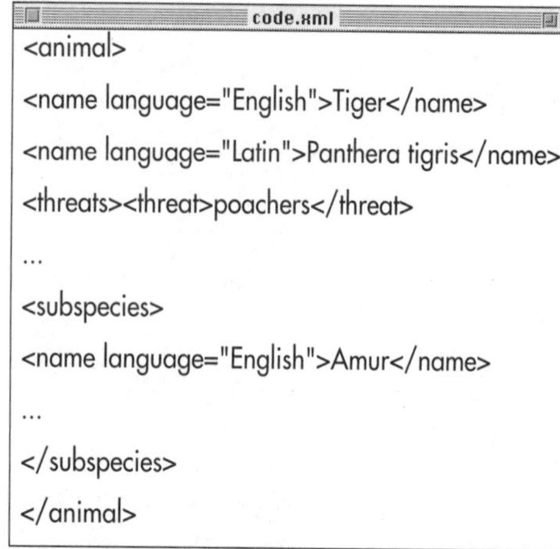

code.xml

```
<animal>
<name language="English">Tiger</name>
<name language="Latin">Panthera tigris</name>
<threats><threat>poachers</threat>
...
<subspecies>
<name language="English">Amur</name>
...
</subspecies>
</animal>
```

Figure 7.15 *Both* `name` *elements must follow the rules defined for it in the complex type definition (not shown). In addition, they are subject to the individual* `minOccurs` *and* `maxOccurs` *attribute values. In this case, according to the schema in Figure 7.14,* `name` *must appear at least twice in an* `animal` *element but only needs to appear once when contained in a* `subspecies` *element.*

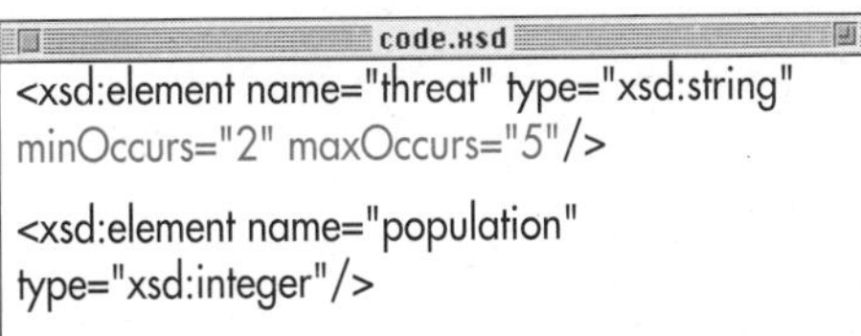

```
code.xsd
<xsd:element name="threat" type="xsd:string"
minOccurs="2" maxOccurs="5"/>

<xsd:element name="population"
type="xsd:integer"/>
```

Figure 7.16 *The* `minOccurs` *and* `maxOccurs` *attributes let you control how many times an element should appear.*

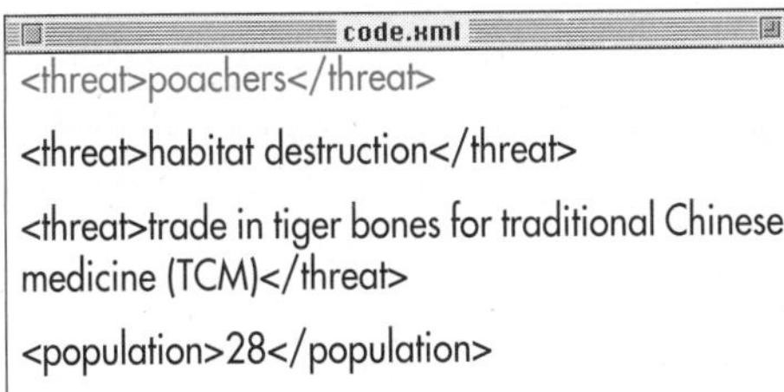

```
code.xml
<threat>poachers</threat>

<threat>habitat destruction</threat>

<threat>trade in tiger bones for traditional Chinese
medicine (TCM)</threat>

<population>28</population>
```

Figure 7.17 *Since there must be at least 2 and at most 5 threats, these three* `threat` *elements are valid. When both* `minOccurs` *and* `maxOccurs` *are omitted (as with the* `population` *element), both values have a default of 1, and thus the element must appear exactly once in the XML document, as it validly does here.*

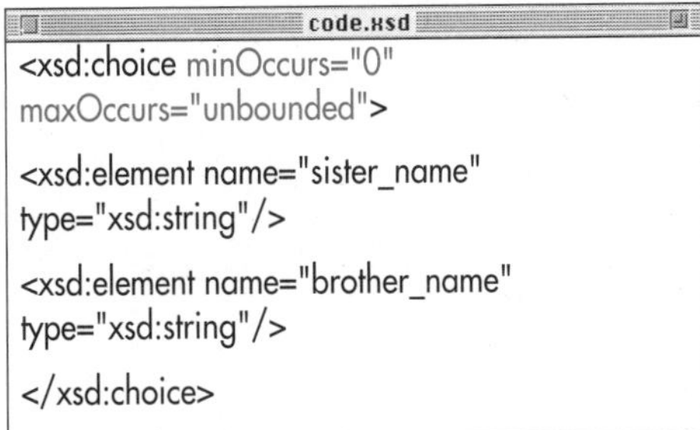

```
code.xsd
<xsd:choice minOccurs="0"
maxOccurs="unbounded">

<xsd:element name="sister_name"
type="xsd:string"/>

<xsd:element name="brother_name"
type="xsd:string"/>

</xsd:choice>
```

Figure 7.18 *The* `minOccurs` *and* `maxOccurs` *attributes can also be applied to sequences, sets of choices, unordered groups, or (references to) named groups. In this example, any number (including zero) of this choice group are allowed, which means that there could be any number of* `sister_name` *and* `brother_name` *elements. This is the equivalent of adding an asterisk to a choice with DTDs (see page 96).*

Controlling How Many

You can control how many times a given element, sequence, set of choices, unordered group, or named group will appear.

To specify the minimum number of times an element or group can appear:

In the element's or group's opening tag, type **minOccurs="n"**, where *n* indicates the fewest number of times the element or group must occur for the document to be considered valid.

To specify the maximum number of times an element or group can appear:

In the element's or group's opening tag, type **maxOccurs="n"**, where *n* is the maximum amount of times the element or group may occur for the document to be considered valid.

✓ Tips

- The `minOccurs` attribute must be a non-negative integer (0, 1, 2, 3, or higher).
- The `maxOccurs` attribute can be any non-negative integer, or the word **unbounded** to indicate that the element can appear any number of times.
- The default value for both `minOccurs` and `maxOccurs` is 1.
- The `minOccurs` and `maxOccurs` attributes can not be used with globally declared elements (that is, those declared just one level below the `xsd:schema` element). They only make sense with locally declared elements and with references to global ones.
- These attributes can also be used in `xsd:sequence`, `xsd:choice`, `xsd:all`, and in *references* to named groups.

Defining Elements to Contain Only Text

If what you really want is a given simple type—whose content is defined to be a specific kind of text—*but with attributes,* you can derive a text-only complex type to fit the bill.

To define a complex type containing only text:

1. Type **<xsd:complexType**.
2. Then type **name="label"**, where *label* identifies the complex type. (This is not the name of the element since you might use this complex type definition in the declarations of more than one element.)
3. Type **>** to complete the opening tag.
4. Type **<xsd:simpleContent>**.
5. Next type **<xsd:restriction** if you are going to limit the base simple type with additional facets.

   Or type **<xsd:extension** if you are going to expand on the simple type.
6. Type **base="foundation">**, where *foundation* is the simple type definition that you're basing the new complex type on.
7. If you chose `xsd:restriction` in step 5, declare the additional facets *(see pages 83–90)* that should limit the complex type definition.
8. Declare the attributes *(see page 108)* or attribute groups *(see page 111)* that should appear in elements of this type.
9. Then type **</xsd:restriction>** or **</xsd:extension>** to match step 5.
10. Type **</xsd:simpleContent>**.
11. Finally, type **</xsd:complexType>** to complete the declaration.

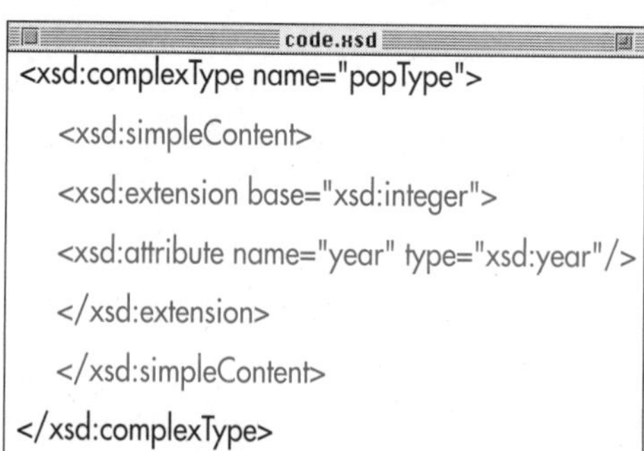

```
code.xsd
<xsd:complexType name="popType">
  <xsd:simpleContent>
  <xsd:extension base="xsd:integer">
  <xsd:attribute name="year" type="xsd:year"/>
  </xsd:extension>
  </xsd:simpleContent>
</xsd:complexType>
```

Figure 7.19 *The* `simpleContent` *element indicates that elements defined with this complex type definition will contain a certain kind of text (based on a simple type) but not other elements. They may also have attributes.*

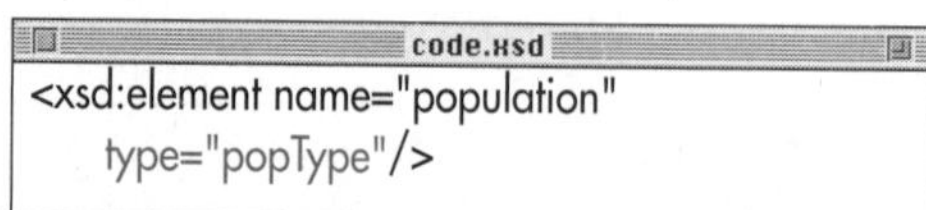

```
code.xsd
<xsd:element name="population"
   type="popType"/>
```

Figure 7.20 *You always have to declare the element that uses the complex type definition (see page 106).*

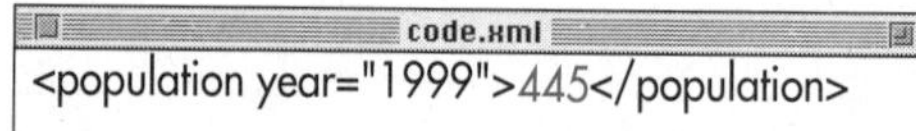

```
code.xml
<population year="1999">445</population>
```

Figure 7.21 *This* `population` *element is valid with the complex type definition in Figure 7.19 because it contains an integer (and has a* `year` *attribute).*

```
code.xml
<population year="1999">Less than
500</population>
```

Figure 7.22 *This* `population` *element, however, is invalid, because "Less than 500" is not an integer, as specified by the simple type upon which the complex type is based.*

code.xsd
```
<xsd:complexType name="sourceType">
    <xsd:complexContent>
    <xsd:extension base="xsd:anyType"/>
    <xsd:attribute name="sectionid"
    type="xsd:integer"/>
    <xsd:attribute name="newspaperid"
    type="xsd:integer"/>
    </xsd:extension>
    </xsd:complexContent>
</xsd:complexType>
```

Figure 7.23 *The* `complexContent` *element is used when you need to declare attributes, but no contained elements.*

code.xsd
```
<xsd:element name="source"
    type="sourceType"/>
```

Figure 7.24 *You have to declare the element in the location where it should appear.*

code.xml
```
<source sectionid="101" newspaperid="21"/>
```

Figure 7.25 *Once declared, you can use the* `source` *element in your XML document.*

Defining Empty Elements

Elements that can contain attributes but that have no content between the opening and closing tags are considered *empty*.

To define complex types for empty elements:

1. Type **<xsd:complexType**.
2. Then type **name="label">**, where *label* identifies the complex type. (This is not the name of the element since you might use this complex type definition in the declarations of more than one element.)
3. Type **<xsd:complexContent>**.
4. Type **<xsd:extension base="xsd:anyType"/>** (with no hyphen) to indicate essentially that there is no type upon which this complex type is based. (And since it will have no content, that's just fine.)
5. Declare the attributes, if any, that should appear in elements of this type *(see page 108)*.
6. Type **</xsd:complexContent>**.
7. Then type **</xsd:complexType>** to complete the declaration.

✔ Tip

- For more details on defining complex types, consult *Defining Elements to Contain Only Elements* on page 94 and *Elements with Anonymous Complex Types* on page 107.

Defining Elements with Mixed Content

While pure database-driven content rarely contains elements that contain both other elements and text, more text-centered documents wouldn't find it at all strange. When creating a complex type that will define such an element, you must declare that the content will be *mixed*.

To create complex types with mixed content:

1. Type **<xsd:complexType**.
2. Then type **name="label"**, where *label* identifies the complex type. (This is not the name of the element since you might use this complex type definition in the declarations of more than one element.)
3. Type **mixed="true"** to indicate the element can contain elements, attributes, and may possibly contain text as well.
4. Type **>** to complete the opening tag.
5. Declare a sequence *(see page 95)*, choice *(see page 96)*, or unordered group *(see page 97)* or reference a named group—which might contain any of the former three—*(see page 99)*, in order to specify which elements the complex type will be able to contain.
6. Then declare or reference the attributes *(see page 108)* or attribute groups *(see page 111)* that should appear in elements of this type, if any.
7. Then type **</xsd:complexType>** to complete the declaration.

✔ Tip

- Mixed content elements are ideal for descriptive, text-based chunks of information.

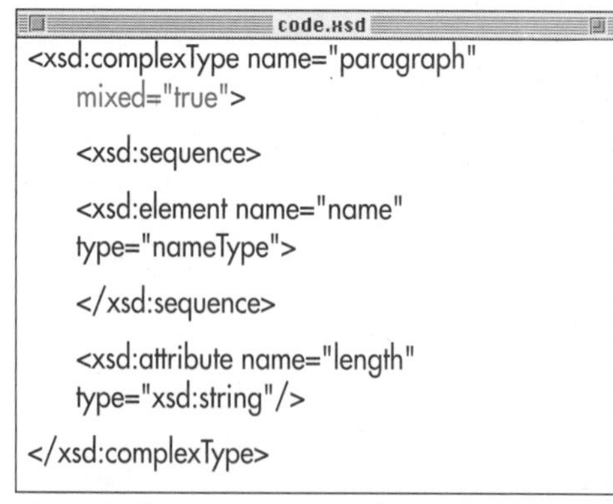

```
code.xsd
<xsd:complexType name="paragraph"
    mixed="true">
    <xsd:sequence>
    <xsd:element name="name"
    type="nameType">
    </xsd:sequence>
    <xsd:attribute name="length"
    type="xsd:string"/>
</xsd:complexType>
```

Figure 7.26 *The* `paragraph` *definition contains an element and an attribute, and thanks to the* `mixed="true"` *attribute, may also contain loose text.*

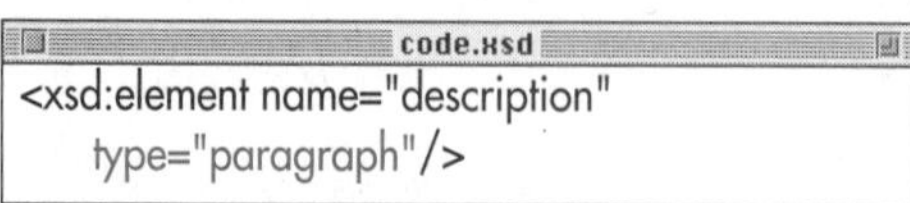

```
code.xsd
<xsd:element name="description"
    type="paragraph"/>
```

Figure 7.27 *You have to declare the element in the location where it should appear.*

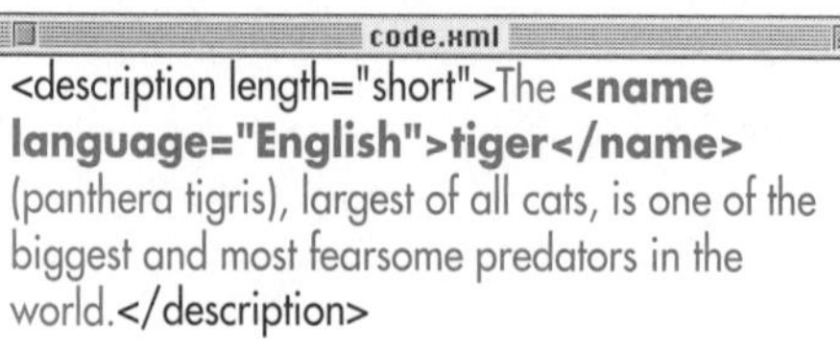

```
code.xml
<description length="short">The <name
language="English">tiger</name>
(panthera tigris), largest of all cats, is one of the
biggest and most fearsome predators in the
world.</description>
```

Figure 7.28 *The* `description` *element contains both loose text (highlighted) and elements (highlighted and in boldface).*

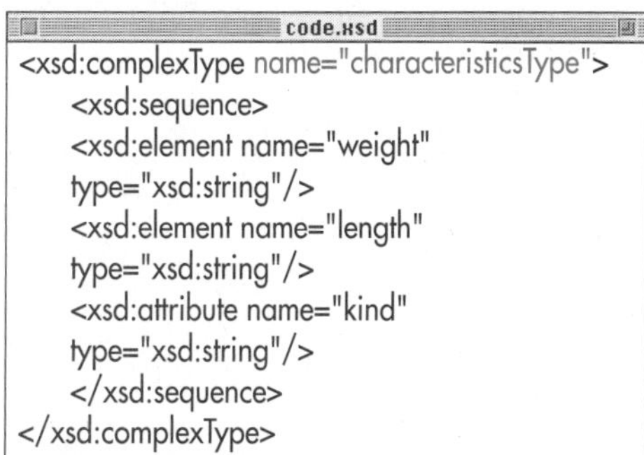

```
<xsd:complexType name="characteristicsType">
    <xsd:sequence>
    <xsd:element name="weight"
    type="xsd:string"/>
    <xsd:element name="length"
    type="xsd:string"/>
    <xsd:attribute name="kind"
    type="xsd:string"/>
    </xsd:sequence>
</xsd:complexType>
```

Figure 7.29 *The* `characteristicsType` *definition requires a sequence of the* `weight` *and* `length` *elements, and a* `kind` *attribute.*

```
<xsd:complexType name="birthType">
    <xsd:complexContent>
    <xsd:extension base="characteristicsType">
    <xsd:sequence>
    <xsd:element name="mother"
    type="xsd:string"/>
    <xsd:element name="birthdate"
    type="xsd:date"/>
    </xsd:sequence>
    </xsd:extension></xsd:complexContent>
    </xsd:complexType>
```

Figure 7.30 *The new* `birthType` *lists only the* additional *elements that will have to appear in the elements it defines.*

```
<xsd:element name="birth_characteristics"
    type="birthType"/>
```

Figure 7.31 *You always have to declare the element that uses the complex type definition (see page 106).*

```
<birth_characteristics kind="normal">
<weight>2-3 pounds</weight>
<length>18-24 inches</length>
<mother>Danai</mother>
<birthdate>1999-06-10</birthdate>
</birth_characteristics>
```

Figure 7.32 *The* `birth_characteristics` *element must contain the features from the* `characteristicsType` *(the* `weight` *and* `length` *elements as well as the* `kind` *attribute), as well as the new features (*`mother` *and* `birthdate`*).*

Basing Complex Types on Complex Types

You can also create complex types from existing complex types. The new complex type begins with all the information from the existing type, and then adds or removes features.

To base complex types on existing types:

1. Type **<xsd:complexType** to begin the definition of the new complex type.
2. Type **name="label">**, where *label* identifies the complex type that you're creating.
3. Type **<xsd:complexContent>**.
4. Type **<xsd:extension** to indicate that the new features of the complex type should be *added* to the existing type.

   Or type **<xsd:restriction** to indicate that (at least some of) the new features of the complex type are more restrictive than the old ones and should *override* these.
5. Type **base="existing"**, where *existing* is the name of the type upon which the complex type will be built.
6. Type **>**.
7. Declare the additional or more restrictive sequences or choices, or reference the named groups that should be part of the new type.
8. Declare or reference the additional attributes that should be part of the new type *(see page 108)*.
9. Type a matching closing tag for step 4.
10. Type **</xsd:complexContent>**.
11. Type **</xsd:complexType>** to complete the complex type definition.

Declaring an Element of Complex Type

Once you've defined a complex type, you can assign it to an element so that the element can then be used in the XML document.

To declare an element of complex type:

1. Type **<xsd:element** to begin the element declaration **(Figure 7.33)**.
2. Type **type="label"**, where *label* matches the identifying word that you used when defining the complex type (e.g., step 2 on page 94).
3. Then type **/>** to complete the element declaration.

✔ Tips

- You can declare elements either globally (at the top level of a schema, just under the `xsd:schema` element) or locally, within a complex type definition *(see page 94)*, a sequence *(see page 95)*, a set of choices *(see page 96)*, an unordered group *(see page 97)*, or a named group definition *(see page 98)*.
- If you are declaring an element locally *(see page 71)*, you can control the number of times the element can appear with the `minOccurs` and `maxOccurs` attributes. For more information, consult *Controlling How Many* on page 101.

```
code.xsd
<xsd:complexType name="characteristicsType">
    <xsd:sequence>
    <xsd:element name="weight"
    type="xsd:string"/>
    <xsd:element name="length"
    type="xsd:string"/>
    <xsd:attribute name="kind"
    type="xsd:string"/>
    </xsd:sequence>
</xsd:complexType>
```

Figure 7.33 *Here is a typical complex type definition (that we saw earlier in Figure 7.29 on page 105).*

```
code.xsd
<xsd:element name="characteristics"
    type="characteristicsType"/>

<xsd:complexType name="animalType"/>
    <xsd:sequence>
    <xsd:element name="name" type="nameType"
    minOccurs="2"/>
    <xsd:element ref="characteristics"
    minOccurs="1"/>
    ...
```

Figure 7.34 *You can declare the element globally, at the top level of your schema document, in which case you'll need to reference the element in the other components in your schema in order to use it.*

```
code.xsd
<xsd:complexType name="animalType"/>
    <xsd:sequence>
    <xsd:element name="name" type="nameType"
    minOccurs="2"/>
    <xsd:element name="characteristics"
    type="characteristicsType" minOccurs="1"/>
    ...
```

Figure 7.35 *Or, you can declare the element locally, within another component (like a complex type definition as shown, or a named group), in which case the element is automatically referenced.*

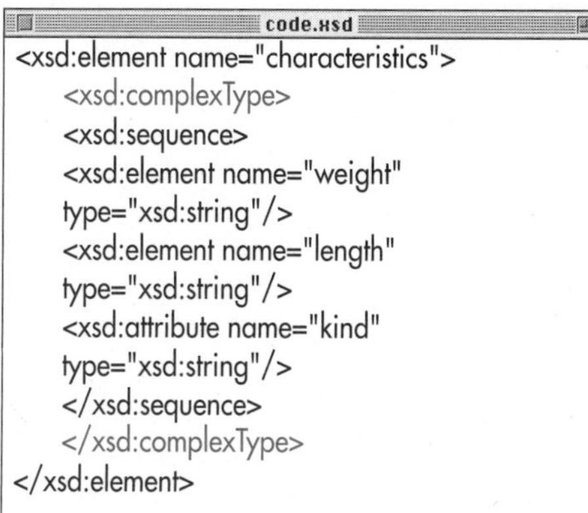

```
code.xsd
<xsd:element name="characteristics">
    <xsd:complexType>
    <xsd:sequence>
    <xsd:element name="weight"
    type="xsd:string"/>
    <xsd:element name="length"
    type="xsd:string"/>
    <xsd:attribute name="kind"
    type="xsd:string"/>
    </xsd:sequence>
    </xsd:complexType>
</xsd:element>
```

Figure 7.36 *This time we redefine the characteristics type as an anonymous type definition. Now we can only use this complex type definition for the element that contains it (*`characteristics`*). The element can be declared either locally or globally.*

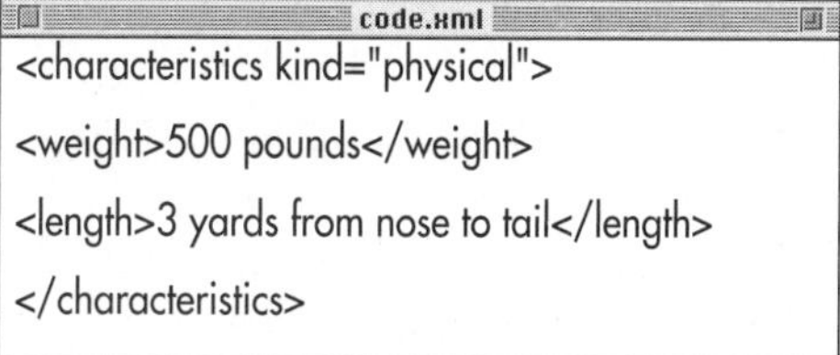

```
code.xml
<characteristics kind="physical">
<weight>500 pounds</weight>
<length>3 yards from nose to tail</length>
</characteristics>
```

Figure 7.37 *Here is a valid instance. It looks the same whether you use a named or anonymous complex type.*

Elements with Anonymous Complex Types

If you don't need to reuse a complex type, it may be faster to create an anonymous complex type within the element declaration.

To declare an element with an anonymous complex type:

1. Type **<xsd:element**.
2. Type **name="label">**, where *label* is the name of the element that you're declaring; that is, in your XML document it will look something like: <label>.
3. Next type **<xsd:complexType>** to begin the anonymous complex type.
4. Declare a sequence *(see page 95)*, choice *(see page 96)*, or unordered group *(see page 97)*, or reference a named group—which might contain any of the former three—*(see page 99)*, in order to specify which elements the complex type will be able to contain.
5. Then declare or reference the attributes *(see page 108)* or attribute groups *(see page 111)* that should appear in elements of this type, if any.
6. Type **</xsd:complexType>** to complete the anonymous complex type definition.
7. Type **</xsd:element>** to complete the declaration of the complex type element.

✔ Tip

- The only difference between named and anonymous complex types is that the former can be used to declare as many different elements as you want, and as the base for additional complex types. The latter can only be used to define the element within which it is found.

Declaring Attributes

While an attribute is always of simple type (since it contains neither other elements nor other attributes), it always appears within an element of complex type, so we discuss how to create it in this chapter rather than the last.

To declare an attribute:

1. Within the definition of the complex type, type **<xsd:attribute**.
2. Then type **name="label"**, where *label* is the name you will use to set the attribute in the XML document.
3. Type **type="simple"**, where *simple* is the simple type to which the attribute belongs. For more details about simple types, consult *Declaring an Element with a Simple Type* on page 76.

   Or type **ref="label"**, where *label* identifies an attribute definition that you've already (globally) declared.
4. Type **>** to complete the opening tag.
5. Add any restraining facets, as desired. For more details, see pages 83–90.
6. Type **</xsd:attribute>**.

✔ Tips

- If there are no restraining facets, you can skip steps 4–6 and type **/>** instead.
- There are several additional built-in simple types, just for attributes. Find them all at *http://www.w3.org/TR/xmlschema-2*.
- You can also define an attribute with an anonymous simple type *(see page 82)*.
- An attribute must be declared at the very end of the complex type to which it belongs, that is, after all of the components in the complex type have been declared.

code.xsd

```
<xsd:element name="source">
    <xsd:complexType>
    <xsd:complexContent>
    <xsd:extension base="xsd:anyType">
    <xsd:attribute name="sectionid"
    type="xsd:string"/>
    <xsd:attribute name="newspaperid"
    type="xsd:string"/>
    </xsd:extension>
    </xsd:complexContent>
    </xsd:complexType>
</xsd:element>
```

Figure 7.38 *An attribute declaration looks like any simple type element declaration.*

Figure 7.39 *Attributes always appear within the opening tag of the containing element.*

```
code.xsd
<xsd:element name="source">
    <xsd:complexType>
    <xsd:complexContent>
    <xsd:extension base="xsd:anyType">
    <xsd:attribute name="sectionid"
    type="xsd:string" use="required"/>
    <xsd:attribute name="newspaperid"
    type="xsd:string"/>
    </xsd:extension>
    </xsd:complexContent>
    </xsd:complexType>
</xsd:element>
```

Figure 7.40 *Since the default is for an attribute to be optional, you must specifically require that it be obligatory.*

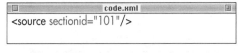

```
code.xml
<source sectionid="101"/>
```

```
code.xml
<source sectionid="101" newspaperid="21"/>
```

Figure 7.41 *Both of these source elements are valid, since only the* `sectionid` *is "required". If an attribute is not specifically required, it is considered optional.*

Requiring an Attribute

Unless you specify otherwise as you are defining an attribute, an attribute is always optional. In other words, it may appear or be absent from the XML document without causing a stir. However, if you'd rather, you can insist that an attribute be present or not when determining if the document is valid.

To require an attribute to be present:

1. While defining the attribute, type **use=**.
2. Next, type **"required"** so that the attribute must appear for the document to be considered valid.
3. If desired, you may add **value="must"**, where *must* is the only acceptable value for the attribute.

To require that an attribute *not* be present:

While defining the attribute, type **use="prohibited"** so that the document can only be considered valid if the attribute is not present.

✔ Tip

- You can also add **use="optional"** to an attribute's definition, but since that's the default value, you'd be doing busy work.

Predefining an Attribute's Content

There are two ways to use a schema to predefine what an attribute's content should be. You can either dictate the attribute's content (as long as the attribute appears in the XML), or set an initial value for the attribute regardless of whether it appears or not. The former is called a *fixed* value; the latter is a *default* value.

To dictate an attribute's content:

1. Within the attribute tag, type **use="fixed"**.
2. Type **value="content"**, where *content* determines what the value of the attribute should be (if the attribute appears in the XML document) for the document to be considered valid.

To set an initial value for an attribute:

1. In the attribute tag, type **use="default"**.
2. Type **value="content"**, where *content* determines what the value of the attribute should be set to if the attribute is omitted from the XML document.

✓ Tips

- The `fixed` attribute only sets the content if the attribute actually appears in the XML. If it is omitted, no content is set.
- If the `default` attribute is set but the attribute is omitted from the XML, then the attribute's value is automatically set to the default value.
- If the `default` attribute is set and the attribute does appear in the XML, its content is unrestricted (depending on the value of the `fixed` attribute).

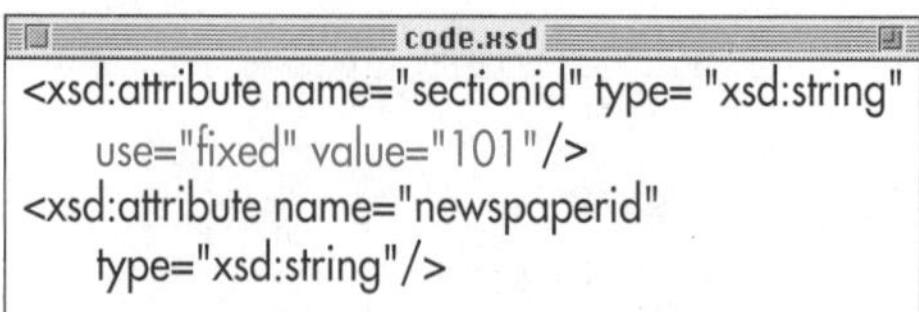

code.xsd

```
<xsd:attribute name="sectionid" type= "xsd:string"
    use="fixed" value="101"/>
<xsd:attribute name="newspaperid"
    type="xsd:string"/>
```

Figure 7.42 *The* `sectionid` *attribute, as long as it appears in the XML document (or is empty), must contain the value "101". The attribute may, however, be omitted altogether. (Note: this is an excerpt of the complex type definition shown in Figure 7.40 on page 109).*

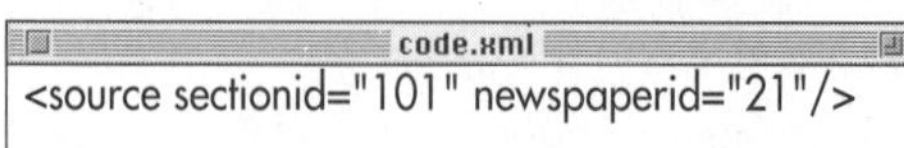

code.xml

```
<source sectionid="101" newspaperid="21"/>
```

Figure 7.43 *This* `source` *element is valid, when compared with the schema data in Figure 7.42. It would also be fine if there were no* `sectionid` *attribute at all.*

code.xml

```
<source sectionid="456" newspaperid="21"/>
```

Figure 7.44 *This is not a valid* `source` *element given the declaration in Figure 7.42.*

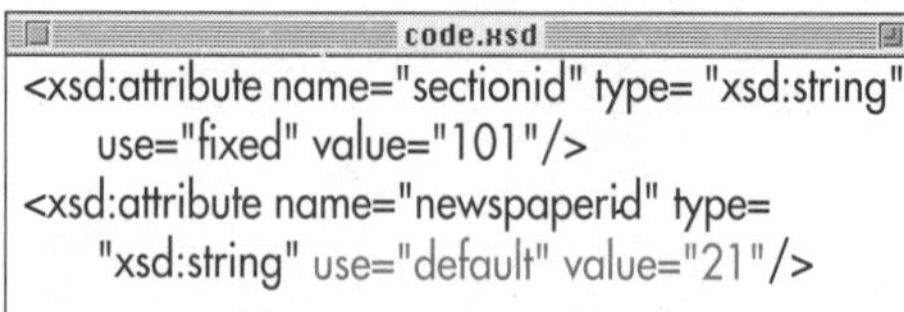

code.xsd

```
<xsd:attribute name="sectionid" type= "xsd:string"
    use="fixed" value="101"/>
<xsd:attribute name="newspaperid" type=
    "xsd:string" use="default" value="21"/>
```

Figure 7.45 *If we define the* `newspaperid` *attribute with a default value, that value will be set as the initial value whether or not the* `newspaperid` *attribute explicitly appears in the XML document. (Note: this is an excerpt of the complex type definition shown in Figure 7.40 on page 109).*

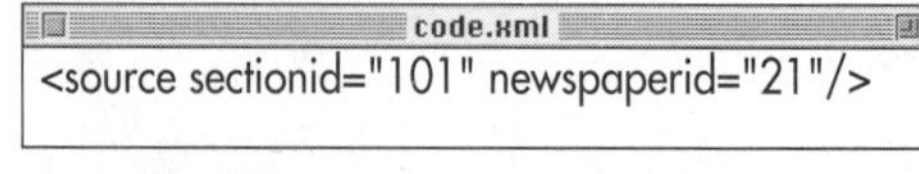

code.xml

```
<source sectionid="101" newspaperid="21"/>
```

code.xml

```
<source sectionid="101" newspaperid="25"/>
```

Figure 7.46 *Both of these* `source` *elements are valid. The default attribute only sets an* initial *value, and any other value is also acceptable.*

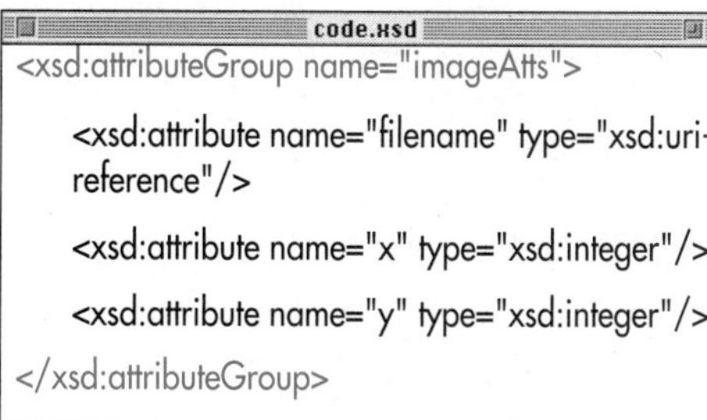

```
code.xsd
<xsd:attributeGroup name="imageAtts">
    <xsd:attribute name="filename" type="xsd:uri-reference"/>
    <xsd:attribute name="x" type="xsd:integer"/>
    <xsd:attribute name="y" type="xsd:integer"/>
</xsd:attributeGroup>
```

Figure 7.47 *By defining a group of attributes with a name, you make it easy to reuse those attributes in multiple type definitions.*

Defining Attribute Groups

If you need to use the same set of attributes in more than one element, it's more efficient to define an attribute group and then reference that group from within the complex type that corresponds to the element.

To define attribute groups:

1. Type **<xsd:attributeGroup name="label">**, where *label* identifies the attribute group.
2. Declare or reference each attribute that belongs to the group *(see page 108)*.
3. Finally, type **</xsd:attributeGroup>** to complete the attribute group definition.

✓ Tips

- An attribute group must be declared globally—at the top level of the schema (just below the `xsd:schema` element).
- Once you declare an attribute group, you must reference it as described on page 112.
- You can only reference globally declared attributes—that is, those that were declared at the top level of the schema. For more details, consult *Local and Global Declarations* on page 71.
- You can, however, declare attributes locally right in the attribute group itself. These attributes will only be available to that particular attribute group, but that might be just enough.
- An attribute group can contain references to other attribute groups.

Referencing Attribute Groups

Once you've defined an attribute group, you can reference it wherever those attributes are needed.

To reference an attribute group:

1. Within a complex type definition, after declaring any elements that should be contained, type **<xsd:attributeGroup**.
2. Then type **ref="label"/>**, where *label* matches the identifying name that you used in step 1 on page 111.

✔ Tips

- Attribute groups are analogous to parameter entities in DTDs *(see page 60)*—but of course, are limited to representing collections of attributes.
- Attributes (and attribute groups) should always be declared at the end of a component, after any elements have been declared.

```
code.xsd
<xsd:element name="picture">
  <xsd:complexType>
  <xsd:complexContent>
  <xsd:extension base="xsd:anyType">
  <xsd:attributeGroup ref="imageAtts"/>
  </xsd:extension>
  </xsd:complexContent>
  </xsd:complexType>
</xsd:element>

<xsd:element name="video">
  <xsd:complexType>
  <xsd:complexContent>
  <xsd:extension base="xsd:anyType">
  <xsd:element name="description"
  type="xsd:string"/>
  <xsd:element name="running_time"
  type="xsd:timeDuration"/>
  <xsd:attributeGroup ref="imageAtts"/>
  <xsd:attribute name="format"
  type="xsd:string"/>
  </xsd:extension>
  </xsd:complexContent>
  </xsd:complexType>
</xsd:element>
```

Figure 7.48 *Typing* `ref="imageAtts"` *is a lot faster and more consistent than redefining the three individual attributes. Note that the* `video` *element has an additional* `format` *attribute declared after the attribute group.*

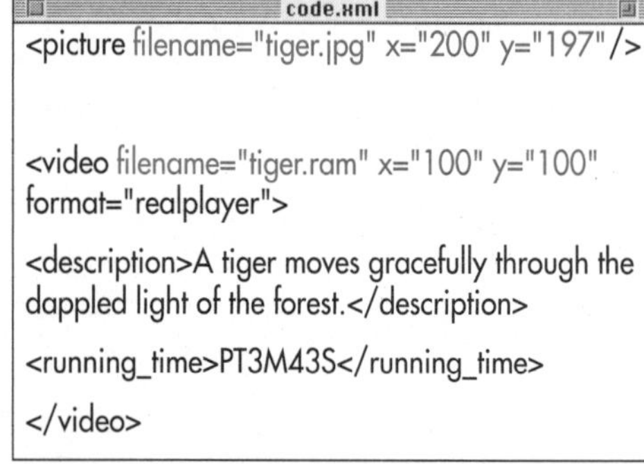

```
code.xml
<picture filename="tiger.jpg" x="200" y="197"/>


<video filename="tiger.ram" x="100" y="100"
format="realplayer">

<description>A tiger moves gracefully through the
dappled light of the forest.</description>

<running_time>PT3M43S</running_time>

</video>
```

Figure 7.49 *Both the* `picture` *and* `video` *elements share the* `filename`, `x`, *and* `y` *attributes, but I only had to define them once.*

8 Using Namespaces in XML


```
code.xsd
<xsd:schema xmlns:xsd="http://www.w3.org/
    2000/10/XMLSchema">
<xsd:element name="name" type="xsd:string"/>
<xsd:element name="source" type="xsd:string"/>
<xsd:element name="river">
    <xsd:complexType>
    <xsd:sequence>
    <xsd:element ref="name"/>
    <xsd:element ref="source"/>
    ...
    </xsd:element>
...
```

Figure 8.1 *In this schema for the fictional "RiversML", each element is declared globally, at the top level of the document, and then referenced in the complex type definitions of the elements in which they will appear.*

```
code.xsd
<xsd:schema xmlns:xsd="http://www.w3.org/
    2000/10/XMLSchema">
<xsd:element name="name" type="xsd:string"/>
<xsd:element name="source" type="xsd:string"/>
<xsd:element name="animal">
    <xsd:complexType>
    <xsd:sequence>
    <xsd:element ref="name"/>
    <xsd:element ref="source"/>
    ...
    </xsd:element>
...
```

Figure 8.2 *In this rendition of the Endangered Species schema, I've declared all the elements globally. If I combine documents created with this schema with documents created with the schema shown in Figure 8.1, the data in both the* `name` *and* `source` *elements will be compromised.*

In the last two chapters, you've learned how to define, in a schema, the set of elements and attributes that make up your XML documents. Now imagine that you want to combine your documents with someone else's documents—but that person, in their schema, has used some of the same names for globally declared elements as you have. For example, my Endangered Species document uses "source" to indicate the source of data on the World Wildlife Fund's Web site, while perhaps you use "source" to indicate the headwaters of a river. If we combine our documents, the `source` element data will become garbled and meaningless.

The solution to this problem is to create a *superlabel* that can distinguish all your elements from mine. For example, I could append the word "Liz" to all my element names (with a colon). Now the `Liz:source` element can't be confused with the `your:source` element. Of course, "Liz" isn't particularly unique (sigh). The name of a superlabel takes the form of a URL, based on a proprietary domain name, in order to ensure that it be both unique (no one else can use names based on your domain name) and permanent (a domain need never change).

The superlabel is called a *namespace* name. The namespace itself is the collection of related element names identified by the namespace name.

(Since locally declared elements are made unique by their context—see page 71—they rarely need to be qualified with a namespace.)

Designing a Namespace Name

Since the whole point of namespaces is to distinguish one similarly titled element from another, a namespace must have an absolutely unique and permanent name. In XML, namespace names are in the form of a URL.

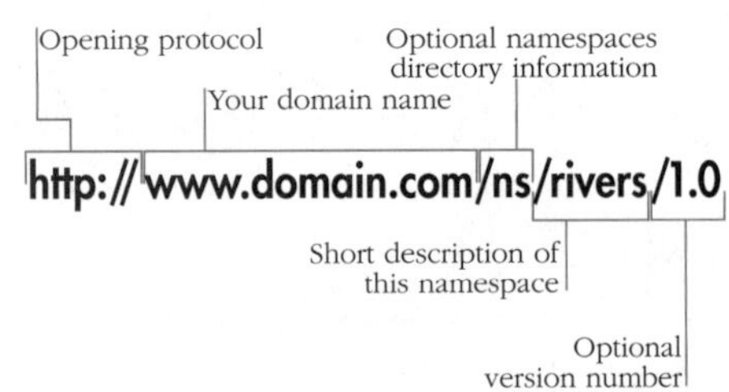

Figure 8.3 *A namespace should be in the form of a URL, typically starting with the standard HTTP protocol, followed by your domain name, an optional namespaces label in the form of a directory name, a very short description of the namespace, and an optional version number. The URL* does not *have to point to an actual file!*

To design a namespace name:

1. Start with your domain name.
2. Add descriptive information (as if it were a path in a URL) to create a unique name for your namespace.

✓ Tips

- Doesn't this sound vague? The truth is that the only official guidelines for creating a namespace name are that it be in the form of a URL, that it be *unique*, and that it be *persistent* (practically permanent). I'd also recommend being *consistent* if you're going to create numerous namespaces.
- You can add version information to your namespace, if desired.
- Using your own domain as the foundation for your namespace name gives you the ability to ensure that the name is unique. No one else can use your domain name.
- Don't use anyone else's domain name to start a namespace name.
- URLs are used for namespace names because they are unique, not because the URL points to anything in particular. While the URL *may* point to a DTD or schema, this is not required, nor is it a goal of the W3C. I recommend choosing a URL that will not ever change and that will never refer to a specific file.

```
<endangered_species>

<animal>

<name language="English">Giant River
    Otter</name>

...

<source sectionid="122" newspaperid="21"
    contentid="630"
    xmlns="http://www.cookwood.com/ns/
    end_species1"/>

<picture filename="otter.jpg" x="200" y="197"/>
```

Figure 8.4 *The* `source` *element is now identified as being part of the* http://www.cookwood.com/ns/end_species1 *namespace. None of the other elements are associated with any namespace. (This is sometimes called being "in no namespace".)*

```
<endangered_species
    xmlns="http://www.cookwood.com/ns/
    end_species1">

<animal>

<name language="English">Giant River
    Otter</name>

<name language="Latin">pteronura
    brasiliensis</name>

<threats><threat>habitat destruction</threat>

<threat>hunting</threat>

<threat>mercury poisoning from gold
    mining</threat>

<threat>pollution from fossil fuel
    extraction</threat>
```

Figure 8.5 *In this example, with the namespace declaration in the root element,* all *of the elements in the document are associated with the* http://www.cookwood.com/ns/end_species1 *namespace. (We'll see in how to override such a* default *namespace on pages 116–117.)*

Declaring Default Namespaces

Once you've designed a namespace name, you can declare it as the default for the whole document, or any part thereof.

To declare a default namespace for an element and all its children:

1. Within the opening tag of the element that you want to label with the namespace, type **xmlns=**.
2. Then type **"URL"**, where *URL* is the name of your namespace *(see page 114)*.

✓ Tips

- Labeling an element with a namespace as described above affects not only that particular element but all of the elements *contained in that element*—as long as these are not labeled with some other namespace.
- So, if you declare a default namespace for the root element, all of the elements in the document are considered to be from that namespace (unless labeled otherwise—see pages 116–117).
- A namespace declared for an entire document (or section thereof) is called a *default namespace* since it applies to all the document's (section's) elements unless some other namespace is also applied.
- You can override a default namespace (or no namespace) by specifying a prefixed namespace for an individual element, as described on pages 116–117. The child elements are not affected.

Namespaces for Individual Elements

If you want to label specific individual elements in your document with a namespace, without affecting those elements' children, you can declare a special nickname or *prefix* for the namespace and then use that prefix to label the individual elements.

To declare a prefix for a namespace name:

1. In the document's root element, type **xmlns:prefix**, where *prefix* will be the nickname for this namespace.
2. Then type **="URL"**, where *URL* is the name of the namespace to which the prefix will refer.

✔ Tips

- Prefixes may not begin with *x*, *m*, and *l*, in that order, in upper- or lowercase.
- You may use a prefix in any element contained within the element in which you declared the prefix, including the containing element itself. That is, if you declare a prefix in the root element, you can use the prefix in any element or attribute in the document, including the root element itself. If you declare the prefix in some other element, it can only be used in that element or in that element's children elements.
- You can declare as many prefixed namespaces as necessary in any element.

code.xml

```
<endangered_species xmlns="http://www.
cookwood.com/ns/ end_species1"

xmlns:rivers="http://www.cookwood.com/ns/
rivers1">

<animal>

<name language="English">Giant River
Otter</name>...

<source sectionid="122" newspaperid="21"
```

Figure 8.6 *By declaring the* `rivers1` *namespace in the document's root element, and assigning it a prefix, I can then use that prefix throughout the document to indicate that individual elements belong to the* `rivers1` *namespace (Figure 8.8 on page 117). Declaring the* `rivers1` *namespace in the* `endangered_species` *element has no effect on the namespace of the* `endangered_species` *element itself.*

code.xml

```
<endangered_species xmlns="http://www.
cookwood.com/ns/ end_species1">

<animal>

<name language="English">Giant River
Otter</name>...

<source sectionid="122" newspaperid="21"
contentid="630"/>

...

<rivers:habitat xmlns:rivers=
"http://www.cookwood.com/ns/rivers1">
<rivers:river><rivers:name>Amazon</rivers:name
>

<rivers:source>Andes Mountain in
Peru</rivers:source>...
```

Figure 8.7 *Since the* `rivers1` *namespace is declared in the* `rivers:habitat` *element, it can only be used within that element and the elements that it contains. It could not be used outside the* `rivers:habitat` *element.*

```
code.xml
<endangered_species
    xmlns="http://www.cookwood.com/ns/
    end_species/1.0"
xmlns:rivers="http://www.cookwood.com/ns/
    rivers/1.0">
<animal>
<name language="English">Giant River
    Otter</name>
<name language="Latin">pteronura
    brasiliensis</name>
<threats><threat>habitat destruction
<rivers:name>Amazon</rivers:name>
<rivers:source>Andes Mountains</rivers:source>
</threat>
<threat>hunting</threat>
<threat>overfishing</threat>
<threat>infection by canine distemper
    virus</threat>
</threats>
<source sectionid="122" newspaperid="21"
    contentid="630"/>
<picture filename="otter.jpg" x="200" y="197"/>
<rivers:picture file="amazon.jpg" x="200"
    y="197"/>
<weight>60 pounds</weight>
<length>8 feet long</length>
<diet><rivers:fauna>fish,
    crustaceans</rivers:fauna></diet>
...
</animal>
```

Figure 8.8 *Each element in the* rivers1 *namespace is preceded by* rivers: *to show that it belongs to the* rivers1 *namespace. While typing* rivers: *a bunch of times is a bit of a pain, typing* http://www.cookwood.com /ns/rivers1 *would be even worse.*

Once you've declared a prefix and the namespace that it refers to, you can use that prefix to label individual elements with different namespaces in your XML—without affecting the children of those elements.

To label individual elements with different namespaces:

1. Type **<** to begin the element.
2. Type **prefix:**, where *prefix* indicates the namespace to which this element belongs, as declared on the previous page.
3. Type **element**, where *element* is the name of the element you want to use.
4. Complete the element as usual. (You may want to add attributes to the element, you may need to close the opening tag with a > or with a /> if it's empty, etc. See Chapter 1, *Writing XML*, for more details.)

✓ Tips

- Only those elements whose names are preceded with a prefix are identified with the namespace declared with that prefix.
- The XML processor considers unprefixed elements to belong to the default namespace *(see page 115)*, if there is one, or to no namespace, if there's not.
- An XML processor considers the prefix an integral part of the element's name. Therefore, the closing tag must match the opening tag. If you've typed **<rivers:source>** for the name of the opening tag, use **</rivers:source>** for the closing tag.
- If you are using a lot of elements and attributes from a given namespace in one contained section, it may be easier to declare a default namespace for the section in its uppermost element *(see page 115)*.

How Namespaces Affect Attributes

While you *could* associate an attribute with a specific namespace, by prefixing it with the appropriate prefix, it's almost never necessary since attributes are already made unique by the element that contains them.

For example, when you see the `sectionid` attribute within the `source` element, you know that it belongs to the `source` element, which belongs to the `end_species1` namespace. There is no confusion. If there were another `sectionid` attribute, say, in an `orange` element, you'd still recognize that `sectionid` attribute as being part of the `orange` element, without any other necessary clues, simply because it is physically contained within the `orange` element.

That said, you should know that default namespaces do not apply to attributes. If the attribute has no prefix (which they rarely have), then it is considered to be "in no namespace" and thus *locally scoped*, which is a fancy way of saying that it is identified by the element that contains it.

In fact, the situation of attributes is not so different from that of locally declared elements. These, too, are identified by the element that contains them and so rarely need to be qualified with a namespace.

code.xml

```
<source sectionid="122" newspaperid="21"
contentid="630"/>

<orange sectionid="3A"/>
```

Figure 8.9 *Even though* `source` *and* `orange` *both have* `sectionid` *attributes, they don't overlap in the same way that identically named elements do. It's obvious by their location that the first* `sectionid` *pertains to the* `source` *and the second to the* `orange`*. And therefore, it's not necessary to identify them with a particular namespace.*

Namespaces, DTDs, and Valid Documents

While you may think of the element as just its name alone, the XML processor considers the element to be called **prefix:element**. If you want to validate your document against a DTD (as opposed to an XML Schema schema), you will have to declare each prefixed element in the DTD.

In addition, it is necessary to declare the attribute with which you declare the namespace, either **xmlns** or **xmlns:prefix**, depending on whether it's a default namespace or one that is called sporadically.

If you think this is kind of a pain, you're not alone. The lack of direct support for namespaces is one of the main reasons that DTDs are being supplanted by schemas written in XML Schema.

For more information on DTDs, see Part 2, *DTDs*, beginning on page 33.

9

NAMESPACES, SCHEMAS, AND VALIDATION

In Chapter 6, *Defining Simple Types*, and Chapter 7, *Defining Complex Types*, you learned how to define a kind or *class* of XML documents by creating a schema that specifies the elements and attributes of which the XML documents are composed. You can compare each of these individual XML documents, officially called *instances*, with the schema to see if it is *valid*, that is, to see if it conforms to what that kind of XML document should be *(see page 73)*. It's a great way to keep your data consistent.

However, if the XML document is made up of elements from different namespaces, as was described in Chapter 8, *Using Namespaces in XML*, validating the document becomes a bit more complicated.

You'll find all the details about setting up documents for validation in this chapter.

(For more information on how to use a schema validator to perform the actual validation, consult *Validating XML with a Schema* on page 245.)

Schemas and Namespaces

As we saw in the previous chapter, a namespace is a collection of related elements and attributes, identified by a common "URL-shaped" name. Namespaces are most often used to distinguish similarly named globally declared elements from one another. (Locally declared elements are generally made unique by their context.) Because a namespace name is always unique, the namespace plus the element name must also be unique.

When you *validate* a document whose elements are identified with a namespace, it's not enough to know that a particular element is unique, you also need to know how it is defined: when and how often it should occur, what other elements it must contain, if any, which attributes it will contain, if any, and so on. All that information is contained in a given schema, the schema in which a particular namespace's elements are defined.

So, while a schema defines what an XML document should look like, it can *simultaneously* create or "populate" a namespace with the elements that the schema contains (and defines). Once a schema's elements are associated with a particular namespace, the namespace-prefixed elements can be used in other documents, and those documents can be validated by looking at the schema(s) that populated the namespace.

```
code.xsd
<?xml version="1.0" ?>

<xsd:schema xmlns:xsd="http://www.w3.org/
    2000/10/XMLSchema"

targetNamespace="http://www.cookwood.com/
    ns/end_species1">

<xsd:element name="endangered_species">
    <xsd:complexType>
    <xsd:sequence>
    <xsd:element name="animal"
    type="animalType"
    maxOccurs="unbounded"/>
    </xsd:sequence>
    </xsd:complexType>
    </xsd:element>

<xsd:complexType name="animalType">
    <xsd:sequence>
    <xsd:element name="name" type="nameType"
    minOccurs="2"/>
    <xsd:element name="threats"
    type="threatsType"/>
    <xsd:element name="weight"
    type="xsd:string" minOccurs="0"
    maxOccurs="1"/>
    ...
    </xsd:sequence>
    </xsd:complexType>

...
```

Figure 9.1 *In this example, the* `endangered_species` *element and the* `animalType` *complex type are now identified with the* `http://www.cookwood.com/ns/end_species1` *namespace. The* `animal`, `threats`, *and* `weight` *elements are not identified with the namespace since they are not top-level elements.*

Populating a Namespace

You can associate the globally declared (top-level) components of your schema with a namespace in order to be able to use those components in other schema documents. A globally declared component is any direct child of the `xsd:schema` element, and could be element declarations, attribute declarations, complex or simple type definitions, named group definitions, and attribute group definitions.

While you don't have to do anything special in the actual definition or declaration, that is, you can simply follow the instructions in Chapters 6 and 7, you do have to specify the *target namespace* with which you want to associate the component.

To specify a target namespace:

In the root element of your schema document, type **targetNamespace="URL"**, where *URL* is the namespace with which you want to associate the components defined in this schema. This is called "populating" a namespace.

✔ Tip

- Only, and I mean *only* the globally declared (top-level) components are associated with the namespace. This does not mean you cannot use or validate the locally declared, and thus, unassociated items, like the `animal` element in Figure 9.1. When we validate an XML instance against the schema shown in the figure, the processor will know where to look for the definition of the `endangered_ species` element, and it will know that the `endangered_species` element must contain an *unqualified* `animal` element (that is, one that is not associated with a namespace).

Populating a Namespace

Adding All Locally Declared Elements

By default, only the globally declared (top-level) components are associated with the target namespace. If you want to add local element declarations and definitions (i.e., those that are one or more levels down), you can add all the elements at once or add all the attribute declarations at once as shown below, or add elements and/or attributes individually as shown on page 125.

To add all the locally declared elements to the target namespace:

In the `xsd:schema` element, type **elementFormDefault="qualified"**.

To add all the locally declared attributes to the target namespace:

In the `xsd:schema` element, type **attributeFormDefault="qualified"**.

✔ Tip

- As we've seen, the default value for each of these attributes is *unqualified*, which means that only globally declared (top-level) components are associated with the target namespace unless you specify otherwise.

code.xsd

```
<?xml version="1.0" ?>

<xsd:schema xmlns:xsd="http://www.w3.org/
    2000/10/XMLSchema"

targetNamespace="http://www.cookwood.com
    /ns/end_species1"

elementFormDefault="qualified">

<xsd:element name="endangered_species">
    <xsd:complexType>
    <xsd:sequence>
    <xsd:element name="animal"
    type="animalType"
    maxOccurs="unbounded"/>
    </xsd:sequence>
    </xsd:complexType>
    </xsd:element>

<xsd:complexType name="animalType">
    <xsd:sequence>
    <xsd:element name="name" type="nameType"
    minOccurs="2"/><xsd:element
    name="threats" type="threatsType"/>
    <xsd:element name="weight"
    type="xsd:string" minOccurs="0"
    maxOccurs="1"/>
    ...
    </xsd:sequence>
    </xsd:complexType>

...
```

Figure 9.2 *Now the locally declared elements,* `animal`, `threats`, *and* `weight` *are associated with the namespace and can be referred to accordingly in an XML document.*

```
code.xsd
<?xml version="1.0" ?>

<xsd:schema xmlns:xsd="http://www.w3.org/
    2000/10/XMLSchema"

targetNamespace="http://www.cookwood.com
    /ns/end_species1"

elementFormDefault="qualified">

<xsd:element name="endangered_species">
    <xsd:complexType>
    <xsd:sequence>
    <xsd:element name="animal"
    type="animalType"
    maxOccurs="unbounded"/>
    </xsd:sequence>
    </xsd:complexType>
    </xsd:element>

<xsd:complexType name="animalType">
    <xsd:sequence>
    <xsd:element name="name" type="nameType"
    minOccurs="2"/>
    <xsd:element name="threats"
    type="threatsType" form="unqualified"/>
    <xsd:element name="weight"
    type="xsd:string" minOccurs="0"
    maxOccurs="1" form="unqualified"/>
    ...
    </xsd:sequence>
    </xsd:complexType>

...
```

Figure 9.3 *Despite the* `elementFormDefault` *setting in the* `xsd:schema` *element, neither the* `threats` *nor* `weight` *elements will be associated with the target namespace because their* `form` *attributes override the* `elementFormDefault` *value.*

Adding Particular Locally Declared Elements

The form attribute is useful for specifying whether a particular, individual, locally declared element should be associated with the target namespace, regardless of the default *(see page 124)*.

To add a particular locally declared element to the target namespace:

In the element's declaration, type **form="qualified"**. Regardless of where that element is declared, it will be associated with the target namespace.

If you've used the `elementFormDefault="qualified"` attribute in the `xsd:schema` element, you can use the `form` attribute to keep a particular locally declared element from being associated with the target namespace.

To keep a particular locally declared element from being associated with a target namespace (despite the default):

In the element's declaration, type **form="unqualified"**.

Referencing Components with Namespaces

Once you have associated schema components (simple or complex named types; element, attribute, attribute group, and named groups) with a namespace *(see page 123)*, you can refer to them within that or other schemas. And since they are associated with a namespace, you *have to specify the namespace* when you refer to them.

In this book, I've been using the *xsd* prefix for all the XML Schema elements, and duly declaring the XML Schema schema (generally called the *schema of schemas*) in the schema's root element. That is why, when I refer to built-in types (that is, types that are already defined in the schema of schemas), I need to prefix them with *xsd*. That way, the schema knows where to find their definitions.

But what about the custom types (both simple and complex) that you derive yourself? Or element or attribute declarations that you want to reference? Or groups that you want to reference? References to any of these must include information about the namespace with which they are associated.

To specify a default namespace for referenced components and then reference those components in the schema:

1. In the root element of the schema document, type **xmlns="URL"**, where *URL* is the namespace with which the referenced components are associated.

2. In the *value* of the `type` and `ref` attributes, type **reference** (with no prefix), where *reference* is the name of the component that is associated with that default namespace.

```
code.xsd
<?xml version="1.0" ?>

<xsd:schema xmlns:xsd="http://www.w3.org/
    2000/10/XMLSchema"

targetNamespace="http://www.cookwood.com/
    ns/end_species1"

xmlns="http://www.cookwood.com/
    ns/end_species1">

<xsd:element name="endangered_species">
    <xsd:complexType>
    <xsd:sequence>
    <xsd:element name="animal"
    type="animalType"
    maxOccurs="unbounded"/>
    </xsd:sequence>
    </xsd:complexType>
    </xsd:element>

<xsd:complexType name="animalType">
    <xsd:sequence>
    <xsd:element name="name" type="nameType"
    minOccurs="2"/>
    <xsd:element name="threats"
    type="threatsType"/>
    <xsd:element name="weight"
    type="xsd:string" minOccurs="0"
    maxOccurs="1"/>
    ...
    </xsd:sequence>
    </xsd:complexType>

...
```

Figure 9.4 *In the root element of the schema, I've declared the default namespace,* `end_species1`, *for this schema document. That means the definitions of the unprefixed types (*`animalType`, `nameType`, *and* `threatsType`*) can be found in the schema that corresponds to the* `end_species1` *namespace. (The definition of the prefixed types,* `xsd:string`, *is found in the schema that corresponds to the* `XMLSchema` *namespace.)*

```
code.xsd
<?xml version="1.0" ?>

<xsd:schema xmlns:xsd="http://www.w3.org/
    2000/10/XMLSchema"

targetNamespace="http://www.cookwood.com/
    ns/end_species1"

xmlns:end="http://www.cookwood.com/
    ns/end_species1">

<xsd:element name="endangered_species">
    <xsd:complexType>
    <xsd:sequence>
    <xsd:element name="animal"
    type="end:animalType"
    maxOccurs="unbounded"/>
    </xsd:sequence>
    </xsd:complexType>
    </xsd:element>

<xsd:complexType name="animalType">
    <xsd:sequence>
    <xsd:element name="name"
    type="end:nameType" minOccurs="2"/>
    <xsd:element name="threats"
    type="end:threatsType"/>
    <xsd:element name="weight"
    type="xsd:string" minOccurs="0"
    maxOccurs="1"/>
    ...
    </xsd:sequence>
    </xsd:complexType>

...
```

Figure 9.5 *This document is equivalent to the one in Figure 9.4 on page 126. This time, I've defined the prefix* end *for referring to the* `end_species1` *namespace. So I have to use the prefix to indicate that* `end:animalType`, `end:nameType`, *and* `end:threatsType` *all belong to the* `end_species1` *namespace. Note, however, that the elements belong to the same namespace as before (which is controlled by the targetNamespace attribute). I've simply changed the way of* identifying *them.*

To declare a namespace with a prefix and then use that prefix to qualify referenced components in the schema:

1. In the root element of your XML document, type **xmlns:prefix="URL"**, where *prefix* is how you will mark the definitions in this schema that belong to the namespace indicated by *URL*.

2. In the *value* of the `type` and `ref` attributes, type **prefix:reference**, where *reference* is the name of the component associated with the namespace that corresponds to the *prefix* (and the *prefix* is the same as in step 1).

✓ Tips

- You can declare as many namespaces as you need and then use definitions defined within them by using the corresponding prefix.
- It does not seem at all intuitive to me that the *value of an attribute* should be associated with a namespace (or with no namespace). But that's the way it works.
- Remember this important distinction: the target namespace is the one that actually and actively *associates* or links a component with a namespace. A namespace declaration, like **xmlns="URL"** or **xmlns:end="URL"**, simply indicates which namespace a component *has been* associated with.

The Schema of Schemas as the Default

There's no law that says I have to prefix elements and types from the schema of schemas with *xsd*. I could just as easily use *zap* or *boffo* or anything else I like. Indeed, if my schema is mostly composed of built-in types, it might be easier and quicker to declare the schema of schemas as the *default namespace*, and then I can forget about prefixing elements from its namespace altogether.

To declare the schema of schemas as the default namespace for a schema:

1. To begin the schema, after the XML declaration, type **<schema** (notice that it's not *xsd:schema*).
2. Next type **xmlns="http://www.w3.org/2000/10/XMLSchema"** to declare the schema of schemas as the default namespace for the schema you're writing.
3. Type **targetNamespace="URL"**, where *URL* is the namespace with which you'd like to associate top-level named type definitions and elements (as usual).
4. Type **xmlns:prefix="URL"**, where *prefix* is how you will mark the definitions in this schema that belong to the namespace indicated by *URL*.
5. Repeat step 4 for each namespace that contains definitions used in this schema.
6. Type **>** to complete the `schema` tag.

✔ Tip

- You will usually need to set one prefix to the target namespace (unless you're importing definitions from another namespace—see page 132 for more details).

```
code.xsd
<?xml version="1.0" ?>

<schema xmlns="http://www.w3.org/
   2000/10/XMLSchema"

targetNamespace="http://www.cookwood.com/
   ns/end_species1"

xmlns:end="http://www.cookwood.com/
   ns/end_species1">

<element name="endangered_species">
   <complexType>
   <sequence>
   <element name="animal"
   type="end:animalType"
   maxOccurs="unbounded"/>
   </sequence>
   </complexType>
   </element>

<complexType name="animalType">
   <sequence>
   <element name="name"
   type="end:nameType" minOccurs="2"/>
   <element name="threats"
   type="end:threatsType"/>
   <element name="weight" type="string"
   minOccurs="0" maxOccurs="1"/>
   ...
   </sequence>
   </complexType>

...
```

Figure 9.6 *This document is exactly equivalent to the one shown in Figure 9.4 on page 126 (and Figure 9.5 on page 127 for that matter). The only difference is one of notation. Here I've declared the schema of schemas as the default namespace, and so I don't need to prefix element names (*`schema`*,* `element`*,* `complexType`*, etc.) or built-in types (*`string`*) with* `xsd`*. On the other hand, I do have to prefix any types that come from other namespaces, as in the case of* `end:animalType`*,* `end:nameType`*, and* `end:threatsType`.

```
code.xml
<?xml version="1.0" ?>
<end:endangered_species
   xmlns:end="http://www.cookwood.com/ns/
   end_species1">
<animal>
<name language="English">Tiger</name>
<name language="Latin">panthera tigris</name>
<threats>
   <threat>poachers</threat>
   <threat>habitat destruction</threat>
   <threat>trade in tiger bones for traditional
   Chinese medicine (TCM)</threat>
   </threats>
<weight>500 pounds</weight>
<length>3 yards from nose to tail</length>
...
</end:endangered_species>
```

Figure 9.7 *In the schema shown in Figure 9.4 on page 126—and because of the targetNamespace attribute in that schema—the* `endangered_species` *element was associated with the namespace* http://www.cookwood.com/ns/end_species1. *If we now wish to validate a document that contains this element (like the XML instance shown), we have to qualify* `endangered_species` *accordingly. Because* `animal` *(and the other elements) was not associated with the target namespace, it requires no such indication here either.*

Namespaces and Validating XML

So, you *qualify* a set of components (identify them with a namespace) and now you're ready to validate a document that uses those components. When validating the documents in Chapters 6 and 7, you didn't have to worry about namespaces because you never associated any of the components you were defining with a target namespace. Now that all or some of your components belong to a namespace, you'll have to specify that namespace for those components in your XML documents when validating those documents.

You may also need to specify where the processor can find the schema document in which the namespace's associated components are defined.

To write valid XML documents with qualified components:

1. You must indicate the namespace of the desired components either by declaring a default namespace (**xmlns="URL"**) and using no prefix with the components, or by declaring a namespace with a prefix (**xmlns:prefix="URL"**) and then prefixing the desired components. Chapter 8, *Using Namespaces in XML*, describes this process in more detail.

2. It is sometimes also necessary to indicate where (e.g., on the server) the schema document can be found that defines or *populates* the namespace being used to qualify the elements *(see page 130)*.

✓ Tip

- Remember to qualify only those elements that are actually associated with the namespace.

Indicating Where a Schema Is

You've already seen how to indicate a schema's location when there are no qualified elements in the XML document *(see page 73)*. Specifying the location of a schema for an XML document that contains qualified elements is pretty similar.

To indicate where the schema for qualified elements can be found:

1. In the root element of the XML document, after the declaration of the namespace that is associated with the qualified elements, type **xmlns:xsi= "http://www.w3. org/2000/10/ XMLSchema-instance"** to declare the namespace of the attribute with which you'll indicate the schema location.
2. Then, type **xsi:schemaLocation="URL**, where *URL* is the name of the namespace whose schema document you're about to give the location of. (Notice that there is no closing double quotation mark.)
3. Type a space (or a return, if you prefer).
4. Now type **file.xsd"**, where *file.xsd* is the URL of the actual file that contains the schema that defines the namespace used in this XML document. (Note that there is no opening double quotation mark.)
5. You can repeat steps 2–4 for as many schemas as the XML document needs.

✔ Tip

- While most XML processors will check the `xsi:schemaLocation` attribute to find the corresponding schema file, not all will. Consult your XML processor's documentation for further details.

code.xml

```
<?xml version="1.0" ?>

<end:endangered_species
    xmlns:end="http://www.cookwood.com/ns/
    end_species1"

xmlns:xsi="http://www.w3.org/2000/10/
    XMLSchema-instance"

xsi:schemaLocation="http://www.cookwood.com/
    ns/end_species1

http://www.cookwood.com/xml/schemas/
    end_species1.xsd">

<animal>

<name language="English">Tiger</name>

<name language="Latin">panthera tigris</name>

<threats>
    <threat>poachers</threat>
    <threat>habitat destruction</threat>
    <threat>trade in tiger bones for traditional
    Chinese medicine (TCM)</threat>
    </threats>

<weight>500 pounds</weight>

<length>3 yards from nose to tail</length>

...
```

Figure 9.8 *The first highlighted line declares the namespace for* xsi*-prefixed items. The second indicates the namespace for which the third line indicates the actual file out on a server somewhere with which that namespace is defined.*

```
code.xsd
<?xml version="1.0" ?>
<xsd:schema xmlns:xsd="http://www.w3.org/
    2000/10/XMLSchema"
targetNamespace="http://www.cookwood.com/
    ns/end_species1">
<xsd:complexType name="threatsType">
    <xsd:sequence>
    <xsd:element name="threat"
    maxOccurs="unbounded"/>
    </xsd:sequence>
    </xsd:complexType>
```

Figure 9.9 *First I create a new file* (threats.xsd, *shown here) with the* `threatsType` *complex type definition. Now, I can use this definition in other schemas.*

```
code.xsd
<?xml version="1.0" ?>
<xsd:schema xmlns:xsd="http://www.w3.org/
    2000/10/XMLSchema"
targetNamespace="http://www.cookwood.com/
    ns/end_species1"
xmlns="http://www.cookwood.com/
    ns/end_species1">
<xsd:include schemaLocation=
    "http://www.cookwood.com/xml/schemas/
    threats.xsd"/>
<xsd:element name="endangered_species">
    <xsd:complexType><xsd:sequence>
    <xsd:element name="animal"
    type="animalType"
    maxOccurs="unbounded"/>
    </xsd:sequence></xsd:complexType>
    </xsd:element>
<xsd:complexType name="animalType">
    <xsd:sequence>
    <xsd:element name="name" type="nameType"
    minOccurs="2"/>
    <xsd:element name="threats"
    type="threatsType"/>
...</xsd:complexType>
```

Figure 9.10 *You can include schema components from other schemas with the same target namespace by using the* `xsd:include` *element.*

Schemas in Multiple Files

You can divide a schema's components into various individual files (officially called *schema documents*) in order to reuse them in several different schemas and documents, or simply to make it easier to handle large schemas.

To include schema components:

1. Divide the schema components among files. Each file should be text only and be saved with the .xsd extension.
2. In the schema document in which you wish to include components, directly after the `xsd:schema` element, type **<xsd:include schemaLocation="included-file.xsd"/>**, where *includedfile.xsd* is the URL of the schema document that contains the components you wish to include.

✔ Tips

- The `targetNamespace` attribute of the included schema document must be the same as the schema document receiving the components. To add schema components with different target namespaces, consult *Importing Components* on page 132.
- If the included schema has no target namespace specified, it is assumed that its target namespace is the same as the one for the schema document in which it is being included.

Schemas in Multiple Files

Importing Components

You can import top-level schema components from other schemas with different target namespaces in order to validate XML documents whose elements are associated with more than one namespace.

To import components from schemas with different target namespaces:

1. Directly after the `xsd:schema` element in the schema document into which you're importing the schema components, type **<xsd:import**.
2. Then type **namespace="URL"**, where *URL* indicates the name of the namespace to which the imported schema components are associated.
3. Then, if necessary, specify the location of the file that contains the schema that defines the namespace in step 2 by typing **xsi:schemaLocation="URL**, where *URL* is the name of the namespace whose schema document you're about to give the location of.
4. Type a space (or a return, if you prefer).
5. Now type **file.xsd"**, where *file.xsd* is the URL of the actual file that contains the schema whose components you want to import.
6. Type **/>** to complete the `xsd:import` tag.
7. As described on page 126, declare a prefix for the imported namespace so that you can refer to the imported components in your schema.

✔ Tip

- If you haven't done so already, you should also declare the XML Schema-instance namespace as described in step 1 on page 130.

```
code.xsd
<?xml version="1.0" ?>

<xsd:schema xmlns:xsd="http://www.w3.org/
   2000/10/XMLSchema"
   xmlns:xsi="http://www.w3.org/2000/10/
   XMLSchema-instance"
   targetNamespace="http://www.cookwood.
   com/ns/end_species1"
   xmlns="http://www.cookwood.com/
   ns/end_species1"
   xmlns:rivers="http://www.cookwood.com/
   ns/rivers1">

<xsd:import namespace=
   "http://www.cookwood.com/ns/rivers1"
   xsi:schemaLocation=
   "http://www.cookwood.com/ns/rivers1
   http://www.cookwood.com/xml/schemas/
   rivers.xsd"/>

<xsd:element name="endangered_species">
   <xsd:complexType><xsd:sequence>
   <xsd:element name="animal"
   type="animalType"
   maxOccurs="unbounded"/>
   </xsd:sequence></xsd:complexType>
   </xsd:element>

<xsd:complexType name="animalType">
   <xsd:sequence><xsd:element name="name"
   type="nameType" minOccurs="2"/>
   <xsd:element name="threats"
   type="threatsType"/>
   ...
   <xsd:element name="habitat"
```

Figure 9.11 *Importing one schema into another makes the components from one schema available for defining components in the containing schema.*

PART 4: XSLT AND XPATH

10

XSLT

The complete and official proposal for transforming and formatting XML documents was originally to be contained in a specification called *XSL*, which stands for *Extensible Style Language*. However, because it was taking so long to finalize, the W3C divided XSL into two pieces: XSLT (for *T*ransformation) and XSL-FO (for *F*ormatting *O*bjects).

This chapter, and the two that follow, explain how to use XSLT to transform XML documents. The end result might be another XML document or more commonly an HTML document for viewing in both the newest and the not-so-new browsers. *Transforming* an XML document means analyzing its contents and taking certain actions depending on what elements are found. You can use XSLT to reorder the output according to a specific criteria, to only display certain pieces of information, and much more.

Since XSL-FO is not yet formalized nor supported by any browsers, it is not covered in this book. You can find information about its current status at *http://www.w3.org/Style/XSL/*. Meanwhile, XSLT is often used in conjunction with the much more widely known CSS, or *Cascading Style Sheets*, which handles the actual formatting. For more information on CSS, see Part 5, beginning on page 175.

The examples in this part of the book are based on a single XML file and a sequential set of XSLT files, in which each one builds on the previous one. I recommend downloading and printing out at least the XML file, if not all of the XSLT files as well *(see page 18)*.

Transforming XML with XSLT

Let's start with an overview of the whole transformation process. Then you can go through the rest of this chapter (and the two that follow) to dig into the details.

To perform the actual transformation, you'll need an XSLT processor. There are a number of these available online, including Instant Saxon (written by Michael Kay). For more details, consult *Transforming XML with an XSLT Processor* on page 246.

The first thing the XSLT processor does is analyze the XML document **(Figure 10.1)** and convert it into a node tree **(Figure 10.2)**. A *node* is nothing more than one individual piece of the XML document (like an element, an attribute, or some text content). A *node tree* is a hierarchical representation of the entire XML document.

Once the processor has identified the nodes in the source XML, it then looks to a XSLT style sheet for instructions on what to do with those nodes. Those instructions are contained in *templates*. Each template has two parts: first, a sort of label that identifies the nodes in the XML document that the template can be applied to, and second, instructions about the actual transformation that should take place.

The processor automatically looks for a *root template*, which it then applies to the *root node* of the XML document (the one that contains the outermost element). The root template generally contains a combination of *literal elements*, that should be output as is, and *XSLT instructions* that output or further process the nodes in the source document.

```
code.xml
<?xml version="1.0"?>
<endangered_species>

<animal>
<name language="English">Tiger</name>
<name language="Latin">panthera
tigris</name>
<threats><threat>poachers</threat>
<threat>habitat destruction</threat>
<threat>trade in tiger bones for traditional
Chinese medicine (TCM)</threat>
</threats>

...
```

Figure 10.1 *You can find the full XML document used in the examples in this chapter on the book's Web site (see page 18). I recommend downloading and printing out a copy for easy reference as you go through the examples.*

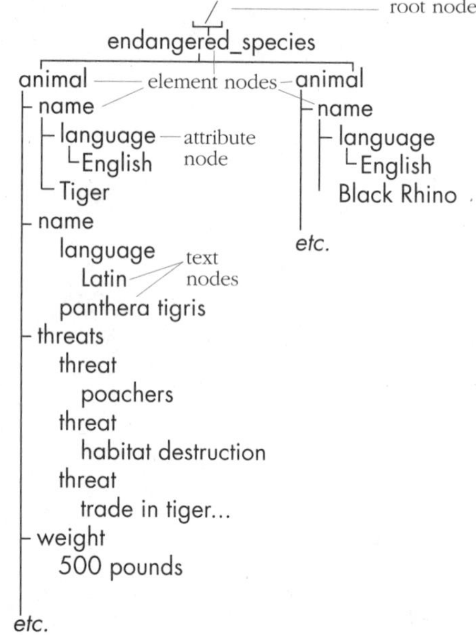

Figure 10.2 *Here is a partial representation of the node tree that corresponds to the XML document shown in Figure 10.1.*

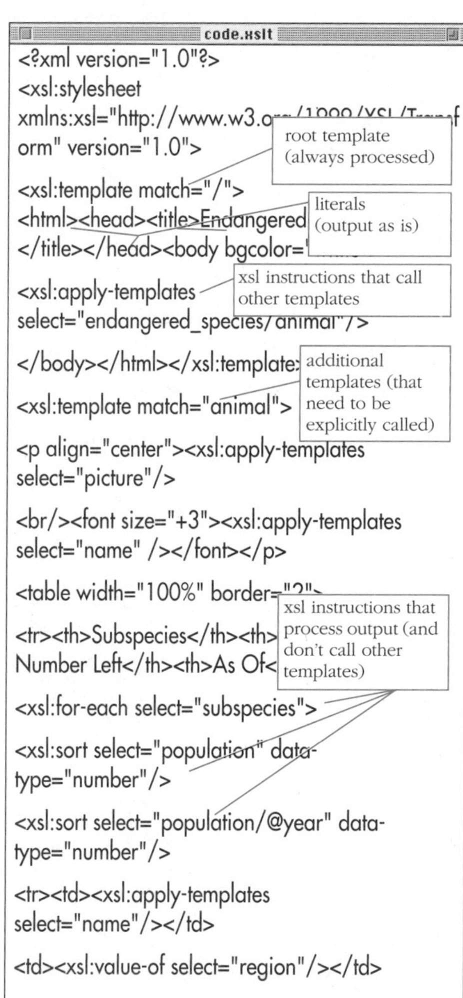

Figure 10.3 *The complete XSLT style sheet can also be found on the book's Web site (see page 18) and should also be downloaded and printed for your convenience.*

One special kind of XSLT instruction (`xsl:apply-templates`) identifies a set of nodes (aptly called a *node set*) and specifies that those nodes should be processed at that point with the *most appropriate* template(s) available. Each of these "subtemplates" can include additional `xsl:apply-templates` instructions that point to other subtemplates. This lets you control the order (and manner) in which the contents of the source document are processed and output.

You identify and select node sets and their corresponding templates by using expressions and patterns, respectively. These are written in XPath syntax and are sufficiently complex to warrant their own chapters: *XPath: Patterns and Expressions*, which begins on page 153 and *Test Expressions and Functions*, which begins on page 163.

The transformed data is then either displayed or saved to another file.

While you can use XSLT to convert almost any kind of document into almost any other kind of document, that's a pretty vague topic to tackle. In this book, I'll focus on using XSLT to convert XML into HTML. This lets you use the strengths and flexibility of XML for handling your data and the compatibility of HTML so that visitors to your site can actually access that data.

Beginning an XSLT Style Sheet

Every XSLT style sheet is an XML document in itself and therefore should begin with a standard XML declaration. Once that's out of the way, you must define the namespace for the style sheet.

To begin an XSLT style sheet:

1. Type **<?xml version="1.0"?>** to indicate that the XSLT style sheet is an XML document. For more details see *Declaring the XML Version* on page 24.

2. Next, type **<xsl:stylesheet xmlns:xsl= "http://www.w3.org/1999/XSL/ Transform" version="1.0">** to specify the namespace for the style sheet and declare its prefix (xsl).

3. Leave a few empty lines where you will create the style sheet (with the instructions contained in this and the two following chapters).

4. Type **</xsl:stylesheet>** to complete the style sheet.

✓ Tips

- There is no space in `xsl:stylesheet`. (It's *not* `xsl:style sheet`.) Nevertheless, I do use two words to refer to *style sheets* when talking about them in this book (as is the convention).

- If you use Internet Explorer 5 for XSLT processing, you'll probably have to use the following namespace declaration: **<xsl:stylesheet xmlns:xsl= "http://www.w3.org/TR/WD-xsl">**.

- For more information on declaring namespaces, Chapter 8, *Using Namespaces in XML.*

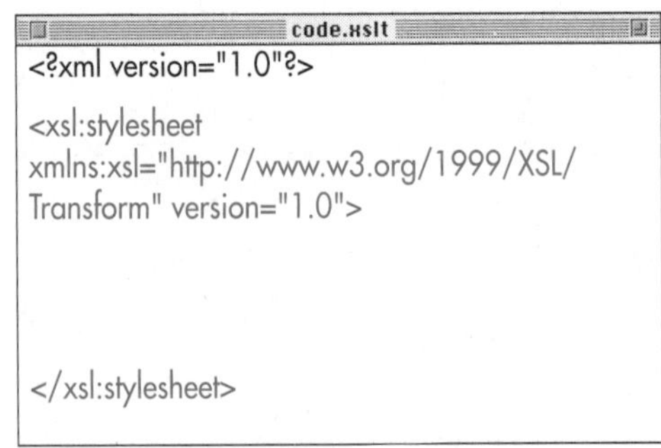

Figure 10.4 *The header for a style sheet is almost always the same. You can just copy and paste this information from one style sheet to the next.*

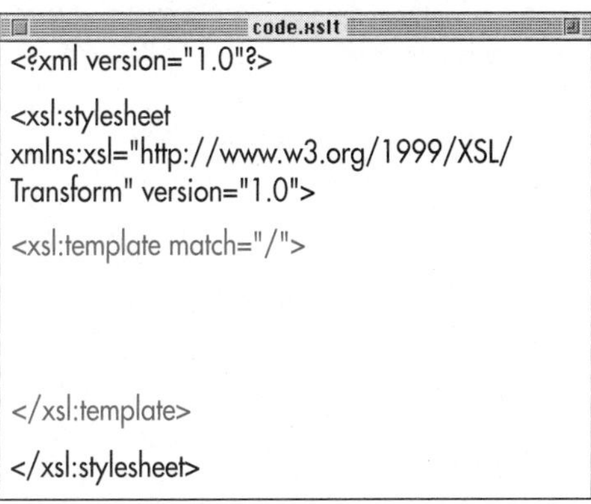


```
<?xml version="1.0"?>

<xsl:stylesheet
xmlns:xsl="http://www.w3.org/1999/XSL/
Transform" version="1.0">

<xsl:template match="/">



</xsl:template>

</xsl:stylesheet>
```

Figure 10.5 *The root template is the only template that is invoked automatically by the XSLT processor.*

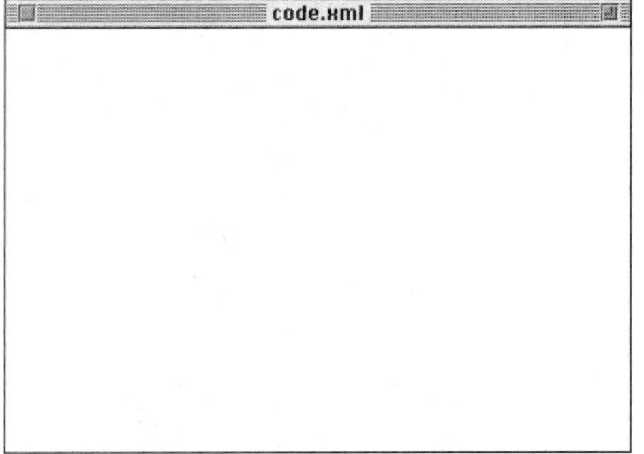

Figure 10.6 *If you process an XML document with this style sheet and most basic of root templates, you'll get an empty document. That's what the template in Figure 10.5 says: output two blank lines.*

Creating the Root Template

The first thing that the XSLT processor looks for in a style sheet is a template that it can apply to the root node of the XML document. I call this template the *root template*.

To create the root template:

1. Type **<xsl:template**.
2. Type **match="/"**. The forward slash is a pattern that matches the root node of the XML document.
3. Type **>**.
4. Leave a few lines for specifying what should happen with the XML document (we'll get there on pages 140–151).
5. Type **</xsl:template>** to complete the root template.

✔ Tips

- While the XSLT processor doesn't really care where this template appears in your XSLT style sheet, it's probably most clear to you (and people who work with you) if you put it up at the very top.
- If you do not include a template that matches the root node of the XML document, a built-in template is used which basically tries to find appropriate templates for each of the root node's child nodes. (This built-in root template is equivalent to **<xsl:template><xsl:apply-templates/></xsl:template>**.) For more information on `xsl:apply-templates`, consult *Creating and Applying Template Rules* on page 144.

Outputting HTML Code

There are basically two kinds of components in an XSLT style sheet: instructions and literals. The XSLT instructions describe how the source XML document will be transformed. The literals—typically HTML code and text—are output just as they appear in the style sheet.

In your root template, you create the structure for the final transformed document. For HTML output, you'll want to add HTML header information (`head`, `body`, etc.) at the very least. And if you like, you can add extensive HTML formatting as well.

In templates other than the root template, you can add whatever HTML formatting is necessary to set up your output, but probably not the `html`, `head`, or `body` elements.

To add HTML code to the output:

Within a template rule tag (that is, between `<xsl:template match="...">` and `</xsl:template>`, add the HTML code that you would like to output when that particular template is invoked.

code.xslt

```
<xsl:template match="/">

<html><head><title>Endangered
Species</title></head><body bgcolor="white">

<p>Endangered animals face numerous threats.
For more information, check out the World Wildlife
Federation's <a
href="http://www.worldwildlife.org/
species/species.cfm?"> pages</a>.

</p><hr/></body></html>

</xsl:template>
```

Figure 10.7 *Anything that is not an xsl instruction will be outputted as is. It's an easy way to add HTML coding and text. The HTML must be well-formed, e.g., the* `<p>` *tags must have matching* `</p>` *tags and I've used* `<hr/>` *and not* `<hr>`.

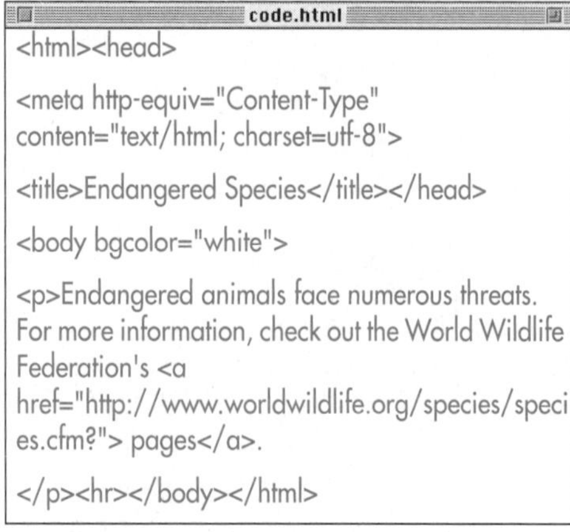

code.html

```
<html><head>

<meta http-equiv="Content-Type"
content="text/html; charset=utf-8">

<title>Endangered Species</title></head>

<body bgcolor="white">

<p>Endangered animals face numerous threats.
For more information, check out the World Wildlife
Federation's <a
href="http://www.worldwildlife.org/species/speci
es.cfm?"> pages</a>.

</p><hr></body></html>
```

Figure 10.8 *The XSLT processor (Saxon, in this case) still hasn't gotten its hands on the XML but contents itself with outputting all of the HTML tags and text. Notice how Saxon adds the* `<meta>` *tag automatically, once it sees the* `<html>` *tag and realizes that we're outputting HTML code. It also changes* `<hr/>` *back into the more recognized and better supported* `<hr>`.

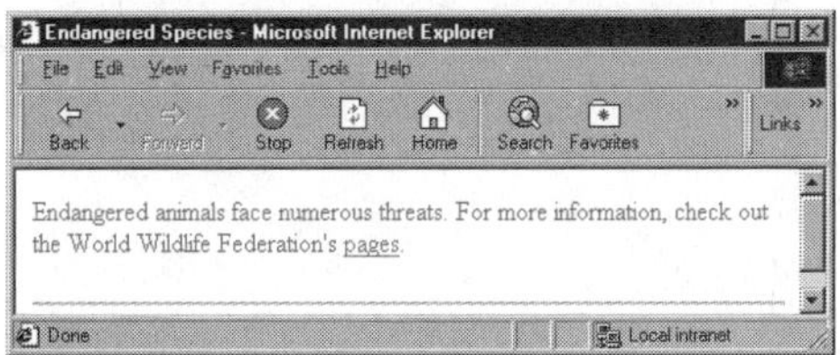

Figure 10.9 *Here's what it looks like so far in a browser. It's not very exciting yet, but we're getting somewhere.*

✔ Tips

- Your HTML code must adhere to XML rules for well-formedness. And while it doesn't have to be XHTML (the only additional change would be to write all your element and attribute names in lowercase letters), it's probably a good idea. For more information on writing HTML according to XML rules, consult Chapter 1, *Writing XML*, in general, and *Rules for Writing XML*, on page 23, in particular. You might also want to look over Appendix A, *XHTML*.
- I don't specify what the match attribute is equal to in the instructions since you can add HTML output to any template, not just the root template.
- You can actually create any kind of node this way. Anything that is not an XSL instruction is output *as is* in the final document.
- You can also create elements (and attributes and text) by using `xsl:element`, `xsl:attribute` *(see page 151)*, and `xsl:text`, but they are a bit more complicated and generally reserved for special cases.
- For more information about how to write HTML, you might want to consult my bestselling *HTML 4 for the World Wide Web: Visual QuickStart Guide, Fourth Edition*. For more information, jump to *http://www.cookwood.com/html4_4e/*.

Outputting HTML Code

Outputting a Node's Content

Once you've created the HTML code that will format a given node's content, you'll want to actually output that content (called its *string value*). The simplest way to add the content of a node (like an element) to the output document is to write it out just as it is.

To output a node's content:

1. If desired, create the HTML code that will format the content *(see page 140)*.
2. Type **<xsl:value-of**.
3. Type **select="expression"**, where *expression* identifies the node set from the XML source document whose content should be output at this point.
4. Type **/>**.

✔ Tips

- Use **select="."** to output the content of the current node. For more information on writing expressions, consult Chapter 11, *XPath: Patterns and Expressions.*
- If the node set identified by the expression has more than one node, only the first node's string value is output. (In the example in Figure 10.11, a node set with two nodes are found since there are two nodes that satisfy the expression. However, because of this rule, only the value of the first ("Tiger") is output.
- The string value of a node is generally the text that that node contains. If the node has child elements, however, the string value *includes* the text contained in those child elements as well.
- If the node set is empty, there is nothing to output.

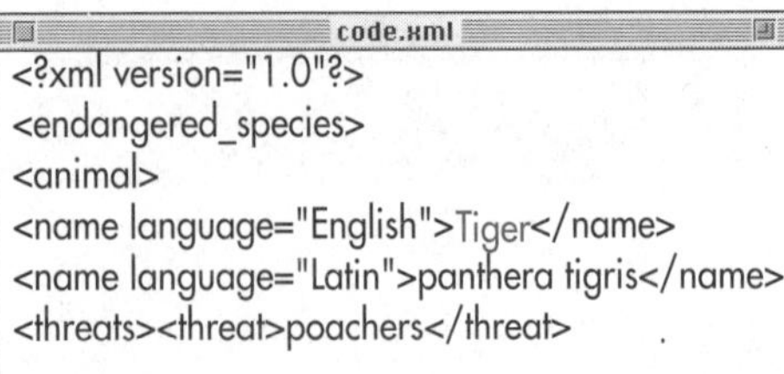

```
code.xml
<?xml version="1.0"?>
<endangered_species>
<animal>
<name language="English">Tiger</name>
<name language="Latin">panthera tigris</name>
<threats><threat>poachers</threat>
```

Figure 10.10 *An excerpt of the XML source document shows the name element and its contents.*

```
code.xslt
<xsl:template match="/">

<html><head><title>Endangered Species
</title></head><body bgcolor="white">

<p>The mighty <xsl:value-of
select="endangered_species/animal/name
[@language='English']"/> faces numerous threats.
For more information, check out the World Wildlife
Federation's <a
href="http://www.worldwildlife.org/
species/species.cfm?"> pages</a>.

</p><hr/>

</body>

</html>

</xsl:template>
```

Figure 10.11 *Instead of the generic "Endangered animals", we're going to grab the contents of the* `name` *element (that is within an* `animal` *element within an* `endangered_species` *element, and has a* `language` *attribute with the value set to* English*).*

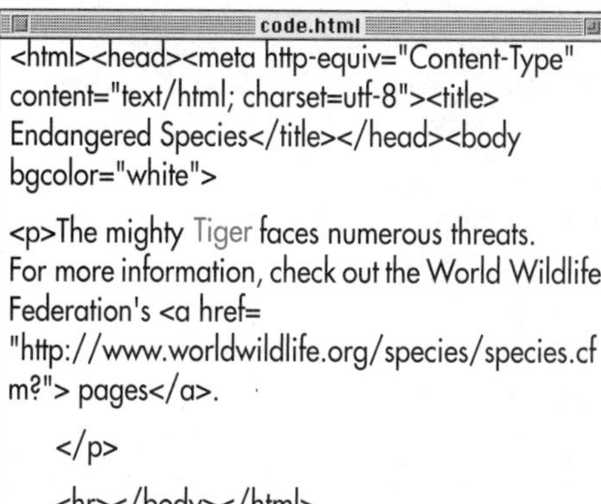

```
code.html
<html><head><meta http-equiv="Content-Type"
content="text/html; charset=utf-8"><title>
Endangered Species</title></head><body
bgcolor="white">

<p>The mighty Tiger faces numerous threats.
For more information, check out the World Wildlife
Federation's <a href=
"http://www.worldwildlife.org/species/species.cf
m?"> pages</a>.

    </p>

    <hr></body></html>
```

Figure 10.12 *When the XSLT processor applies the root template, it first outputs all the HTML header stuff, and then when it gets to the* `xsl:value-of` *element, it finds a nodeset with two nodes: the content of the* `animal name` *elements whose* `language` *is set to English. It then outputs the value of just the first of these nodes, which is* Tiger.

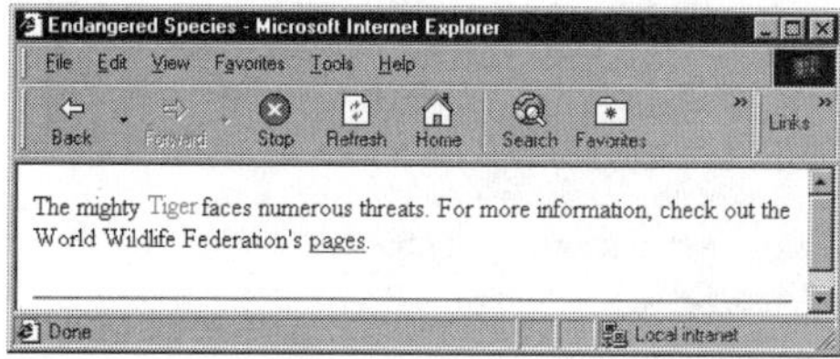

Figure 10.13 *And now our output actually uses input from the source XML document. There's definite potential here.*

- Some versions of Explorer's XSLT processor don't require the select attribute (and assume the current node if it is missing). It is, however, officially required.
- Since the `<xsl:value-of>` element never has any content, you can always combine the opening and closing tags as shown in step 4 above.
- If the expression evaluates to a boolean, the output may be either "true" or "false". If the expression is a number, the number is converted to a string.
- You can also create an expression that calculates a value using functions. For more details, consult Chapter 12, *Test Expressions and Functions.*

Creating and Applying Template Rules

Template rules are modules that describe how a particular part of your source XML should be output. A template rule has three parts: the opening tag describes which part(s) of your XML document the template should be applied to, the middle bit describes what should happen once a match is found, and the closing tag completes the template.

To create a template rule:

1. Type **<xsl:template** to begin the template rule.
2. Type **match="pattern"**, where *pattern* identifies the sections of the XML document to which the template may be applied. The syntax for describing patterns is described on pages 154–161.
3. Type **>**.
4. Specify what should happen when a node is found that matches the pattern in step 2. The possibilities are discussed in the rest of this chapter.
5. Type **</xsl:template>** to complete the template rule.

✓ Tips

- The root template which you saw on page 139 is nothing more than a template with a pattern that matches the root node.
- Only the root template is called automatically. All other templates must be invoked manually *(see page 145)*. Otherwise, they are simply ignored.
- The order of the templates in a style sheet is completely irrelevant. It is the order and position of the `xsl:apply-templates` elements which determines the order in which templates are processed.

```
code.xslt
<xsl:template match="/"><html><head>
<title>Endangered Species</title></head> <body
bgcolor="white">

<xsl:apply-templates
select="endangered_species/animal"/>
</body></html>
</xsl:template>

<xsl:template match="animal">
<p align="center">
<br/><font size="+3"><xsl:apply-templates
select="name" /></font></p>
<p>The mighty <xsl:value-of
select="name[@language='English']"/> faces
numerous threats. For more information, check out
the World Wildlife Federation's <a
href="http://www.worldwildlife.org/species/speci
es.cfm?"> pages</a>. </p><hr/>
</xsl:template>

<xsl:template match="name[@language=
'English']"><nobr><b><xsl:value-of select="."/>:
</b> </nobr></xsl:template>

<xsl:template match="name[@language=
'Latin']"><nobr><i><xsl:value-of select="."/></i>
</nobr></xsl:template>
```

Figure 10.14 *In this excerpt of the XSLT style sheet, there are four template rules, the root template, one for* `animal` *nodes, one for* `name` *nodes with the* `language` *attribute set to* English, *and one for* `name` *nodes with the* `language` *attribute set to* Latin. *The latter three, non-root templates must be explicitly called (Figure 10.15).*

```
code.xslt
<xsl:template match="/"><html><head>
<title>Endangered Species</title></head> <body
bgcolor="white">
<xsl:apply-templates
select="endangered_species/animal"/>
</body></html>
</xsl:template>

<xsl:template match="animal">
<p align="center">
<br/><font size="+3"><xsl:apply-templates
select="name" /></font></p>
```

Figure 10.15 *This is part of the same style sheet as shown in Figure 10.14, with the corresponding* `xsl:apply-templates` *elements highlighted.*

code.html

```
<body bgcolor="white">

<p align="center"><br><font size="+3">
<nobr><b>Tiger: </b></nobr><nobr>
<i>panthera tigris</i></nobr>
</font></p>

<p>The mighty Tiger faces numerous threats. For
more information, check out the World Wildlife
Federation's <a
href="http://www.worldwildlife.org/species/
species.cfm?"> pages</a>. </p>

<hr>

<p align="center"><br><font size="+3">
<nobr><b>Black Rhino: </b></nobr>
<nobr><i>diceros bicornis</i></nobr>
</font></p>

<p>The mighty Black Rhino faces numerous threats.
For more information, check out the World Wildlife
Federation's <a
```

Figure 10.16 *The light red is what has been generated for each* `animal` *node (there are two in this XML document). The boldface is what resulted from the* `name` *templates.*

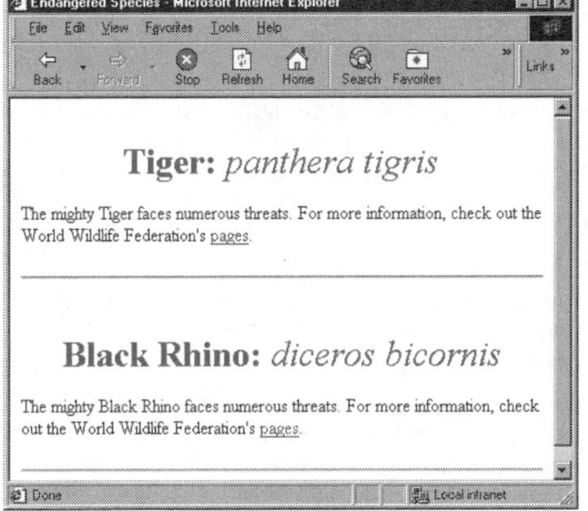

Figure 10.17 *Note that the* `endangered_species/animal` *node set includes* both `animal` *nodes (the* Tiger *one and the* Black Rhino *one), and therefore, in contrast to Figure 10.13 on page 143, both sets of information are output. The* `name` *templates are called each time an* `animal` *node is processed (and that's how you get those great titles!).*

Creating a template rule isn't enough; you also have to invoke the template rule in a specific situation. This is how you control *where* the transformation described by the template is output in the final document.

To apply a template rule:

1. Within a template rule, type **<xsl:apply-templates**.
2. If desired, type **select="expression"**, where *expression* identifies the elements of the XML document whose templates should be applied.
3. Type **/>** to complete the tag.

✔ Tips

- If you don't specify the `select` attribute in step 2, the processor will look for and apply a template to each and every one of the current node's descendants.
- The `xsl:apply-templates` element looks for and invokes the *most appropriate* template rule for each node it must process. It decides which nodes to process by looking at its own expression. It decides which templates to use by looking at their patterns and finding the one that best matches each node in the node set. It is quite possible that a different template be used for each different node.
- If there is no matching template available, a built–in template is invoked. For a root or element node, that means finding appropriate templates for all the child nodes. For a text node, it means outputting the text as is. For an attribute node, it means outputting the attribute as text.
- The `xsl:apply-templates` element may contain `xsl:sort` *(see page 150)*.

Batch-Processing Nodes

The `xsl:for-each` element also processes all the nodes in a given set in the same way, one after the other. Its primary difference from `xsl:apply-templates` is one of method, not results.

To batch-process nodes:

1. Within a template rule, type **<xsl:for-each**.
2. Type **select="expression"**, where *expression* identifies the set of nodes that will be processed.
3. Type **>**.
4. Specify what processing should take place.
5. Type **</xsl:for-each>**.

```
code.xslt
<xsl:template match="animal">
<p align="center"><br/><font
size="+3"><xsl:apply-templates select="name"
/></font></p>
<table width="100%" border="2">
<tr><th>Subspecies</th><th>Region</th><th>Nu
mber Left</th><th>As Of</th></tr>
<xsl:for-each select="subspecies">
<tr><td><xsl:apply-templates
select="name"/></td>
<td><xsl:value-of select="region"/></td>
<td><xsl:value-of select="population"/></td>
<td><xsl:value-of
select="population/@year"/></td></tr>
</xsl:for-each>
</table>
<p>The mighty <xsl:value-of
```

Figure 10.18 *Notice that the* `<table>` *and its first row come before the* `xsl:for-each` *instruction, and that the closing* `</table>` *tag comes after it. Within the* `xsl:for-each` *instruction go all of the things that should happen for each and every node in the selected set (in this case, each* `subspecies` *for the current* `animal`*).*

The first line outputs the first row of the table, the first cell of that row, then processes the `name` *node set, and closes the cell.*

The second line creates another table cell, inserts the value of the `region` *node within it, and closes the cell.*

The third line creates another table cell, inserts the value of the `population` *node within it, and closes the cell.*

The fourth line creates another table cell, inserts the value of the `population` *element's* `year` *attribute, and then it completes the table row.*

Each line is processed for each node in the selected node set (`subspecies`*, here), which, in effect, creates a separate row for each of an animal's subspecies.*

code.html

```
<i>panthera tigris</i></nobr></font></p>
<table width="100%" border="2">
<tr><th>Subspecies</th>
<th>Region</th>
<th>Number Left</th>
<th>As Of</th></tr>
<tr><td><nobr><b>Amur or Siberian: </b>
</nobr><nobr><i>P.t. altaica</i></nobr></td>
<td>Far East Russia</td>
<td>445</td>
<td>1999</td>
</tr>
<tr><td><nobr><b>Balian: </b></nobr>
<nobr><i>P.t. balica</i></nobr></td>
<td>Bali</td>
<td>0</td>
<td>1937</td></tr>
...
</table>
   <p>The mighty Tiger faces numerous threats. For
```

Figure 10.19 *The* `xsl:for-each` *instruction creates a new row for each* `subspecies` *in the current* `animal`*. (Note: not all of them are shown here, due to space constraints.) Once it has processed all the nodes in the selected set, it continues with the rest of the template (and in this case, outputs the closing* `</table>` *tag and then the descriptive paragraph).*

Tiger: *panthera tigris*

Subspecies	Region	Number Left	As Of
Amur or Siberian: *P.t. altaica*	Far East Russia	445	1999
Balian: *P.t. balica*	Bali	0	1937
Javan: *P.t. sondaica*	Java	0	1972
Caspian: *P.t. virgata*	Caspian Sea	0	1950
Bengal: *P.t. tigris*	India	3159	1999
Sumatran: *P.t. sumatrae*	India, Bangladesh	400	1999
Amoy: *P.t. amoyensis*	South China	20	1999
Indo-chinese: *P.t. corbetti*	Indo-China	1227	1998

The mighty Tiger faces numerous threats. For more information, check out the World Wildlife Federation's pages.

Black Rhino: *diceros bicornis*

Figure 10.20 *There is a whole other table of data about the Black Rhino below its title, hidden from view.*

✔ Tips

- The `xsl:for-each` element is typically used to create HTML tables, with the opening and closing `table` tags preceding and following the element, respectively, and with the `tr` and `td` tags as part of the processing as described in step 4 above.
- In general, place the `xsl:for-each` right before the rules that should be repeated for each node found. You may want to add framing material (like a table or whatever) before and after the opening and closing tags, respectively.
- Since the HTML table is part of the XSLT file, which must follow XML's syntax rules, you'll have to keep these rules in mind as you set up your table. In particular, remember that every opening tag must have a matching closing tag and that elements may not overlap. For more details, consult *Rules for Writing XML* on page 23.

Processing Nodes Conditionally

It's not uncommon to want to process a node or a set of nodes only if a certain condition is met. The condition is written as an expression. For example, you might want to perform a certain action if a particular node set is not empty, or if the string value of a node is equal to a particular word.

To process nodes conditionally:

1. Within a template rule, type **<xsl:if**.
2. Type **test="expression"**, where *expression* specifies a node set, a string, or a number. See Chapter 11, *XPath: Patterns and Expressions* for more details on writing expressions.
3. Type **>**.
4. Specify what should happen if the node set, string or number specified in step 2 is not empty (or not equal to zero, in the case of a number).
5. Type **</xsl:if>**.

✔ Tips

- How do you know when the expression is true? A node set is considered true if it is not empty, that is, it contains some node.
- If you want to be able to specify an alternate result when the expression is false—e.g., an else condition—use `xsl:choose` *(see page 149)*.
- You can test for all sorts of conditions. Consult Chapter 11, *XPath: Patterns and Expressions*, for details on how to construct test expressions.

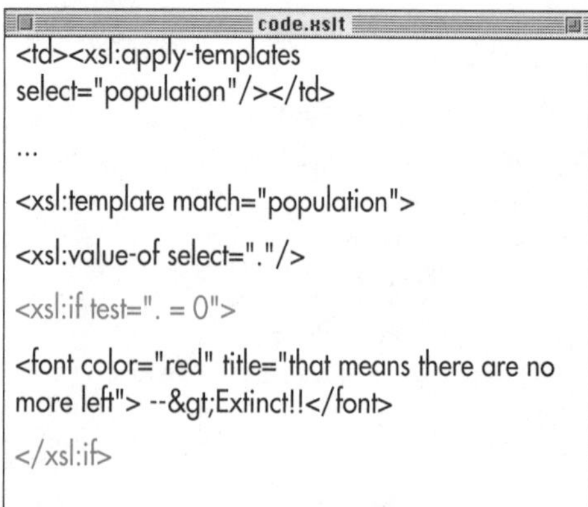

```
code.xslt
<td><xsl:apply-templates
select="population"/></td>

...

<xsl:template match="population">

<xsl:value-of select="."/>

<xsl:if test=". = 0">

<font color="red" title="that means there are no
more left"> --&gt;Extinct!!</font>

</xsl:if>
```

Figure 10.21 *Now instead of just outputting the value of* `population`, *we'll apply a template. In the template, first we output the value. Then we test to see if the* `population` *is zero. If it is, we add "-->Extinct" in red (with a title) to make that zero more noticeable. Note that the less-than sign must be written as* >.

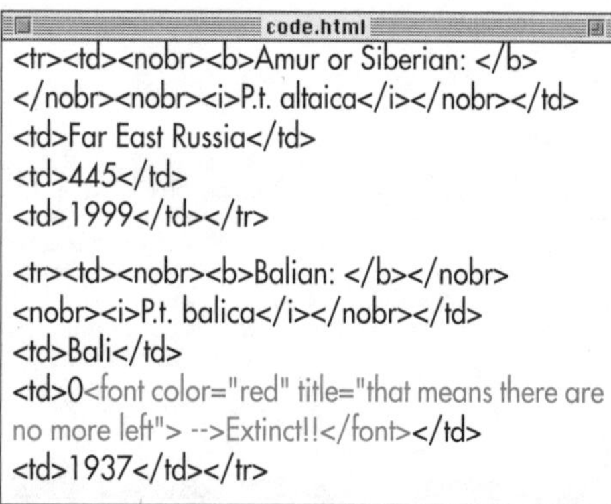

```
code.html
<tr><td><nobr><b>Amur or Siberian: </b>
</nobr><nobr><i>P.t. altaica</i></nobr></td>
<td>Far East Russia</td>
<td>445</td>
<td>1999</td></tr>

<tr><td><nobr><b>Balian: </b></nobr>
<nobr><i>P.t. balica</i></nobr></td>
<td>Bali</td>
<td>0<font color="red" title="that means there are
no more left"> -->Extinct!!</font></td>
<td>1937</td></tr>
```

Figure 10.22 *The extra text in red is only added if the* `population` *is equal to zero. (The Amur or Siberian tigers get no extra text since there are still a whopping 445 left.)*

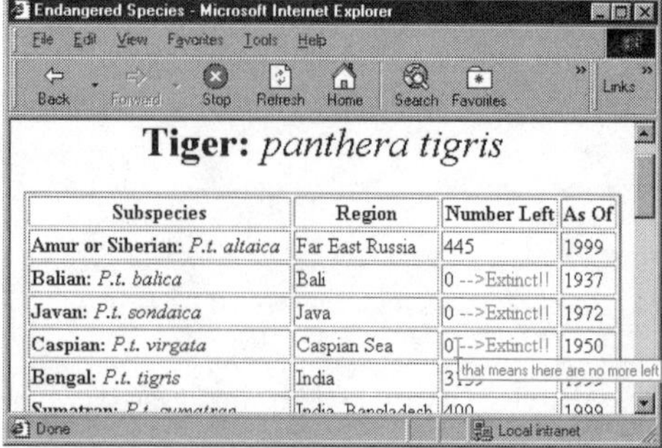

Subspecies	Region	Number Left	As Of
Amur or Siberian: *P.t. altaica*	Far East Russia	445	1999
Balian: *P.t. balica*	Bali	0 -->Extinct!!	1937
Javan: *P.t. sondaica*	Java	0 -->Extinct!!	1972
Caspian: *P.t. virgata*	Caspian Sea	0 -->Extinct!!	1950
Bengal: *P.t. tigris*	India	3	

Figure 10.23 *If the* `population` *is equal to zero, the extra text (and* `title` *attribute) is added to make the information stand out.*

```
code.xslt
<xsl:template match="population">
<xsl:choose>
<xsl:when test=". = 0">
<font color="red" title="that means there are
no more left">Extinct</font>
</xsl:when>

<xsl:when test=". &gt; 0 and . &lt; 50">
<font title="they're almost gone"><xsl:value
of select="."/></font>
</xsl:when>

<xsl:otherwise>
<xsl:value-of select="."/>
</xsl:otherwise></xsl:choose>
</xsl:template>
```

Figure 10.24 *First the XSLT processor checks if the* `population` *is zero. If it is, it outputs* Extinct *(in red with a tooltip). If the* `population` *is not zero, it checks to see if its greater than 0 and less than 50, and if so, adds a cautionary tooltip around the value. In all other cases, the processor simply outputs the value.*

```
code.html
<tr><td><nobr><b>Balian: </b></nobr>
<nobr><i>P.t. balica</i></nobr></td>
<td>Bali</td>
<td><font color="red" title="that means there are
no more left">Extinct</font></td>
<td>1937</td></tr>
```

Figure 10.25 *In this tiny excerpt, you can see that instead of adding* Extinct *after the value (as in Figure 10.22 on page 148), only the word* Extinct *is output when the* `population` *is zero.*

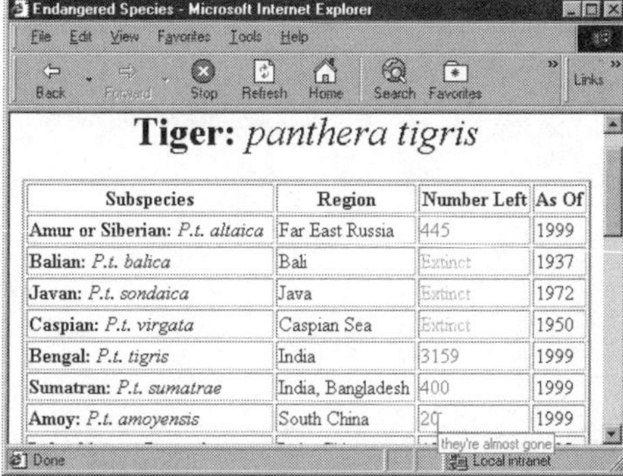

Subspecies	Region	Number Left	As Of
Amur or Siberian: *P.t. altaica*	Far East Russia	445	1999
Balian: *P.t. balica*	Bali	Extinct	1937
Javan: *P.t. sondaica*	Java	Extinct	1972
Caspian: *P.t. virgata*	Caspian Sea	Extinct	1950
Bengal: *P.t. tigris*	India	3159	1999
Sumatran: *P.t. sumatrae*	India, Bangladesh	400	1999
Amoy: *P.t. amoyensis*	South China	20	1999

Figure 10.26 *There are now three actions, depending on the value for* `population`. *We've added a tooltip to highlight very low* `population` *values.*

Adding Conditional Choices

The `xsl:if` instruction described on the previous page only allows for one condition and one resulting action. You can use `xsl:choose` when you want to test for several different situations, and react accordingly to each one.

To add conditional choices:

1. Within a template rule, type **<xsl:choose>**.
2. Then type **<xsl:when** to begin the first condition.
3. Type **test="expression"**, where *expression* specifies a node set, a string, or a number. See Chapter 11, *XPath: Patterns and Expressions* for more details on writing expressions.
4. Type **>** to complete the `xsl:when` element.
5. Specify the processing that should take place if the node set, string, or number tested in step 3 is not empty (or equal to zero, in the case of numbers).
6. Type **</xsl:when>**.
7. Repeat steps 2–6 for each condition.
8. If desired, type **<xsl:otherwise>**.

   Specify what should happen if none of the conditions specified by the `xsl:when` elements are true.

   Type **</xsl:otherwise>**.
9. Type **</xsl:choose>**.

✔ Tip

- The action contained in the first true condition that is found is performed. All the following conditions are then ignored.

Sorting Nodes Before Processing

By default, the nodes are processed in the order in which they appear in the document. If you'd like to process them in some other order, you can add an `xsl:sort` element to the `xsl:apply-templates` or `xsl:for-each` elements.

To sort nodes before processing:

1. Directly after an `xsl:apply-templates`, `xsl:for-each`, or in fact, another `xsl:sort` element, type **<xsl:sort**.
2. Type **select="criteria"**, where *criteria* is an expression that specifies the key on which the nodes to be processed should be sorted.
3. If desired, type **order="descending"**. The default is for keys to be sorted in ascending order.
4. If desired, type **data-type="text"** or **data-type="number"** depending on what you're sorting.
5. Type **/>** to complete the `xsl:sort` element.
6. Repeat steps steps 1–5 to define as many keys as desired.

✔ Tips

- Be sure to specify the correct data-type in step 4. Sorting numbers as text has such erroneous results as 100, 7, 89. Sorting text as numbers is equally ineffective.
- Descending means you go from high numbers to low, and from Z to A. Ascending means the low numbers (and letters) appear at the top.

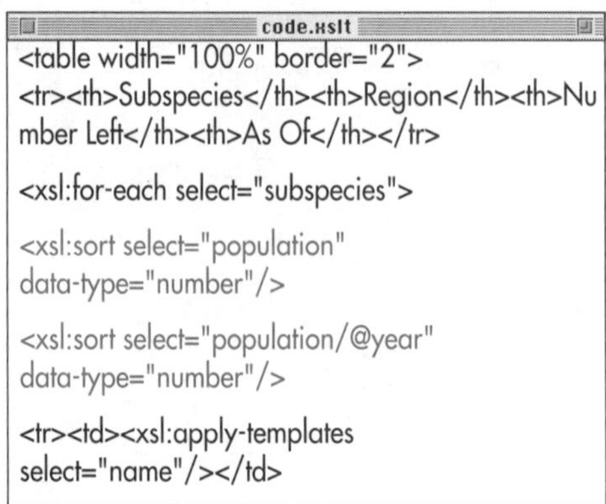

code.xslt

```
<table width="100%" border="2">
<tr><th>Subspecies</th><th>Region</th><th>Nu
mber Left</th><th>As Of</th></tr>
<xsl:for-each select="subspecies">
<xsl:sort select="population"
data-type="number"/>
<xsl:sort select="population/@year"
data-type="number"/>
<tr><td><xsl:apply-templates
select="name"/></td>
```

Figure 10.27 *Back up at the top of our XSLT style sheet, we add two* `xsl:sort` *instructions right after the* `xsl:for-each` *element but before the output is generated.*

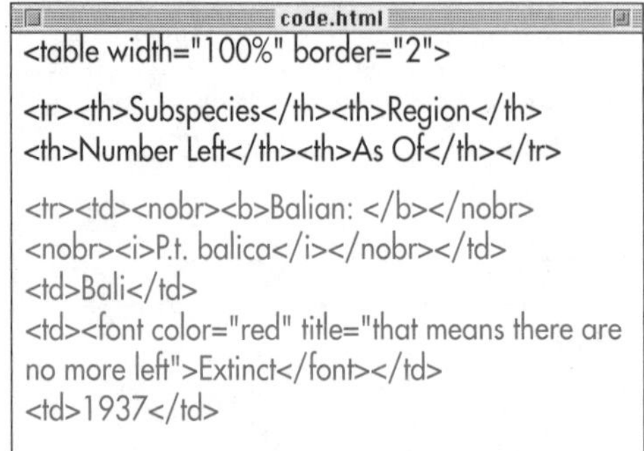

code.html

```
<table width="100%" border="2">
<tr><th>Subspecies</th><th>Region</th>
<th>Number Left</th><th>As Of</th></tr>
<tr><td><nobr><b>Balian: </b></nobr>
<nobr><i>P.t. balica</i></nobr></td>
<td>Bali</td>
<td><font color="red" title="that means there are
no more left">Extinct</font></td>
<td>1937</td>
```

Figure 10.28 *Now the Bali tiger (the first tiger to go extinct) is the first to be processed and will thus appear at the top of the table.*

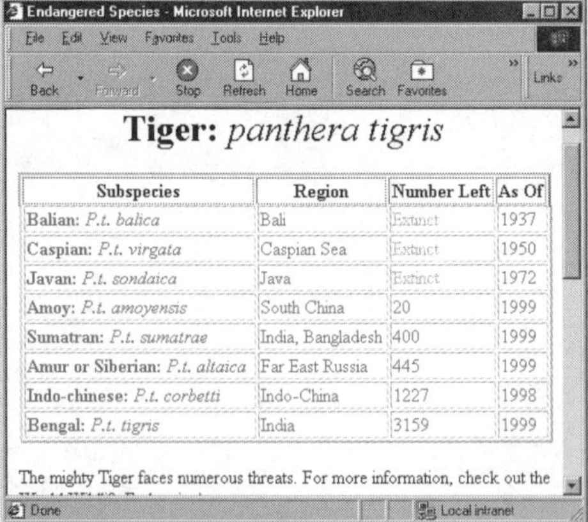

Figure 10.29 *Now the world's tigers are listed first in order of population and second by the year they went extinct. (Note: This table contains real data and represents the* entire *world tiger population in the wild.)*

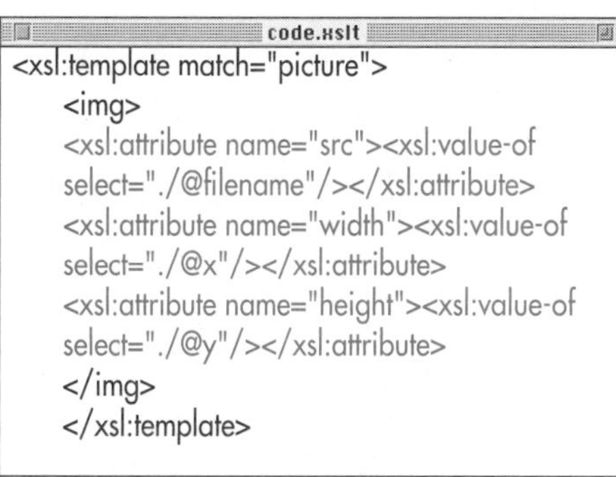

```
code.xslt
<xsl:template match="picture">
    <img>
    <xsl:attribute name="src"><xsl:value-of
    select="./@filename"/></xsl:attribute>
    <xsl:attribute name="width"><xsl:value-of
    select="./@x"/></xsl:attribute>
    <xsl:attribute name="height"><xsl:value-of
    select="./@y"/></xsl:attribute>
    </img>
    </xsl:template>
```

Figure 10.30 *Here I've created a template that converts my* `picture` *elements into standard HTML* `img` *tags. The expression "./@filename" means "select the* `filename` *attribute of the current node" (in this case the* `picture` *node). For more on selecting a node's attributes, see page 160.*

```
code.html
<body bgcolor="white">
<p align="center">
<img src="tiger.jpg" width="200" height="197">
<br><font size="+3">
<nobr><b>Tiger: </b></nobr>
```

Figure 10.31 *Voilà! A perfectly valid HTML img tag.*

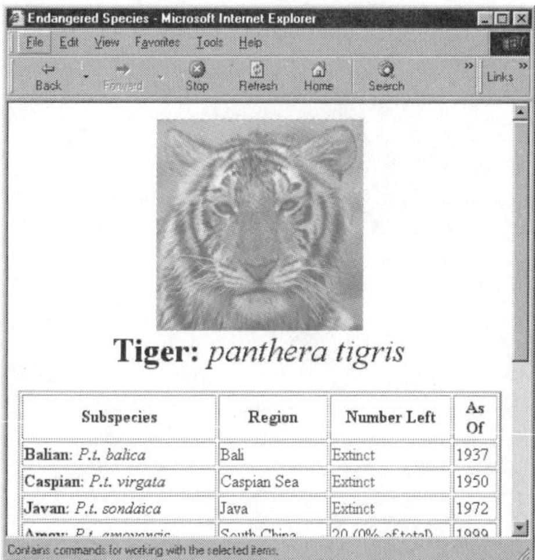

Figure 10.32 *The majestic tiger picture appears as requested.*

Generating Attributes

It's often useful to be able to add attributes (and their values) to a given element.

To generate attributes:

1. Directly after the opening tag of the element in which the new attribute should appear, type **<xsl:attribute**.
2. Type **name="att_name"**, where *att_name* is the name that the attribute should have in the element.
3. Type **>**.
4. Then either type or output the value of the new attribute.
5. Finally, type **</xsl:attribute>**.

✔ Tips

- You can use the `xsl:value-of` element in step 4 to generate the value of the attribute from content that comes from your XML document.
- This is a great way to convert custom image elements into standard HTML `img` tags.

XPath: Patterns and Expressions

11

In the previous chapter, XSLT, you learned about creating and applying templates in order to transform the information in your XML document. Actually, it's important to remember that when you "apply a template", you're actually specifying that a set of nodes be processed by *whatever templates (in the plural) are appropriate*, and not simply executing a given template. In other words, you say, "process all of the `name` nodes with whatever template best suits them" and not "fire up the *name[language='English']* template". The difference is subtle but important.

When you create a template, you use a *pattern* to specify the nodes that the template can be applied to. When you call a template (say, with `xsl:apply-templates`), you use an *expression* to specify the node set that should be processed (with appropriate templates). You also use expressions in other xsl instructions to isolate and then further process given node sets.

You write both patterns and expressions using XPath syntax, a system of describing the node sets by specifying their location in the XML document which is described in detail in this chapter. The main difference between patterns and expressions is that the former are basically context-free, which means that a pattern like **"name"** matches *any* `name` element in the XML document regardless of its location. Expressions, on the other hand, can only be evaluated by looking at the context in which they appear. An expression like **"name"** might refer only to `name` nodes within `subspecies` elements, depending on where it is used.

Determining the Current Node

As the XSLT processor goes through your stylesheet and XML document, it works on one node at a time. It's usually easiest to specify what needs to be processed next with respect to the *current node*, that is, the node the processor is presently working on. Of course, before you can do that, you need to know how to identify the current node.

To determine the current node:

1. By default, the current node is the one that is specified by the template currently being processed. In other words, the current node is specified in the template's match attribute.

2. If there is an `xsl:apply-templates` instruction, the current node becomes the one that is matched by the corresponding template (and thus, the one specified by the `xsl:apply-templates` instruction). When you have "returned" from that `xsl:apply-templates` instruction, the current node reverts back to the old template's match attribute.

3. If there is an `xsl:for-each` instruction, the current node changes to the one specified by the `xsl:for-each`'s select attribute. After the `xsl:for-each` instruction, the current node reverts back to whatever it was before that instruction was processed.

✔ Tip

- The `xsl:apply-templates` instruction may process more than one node (one after the other). So, each of those nodes to be processed will be the current node in turn.

code.xslt

```
<?xml version="1.0"?>

<xsl:stylesheet xmlns:xsl="http://www.w3.org/
1999/XSL/Transform" version="1.0">
<xsl:template match="/">  1
<html><head><title>Endangered Species
</title></head><body bgcolor="white">

<xsl:apply-templates  1a
select="endangered_species/animal"/>

</body></html></xsl:template>

<xsl:template match="animal">  2

<p align="center">

<br/><font size="+3"><xsl:apply-templates
select="name" /></font></p>  2a

<table width="100%" border="2">

<tr><th>Subspecies</th><th>Region</th><th>Nu
mber Left</th><th>As Of</th></tr>

<xsl:for-each select="subspecies">  2b

<xsl:sort select="population" data-
type="number"/>
```

Figure 11.1 *At point 1, the current node is / (the root node) as specified by the template. When the processor reaches point 1a (and consequently point 2), the current node becomes the first* `animal` *element contained in the* `endangered_species` *element. Once that first* `animal` *element is processed, the second* `animal` *element becomes the current node, and so on until all the* `animal` *elements have been processed (and taken their turn as the current node).*

At point 2a, the first `name` *element in the* `animal` *element being processed becomes the current node. We go off to the* `name` *templates (could be a point 3, but it's not shown) and follow the instructions there. Then the second* `name` *element is processed, and so on.*

After we "return" from the `name` *templates applied in point 2a, the current node becomes the* `animal` *element once again, until we get to point 2b, the* `xsl:for-each` *instruction. At this point, the current node becomes the first* `subspecies` *element in the current animal node. Then the second* `subspecies` *element is processed, and so on until they're all done.*

And so on!

```
code.xslt
<xsl:template match="animal">

<p align="center">

<br/><font size="+3"><xsl:apply-templates
select="name" /></font></p>

...

</xsl:template>

<xsl:template
match="name[@language='English']">

<nobr><b><xsl:value-of select="."/>:
</b></nobr>

</xsl:template>
```

Figure 11.2 *The current node will be the contents of some* `name` *element whose* `language` *attribute is "English". Which* `name` *element it is depends on where we are in the transformation process.*

```
code.html
<body bgcolor="white">

<p align="center"><br><font size="+3">
<nobr><b>Tiger: </b></nobr><nobr>
<i>panthera tigris</i></nobr></font></p>

<table width="100%" border="2">

<tr><th>Subspecies</th><th>Region</th>
<th>Number Left</th><th>As Of</th></tr>

<tr><td><nobr><b>Balian: </b></nobr>
<nobr><i>P.t. balica</i></nobr></td>
```

Figure 11.3 *The first highlighted material (*Tiger *and* panthera tigris*) comes when we apply the* `name` *template at the beginning of the* `animal` *template. The next output is when we call the* `name` *template from inside the* `xsl:for-each` *instruction as we work on the* `subspecies` *elements, and so the current node is each* `name` *element (in turn) inside each* `subspecies` *element (as with* Balian *and* P.t. balica*, shown here).*

Referring to the Current Node

If you're currently processing the node that you want to use in a `select` attribute, it's much easier to use the shortcut for the node than to reference it's entire location from the root.

To refer to the current node:

1. Type **.** (that's a single period).

✔ Tips

- You don't always want to select the entire node set. You can add a test, called a predicate, to get a subset of the current node. For more details, consult *Selecting Subsets* on page 161.
- You can also use . in a predicate to refer to the context node (that is, the node that is being tested by the predicate).

Selecting a Node's Children

If the current node actually contains the elements that you want to select—that is, they are the node's *children*—you can select the desired child nodes by using just their name, instead of the complete path from the root.

To get a node's children:

1. Make sure you know what the current node is *(see page 154)*, and that the node set you're interested in is a child (or some descendant) of the current node.
2. Type **child**, where *child* is the name of the element that is contained within the elements referred to by the current node.
3. If desired, you can type **/grandchild**, where *grandchild* is a node set contained in the child set referenced in step 2 in order to dig deeper into the hierarchy and reference node sets further down.
4. Repeat step 3 until you get to the level you want.

✓ Tips

- Of course, before you ask for children, it's important to know which is the current node. See page 154 for details.
- Type * (an asterisk) to select all of the node's children.
- You could conceivably use **./child** to do this as well, but why bother? Just **child** is so much simpler and exactly equivalent.

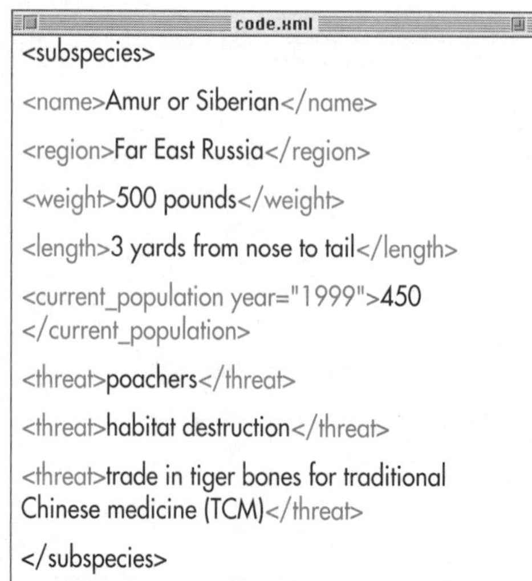

code.xml

```
<subspecies>
<name>Amur or Siberian</name>
<region>Far East Russia</region>
<weight>500 pounds</weight>
<length>3 yards from nose to tail</length>
<current_population year="1999">450
</current_population>
<threat>poachers</threat>
<threat>habitat destruction</threat>
<threat>trade in tiger bones for traditional
Chinese medicine (TCM)</threat>
</subspecies>
```

Figure 11.4 *Here is an excerpt from the XML document. This subspecies element has eight child elements.*

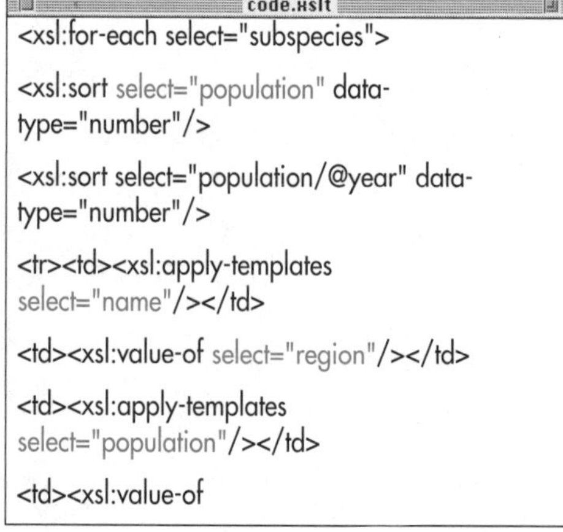

code.xslt

```
<xsl:for-each select="subspecies">
<xsl:sort select="population" data-
type="number"/>
<xsl:sort select="population/@year" data-
type="number"/>
<tr><td><xsl:apply-templates
select="name"/></td>
<td><xsl:value-of select="region"/></td>
<td><xsl:apply-templates
select="population"/></td>
<td><xsl:value-of
```

Figure 11.5 *When we get to the* `for-each`, `subspecies` *becomes the current node. The* `select` *attribute in the first* `xsl:sort` *instruction selects all the* `population` *nodes that are children of the* `subspecies` *node being processed. The* `select` *attribute in the* `apply-templates` *instruction looks for all the* `name` *nodes that are children of the* `subspecies` *element.*

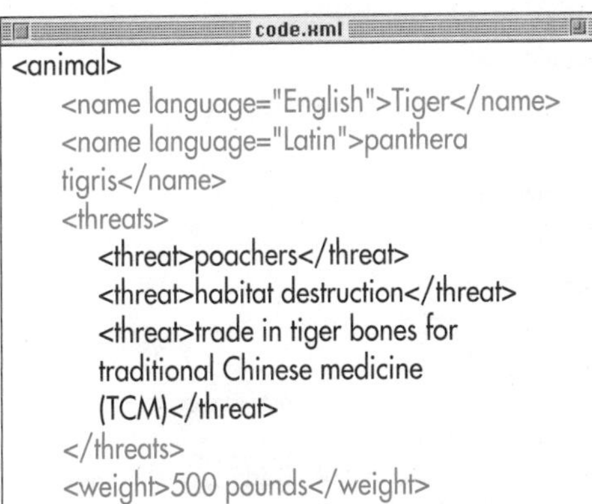

```
code.xml
<animal>
    <name language="English">Tiger</name>
    <name language="Latin">panthera
    tigris</name>
    <threats>
        <threat>poachers</threat>
        <threat>habitat destruction</threat>
        <threat>trade in tiger bones for
        traditional Chinese medicine
        (TCM)</threat>
    </threats>
    <weight>500 pounds</weight>
```

Figure 11.6 *Notice that the* `threats` *and* `name` *elements are both children of (contained directly in) the* `animal` *element—and thus are siblings.*

```
code.xslt
<xsl:template match="threats">
<ul>The mighty <xsl:value-of
select="../name[@language='English']"/> faces
numerous threats: <xsl:for-each select="threat">
<li><xsl:value-of select="."/></li>
</xsl:for-each></ul>
For more information, check out the World Wildlife
```

Figure 11.7 *When we apply this new* `threats` *template,* `threats` *becomes the current node. If we then want to reference the* `name` *element (which is its sibling), we have to use* **..** *to go up one level (to the parent element,* `animal`*) and then* **/** *to get to a different child, and then* `name` *to specify which child.*

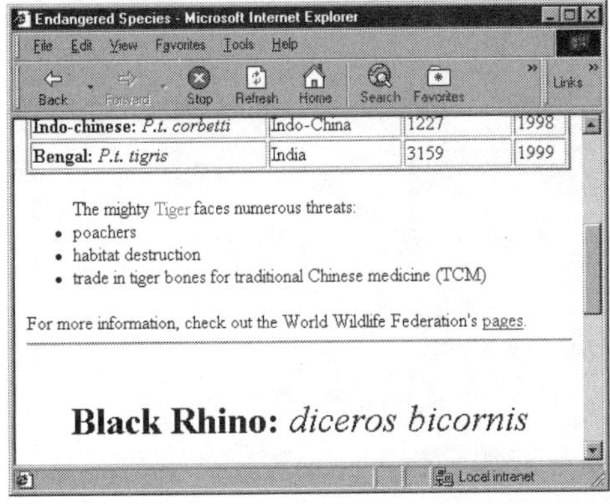

Figure 11.8 *Although the context has changed (we're in the* `threats` *template, not the* `animal` *template now), as long as we specify the new relationship, the value is output properly. I've also added some fancier formatting of the individual* `threats`.

Selecting a Node's Parent or Siblings

Again, if the relationship between the current node *(see page 154)* and the desired node is quite clear, it's much easier to use a shortcut than to write the complete, absolute relationship starting from the root.

To select a node's parent:

1. Make sure you know what the current node is, and that the node set you're interested in is a parent (or some ancestor) of the current node.
2. Type **..** (that's two periods) to select the node's parent.

To select a node's siblings:

1. After you've gotten to the node's parent in step 2 above, type **/sibling**, where *sibling* is the name of the desired node (which is contained in the current node's parent, but isn't the current node).
2. If desired, type **/niece**, where *niece* is a node that is the child of the sibling of the current node.
3. Repeat step 2 as necessary.

✔ Tips

- The **..** is often combined with the attribute axis to find the attribute of the parent node (**../@name**). More on this when we get to attributes *(see page 160)*.
- You can also use an asterisk as a wildcard within the path. For example, **/*/nephew** would select all the *nephew* elements of *all of the siblings* of the current node.

Selecting All of the Descendants

The double forward slash comes in handy when you need to select all of the descendants of a particular node. Like most of the other symbols, you can use it either in an absolute or relative path.

To select all of the descendants of the root node:

Type **//** (that's two forward slashes).

To select all of the descendants of the current node:

Type **.//** (a period followed by two forward slashes).

To select all the descendants of any node:

1. Use the techniques in the previous pages to get to the node whose descendants you're interested in.
2. Then type **//** (two forward slashes).

To select some of the descendants of any node:

1. Create the path to the node whose descendants you're interested in using the techniques described on earlier pages.
2. Type **//**.
3. Then type the name of the descendant elements that you're interested in.

✔ Tip

- This last technique is a great way to get to a node when you don't know (or don't care) where it is in the document. An expression like **//name** will output *all* the name elements, wherever they may be **(Figure 11.11)**.

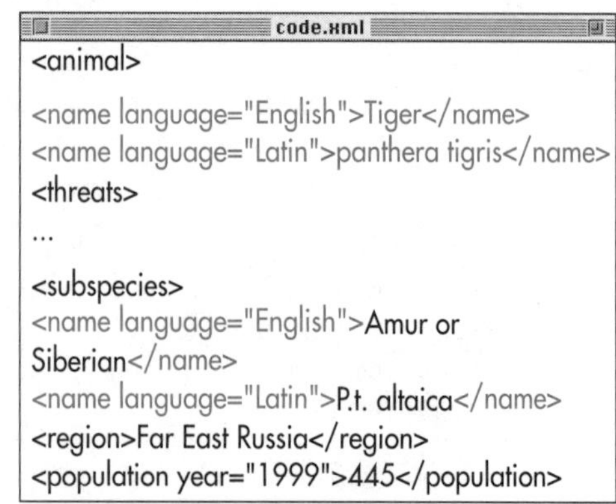

```
code.xml
<animal>
<name language="English">Tiger</name>
<name language="Latin">panthera tigris</name>
<threats>
...
<subspecies>
<name language="English">Amur or Siberian</name>
<name language="Latin">P.t. altaica</name>
<region>Far East Russia</region>
<population year="1999">445</population>
```

Figure 11.9 *There are* `name` *elements in the* `animal` *element, and there are* `name` *elements in the* `subspecies` *element.*

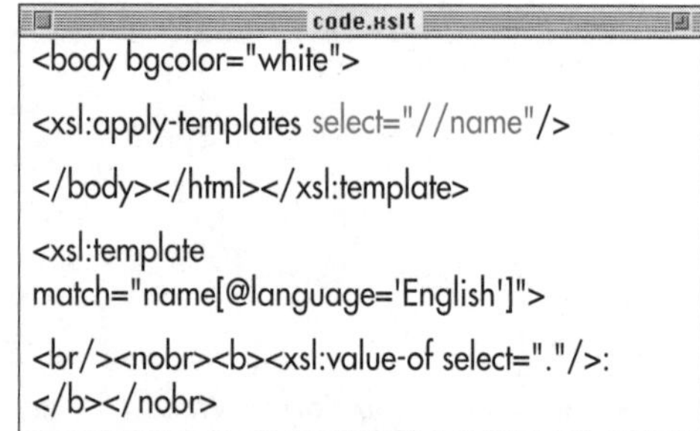

```
code.xslt
<body bgcolor="white">
<xsl:apply-templates select="//name"/>
</body></html></xsl:template>
<xsl:template match="name[@language='English']">
<br/><nobr><b><xsl:value-of select="."/>:
</b></nobr>
```

Figure 11.10 *The* `select` *attribute that is highlighted matches all of the* `name` *elements no matter where they appear in the source document. (Note that I've eliminated the* `animal` *template completely and added a* `<br/>` *to the English* `name` *template to make the example more obvious.)*

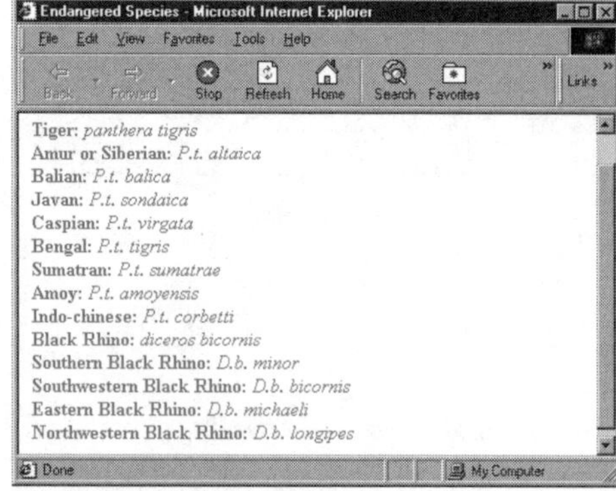

Figure 11.11 *Notice that all of the* `name` *elements (both English and Latin) are contained in* `animal` *(Tiger, Black Rhino, etc.) and the* `name` *elements contained in* `subspecies` *(Amur, Balian, Southern Black Rhino, etc.) are displayed here.*

```
code.xslt
<xsl:template match="animal">
<p align="center">
<br/><font size="+3"><xsl:apply-templates
select="name" /></font></p>

<table width="100%" border="2">

<tr><th>Subspecies</th><th>Region</th><th>Nu
mber Left</th><th>As Of</th></tr>

<xsl:for-each select="/endangered_species/
animal/subspecies">

<xsl:sort select="population" data-type=
```

Figure 11.12 *Back to the* `animal` *template, I've written the path to the* `subspecies` *node set from the root.*

```
code.html
<tr><td><nobr><b>Javan: </b></nobr>
<nobr><i>P.t. sondaica</i></nobr></td>
<td>Java</td>
<td><font color="red" title="that means there are
no more left">Extinct</font></td>
<td>1972</td></tr>

<tr><td><nobr><b>Northwestern Black Rhino:
</b></nobr><nobr><i>D.b.
longipes</i></nobr></td>
```

Figure 11.13 *Notice how we've got the Northwestern Black Rhino being processed right after one of the subspecies of tiger.*

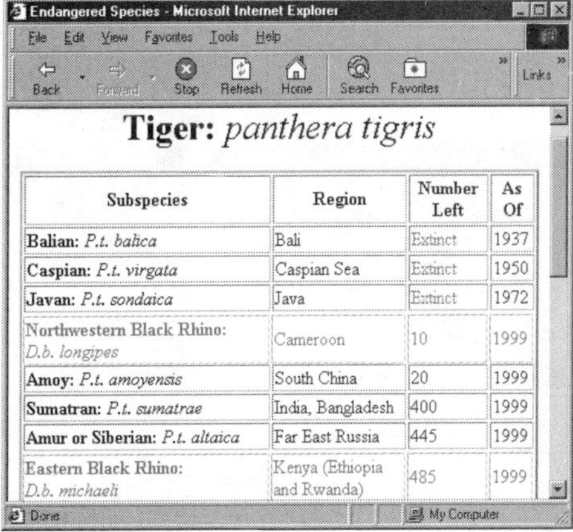

Tiger: *panthera tigris*

Subspecies	Region	Number Left	As Of
Balian: *P.t. balica*	Bali	Extinct	1937
Caspian: *P.t. virgata*	Caspian Sea	Extinct	1950
Javan: *P.t. sondaica*	Java	Extinct	1972
Northwestern Black Rhino: *D.b. longipes*	Cameroon	10	1999
Amoy: *P.t. amoyensis*	South China	20	1999
Sumatran: *P.t. sumatrae*	India, Bangladesh	400	1999
Amur or Siberian: *P.t. altaica*	Far East Russia	445	1999
Eastern Black Rhino: *D.b. michaeli*	Kenya (Ethiopia and Rwanda)	485	1999

Figure 11.14 *Make sure you know what you're doing when you disregard the current node. It may give you the structure that you need to avoid a mess like the one shown.*

Disregarding the Current Node

All of the patterns and expressions that we've created so far have been dependant on the current node. For example, choosing `name` inside the `animal` template only matches the `name` elements that are within the current `animal` element being processed. You can completely disregard the current node by writing the path to the desired node all the way from the root.

To disregard the current node by writing the path from the root:

1. Start by typing **/** to note that you'll be starting at the root of the XML document.
2. Type **root**, where *root* is the root element of your XML document *(see page 25)*.
3. Type **/** to indicate that you're going down one level in your XML document's hierarchy.
4. Type **container**, where *container* is the name of the element on the next level that contains the desired element.
5. Repeat steps 3–4 until you have specified all of the ancestors of the element you're interested in.
6. Type **/element**, where *element* is the name of the element that you want to match.

✓ Tips

- At any point in the path, you can use * as a wildcard to specify all the elements at that level.
- You may skip steps 3–5 if the desired element is a child of the root element itself.

Selecting a Node's Attributes

If you're interested in a node's attributes rather than the element itself, you can use the @ to specify the attribute axis.

To select a node's attribute(s):

1. Write the path to the node, using the techniques described in this chapter.
2. Type **/@** to indicate that you're interested in attributes.
3. Type **attribute**, where *attribute* is the name of the attribute you're interested in.

   Or type * (that's an asterisk) as a wildcard to select all of the node's attributes.

✓ Tip

- You can combine this technique with the `xsl:attribute` element to create custom attributes within a new tag. For example, you could convert unorthodoxly formatted picture data into a standard HTML `img` tag. For more details about the `xsl:attribute` element, consult *Generating Attributes* on page 151.

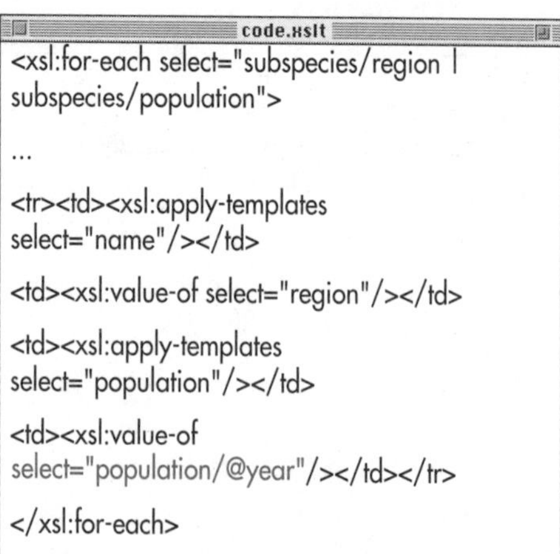

code.xslt

```
<xsl:for-each select="subspecies/region |
subspecies/population">

...

<tr><td><xsl:apply-templates
select="name"/></td>

<td><xsl:value-of select="region"/></td>

<td><xsl:apply-templates
select="population"/></td>

<td><xsl:value-of
select="population/@year"/></td></tr>

</xsl:for-each>
```

Figure 11.15 *To get the attribute(s) of an element, use the @ sign followed by the name of the attribute.*

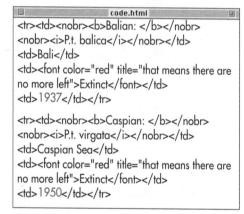

code.html

```
<tr><td><nobr><b>Balian: </b></nobr>
<nobr><i>P.t. balica</i></nobr></td>
<td>Bali</td>
<td><font color="red" title="that means there are
no more left">Extinct</font></td>
<td>1937</td></tr>

<tr><td><nobr><b>Caspian: </b></nobr>
<nobr><i>P.t. virgata</i></nobr></td>
<td>Caspian Sea</td>
<td><font color="red" title="that means there are
no more left">Extinct</font></td>
<td>1950</td></tr>
```

Figure 11.16 *The contents of the attribute are output.*

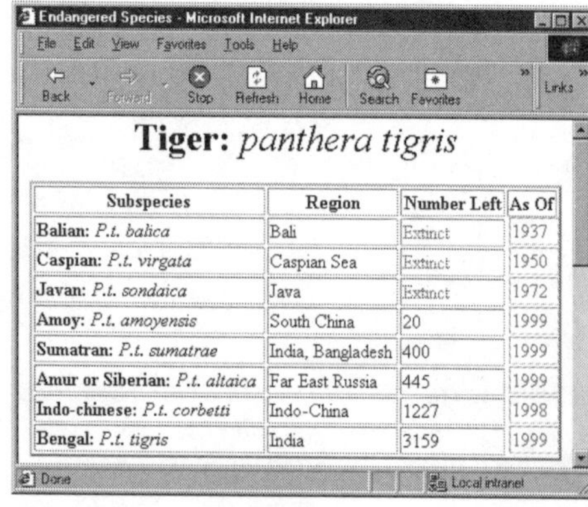

Subspecies	Region	Number Left	As Of
Balian: *P.t. balica*	Bali	Extinct	1937
Caspian: *P.t. virgata*	Caspian Sea	Extinct	1950
Javan: *P.t. sondaica*	Java	Extinct	1972
Amoy: *P.t. amoyensis*	South China	20	1999
Sumatran: *P.t. sumatrae*	India, Bangladesh	400	1999
Amur or Siberian: *P.t. altaica*	Far East Russia	445	1999
Indo-chinese: *P.t. corbetti*	Indo-China	1227	1998
Bengal: *P.t. tigris*	India	3159	1999

Figure 11.17 *On the Web page, it doesn't matter whether the data was originally an attribute or an element in the XML document.*

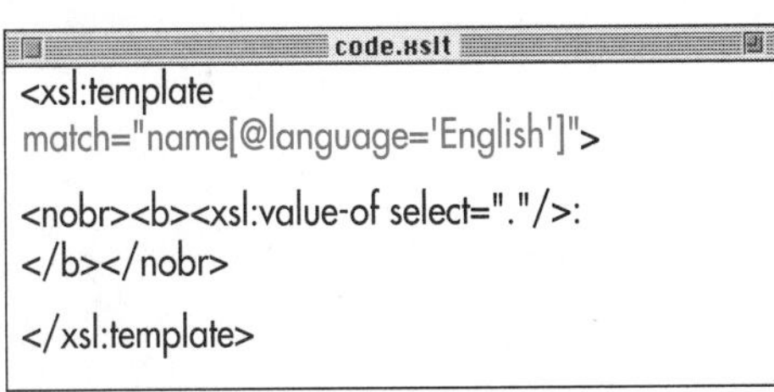

```
code.xslt
<xsl:template
match="name[@language='English']">

<nobr><b><xsl:value-of select="."/>:
</b></nobr>

</xsl:template>
```

Figure 11.18 *This template will only be applied to those* `name` *elements that have a* `language` *attribute equal to* English.

```
code.xml
<animal>
<name language="English">Tiger</name>
<name language="Latin">panthera tigris</name>
<threats><threat>poachers</threat>
<threat>habitat destruction</threat>
<threat>trade in tiger bones for traditional Chinese
medicine (TCM)</threat>
</threats>
<weight>500 pounds</weight>
<length>3 yards from nose to tail</length>
<source sectionid="120"
newspaperid="21"></source>
<picture filename="tiger.jpg" x="200" y="197"/>

<subspecies>
<name language="English">Amur or
Siberian</name>
<name language="Latin">P.t. altaica</name>

<region>Far East Russia</region>
```

Figure 11.19 *The template shown in Figure 11.18 will only be applied to the highlighted items (and not to the* `name` *elements whose* `language` *attribute is set to* Latin).

Endangered Species - Microsoft Internet Explorer

Tiger: *panthera tigris*

Subspecies	Region	Number Left	As Of
Balian: *P.t. balica*	Bali	Extinct	1937
Caspian: *P.t. virgata*	Caspian Sea	Extinct	1950

Figure 11.20 *The English names are displayed in boldface and are followed by a colon, as is stipulated by their template.*

Selecting Subsets

It's not always precise enough to select an entire node set. You can create boolean expressions (called *predicates*) to test a condition and then select a subset of the node depending on the results of that test.

To select a subset:

1. Create the path to the node that contains the desired subset following the instructions in the rest of this chapter.
2. Type **[** (that's a left square bracket--to the right of the *p* on your keyboard).
3. Type the expression that identifies the subset.
4. Type **]** (the right square bracket).

✔ Tips

- The expression that identifies the subset needn't be a comparison. It's enough to say **[@language]**, which would, in our example, select all the `name` elements *that have* a `language` attribute (regardless of its value).
- You can use functions to write more complicated predicates. For more details, see Chapter 12, *Test Expressions and Functions.*
- Make sure you type square brackets and not curly ones or parentheses.
- Use multiple predicates to narrow the search. **name[@language='English'] [position() = last()]** would select the `name` elements that have a `language` attribute equal to *English* and that are the last node in the set.
- You can also add an attribute selector after the predicate, if desired. For example, to get all the attributes of the last element of the current node set, use **[last ()]/@***.

12

TEST EXPRESSIONS AND FUNCTIONS

You've already seen how you can extract the contents of a node with `xsl:value-of`. In fact, `xsl:value-of` outputs the string value of the first node in a node set. You can perform one or more operations on that string before it is output, using functions, as described throughout this chapter.

Sometimes, you don't need to output the data, but instead want to use it as a test condition in an `xsl:if` or `xsl:when` instruction. Functions let you test for more complicated situations.

You can also use functions in a predicate to select a subset of the nodes in a node set.

The official specifications for functions can be found at the World Wide Web Consortium site: *http://www.w3.org/TR/xpath#corelib*.

Comparing Two Values

Perhaps the most common test that you can perform is whether one value is bigger than another. You can then use the answer to determine which actions should result.

To compare two values:

1. Create the path to the first node set that you want to compare.
2. Type **=** (equals), **!=** (not equal to), **>** (greater-than), **>=** (greater-than or equals), **<** (less-than), or **<=** (less-than or equals), depending on how you want to compare the two values.
3. Type the path to the node set or the value that you want to compare with the node set in step 1.

✔ Tips

- If you just want to test that a node set exists (regardless of its contents), skip steps 2–3.
- String and text values in step 3 should be enclosed in single quotes.
- Use `and` to test that all of a series of multiple conditions are true. Use `or` to test if at least one of a series of multiple conditions is true.

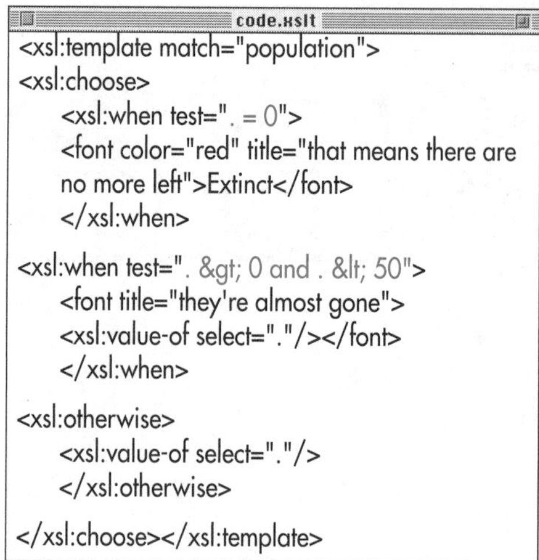

code.xslt

```
<xsl:template match="population">
<xsl:choose>
   <xsl:when test=". = 0">
   <font color="red" title="that means there are
   no more left">Extinct</font>
   </xsl:when>
<xsl:when test=". &gt; 0 and . &lt; 50">
   <font title="they're almost gone">
   <xsl:value-of select="."/></font>
   </xsl:when>
<xsl:otherwise>
   <xsl:value-of select="."/>
   </xsl:otherwise>
</xsl:choose></xsl:template>
```

Figure 12.1 *In the first example, we test to see if the current node (represented by the period) is equal to zero. If it is, the word* Extinct *is output. In the second example, we check to see if the current node is greater than 0 and less than 50, in which case a tooltip with "they're almost gone" is output. (Yes, you've seen this example, in Adding Conditional Choices* on *page 149 when we were going over* `xsl:choose`*.)*

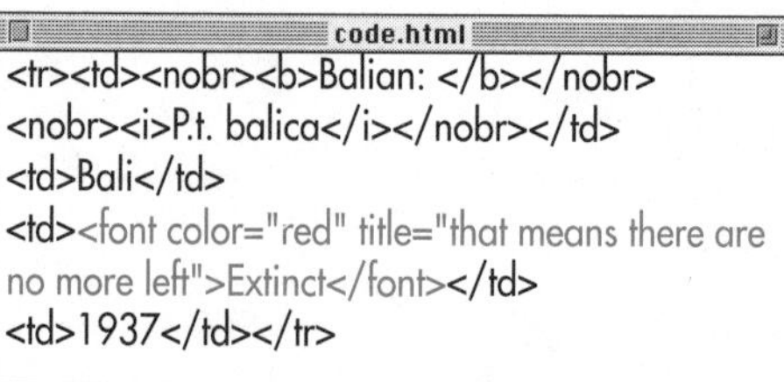

code.html

```
<tr><td><nobr><b>Balian: </b></nobr>
<nobr><i>P.t. balica</i></nobr></td>
<td>Bali</td>
<td><font color="red" title="that means there are
no more left">Extinct</font></td>
<td>1937</td></tr>
```

Figure 12.2 *Since the Balian tiger became extinct in 1937 and its population is therefore equal to zero, the word* Extinct *is output (in red with a tooltip).*

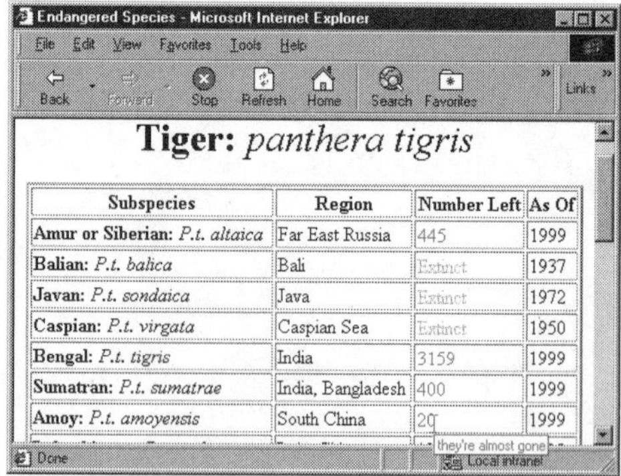

Figure 12.3 *Comparing one value with another is a common kind of test.*

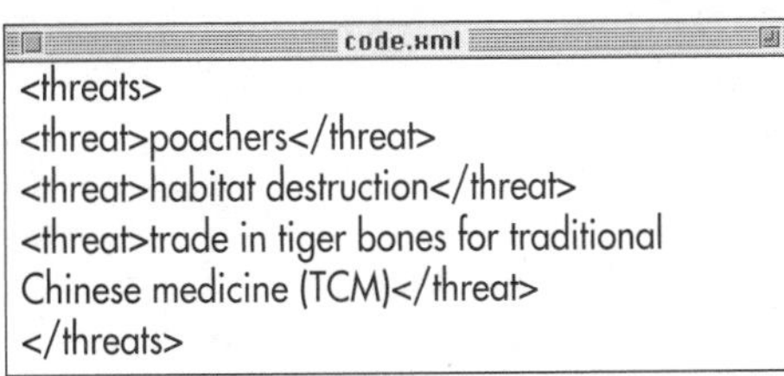

code.xml

```
<threats>
<threat>poachers</threat>
<threat>habitat destruction</threat>
<threat>trade in tiger bones for traditional
Chinese medicine (TCM)</threat>
</threats>
```

Figure 12.4 *An excerpt of the XML document shows three* `threat` *elements contained in the* `threats` *element.*

code.xslt

```
<xsl:template match="threats">
<p>The mighty <xsl:value-of
select="../name[@language='English']"/> faces
numerous threats, among them <xsl:for-each
select="threat">
<xsl:value-of select="."/>
<xsl:choose>
<xsl:when test="position()=last()">.</xsl:when>
<xsl:when test="position()=last()-1">, and
</xsl:when>
<xsl:otherwise>, </xsl:otherwise>
</xsl:choose>
</xsl:for-each></p></xsl:template>
```

Figure 12.5 *It's important that the template be for the* `threats` *element (and not the* `threat` *element). If we applied a* `threat` *template to each* `threat`*, each one would be in the first position. In a* `threats` *template, the individual* `threat` *elements are numbered 1, 2 and, 3.*

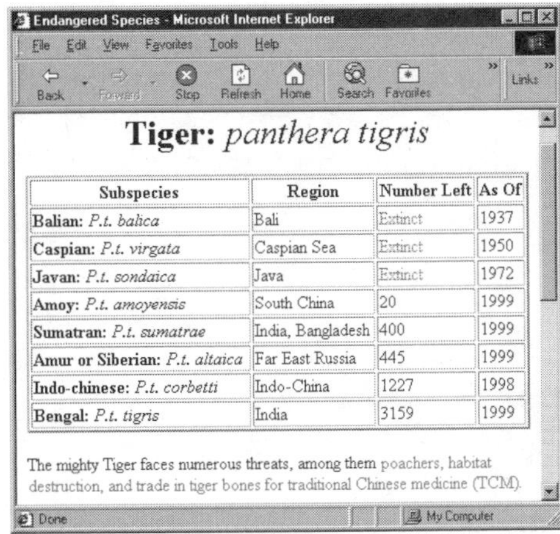

Subspecies	Region	Number Left	As Of
Balian: *P.t. balica*	Bali	Extinct	1937
Caspian: *P.t. virgata*	Caspian Sea	Extinct	1950
Javan: *P.t. sondaica*	Java	Extinct	1972
Amoy: *P.t. amoyensis*	South China	20	1999
Sumatran: *P.t. sumatrae*	India, Bangladesh	400	1999
Amur or Siberian: *P.t. altaica*	Far East Russia	445	1999
Indo-chinese: *P.t. corbetti*	Indo-China	1227	1998
Bengal: *P.t. tigris*	India	3159	1999

Figure 12.6 *The* `threat` *itself is output no matter what. If it's in the last position, a period is also output. If it's in the second to last position (*`position ()-1`*), a comma and space are output after it, and if it's in any other position, nothing else is added.*

Testing the Position

You can also choose to select the first, second, or even the last child of a node.

To test a node's position:

Type **position() = n**, where *n* is the number that identifies the position of the node within the current node set.

To find the last node in a node set:

Type **last()** to get the last node.

✔ Tips

- You never put anything between the parentheses in the `position` or `last` functions. (In other, more formal, words, they never take *arguments.*)
- You can also use **n** as an abbreviation for **position()=n**, but only in a predicate. For example, **subspecies[1]** would result in the first `subspecies` node. (You can't use the abbreviation in `xsl:if` or `xsl:when` test expressions, or even in an `xsl:value-of` instruction.)

Subtotaling Values

You can use the sum() function to actually add up all the values of the nodes in a node set. It's great for tabular data.

To subtotal values:

1. Type **sum(**.
2. Type the path to the node set whose nodes should be totaled.
3. Type **)** to complete the function.

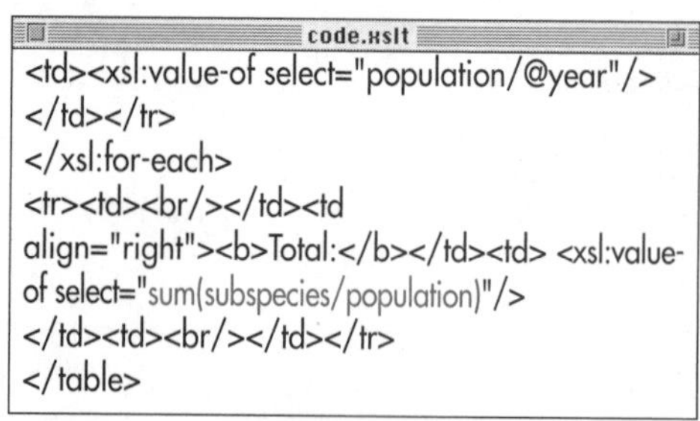

```
code.xslt
<td><xsl:value-of select="population/@year"/>
</td></tr>
</xsl:for-each>
<tr><td><br/></td><td
align="right"><b>Total:</b></td><td> <xsl:value-
of select="sum(subspecies/population)"/>
</td><td><br/></td></tr>
</table>
```

Figure 12.7 *After the closing* `xsl:for-each` *element but before the end of the table, I've added this* `xsl:value-of` *instruction to output the sum of the populations of each animal.*

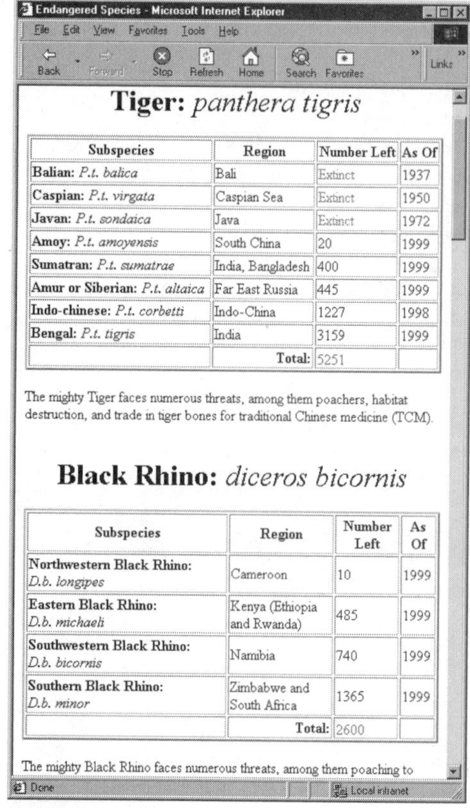

Tiger: *panthera tigris*

Subspecies	Region	Number Left	As Of
Balian: *P.t. balica*	Bali	Extinct	1937
Caspian: *P.t. virgata*	Caspian Sea	Extinct	1950
Javan: *P.t. sondaica*	Java	Extinct	1972
Amoy: *P.t. amoyensis*	South China	20	1999
Sumatran: *P.t. sumatrae*	India, Bangladesh	400	1999
Amur or Siberian: *P.t. altaica*	Far East Russia	445	1999
Indo-chinese: *P.t. corbetti*	Indo-China	1227	1998
Bengal: *P.t. tigris*	India	3159	1999
	Total:	5251	

The mighty Tiger faces numerous threats, among them poachers, habitat destruction, and trade in tiger bones for traditional Chinese medicine (TCM).

Black Rhino: *diceros bicornis*

Subspecies	Region	Number Left	As Of
Northwestern Black Rhino: *D.b. longipes*	Cameroon	10	1999
Eastern Black Rhino: *D.b. michaeli*	Kenya (Ethiopia and Rwanda)	485	1999
Southwestern Black Rhino: *D.b. bicornis*	Namibia	740	1999
Southern Black Rhino: *D.b. minor*	Zimbabwe and South Africa	1365	1999
	Total:	2600	

The mighty Black Rhino faces numerous threats, among them poaching to

Figure 12.8 *The populations of each species are subtotaled and output. (These are real numbers.)*

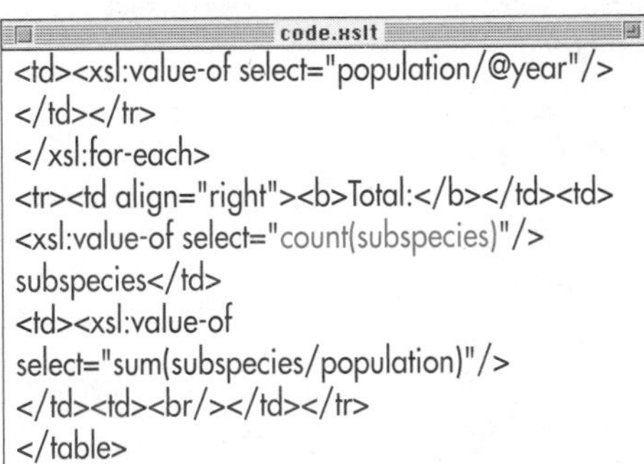

```
<td><xsl:value-of select="population/@year"/>
</td></tr>
</xsl:for-each>
<tr><td align="right"><b>Total:</b></td><td>
<xsl:value-of select="count(subspecies)"/>
subspecies</td>
<td><xsl:value-of
select="sum(subspecies/population)"/>
</td><td><br/></td></tr>
</table>
```

Figure 12.9 *Remember that this excerpt is within the* `animal` *template, and therefore, we'll be counting the number of* `subspecies` *elements in each* `animal` *element that's processed.*

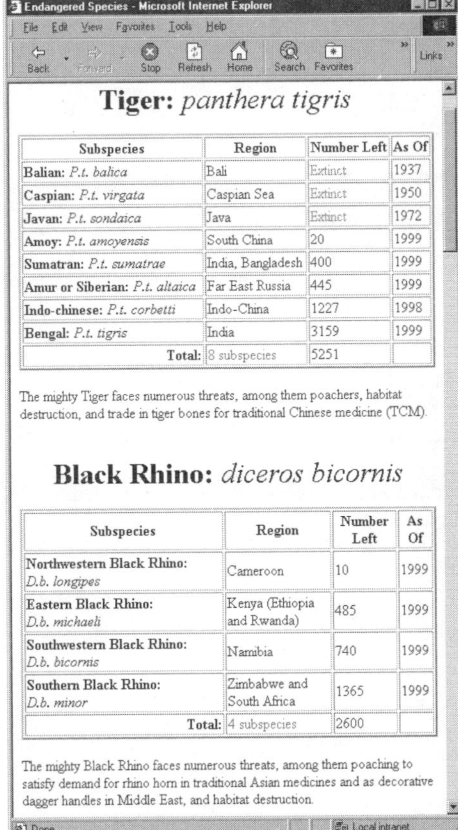

Tiger: *panthera tigris*

Subspecies	Region	Number Left	As Of
Balian: *P.t. balica*	Bali	Extinct	1937
Caspian: *P.t. virgata*	Caspian Sea	Extinct	1950
Javan: *P.t. sondaica*	Java	Extinct	1972
Amoy: *P.t. amoyensis*	South China	20	1999
Sumatran: *P.t. sumatrae*	India, Bangladesh	400	1999
Amur or Siberian: *P.t. altaica*	Far East Russia	445	1999
Indo-chinese: *P.t. corbetti*	Indo-China	1227	1998
Bengal: *P.t. tigris*	India	3159	1999
Total:	8 subspecies	5251	

The mighty Tiger faces numerous threats, among them poachers, habitat destruction, and trade in tiger bones for traditional Chinese medicine (TCM).

Black Rhino: *diceros bicornis*

Subspecies	Region	Number Left	As Of
Northwestern Black Rhino: *D.b. longipes*	Cameroon	10	1999
Eastern Black Rhino: *D.b. michaeli*	Kenya (Ethiopia and Rwanda)	485	1999
Southwestern Black Rhino: *D.b. bicornis*	Namibia	740	1999
Southern Black Rhino: *D.b. minor*	Zimbabwe and South Africa	1365	1999
Total:	4 subspecies	2600	

The mighty Black Rhino faces numerous threats, among them poaching to satisfy demand for rhino horn in traditional Asian medicines and as decorative dagger handles in Middle East, and habitat destruction.

Figure 12.10 *Note that the word "subspecies" is not generated by the* `count` *function. It's just a literal word, and appears in the stylesheet above. (Note that I've moved the word "Total" over to the first column in the table so that there's room for the subspecies count.)*

Counting Nodes

Often, rather than subtotalling a set of nodes, you simply want to know how many there are.

To count nodes:

1. Type **count(**.
2. Type the path to the node set whose nodes should be counted.
3. Type **)** to complete the function.

Multiplying, Dividing, Adding, Subtracting

You can add simple arithmetic operations to your expressions to test for slightly more complicated conditions.

To multiply, divide, add, or subtract:

1. Type the first operand. It can be a numerical constant like 12 or a node set (in which case the string value of the first node is used).
2. Type the mathematical operator: * (for multiplication), **div** (for division, since / is already fraught with meaning), **+** (for addition), or **-** (for subtraction).
3. Type the second operand.

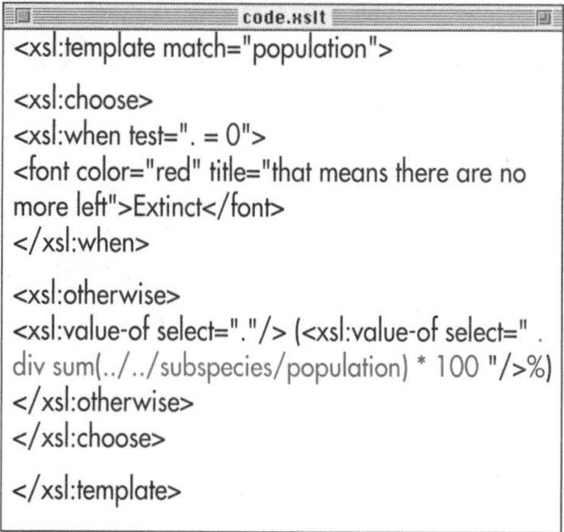

```
code.xslt
<xsl:template match="population">

<xsl:choose>
<xsl:when test=". = 0">
<font color="red" title="that means there are no
more left">Extinct</font>
</xsl:when>

<xsl:otherwise>
<xsl:value-of select="."/> (<xsl:value-of select=" .
div sum(../../subspecies/population) * 100 "/>%)
</xsl:otherwise>
</xsl:choose>

</xsl:template>
```

Figure 12.11 *In the* `population` *template, as long as the population is not equal to zero, we divide the current node (that period)—which is the population of the subspecies being processed—by the sum of that animal's subspecies' populations and then multiply the result by 100. (Notice that I got rid of one of the* `xsl:when` *instructions for simplicity's sake.)*

✔ Tips

- Numbers are always double-length floating point which makes for really ugly division **(Figure 12.12)**. You'll want to combine `div` with other functions *(see pages 169–170)*.
- As usual, multiplication and division are performed before addition and subtraction. In other words, 4+5*3 is 19 and not 27. You can use parentheses to override the default. So, (4+5)*3 is, in fact, 27.
- There is a fifth operator, **mod**, for obtaining the remainder of a division. So, **20 mod 4** is 0 (since 4 divides evenly into 20), but **20 mod 3** is 2 since 20/3 is 6 with a remainder of 2.

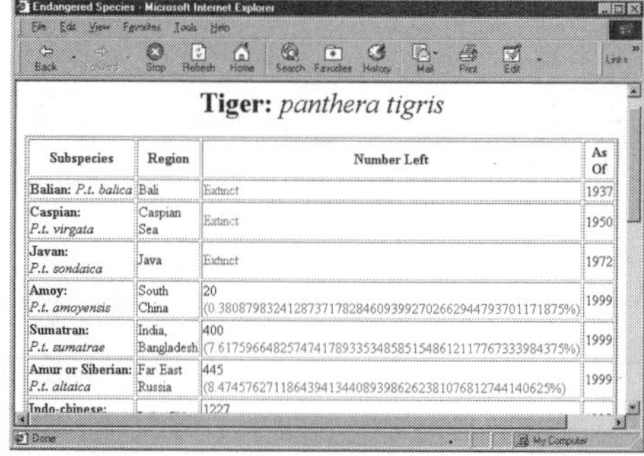

Figure 12.12 *The percentages while correct are awfully ugly. We'll make them look better on the next page.*

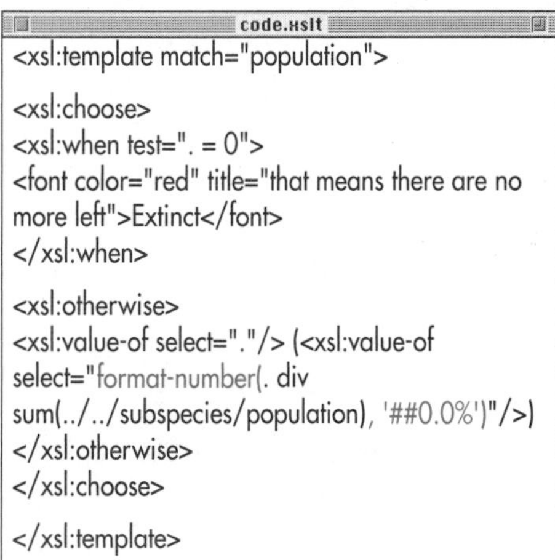

```
code.xslt
<xsl:template match="population">

<xsl:choose>
<xsl:when test=". = 0">
<font color="red" title="that means there are no
more left">Extinct</font>
</xsl:when>

<xsl:otherwise>
<xsl:value-of select="."/> (<xsl:value-of
select="format-number(. div
sum(../../subspecies/population), '##0.0%')"/>)
</xsl:otherwise>
</xsl:choose>

</xsl:template>
```

Figure 12.13 *The number being formatted is exactly the same as in Figure 12.11 on page 168. Now it will be formatted as a percentage with at least one digit to the left of the decimal point (but numbers are never truncated to the left) and exactly one digit to the right of the decimal point.*

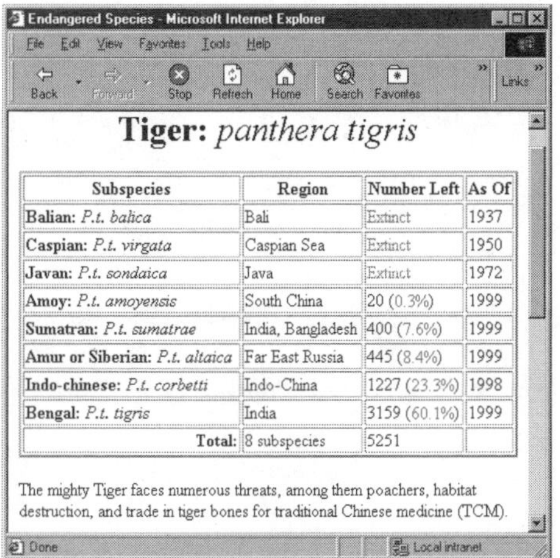

Endangered Species - Microsoft Internet Explorer

Tiger: *panthera tigris*

Subspecies	Region	Number Left	As Of
Balian: *P.t. balica*	Bali	Extinct	1937
Caspian: *P.t. virgata*	Caspian Sea	Extinct	1950
Javan: *P.t. sondaica*	Java	Extinct	1972
Amoy: *P.t. amoyensis*	South China	20 (0.3%)	1999
Sumatran: *P.t. sumatrae*	India, Bangladesh	400 (7.6%)	1999
Amur or Siberian: *P.t. altaica*	Far East Russia	445 (8.4%)	1999
Indo-chinese: *P.t. corbetti*	Indo-China	1227 (23.3%)	1998
Bengal: *P.t. tigris*	India	3159 (60.1%)	1999
Total:	8 subspecies	5251	

The mighty Tiger faces numerous threats, among them poachers, habitat destruction, and trade in tiger bones for traditional Chinese medicine (TCM).

Figure 12.14 *The percentages look much better without quite so many digits. (Also note that the parentheses around the percentages are simple literal elements that I typed in the stylesheet around the* `xsl:value-of` *element that creates the number itself.)*

Formatting Numbers

Instead of manually formatting percentages and other kinds of numbers as we attempted on the previous page, it's much easier to use the format-number function.

To format numbers:

1. Type **format-number(**.
2. Type the expression which contains the number to be formatted.
3. Type **, '** (a comma, space, and single quote).
4. Type **0** for each digit that should always appear, **#** for each digit that should only appear when not zero (and not significant), **.** (a period), if desired, to separate the integer part of a number from the fractional part, **,** (a comma), if desired, to separate groups of digits in the integer part, and **%** (the percent sign), if desired, to display the number as a percentage.
5. Type **')** (a single quote followed by right parentheses) to complete the number pattern and then close the function.

✓ Tips

- So, use #,##0.00 to output at least one digit in the integer, with commas separating every 3 digits, and exactly two digits in the fractional part of the number (as in dollars and cents: 269.40). With #,000.0#, the numbers with tenths but no hundredths would have no final 0: 269.4.
- Negative numbers are preceded by a minus sign (-) by default. If you'd rather they be surrounded by parentheses, add **;(0)** after step 4 above.

Rounding Numbers

There are three functions for rounding numbers. You can either always round up (ceiling), always round down (floor), or round to the nearest integer (round).

To round numbers:

1. Type **ceiling(**, **floor(**, or **round(**, depending on whether you want to round up, down, or to the nearest integer.
2. Type the expression which contains the number to be formatted.
3. Type **)** to complete the function.

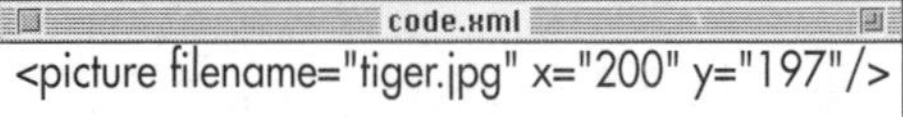

```
code.xml
<picture filename="tiger.jpg" x="200" y="197"/>
```

Figure 12.15 *In this excerpt of the XML file, we see that the image's original size was 200 pixels wide by 197 pixels tall.*

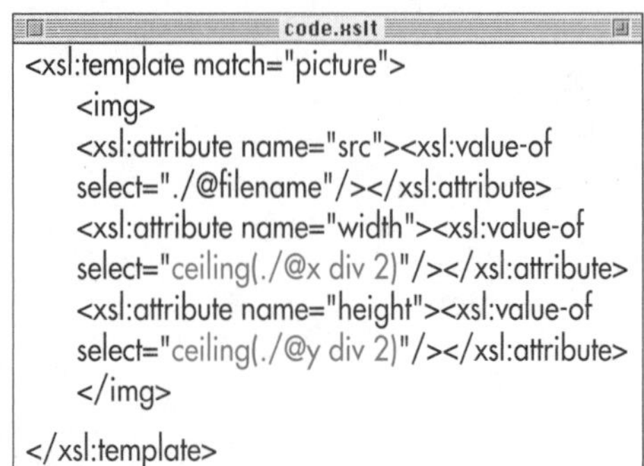

```
code.xslt
<xsl:template match="picture">
    <img>
    <xsl:attribute name="src"><xsl:value-of
    select="./@filename"/></xsl:attribute>
    <xsl:attribute name="width"><xsl:value-of
    select="ceiling(./@x div 2)"/></xsl:attribute>
    <xsl:attribute name="height"><xsl:value-of
    select="ceiling(./@y div 2)"/></xsl:attribute>
    </img>
</xsl:template>
```

Figure 12.16 *On the main page, I'd like the pictures to be shown at half their regular size. Since the HTML tags,* `width` *and* `height`*, only accept integers, I use the* `ceiling` *function to round the division up to the nearest integer. (Compare with Figure 10.30 on page 151.)*

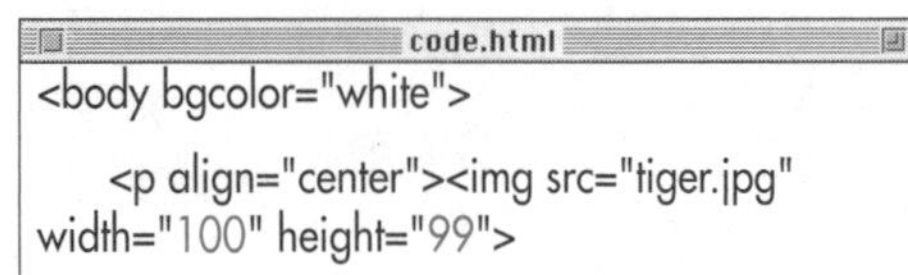

```
code.html
<body bgcolor="white">

    <p align="center"><img src="tiger.jpg"
width="100" height="99">
```

Figure 12.17 *The value for the height of the image becomes 99, which is the next highest integer after 98.5 (197 divided by two).*

Figure 12.18 *The tiger image on the main page now measures approximately half of its normal size: 100 by 99 pixels.*

```
code.xml
<animal>
<name language="English">Tiger</name>
<name language="Latin">panthera tigris</name>
<threats><threat>poachers</threat>

...

<subspecies>

<name language="English">Amur or
Siberian</name>
<name language="Latin">altaica</name>
<region>Far East Russia</region>

<population year="1999">445</population>
```

Figure 12.19 *In the XML document, the Latin animal name has always contained the full genus and species names. Now, we remove the initials from each subspecies' Latin name in the XML document so that they're not duplicated when we generate them with XSLT.*

```
code.xslt
<xsl:template match="name[@language='Latin']">
<nobr><i><xsl:value-of select="."/>
</i></nobr></xsl:template>

<xsl:template
match="subspecies/name[@language='Latin']">
<nobr><i><xsl:value-of select="substring
(../../name[@language='Latin'],1,1)"/>
<xsl:value-of select="."/></i></nobr>

</xsl:template>
```

Figure 12.20 *In a new template just for the subspecies' Latin names, we use* `substring` *to extract the first letter of the animal's Latin name.*

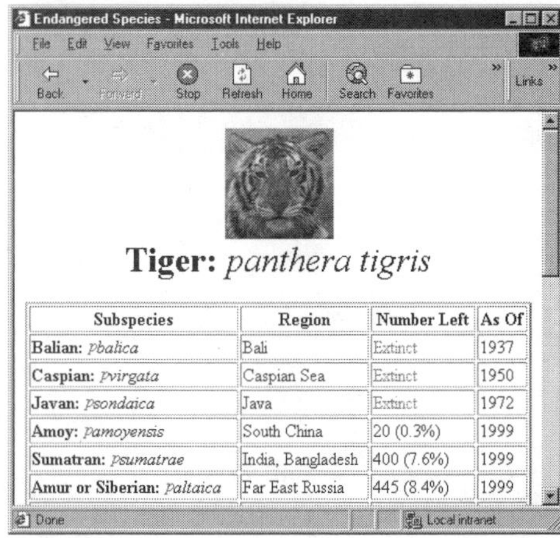

Figure 12.21 *Now we've got a lower case* p *in front of each subspecies' Latin name. It's a start.*

Extracting Substrings

It's often useful to dig into a string and take out only the bit that you need. In our example, we can generate the abbreviated version of the subspecies name by extracting the initials of the genus and species from the animal's Latin name.

To extract substrings:

1. Type **substring(**.
2. Type the expression which contains the source string.
3. Type **, n**, where *n* is the position of the first character that you want to extract. A comma separates each of the arguments in a substring function.
4. If desired, type **, m**, where *m* is the number of characters you want to extract. A comma separates each of the arguments in a substring function.
5. Type **)** to complete the function.

To extract a substring that comes before or after a particular character:

1. Type **substring-after(** or **substring-before(** depending on whether you want to extract the part of the string that comes before or after the character.

2. Type the expression which contains the source string.

3. Type **, c**, where *c* is the character after or before which the substring will be extracted.

4. Type **)** to complete the function.

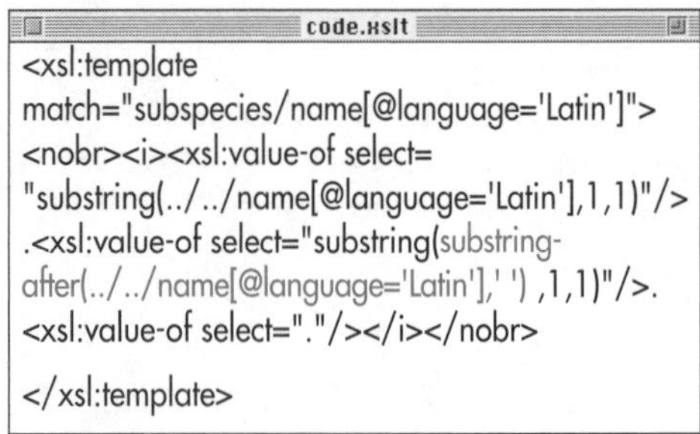

```
code.xslt
<xsl:template
match="subspecies/name[@language='Latin']">
<nobr><i><xsl:value-of select=
"substring(../../name[@language='Latin'],1,1)"/>
.<xsl:value-of select="substring(substring-
after(../../name[@language='Latin'],' ') ,1,1)"/>.
<xsl:value-of select="."/></i></nobr>

</xsl:template>
```

Figure 12.22 *To get the first character of the second word in the animal's Latin name, we'll extract the substring that comes after the space. (Then, we'll use the* `substring` *function to take just the first letter of the result.) Notice also that I've manually added the necessary periods and space.*

Subspecies	Region	Number Left	As Of
Balian: *p.t. balica*	Bali	Extinct	1937
Caspian: *p.t. virgata*	Caspian Sea	Extinct	1950
Javan: *p.t. sondaica*	Java	Extinct	1972
Amoy: *p.t. amoyensis*	South China	20 (0.3%)	1999
Sumatran: *p.t. sumatrae*	India, Bangladesh	400 (7.6%)	1999
Amur or Siberian: *p.t. altaica*	Far East Russia	445 (8.4%)	1999
Indo-chinese: *p.t. corbetti*	Indo-China	1227 (23.3%)	1998

Figure 12.23 *Now we've got the second initial and the punctuation. We're almost there.*

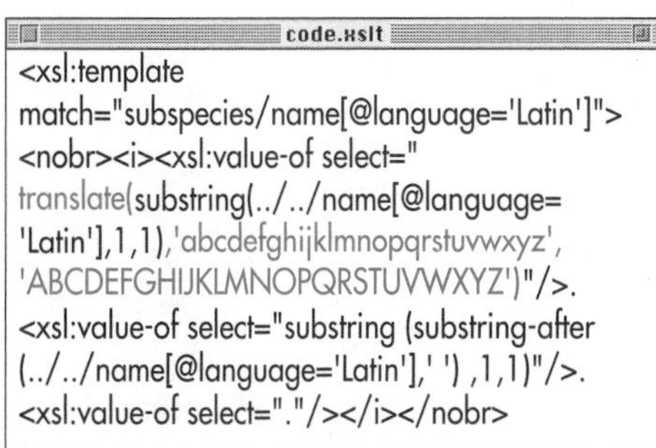

```
<xsl:template
match="subspecies/name[@language='Latin']">
<nobr><i><xsl:value-of select="
translate(substring(../../name[@language=
'Latin'],1,1),'abcdefghijklmnopqrstuvwxyz',
'ABCDEFGHIJKLMNOPQRSTUVWXYZ')"/>.
<xsl:value-of select="substring (substring-after
(../../name[@language='Latin'],' ') ,1,1)"/>.
<xsl:value-of select="."/></i></nobr>
```

Figure 12.24 *Now we use the* `translate` *function on the first initial to change it to uppercase.*

Figure 12.25 *The first initial is now capitalized, as it should be. Big deal, you say, we're back where we started. The difference is that the genus data is no longer duplicated among the animal* `name` *elements and the subspecies* `name` *elements. Whenever possible, data should be stored in one sole location and then leveraged for as many uses as possible. This saves both on data entry and on errors.*

Capitalizing Strings

When manipulating text, it's often important to be able to change letters from upper- to lowercase and back again.

To capitalize strings:

1. Type **translate(**.
2. Type the expression which contains the source string.
3. Type **, 'abcdefghijklmnopqrstuvwxyz'** (that is, a comma, space, and then the string that contains the letters that should be changed).
4. Type **, 'ABCDEFGHIJKLMNOPQRSTUV WXYZ'** (that is, a comma, a space, and a string that contains the letters that the letters in step 3 should be changed into).
5. Type **)** to complete the function.

✓ Tips

- To change letters from lower- to uppercase, reverse step 3 and step 4.
- You can use the `translate` function to translate any character to any other character. Type the letters that should be changed in step 3 and the letters that these should be changed into in step 4.

Part 5: Cascading Style Sheets

13

SETTING UP CSS

```
code.xml
<?xml version="1.0" ?>

<endangered_species>

<intro>The animals and plants on our planet are disappearing at an alarming rate. It's time to do something about it right now!</intro>

<picture filename="panther.jpg" text="Florida Panther" x="216" y="215"/>

<name>Florida Panther</name>

<description>With perhaps no more than <population>50</population> adults left in wild areas of Southwestern Florida, the majestic but
```

Figure 13.1 *Here is the beginning of the XML page that is used for the examples throughout this chapter. You can download it from my Web site and print it for your convenience (see page 18).*

```
code.html
<html><head><title>Panthers and Otters</title></head>

<body>

<p class="intro">The animals and plants on our planet are disappearing at an alarming rate. It's time to do something about it right now!</p>

<img src="panther.jpg" alt="Florida Panther" width="216" height="215" border="0">

<h1>Florida Panther</h1>

<p>With perhaps no more than 50 adults left in wild areas of Southwestern Florida,
```

Figure 13.2 *Here is a rough approximation of the same file (Figure 13.1) written in HTML.*

In HTML, every tag has default formatting built right in. If you don't like that formatting, you can adjust it by adding other tags, or by applying style sheets. In XML, tags start with no style characteristics at all. You must specify exactly how tags should be displayed. In fact, an XML document cannot be shown in a browser until you specify that information.

There are two popular ways to format the tags in an XML document—with Extensible Stylesheet Language - Transformation (XSLT), as we've seen, or with Cascading Style Sheets (CSS). Since XSLT can convert XML documents into HTML documents, it can also be used to apply style formatting (by judicious use of those HTML tags). XSLT does not, however, contain any explicit formatting instructions itself.

CSS, on the other hand, was born to format. It worries about type size and background colors. If you don't need to transform your document, then you can apply formatting directly to XML with CSS. However, since many folks still use browsers that can't read XML directly, this is really more of a future possibility than a practical solution today. Right now, it's much more common to apply CSS to an HTML document that has been generated from an XML document with XSLT.

In the following chapters, I will focus on applying CSS to XML, but will give you all the information you need to apply CSS to HTML as well.

CSS with XML vs. CSS with HTML

The very nature of cascading style sheets is to add formatting information in layers where each succeeding layer overrules the last. One major difference between applying CSS to XML versus applying CSS to HTML is that HTML tags already have some formatting information incorporated in them. XML tags do not.

It's important, then, while writing your CSS, to think about whether the styles will be applied to XML's blank slate **(Figure 13.3)** or to HTML's already colorful palette **(Figure 13.4)**. In particular, pay close attention to the `display` properties *(see page 190)* when writing CSS that will be applied directly to XML. When writing HTML, be aware that your styles will be *added* to the existing formatting, only *overruling* its characteristics when there is a direct conflict.

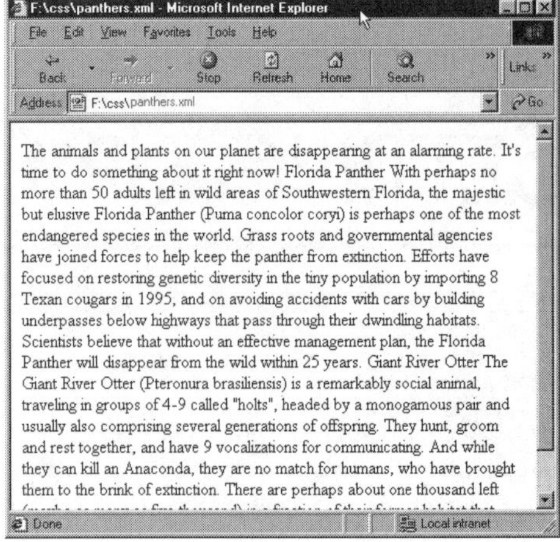

Figure 13.3 *An XML document pointing to an empty style sheet looks pretty bland. No line breaks. No formatting. Nothing. If you don't point the XML document to any CSS file at all, in Explorer, you'll only see a hierarchical view of the XML document's contents. It looks even worse than this: see Figure 13.13 on page 185!*

Images and links in XML documents with CSS

Since no browser yet supports XLink and XPointer*(see page 225)*, XML documents formatted directly with CSS generally cannot include images or links. However, you can use the `background` property to fake embedded images (and for real background images) as I'll show you on page 201.

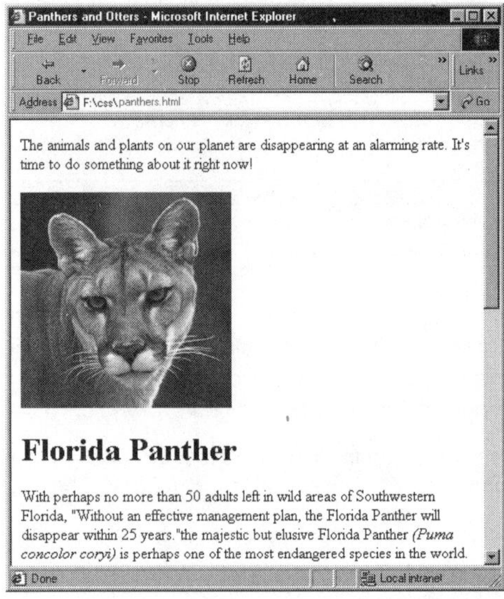

Figure 13.4 *The same information written with HTML tags—but still no CSS—looks a lot different. Starting with HTML—presumably generated with XSLT from your XML document—gives you a head start on formatting (that you may or may not want).*

CSS1, CSS2, and Browsers

Perhaps the most difficult problem to surmount when using CSS is that many browsers support only a subset of its features. While Explorer 5 for Windows and Mac supports most of the features in CSS1, its support for CSS2 is more spotty. Early releases of Mozilla (the engine behind the upcoming Netscape 6) also reveal uneven support. The best thing to do is check one of the many online compatibility charts. (See my Web site for links.) And then restrict your use of CSS to those features that work the best across browsers.

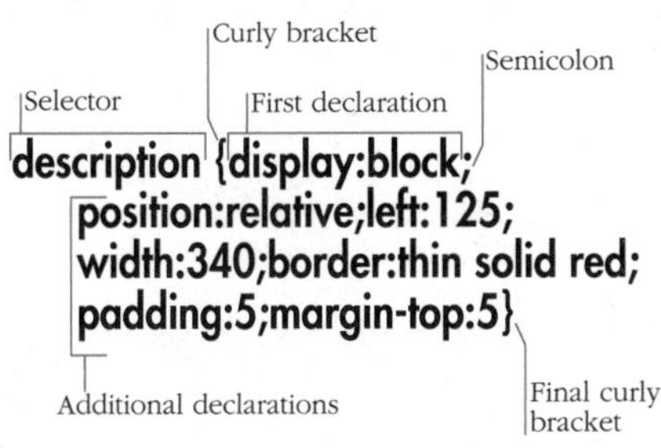

Figure 13.5 *A style is made up of a selector (which points to the element or elements to which the style will apply) and one or more declarations that describe how the element(s) should be formatted.*

The Anatomy of a Style

A style is made up of a *selector* and one or more *declarations*. The selector specifies which elements the style should be applied to (say, all the `subspecies` elements). The declaration determines how the chosen elements should be displayed—perhaps in red, at 12 points, with Lithos Regular.

A selector can be as simple as an element name, like `subspecies` or `threat`, in our example. Or you can combine different kinds of selectors to form a pattern that matches the specific elements that you want to format. For more details, consult *Specifying Where Styles Are To Be Applied* on page 180.

The actual formatting that is applied depends on the *declaration*, which is made up of a *property*, a colon, and one or more *values*. For example, to change the color of text, you use the `color` property with a value of say, "red". The definition would read **color: red**. The space after the colon is optional. Multiple declarations must be separated by semicolons.

Some properties can be grouped together with a special umbrella property (like, `font`, `background`, and `border`, among others). For example, **font: bold 12pt Tekton** is the same as writing **font-size: 12pt; font-weight: bold; font-family: Tekton**.

Many properties are *inherited* from parent elements to child elements. So, if you apply an inheritable property (like `font`) to a parent element, the child element will automatically have that property as well. You can override inherited properties by explicitly applying a different value for the property to the child element.

The available properties and corresponding values that can be used to define styles are described in detail on pages 190–222.

Specifying Where Styles Are To Be Applied

A selector specifies the elements in your document to which the formatting information in the declaration will be applied.

To write a selector that specifies where the style should be applied:

- Type * to apply the style to every element.
- Type **name** to apply the style to every *name* element in the document.
- Type **name1, name2, name3**, and so on, to apply the style to each of the named elements. Each element name should be separated from the last by a comma.
- Type **parent descendant** to apply the style to the *descendant* elements that are contained in a *parent* element. (There may be intermediary containers.)
- Type **parent > child** to apply the style to only those *child* elements that are contained directly within the *parent* element.
- Type **name:first-child** to apply the style to a *name* element when it is the *first child* element of its parent.
- Type **before + after** to apply the style to only those *after* elements that come directly after a *before* element.
- Type **name[att_name]** to apply the style to *name* elements that have an attribute called *att_name*. The value of the attribute is irrelevant.
- Type **name[att_name=att_value]** to apply the style to *name* elements that have an attribute named *att_name* with a value of *att_value*.

Figure 13.6 *In this incredibly simple style sheet, I've declared a style rule for both the* `intro` *and* `latin_name` *elements (they'll be red, but don't worry too much about the declarations themselves yet).*

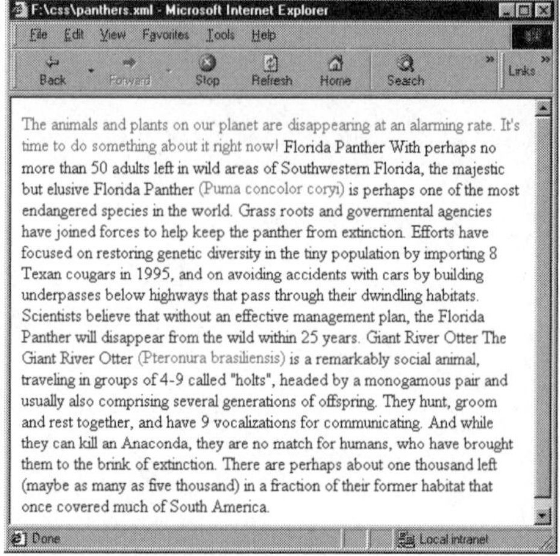

Figure 13.7 *The style is applied to each of the comma separated elements in the selector.*

Figure 13.8 *This rule should be applied to only those picture elements that contain an attribute named* `filename` *with a value set to* panther.jpg.

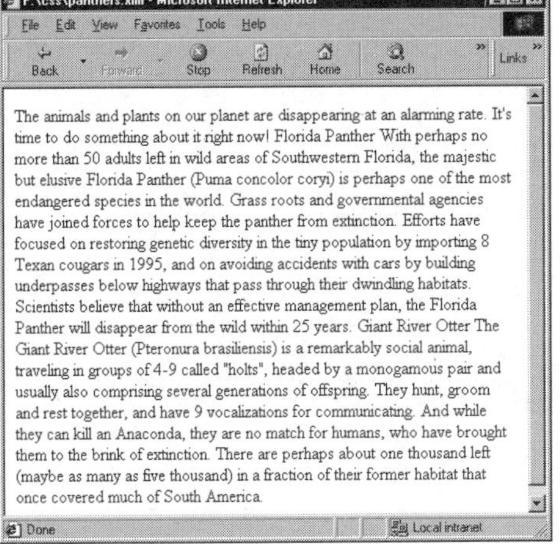

Figure 13.9 *Applying a style to an element depending on the value of an attribute is currently not supported by any major browser, including Explorer 5 for Windows, shown here.*

- Type **name[att_name~=att_value]** to apply the style to *name* elements that have an attribute named *att_name* with a value that contains a set of space separated words, one of which is *att_value.*
- Type **name#id_name** to apply the style to a *name* element with an ID attribute whose value is *id_name.* *(see page 52).*
- Type **name:link** to apply the style to a *name* element that is an as yet unvisited link.
- Type **name:visited** to apply the style to a *name* element that is a visited link.
- Type **name:active** to apply the style to a *name* element that is a link that is being clicked on.
- Type **name:hover** to apply the style to a *name* element that is a link that is being pointed at with the mouse.
- Type **name:focus** to apply the style to a *name* element that is a link that has been tabbed to with the keyboard but not yet activated.

✔ Tips

- Unfortunately, no browser supports all these selectors. Most support the first four and the #.
- Theoretically, you can combine these selectors to more precisely specify the elements to which you wish to apply the style. The reality, however, is that many browsers don't support the standard.
- Note that in an HTML document, you can use **.class_name** (that is, a period followed by the class name) as a shorthand for **[class="class_name"]** (as described in the last procedure on the previous page).

Creating an External Style Sheet

A *style sheet* is a list of the styles (sometimes called *rules*) that you've defined for formatting the elements in your XML documents. Since XML documents are often dynamic, changing collections of information, and specifically designed to be free of formatting to boot, the style sheet is most often a separate, independent, text document.

To create a style sheet:

1. Create a new text document with your text editor of choice.
2. Type the name of the selector that describes the element(s) to which the style should be applied. See page 180 for more details.
3. Type **{** to mark the beginning of the properties that should be applied.
4. Define as many properties as desired, using the instructions in Chapter 14, *Layout with CSS* and Chapter 15, *Formatting Text with CSS*. Separate each property with a semicolon.
5. Type **}** to mark the end of this rule.
6. Repeat steps 2–5 for each style rule.
7. Save the document in text only format in the desired directory. Give the document the extension .css to designate the document as a Cascading Style Sheet.

```
code.css
endangered_species {display:block}
name {display:block;position:absolute;left:9}
intro {display:block;border:medium dotted red;
    padding:5;margin-top:5}
description {display:block;position:relative;
    left:125;width:340;border:thin solid red;
    padding:5;margin-top:5}
picture {display:block}
population {display:inline}
latin_name {display:inline}
more_info {display:inline}
```

Figure 13.10 *A style sheet contains a list of selectors and the declarations that should be applied to the elements they represent. It should be saved as text only with the .css extension.*

✔ Tips

- Make sure you save the style sheet as Text Only (sometimes called Text Document or ASCII) and give it the .css extension. It should be uploaded in ASCII—not Binary—mode.
- For more information on how to write style rules, consult *The Anatomy of a Style* on page 179.
- Each set of properties must begin with an opening curly bracket "**{**" and end with a closing curly bracket "**}**". Each property and its values must be separated with a semicolon "**;**".
- You can also create style sheets within an XML document, and even within an individual tag. For more details, consult *Using Internal Style Sheets* on page 187 and *Applying Styles Locally* on page 188. Local style sheets override internal ones, which in turn override external ones.
- You may apply an external style sheet to as many XML documents as you like. You may also apply multiple style sheets to a single XML document. Each succeeding style sheet has precedence over those declared earlier.

Calling a Style Sheet for an XML Document

You use a special processing instruction to apply a cascading style sheet to an XML document. If the XML document is not pre-processed with XSLT, you'll have to do it manually. Otherwise, follow the second set of instructions to have the XSLT processor add it for you.

To create the processing instruction manually:

1. At the top of your XML document, after the initial XML declaration, if any *(see page 24)*, type **<?xml-stylesheet type="text/css"**.
2. Then type **href="styles.css"**, where *styles.css* is the name of your cascading style sheet.
3. Finally, type **?>** to complete the processing instruction.

To create the processing instruction with XSLT:

1. In the root template of your XSLT style sheet, type **<xsl:processing-instruction name="xml-stylesheet">**. This is the element that creates processing instructions.
2. Then type **type="text/css"** since you're calling a CSS style sheet.
3. Then type **href="styles.css"**, where *styles.css* is the name of your style sheet.
4. And finally, type **</xsl:processing-instruction>**.

code.xml

```
<?xml version="1.0" ?>

<?xml-stylesheet type="text/css"
    href="end_species.css" ?>

<endangered_species>

<intro>The animals and plants on our planet are
disappearing at an alarming rate. It's time to do
something about it right now!</intro>

<picture filename="panther.jpg" text="Florida
Panther" x="216" y="215"/>

<name>Florida Panther</name>

<description>With perhaps no more than
<population>50</population> adults left in wild
areas of Southwestern Florida, the majestic but
elusive Florida Panther <latin_name>(Puma
concolor coryi) </latin_name>is perhaps one of the
```

Figure 13.11 *In an XML document, you can specify the corresponding style sheet explicitly* (end_species.css *in this case).*

code.xslt

```
<?xml version="1.0"?>

<xsl:stylesheet xmlns:xsl="http://www.w3.org/
1999/XSL/Transform" version="1.0">

<xsl:template match="/">

<xsl:processing-instruction name="xml-
stylesheet">

type="text/css" href="end_species.css"

</xsl:processing-instruction>

<xsl:apply-templates
select="endangered_species/animal"/>
</xsl:template>
```

Figure 13.12 *The XML document generated by this XSLT style sheet will contain the line <?xml-stylesheet type="text/css" href="end_species.css" ?> and thus the call to the style sheet in the generated XML document will be identical to that shown in Figure 13.11.*

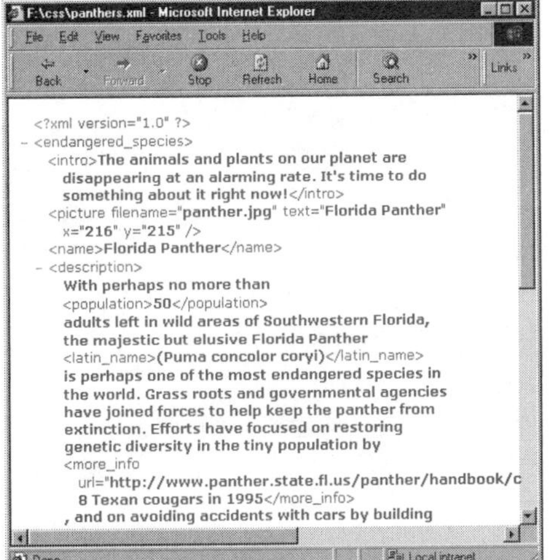

Figure 13.13 *If you don't specify any style sheet at all, Explorer shows the document in hierarchical form. You can collapse and expand the document to see its contents more clearly, but it still looks pretty ugly.*

✓ Tips

- You can call as many style sheets as you like. The later ones have precedence over the earlier ones.
- If you don't call a style sheet for an XML document, Explorer displays it in a hierarchical form **(Figure 13.13)** while Mozilla outputs the entire document as one block of text, with the default size and font.
- If you don't create declarations for each and every element, those elements will be displayed in the default size and font. So, if for some reason, you were to use a blank style sheet, both Internet Explorer and Mozilla would output the document as one block of text, in the default font and size.

Calling a Style Sheet for an HTML Document

If you're using the XSLT processor to convert your XML document into HTML, you can also have it add a call to an external style sheet with the final formatting information.

To call a style sheet for an HTML document:

1. In the `head` section of the HTML code in your XSLT style sheet, type **<link rel="stylesheet" type="text/css"**.
2. Then type **href="styles.css"**, where *styles.css* is the name of your cascading style sheet.
3. If you're adding the code via an XSLT style sheet, you must type **/**. (In straight HTML, of course, you don't usually use one.)
4. Then type **>** to close the `link` element.

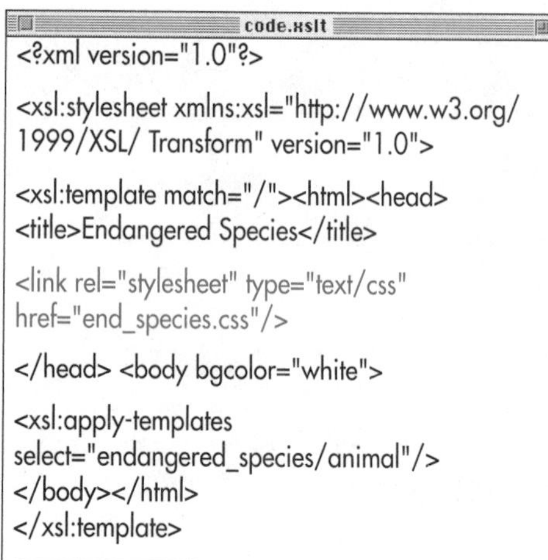

```
code.xslt
<?xml version="1.0"?>

<xsl:stylesheet xmlns:xsl="http://www.w3.org/
1999/XSL/ Transform" version="1.0">

<xsl:template match="/"><html><head>
<title>Endangered Species</title>

<link rel="stylesheet" type="text/css"
href="end_species.css"/>

</head> <body bgcolor="white">

<xsl:apply-templates
select="endangered_species/animal"/>
</body></html>
</xsl:template>
```

Figure 13.14 *The HTML document generated by this XSLT style sheet will contain the line* `<link rel="stylesheet" type="text/css" href= "end_species.css"/>` *which is the standard way for an HTML document to call an external style sheet.*

✔ Tips

- It doesn't make sense to add the `link` element to an XML document. The `link` element has no intrinsic meaning in XML and won't have any effect.
- For more details on adding HTML tags to your output generated with XSLT, consult *Outputting HTML Code* on page 140.

```
code.xslt
<?xml version="1.0"?>
<xsl:stylesheet xmlns:xsl="http://www.w3.org/
1999/XSL/ Transform" version="1.0">
<xsl:template match="/"><html><head>
<title>Endangered Species</title>
<style>
<![CDATA[
<!--
endangered_species {display:block}
name {display:block;position:absolute;left:9}
intro {display:block;border:medium dotted red;
    padding:5;margin-top:5}
description {display:block;position:relative;
    left:125;width:340;border:thin solid red;
    padding:5;margin-top:5}
picture {display:block}
population {display:inline}
latin_name {display:inline}
more_info {display:inline}
-->
]]>
</style>
</head> <body bgcolor="white">
<xsl:apply-templates
select="endangered_species/animal"/>
</body></html>
</xsl:template>
```

Figure 13.15 *The style tag tells the HTML document that style information is coming. The* `<!--` *hides the style information from non-supportive browsers. Finally, the* `<![CDATA[` *bit keeps XML parsers from looking at or trying to analyze the style information.*

Using Internal Style Sheets

In HTML, it's perfectly legal to add a style sheet right inside the document. If you're generating an HTML document with XSLT, you'll have one extra step.

To generate an internal style sheet in an HTML document:

1. In your XSLT style sheet, in the `head` section of the HTML code (that is, presumably in the root template), type **<style>** to begin the internal style sheet.
2. Then type **<![CDATA[** to hide the style information from the XML parser. (This is not always necessary, but is a good precaution.)
3. Then type **<!--** to hide the style information from browsers who don't recognize it. (This is called *commenting out.*)
4. Type the selectors and properties as described in Chapter 14, *Layout with CSS* and Chapter 15, *Formatting Text with CSS.*
5. Next, type **-->** to finish the commenting that hides the styles from non-supportive browsers.
6. Type **]]>** to complete the CDATA section.
7. And last, but not least, type **</style>**.

✔ Tip

- Since internal style sheets can only be used to format the documents within which they reside, this technique is probably not very common. Instead, it often makes more sense to use external style sheets *(see page 182)* that you can apply to more than one document.

Using Internal Style Sheets

Applying Styles Locally

While applying styles to a particular tag within the body of an XML or HTML tag does not take advantage of the efficiency and power of style sheets, it can be a useful and relatively simple way to access the more advanced formatting that style sheets provide. Of course, this will only work in an HTML document (perhaps generated with XSLT).

To apply styles locally:

1. Within the tag that you want to format, type **style="**.
2. Type the selectors and properties as described in Chapter 14, *Layout with CSS* and Chapter 15, *Formatting Text with CSS.*
3. To create additional style definitions, type **;** (a semicolon) and repeat step 2.
4. Type the final **"** (quotation mark).

✔ Tips

- Be careful not to confuse the equals signs with the colon. Since they both assign values, it's easy to interchange them without noticing and cause unpleasant errors.
- Don't forget to separate multiple property definitions with a semicolon.
- Some folks end every property:value pair—including the last one—with a semicolon so that they don't have to remember to add it if they tack on more pairs. That's fine, but is not required.
- Don't forget to enclose your style definitions in straight quotation marks.
- You can create this tag with the `xsl:attribute` element as well *(see page 151).*

code.xslt

```
<xsl:template match="animal">
<p style="background:yellow;color:red;text-transform-capitalize;border:double medium green;font-weight:900;padding:0.5em">
<font size="+3" ><xsl:apply-templates select="name" /></font></p>
<p>The mighty <xsl:value-of select="name[@language='English']"/> faces numerous threats. For more information, check out the World Wildlife Federation's <a href="http://www.worldwildlife.org/species/species.cfm?"> pages</a>. </p><hr/>
</xsl:template>
```

Figure 13.16 *Note that when you apply styles locally, you use straight double quotation marks instead of curly brackets to surround the declarations (which continue to be separated with semicolons).*

14

Layout with CSS

Since XML elements have no default formatting, the first thing you should specify are the very basic layout settings.

Every element styled with CSS is enclosed in an invisible box. You can control the size, color, and spacing of the box, as well as the way it flows with respect to other objects on the page.

An element's box may be *block-level* (thereby generating a new paragraph) or *inline* (not generating a new paragraph).

There are three special areas of the box that you can control. First, surrounding the contents is a space called the *padding*. You can control the padding's width. Around the padding is the *border*. The border can be colored and thickened, and can also have texture. Around the border is a transparent space called the *margin*. Although you can't color the margin, you can change its width and height, thereby controlling the position of the elements on the page.

Some layout styles, especially percentage values, depend on an element's parent. A *parent* is the element that contains the current element. For example, an `animal` element might contain `subspecies` and `name` tags, and thus is a parent to them. However, if the `animal` is sectioned into `subspecies` tags and the `name` tags are enclosed in one of the `subspecies`, then the `subspecies` is the `name`'s parent (and the `animal` is the `subspecies`' parent). Finally, the `name` tag might contain a `language` element, and, in turn, be its parent.

Defining Elements as Block-Level or Inline

In HTML, every element is pre-defined as either *block-level* (that is, it starts at the beginning of a line, and the element that follows it starts at the beginning of a line) or *inline* (it appears within a line). With XML elements, you have to specify this characteristic explicitly.

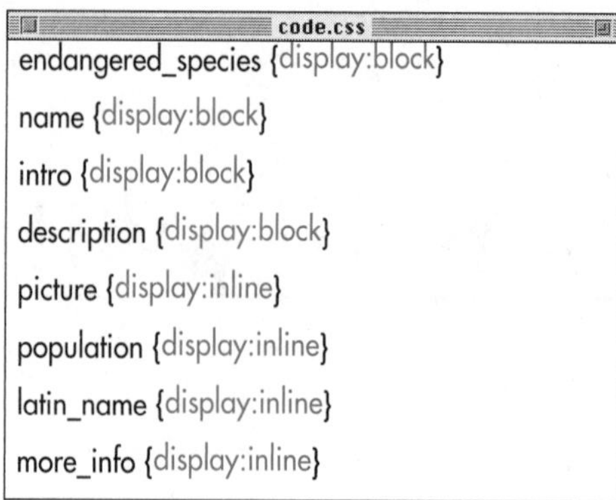

```
code.css
endangered_species {display:block}
name {display:block}
intro {display:block}
description {display:block}
picture {display:inline}
population {display:inline}
latin_name {display:inline}
more_info {display:inline}
```

Figure 14.1 *I want the* `name` *to appear on its own line, so I apply a* `block` *display style to it. Conversely, I want* `latin_name` *to appear inline.*

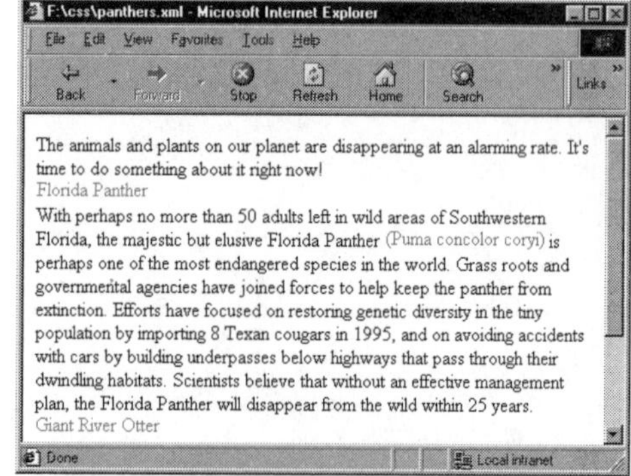

Figure 14.2 *The XML file now shows line breaks before and after each* `name` *element, but not around the* `latin_name` *elements that flow along with the rest of the text.*

To define an element as block-level or inline:

1. Type **display:**.
2. Type **block** to display the element as block-level (it will start on a new line, and the element that follows it will start on a new line).

   Or type **inline** to display the element as inline (it will appear directly after the preceding element). Inline is the default.

✔ Tips

- The default value for `display` is `inline`.
- Theoretically, there are less direct ways of making an element inline. You can use `display:compact`, `display:run-in` and `display:inline-table`. The only problem with these is that no browser currently supports.
- The `display` property can also be used to hide elements completely *(see page 191)* or to display them as list items *(see page 206)*. List items are block-level.
- Netscape 4.x does not support overriding the default display value for HTML elements.

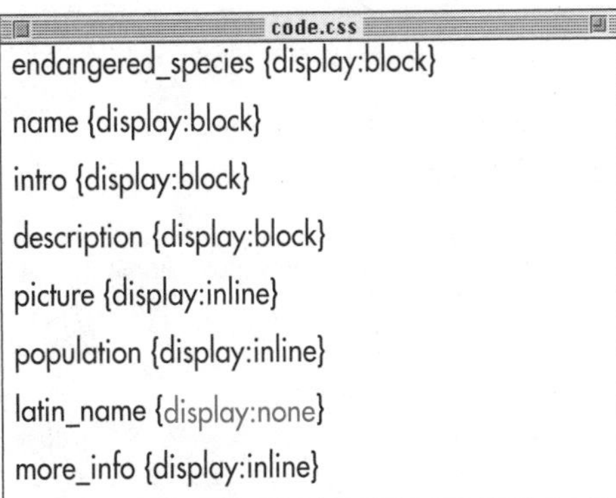
code.css
```
endangered_species {display:block}
name {display:block}
intro {display:block}
description {display:block}
picture {display:inline}
population {display:inline}
latin_name {display:none}
more_info {display:inline}
```

Figure 14.3 *You can hide elements completely by using* `display:none`. *They are taken completely out of the flow; no empty space marks where they should have been.*

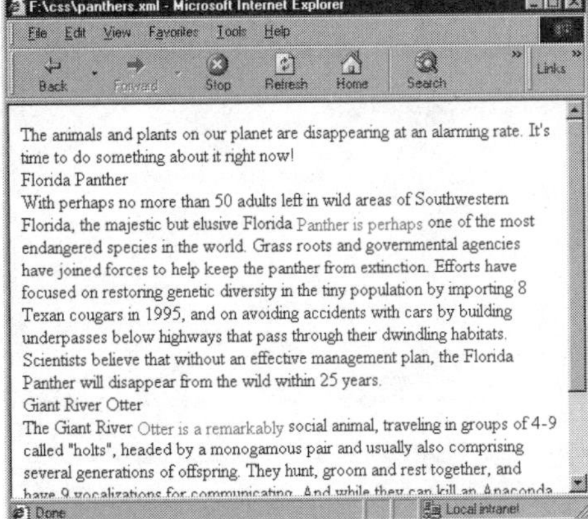

Figure 14.4 *The* `latin_name` *elements disappear.*

Hiding Elements Completely

The one CSS feature that begins to resemble the transformative qualities of XSLT is the ability to not display a given element.

To hide elements completely:

Type **display:none**.

✔ Tips

- If you use `display:none`, no trace remains of the hidden element in the browser window. There is no empty space.
- The `display:none` definition, combined with scripts, is ideal for hiding elements that belong to one of several versions contained in the same document.

Offsetting Elements In the Natural Flow

Each element has a natural location in a page's flow. Moving the element with respect to this original location is called *relative positioning*. The surrounding elements are not affected—at all.

To offset elements within the natural flow:

1. Type **position:relative;** (don't forget the semicolon).
2. Type **top**, **right**, **bottom**, or **left**.
3. Type **:v**, where *v* is the desired distance that you want to offset the element from its natural location, either as an absolute or relative value (10pt, or 2em, for example).
4. If desired, type **;** (semicolon) and repeat steps 2 and 3 for additional directions.

✔ Tips

- The "relative" in *relative positioning* refers to the element's original position, not the surrounding elements. You can't move an element with respect to other elements. Instead, you move it with respect to where it used to be. Yes, this is important!
- The other elements are not affected by the offsets—they flow with respect to the *original* containing box of the element, and may even be overlapped.
- To flow text around another element, that element must be positioned relatively.
- Including **position:relative** enables offsets. Without it, the offsets may not work. (In Explorer, they definitely won't.)

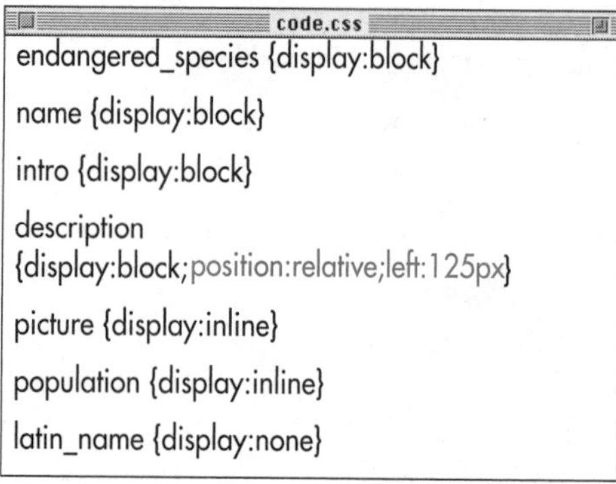

```
code.css
endangered_species {display:block}
name {display:block}
intro {display:block}
description
{display:block;position:relative;left:125px}
picture {display:inline}
population {display:inline}
latin_name {display:none}
```

Figure 14.5 *To indent the* `description` *paragraphs, I position them 125 pixels to the left of where they would normally appear.*

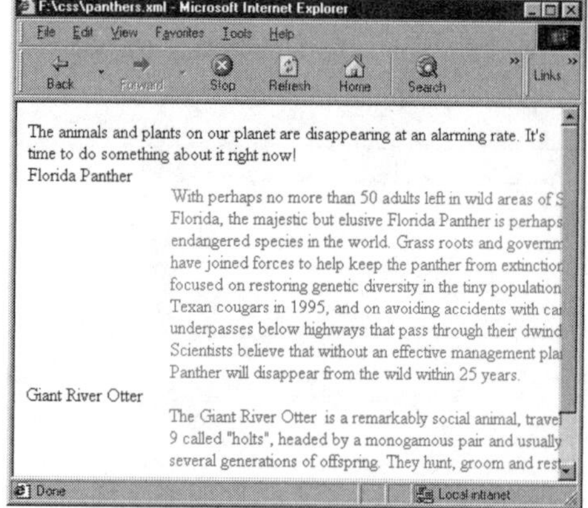

Figure 14.6 *The two* `description` *paragraphs are offset 125 pixels from their original left starting point.*

```
code.css
endangered_species {display:block}
name {display:block;position:absolute;left:9px}
intro {display:block}
description
{display:block;position:relative;left:125px}
picture {display:block}
population {display:inline}
latin_name {display:inline}
more_info {display:inline}
```

Figure 14.7 *I used a value of 9 pixels so that the* `name` *would be flush with the* `intro` *element, which by default is positioned nine pixels to the left of the browser window margin.*

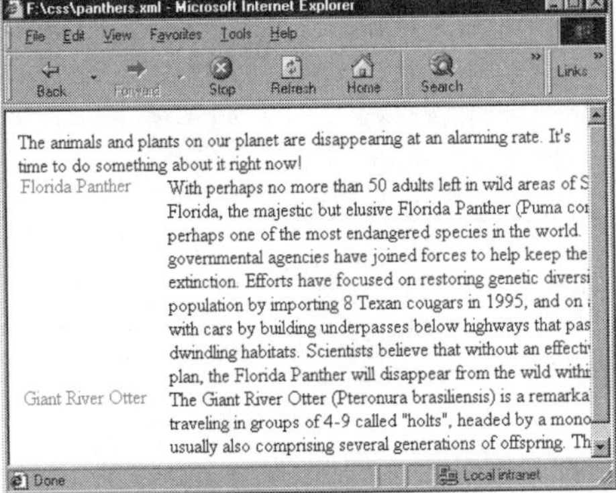

Figure 14.8 *The names are taken completely out of the flow of the document and thus, seemingly float along side the* `description` *paragraphs. Any offsets that are not explicitly set (the right, top, and bottom in this case), come from the position the element would have had if it had not been absolutely positioned.*

Positioning Elements Absolutely

The elements in a document generally flow in the order in which they appear. That is, if the `name` element comes before the `description` element, the name appears before the description. This is called the natural flow. You can take elements out of the natural flow—and position them *absolutely*—by specifying their precise position with respect to their parent element.

To absolutely position elements:

1. Type **position:absolute;** (don't forget the semicolon).
2. Type **top**, **right**, **bottom**, or **left**.
3. Type **:v**, where *v* is the desired distance that you want to offset the element from its parent element, either expressed as an absolute or relative value (10pt, or 2em, for example), or as a percentage of the parent element.
4. If desired, type **;** (semicolon) and repeat steps 2 and 3 for additional directions.

✓ Tips

- For more information on parent elements, see page 179.
- Because absolutely positioned elements are taken out of the flow of the document, they often overlap each other or other elements. (This is not always bad.)
- If you don't specify an offset for an absolutely positioned item, the item appears in its natural position (after the header in this example), but does not affect the flow of subsequent items.

Setting the Height or Width for an Element

You can set the height and width for most elements, including images, form elements, and even blocks of text. If you have several elements on a page that are the same size, you can set their height and width simultaneously. This information helps browsers set aside the proper amount of space necessary and thus view the rest of the page—generally, the text—more quickly.

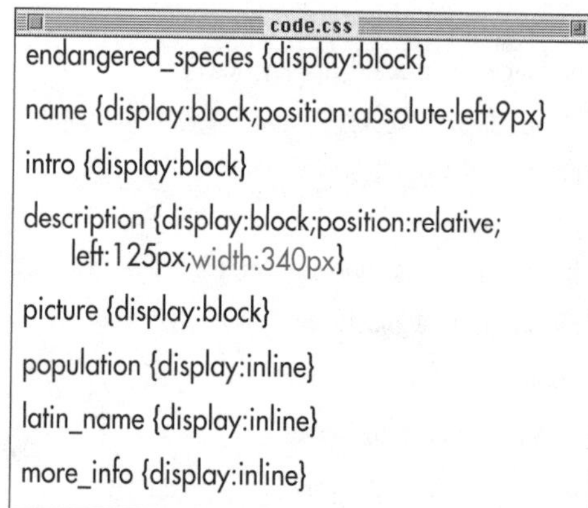

```
endangered_species {display:block}
name {display:block;position:absolute;left:9px}
intro {display:block}
description {display:block;position:relative;
    left:125px;width:340px}
picture {display:block}
population {display:inline}
latin_name {display:inline}
more_info {display:inline}
```

Figure 14.9 *You can keep paragraphs easy to read by setting the width property.*

To set the height or width for an element:

1. Type **width:w**, where *w* is the width of the element, and can be expressed either as an absolute value or as a percentage of the parent element.
2. Type **height:h**, where *h* is the height of the element, and can be expressed only as an absolute value.

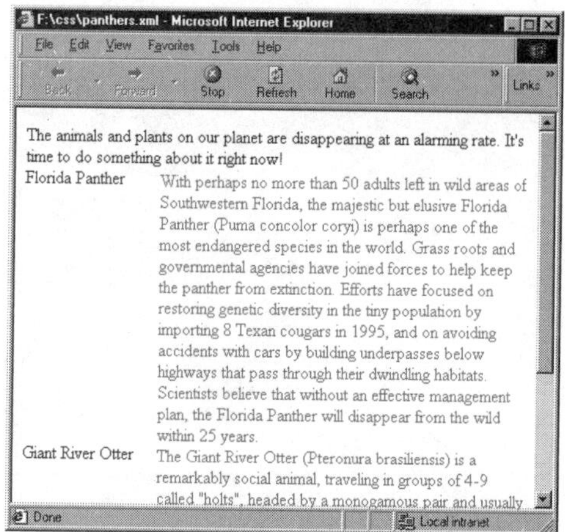

Figure 14.10 *The descriptions are narrower and more legible now that I've adjusted the width.*

✓ Tip

- Using a percentage value for the width property is a little tricky. If you are used to HTML, you might think 50% means half of the original image size. Not so. It means half of the width *of the parent element*— no matter what the original width of the image was. *(For more on parent elements, see page 179.)*

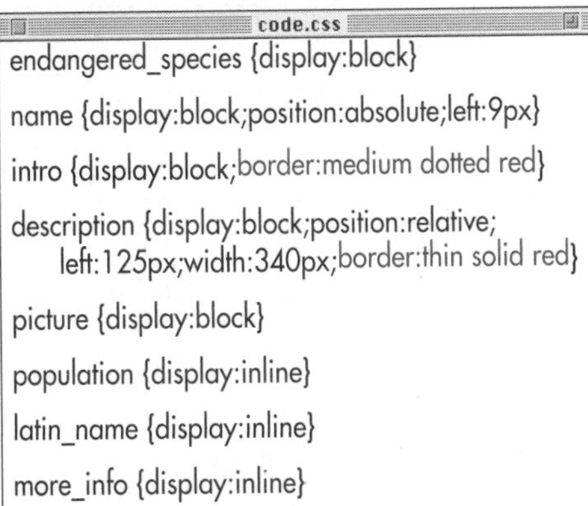

```
endangered_species {display:block}
name {display:block;position:absolute;left:9px}
intro {display:block;border:medium dotted red}
description {display:block;position:relative;
    left:125px;width:340px;border:thin solid red}
picture {display:block}
population {display:inline}
latin_name {display:inline}
more_info {display:inline}
```

Figure 14.11 *Only the border style is required. You can add the position, thickness, and color if desired.*

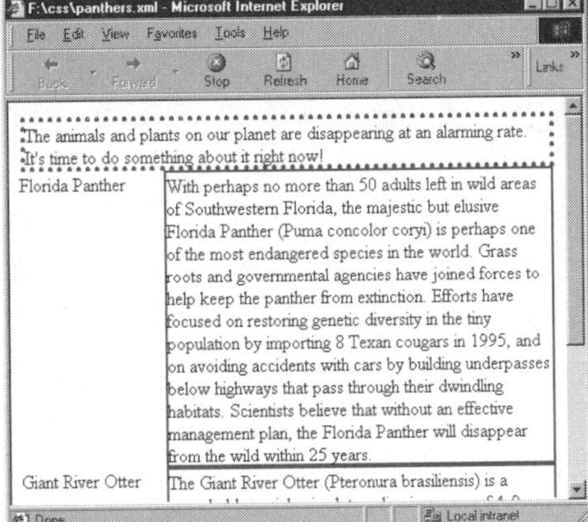

Figure 14.12 *Borders help to delimit blocks of text.*

Setting the Border

You can create a border around an element and then set its thickness, style, and color. If you've specified any padding *(see page 196)* the border encloses both the padding and the contents of the element.

To set the border:

1. Type **border**.
2. If desired, type **-top**, **-bottom**, **-left**, or **-right**, (with no space after **border**) to limit where the border should go.
3. Again, with no spaces, type **:** (a colon).
4. If desired, type **thin**, **medium**, **thick**, or an absolute value (like **4px**) to determine the thickness of the border. Medium is the default.
5. Type **none**, **dotted**, **dashed**, **solid**, **double**, **groove**, **ridge**, **inset**, or **outset** to determine the border style.
6. If desired, type **color**, where *color* is either one of the 16 color names *(see page 251)* or is expressed as described on page 200.

✔ Tips

- You can define any part of the border individually. For example, you can use **border-left-width:5** to set just the width of just the left border. Or use **border-color:red** to set just the color of all four sides. The twenty different properties are border-style (border-top-style, border-right-style, etc.), border-color (border-top-color, etc.), border-width (border-top-width, etc.), and border (border-top, etc.)
- If you don't set the color of the border, the browser uses the color specified for the element's contents *(see page 200)*.

Adding Padding Around an Element

Padding is just what it sounds like: extra space around the contents of an element but inside the border. Think of Santa Claus' belly—nicely padded, while being held in by his belt (the border). You can change the padding's thickness, but not its color or texture.

To add padding around an element:

1. Type **padding**.
2. If desired, type **-top**, **-bottom**, **-left**, or **-right**, (with no space after **padding**) to limit the padding to one side of the object.
3. Type **:x**, where *x* is the amount of desired space to be added, expressed in units or as a percentage of the parent element.

✔ Tips

- There are several shortcuts available for setting the padding values. You can use **padding: t r b l** to set the top, right, bottom, and left values at once, in that order (with just a space separating each value). Or **padding: v h** to set the top and bottom values (v) equally and the right and left values (h) equally. Or type **padding: t h b** to set the top value (t), the left and right values to a single value (h), and then the bottom value (b). Or type **padding: a**, where *a* is the value for all sides.
- The values may be expressed in absolute terms or as a percentage of the corresponding width in the parent element.

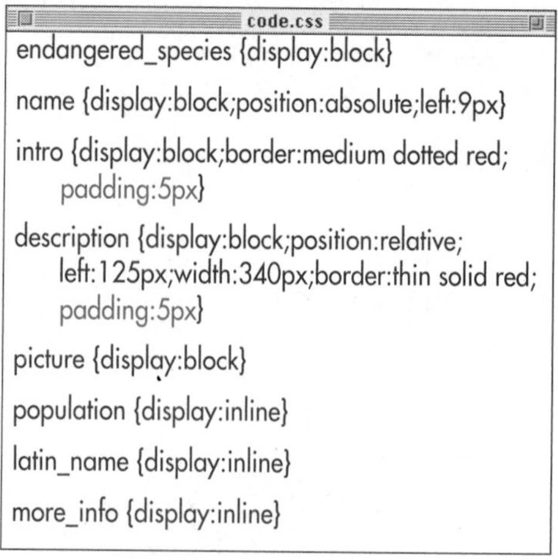

code.css

```
endangered_species {display:block}
name {display:block;position:absolute;left:9px}
intro {display:block;border:medium dotted red;
    padding:5px}
description {display:block;position:relative;
    left:125px;width:340px;border:thin solid red;
    padding:5px}
picture {display:block}
population {display:inline}
latin_name {display:inline}
more_info {display:inline}
```

Figure 14.13 *Padding puts a bit of space (5 pixels in this example) between the border and the text.*

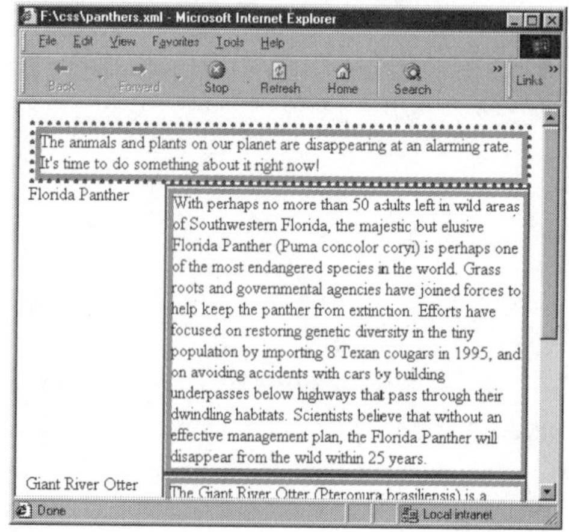

Figure 14.14 *The highlighted areas show the padding inside the border. (It doesn't have any color when viewed outside of this book.)*

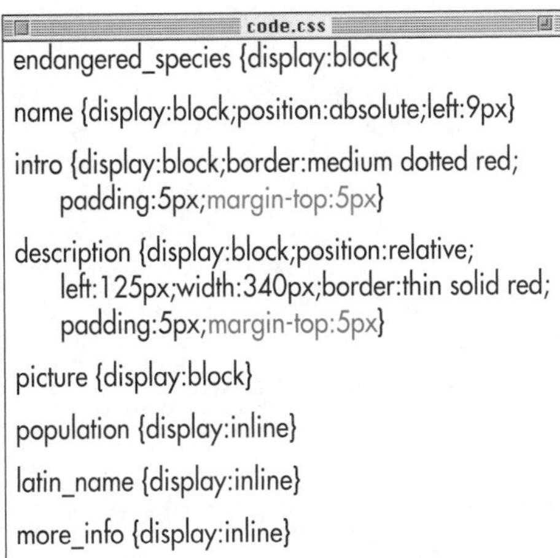

```
code.css
endangered_species {display:block}
name {display:block;position:absolute;left:9px}
intro {display:block;border:medium dotted red;
    padding:5px;margin-top:5px}
description {display:block;position:relative;
    left:125px;width:340px;border:thin solid red;
    padding:5px;margin-top:5px}
picture {display:block}
population {display:inline}
latin_name {display:inline}
more_info {display:inline}
```

Figure 14.15 *Set the margin on just one side of the box by adding top, bottom, left, or right to the word margin.*

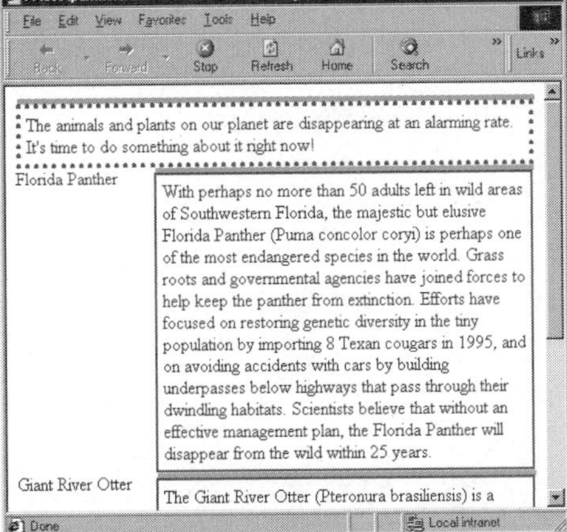

Figure 14.16 *Adding a margin increases the space between elements (not within them, as does padding).*

Setting the Margins around an Element

The margin is the amount of transparent space between one element and the next, in addition to and outside of any padding *(see page 196)* or border *(see page 195)* around the element.

To set an element's margins:

1. Type **margin**.
2. If desired, type **-top**, **-bottom**, **-left**, or **-right**, (with no space after **margin**) to limit where space should be added.
3. Type **:x**, where *x* is the amount of desired space to be added, expressed in units or as a percentage of the width of the corresponding value of the parent element.

✔ Tips

- You can also use **margin: t r b l** to set the top, right, bottom, and left values at once, in that order (with just a space separating each value). Or **margin: v h** to set the top and bottom values (v) equally and the right and left values (h) equally. Or type **margin: t h b** to set the top value (t), the left and right values to a single value (h), and then the bottom value (b). Last but not least, you can type **margin: a**, where *a* is the value to be used for all sides.
- The values may be expressed in absolute terms or as a percentage of the corresponding width in the parent element.
- Margin values for absolutely positioned boxes are specified with the offset properties—top, bottom, right, and left *(see page 193)*.

Wrapping Text around Elements

You can define your elements so that the rest of the document always wraps around them to the left or right, down both sides, or never at all.

To wrap elements around other elements:

1. Type **float:**.
2. Type **left** if you want the element on the left and the rest of the document to flow to its right.

   Or type **right** if you want the element on the right and the rest of the document to flow to its left.

✔ Tips

- Make sure you specify the width of a floated element.
- Remember, the direction you choose applies to the element you're floating, not to the elements that flow around it. When you **float: left**, the rest of the document flows to the right, and vice-versa.
- The trick to making things flow *between* elements is to always put the floating element directly before the content that should flow next to it.

code.xml

```
<description>With perhaps no more than
<population>50</population> adults left in wild
areas of Southwestern Florida, <blurb>"Without an
effective management plan, the Florida Panther will
disappear within 25 years."</blurb> the majestic
but elusive Florida Panther <latin_name>(Puma
concolor coryi) </latin_name>is perhaps one of the
most endangered species in the world. Grass roots
and governmental agencies have joined forces to
help keep the panther from extinction. Efforts have
```

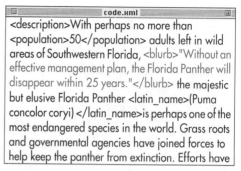

Figure 14.17 *I've added a side-bar type* `blurb` *element to my XML document.*

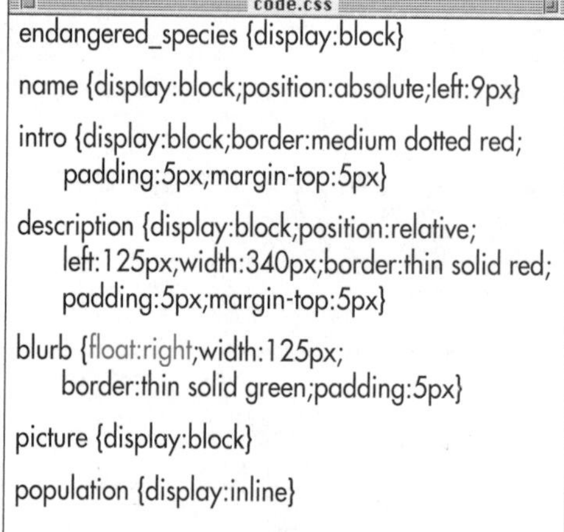

code.css

```
endangered_species {display:block}

name {display:block;position:absolute;left:9px}

intro {display:block;border:medium dotted red;
    padding:5px;margin-top:5px}

description {display:block;position:relative;
    left:125px;width:340px;border:thin solid red;
    padding:5px;margin-top:5px}

blurb {float:right;width:125px;
    border:thin solid green;padding:5px}

picture {display:block}

population {display:inline}
```

Figure 14.18 *Next we set the* `blurb` *to float to the right.*

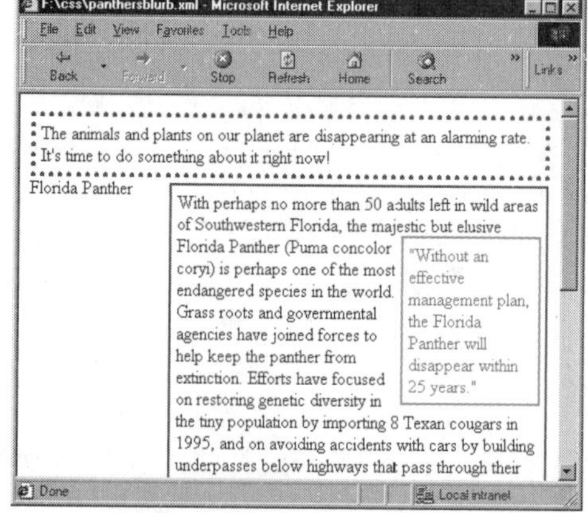

Figure 14.19 *Floating a block of text is a great way to call attention to it.*

```
code.css
endangered_species {display:block}
name {display:block;position:absolute;left:9px}
intro {display:block;border:medium dotted red;
    padding:5px;margin-top:5px}
description {display:block;position:relative;
    left:125px;width:340px;border:thin solid red;
    padding:5px;margin-top:5px}
blurb {float:right;clear:right;width:125px;
    border:thin solid green;padding:5px}
picture {display:block}
population {display:inline}
latin_name {display:inline}
more_info {display:inline}
```

Figure 14.20 *Add* `clear:right` *if you don't want text to flow to the left of an element.*

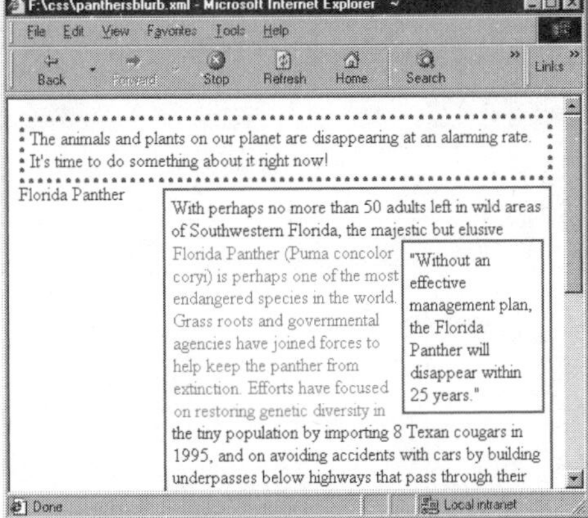

Figure 14.21 *Explorer 5 doesn't support the* `clear` *property. The highlighted text should not begin until below the end of the sidebar (starting where it currently says "the tiny population").*

Stopping Text Wrap

With style sheets you can mark a particular tag so that other elements (like text) cannot flow around it.

To stop text wrap:

1. Type **clear:**.
2. Type **left** to stop the flow until the left side is clear of all elements.

   Or type **right** to stop the flow until the right side is clear of elements.

   Or type **both** to stop the flow until both sides are clear.

   Or type **none** to continue the flow.

✔ Tips

- If you're like me and can never correctly answer 50-50 Trivial Pursuit questions like "Which hand is God holding out to Adam in the Sistine Chapel, his right or his left?", then perhaps this clarification will be useful: When you use **clear: right**, you mean you want to stop text flow *until the right is clear*. Confusingly, the result is that the left *looks clear*.
- The use of the clear style is analogous in HTML to the `br` tag with the `clear` attribute.
- Explorer 5 for Windows doesn't support the `clear` property **(Figure 14.21)**.

Changing the Foreground Color

You can change the color of any element, including horizontal lines, form elements, and tables.

To change the foreground color:

1. Type **color:**.
2. Type **colorname**, where *colorname* is one of the 16 predefined colors *(see page 251)*.

   Or type **#rrggbb**, where *rrggbb* is the hexadecimal representation of the desired color.

   Or type **rgb(r, g, b)**, where *r, g,* and *b* are integers from 0–255 that specify the amount of red, green, or blue, respectively, in the desired color.

   Or type **rgb(r%, g%, b%)**, where *r, g,* and *b* specify the percentage of red, green, and blue, respectively, in the desired color.

✓ Tips

- For more about specifying colors, see Appendix D, *Colors in Hex.*
- If you type a value for r, g, or b higher than 255 it will be replaced with 255. Similarly a percentage higher than 100% will be replaced with 100%.
- You can also use the `color` property to change the color of text *(see page 217).*
- Changing the foreground color of an image doesn't have any effect. (You'll have to do that in an image editing program.) You can, however, change the background color (that is, what will appear through transparent areas). For more information, consult *Changing the Background* on page 201.

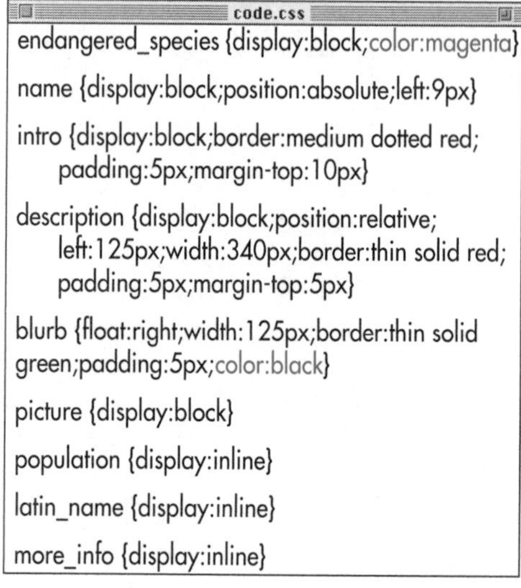

code.css

```
endangered_species {display:block;color:magenta}
name {display:block;position:absolute;left:9px}
intro {display:block;border:medium dotted red;
    padding:5px;margin-top:10px}
description {display:block;position:relative;
    left:125px;width:340px;border:thin solid red;
    padding:5px;margin-top:5px}
blurb {float:right;width:125px;border:thin solid
green;padding:5px;color:black}
picture {display:block}
population {display:inline}
latin_name {display:inline}
more_info {display:inline}
```

Figure 14.22 *Since the* `color` *property is inherited, and I've set it to magenta in the root* `endangered_species` *element, all of the elements will be magenta unless I specify otherwise (as I do for* `blurb`*, which will be black).*

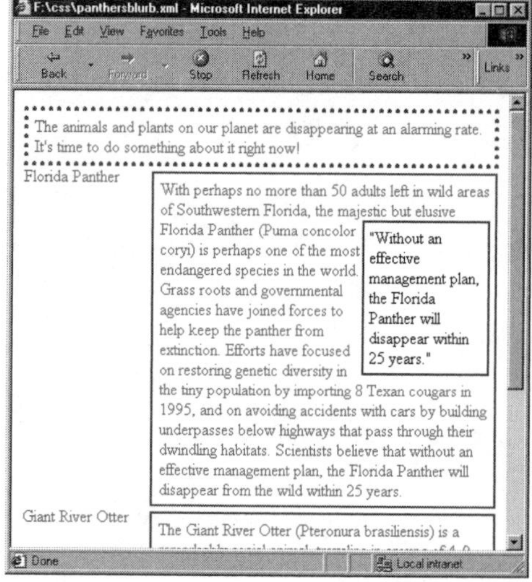

Figure 14.23 *You can also change the color of horizontal rules, form elements, and table cells in HTML.*

code.css

```
endangered_species {display:block;color:black;
    background:url(pantherlight.jpg)}
name {display:block;position:absolute;left:9px}
intro {display:block;border:medium dotted red;
    padding:5px;margin-top:10px}
description {display:block;position:relative;
    left:125px;width:340px;border:thin solid red;
    padding:5px;margin-top:5px}
blurb {float:right;width:125px;border:thin solid
    green;padding:5px;color:black}
picture {display:block}
population {display:inline}
```

Figure 14.24 *The filename of the image goes within parentheses, not quotation marks.*

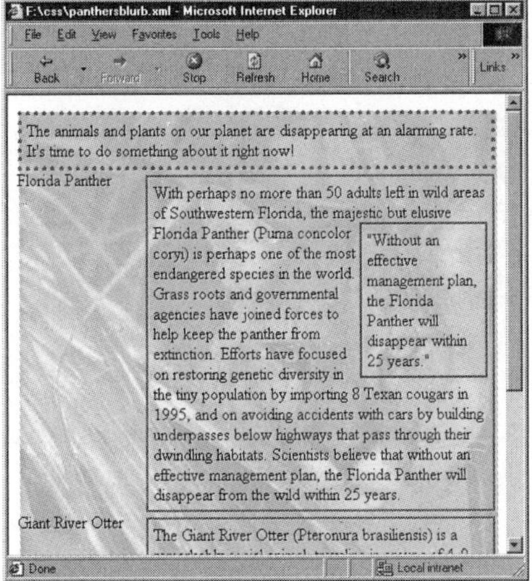

Figure 14.25 *If you are going to use a background image, make sure that it contrasts adequately with any text that is above it.*

Changing the Background

The background refers not to the background of the entire page, but to the background of a particular tag. In other words, you can change the background of any element—including images, form elements, and tables.

To change the background color or image:

1. Type **background:**.
2. If desired, type **transparent** or **color**, where *color* is specified as for the foreground *(see page 200)*.
3. If desired, type **url(image.gif)**, where *image.gif* is the image you wish to use for the background.

   If desired, type **repeat** to tile the image both horizontally and vertically, **repeat-x** to tile the image only horizontally, **repeat-y** to tile the image only vertically, or **no-repeat** to not tile the image.

   If desired, type **fixed** or **scroll** to determine whether the background should scroll along with the canvas.

   If desired, type **x y** to set the position of the background image, where *x* and *y* can be expressed as a percentage or as an absolute distance. Or use values of *top, center,* or *bottom* for *x* and *left, center,* and *right* for *y*.

✓ Tips

- You can apply a background image to a `picture` element to fake an embedded image. Use # in the selector to limit the image to a particular `picture` element.
- If you specify both a color and a URL for the background, the color will be used until the URL is loaded, and through any transparent portions of the image.

Positioning Elements in 3D

Earlier we discussed relative and absolute positioning, but both of these are solely concerned with two dimensions, height and width. CSS also lets you set the position of elements in the third dimension (depth), so that you can control any elements that may be overlapping.

To position elements in 3D:

1. Type **z-index:**.
2. Type **n**, where *n* is a number that indicates the element's level in the stack of objects.

✔ Tips

- The higher the z-index, the higher up the element will be in the stack.
- You can use both positive and negative values for z-index.

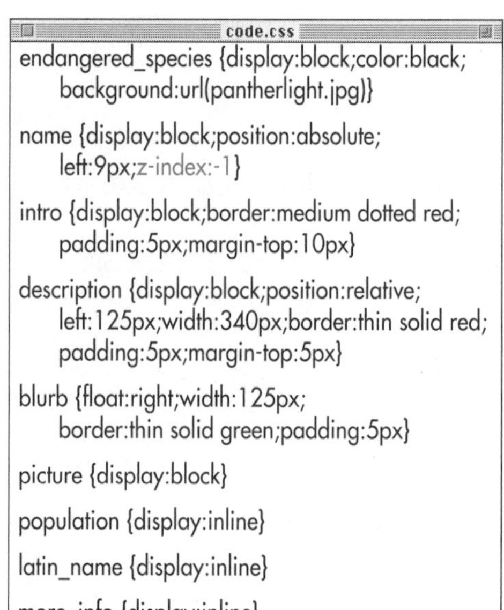

```
code.css
endangered_species {display:block;color:black;
    background:url(pantherlight.jpg)}
name {display:block;position:absolute;
    left:9px;z-index:-1}
intro {display:block;border:medium dotted red;
    padding:5px;margin-top:10px}
description {display:block;position:relative;
    left:125px;width:340px;border:thin solid red;
    padding:5px;margin-top:5px}
blurb {float:right;width:125px;
    border:thin solid green;padding:5px}
picture {display:block}
population {display:inline}
latin_name {display:inline}
more_info {display:inline}
```

Figure 14.26 *Use a negative number for the* `z-index` *to ensure that it will be the bottom-most element.*

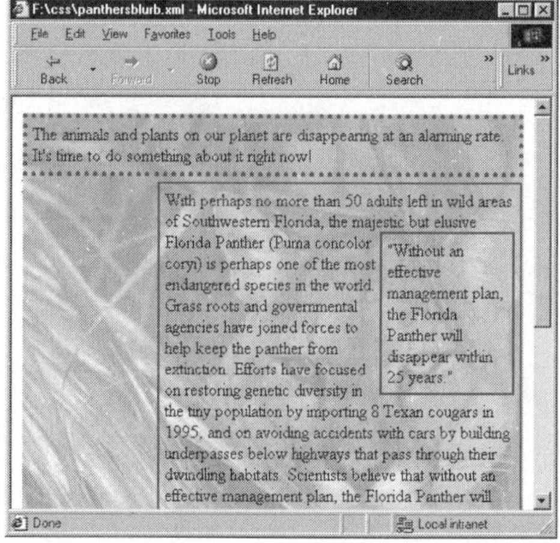

Figure 14.27 *The* Florida Panther *text is invisible now because it's below the background. (Compare with Figure 14.25 on page 201.)*

```
code.css
endangered_species {display:block}

name {display:none;position:absolute;left:9px;
z-index:-1}

intro {display:block;border:medium dotted
red;padding:5px;margin-top:5px}

description {display:inline;width:200px;
border:thin solid red;padding:5px;margin-
top:5px; vertical-align:top}

picture {display:none}

population {display:inline}

latin_name {display:inline}

more_info {display:inline}
```

Figure 14.28 *Because you can only vertically align inline elements, I've hidden the* `name` *and* `picture` *elements. Finally, I made the width of the* `description` *boxes narrower so that they'd fit on the screen next to each other.*

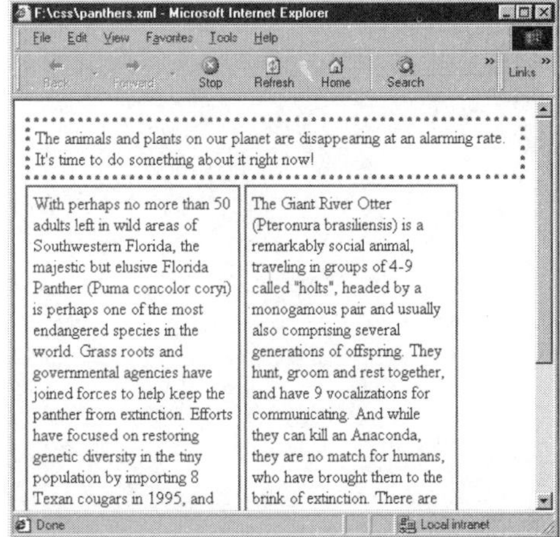

Figure 14.29 *These two* `description` *boxes (since nothing else separates them now that I've hidden all the other pieces) are aligned at their top edge.*

Aligning Elements Vertically

If you have elements on your page that you would like aligned in the same way, you can use the `vertical-align` property to display the element accordingly.

To position text:

1. Type **vertical-align:**
2. Type **baseline** to align the element's baseline with the parent's baseline.

   Or type **middle** to align the middle of the element with the middle of the parent.

   Or type **sub** to position the element as a subscript with respect to the parent.

   Or type **super** to position the element as a superscript with respect to the parent.

   Or type **text-top** to align the top of the element with the top of the parent.

   Or type **text-bottom** to align the bottom of the element with the bottom of the parent.

   Or type **top** to align the top of the element with the top of the tallest element on the line.

   Or type **bottom** to align the bottom of the element to the bottom of the lowest element on the line.

   Or type a percentage of the line height of the element, which may be positive or negative.

✔ Tip

- You can only vertically align inline elements. (It wouldn't make sense to vertically align elements that start on separate lines.)

Determining Where Overflow Should Go

If you make an element's box smaller than its contents with the height and width properties *(see page 194)*, the excess content has to go somewhere. You can decide where it should go with the overflow property.

To determine where overflow should go:

1. Type **overflow:**.
2. Type **visible** to expand the element box so that its contents fit. This is the default option.

   Or type **hidden** to hide any contents that don't fit in the element box.

   Or type **scroll** to add scroll bars to the element so that the visitor can access the overflow if they so desire.

✔ Tip

- If you don't specify the overflow property, excess content will flow below (but not to the right of) the element's box. This is one of the reasons that assigning a height to text sometimes seems like it has no effect.

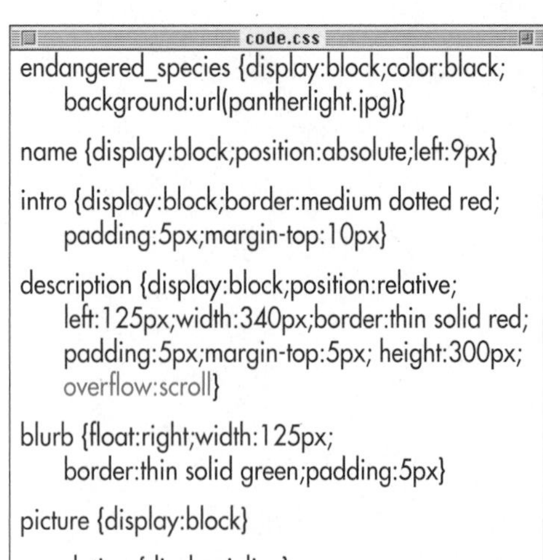

```
code.css
endangered_species {display:block;color:black;
    background:url(pantherlight.jpg)}

name {display:block;position:absolute;left:9px}

intro {display:block;border:medium dotted red;
    padding:5px;margin-top:10px}

description {display:block;position:relative;
    left:125px;width:340px;border:thin solid red;
    padding:5px;margin-top:5px; height:300px;
    overflow:scroll}

blurb {float:right;width:125px;
    border:thin solid green;padding:5px}

picture {display:block}

population {display:inline}
```

Figure 14.30 *It only makes sense to apply the* `overflow` *property where you've restricted the height.*

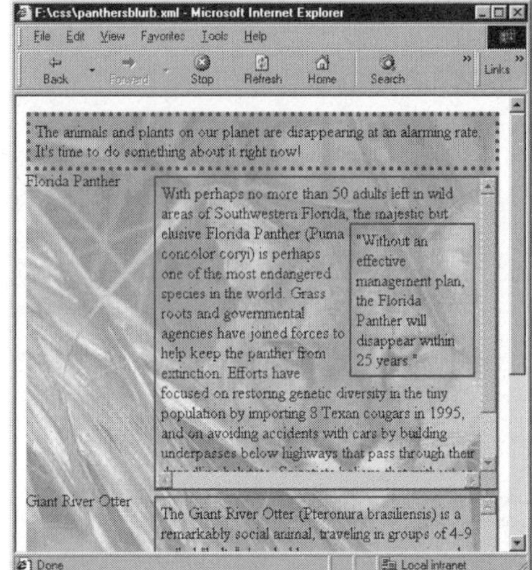

Figure 14.31 *If you restrict the height of a text box so that not all of the text is visible, one option is to provide scroll bars in order to give access to the rest of the text.*

```
code.css
endangered_species {display:block;color:black;
    background:url(pantherlight.jpg)}

name {display:block;position:absolute;left:9;
    background:white;clip:rect(5 80 15 20)}

intro {display:block;border:medium dotted red;
    padding:5;margin-top:10}

description {display:block;position:relative;
    left: 125;width:340;border:thin solid red;
    padding:5; margin-top:5;height:300;
    overflow:scroll}

blurb {float:right;width:125;
    border:thin solid green;padding:5;color:black}

picture {display:block}
```

Figure 14.32 *I also changed the background of the* `name` *element to* white *so it would be easier to see the effect of the* `clip` *property.*

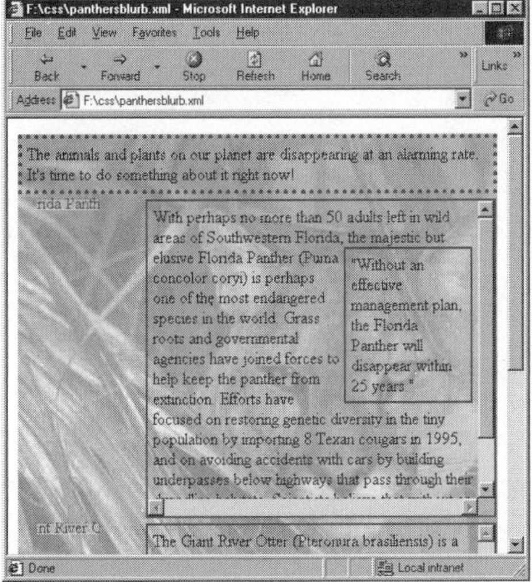

Figure 14.33 *I still haven't found a good use for clip. Suggestions welcome!*

Clipping an Element

You can create a window that only reveals a particular section of the element. Currently, the window must be a rectangle, but the idea is that other shapes will be available in future revisions of CSS.

To clip an element:

1. Type **clip:rect(**.
2. Type **t r b l**, where *t*, *r*, *b*, and *l* are the top, right, bottom, and left coordinates of the rectangular portion of the element that you want to display.
3. Type the final **)**.

✓ Tips

- Presently, an element has to be positioned absolutely *(see page 193)* before you can clip it.
- Remember not to add commas between the offset values.
- The offset values can be absolute (3px) or relative (3em).
- Clipping does not just affect the element's content. It also hides padding and borders.
- Clipping is currently under review by the World Wide Web Consortium and may have changed by the time you read this.

Setting List Properties

There are several bullet styles for unordered lists, and several number styles for numbered lists. You can set these styles globally with the list-style property.

To set list properties:

1. Type **display:list-item;** to indicate that the element should be displayed as a list (not block or inline).
2. Next type **list-style:**.
3. To set the list item property to a solid, round circle, type **disc**.

   Or type **circle** to use an empty, round circle.

   Or type **square** to use a solid square.

   Or type **decimal** to use arabic numerals (1, 2, 3, etc.).

   Or type **lower-alpha** to use lowercase letters (a, b, c, etc.).

   Or type **upper-alpha** to use uppercase letters (A, B, C, etc.).

   Or type **lower-roman** to use lowercase Roman numerals (i, ii, iii, etc.).

   Or type **upper-roman** to use uppercase Roman numerals (I, II, III, etc.).

   Or type **url(image.gif)**, where *image.gif* is the URL of the image that you want to use as a marker for your lists.
4. If desired, type **outside** to hang the marker to the left of the list items. Type **inside** to align the marker flush left together with all the other lines in the list item.

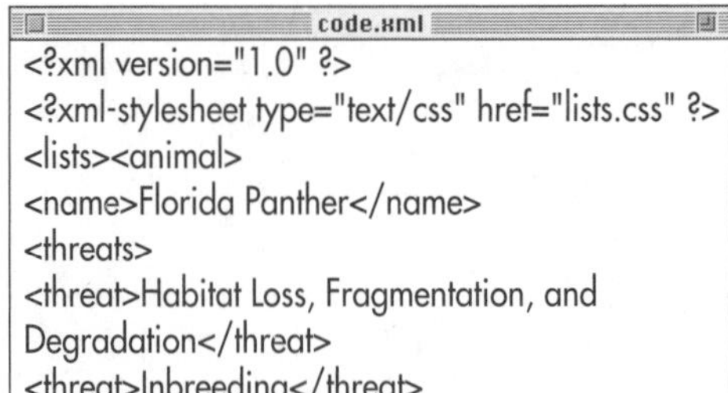

```
code.xml
<?xml version="1.0" ?>
<?xml-stylesheet type="text/css" href="lists.css" ?>
<lists><animal>
<name>Florida Panther</name>
<threats>
<threat>Habitat Loss, Fragmentation, and
Degradation</threat>
<threat>Inbreeding</threat>
```

Figure 14.34 *Here's the XML code for the lists.*

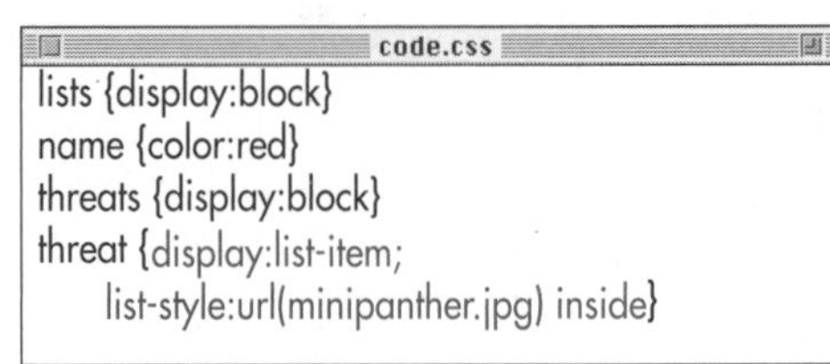

```
code.css
lists {display:block}
name {color:red}
threats {display:block}
threat {display:list-item;
    list-style:url(minipanther.jpg) inside}
```

Figure 14.35 *We have to define the* `threat` *element to display as a list item, and then we give it an image (for bullets) and specify that they be shown inside the text.*

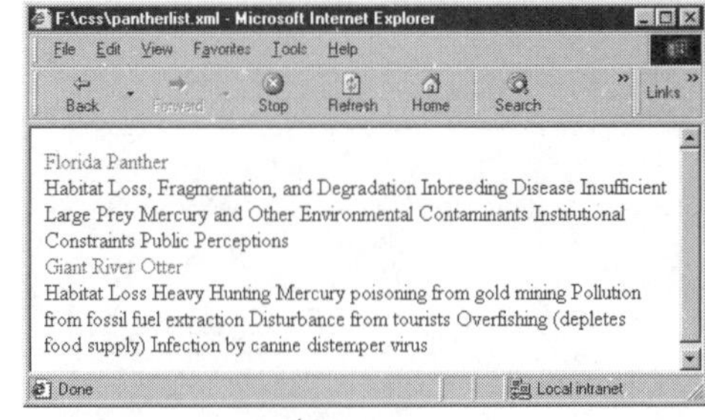

Figure 14.36 *IE doesn't support the* `display:list-item` *rule and thus cannot display lists properly in an XML document (cf. Figure 14.38 on page 207).*

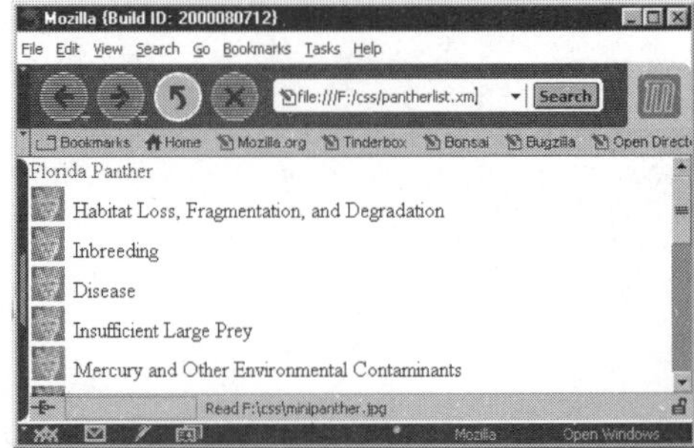

Figure 14.37 *This early version of Netscape 6 supports image bullets but strangely enough, not regular ones.*

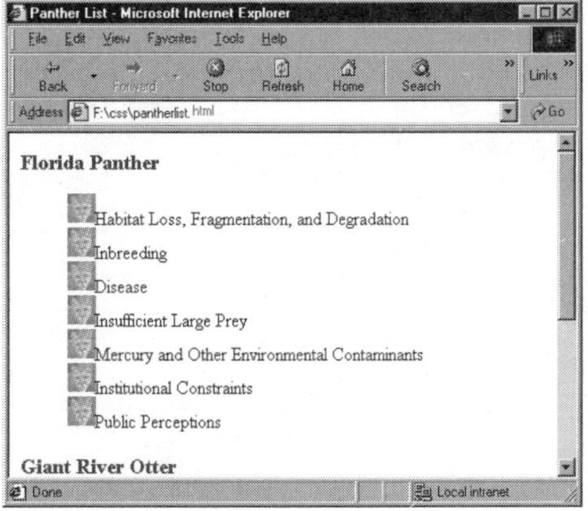

Figure 14.38 *Explorer doesn't have any problem with the* `list-style` *property—as long as you apply it to the* `li` *items in an HTML document.*

✓ Tips

- Explorer *does* support fancy lists in HTML documents **(Figure 14.38)**. But since it doesn't currently support **display:list-item**, it can't understand what to apply the properties to in an XML document.
- The `outside` value won't create hanging indents properly if you use big images for bullets. Until it does, `inside` looks better.
- The `list-style` property can be divided into `list-style-type`, `list-style-image`, and `list-style-position`. These might be useful when overriding individual aspects of inherited list styles. In most cases, however, it's easier to just use `list-style`.

Specifying Page Breaks

At some point, your visitors may decide to print your Web page. Most browsers will automatically adjust the contents on a page in order to best fit the paper size the visitor has chosen in the Page Setup dialog box. With CSS2 you can specify exactly where you want the page to break when your visitor goes to print it out.

To specify a page break after a given tag:

Type **page-break-after:always**.

To specify a page break before a given tag:

Type **page-break-before:always**.

To remove page breaks:

Type **page-break-after:auto** or **page-break-before:auto**.

```
code.css
lists {display:block}
animal {page-break-after:always}
name {color:red}
threats {display:block}
threat {display:list-item;
    list-style:url(minipanther.jpg) inside}
```

Figure 14.39 *After each* `animal` *element, there should be a page break.*

Formatting Text with CSS

Styles offer many more possibilities than HTML tags and extensions ever did. Now you can change the size, weight, slant, line height, foreground and background color, spacing, and alignment of text, decide whether it should be underlined, overlined, struck through, or blinking, and convert it to all uppercase, all lowercase, or small-caps.

Remember that using CSS on an XML document is like painting on a blank slate. Since XML elements, unlike HTML tags, have no default formatting, you'll have to define *every* characteristic you want the text to have.

Choosing a Font Family

Because not everyone has the same set of fonts, the `font-family` property has a special characteristic: you can specify more than one font, in case the first is not available in your visitor's system. You can also have a last ditch attempt at controlling the display in the visitor's system by specifying a generic font style like *serif* or *monospace.*

To set the font family:

1. Type **font-family:familyname**, where *familyname* is your first choice of font.
2. If desired, type **, familyname2**, where *familyname2* is your second font choice. Separate each choice with a comma.
3. Repeat step 2 as desired.

✔ Tips

- It's a good idea to specify at least two font choices, one of them a common font, so that you maintain some control over how the document is displayed. Common fonts in Macintosh systems are Times and Palatino for serif fonts and Helvetica for sans-serif. Most Windows systems contain Times as well, but Arial is more prevalent as a sans-serif choice.
- You can use the following generic font names—**serif**, **sans-serif**, **cursive**, **fantasy**, and **monospace**—as a last ditch attempt to influence which font is used for display.
- You can set the font family, font size, and line height all at once, using the general font style *(see page 216)*.
- Child elements inherit the `font-family` from their parent elements.
- Quotes (either single or double) are not required, but may help some browsers understand font names with spaces.

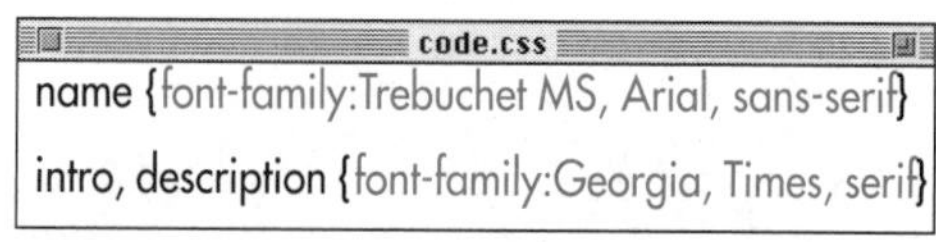

```
code.css
name {font-family:Trebuchet MS, Arial, sans-serif}
intro, description {font-family:Georgia, Times, serif}
```

Figure 15.1 *Notice how I apply the Georgia font family to both the* `intro` *and the* `description` *elements. (For more details about complex selectors, see page 180.)*

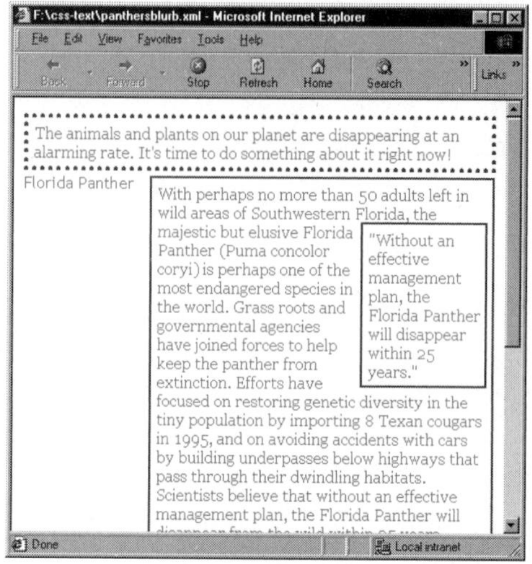

Figure 15.2 *Notice that Georgia is also used for the blurb. That's because a font family is inherited from an element's parent.*

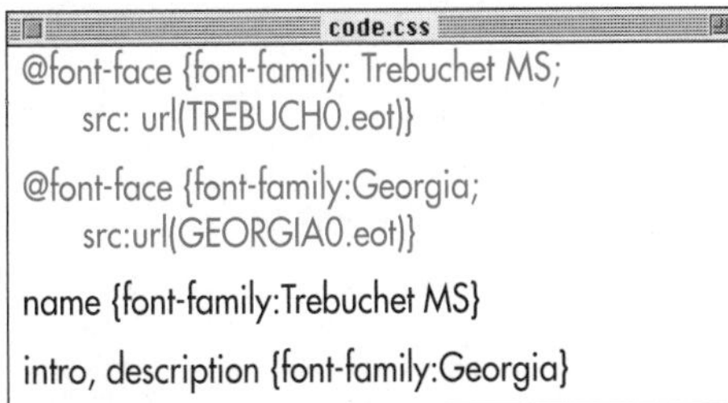

```
@font-face {font-family: Trebuchet MS;
    src: url(TREBUCH0.eot)}

@font-face {font-family:Georgia;
    src:url(GEORGIA0.eot)}

name {font-family:Trebuchet MS}

intro, description {font-family:Georgia}
```

Figure 15.3 *Be careful to use the exact name of the font as well as the path to the embedded file.*

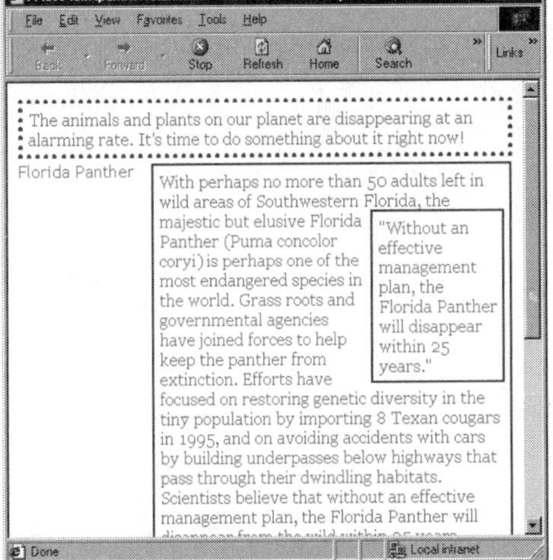

Figure 15.4 *The proper fonts will be displayed even on systems that don't have Trebuchet or Georgia installed.*

Embedding Fonts on a Page

You can choose whatever font you want, but if your visitors don't have it installed on their computers, they won't be able to view it. One solution is to embed a font in a page.

To embed fonts on a page:

1. Type **@font-face {font-family:**.
2. Type the full name of the font that you wish to embed.
3. Type **; src:url(**.
4. Type the URL of the font.
5. Type **)}**.
6. Use the font name from step 2 in other style definitions, as desired.

✔ Tips

- You can't just choose any font file as the source for an embedded font (in step 4). You have to use a special format of the font. Internet Explorer requires fonts to be in the .eot format. You can convert your installed fonts into .eot with a program called WEFT. For more information, see *www.microsoft.com/typography/web/embedding/*.
- Bitstream has developed WebFont Maker that allows you to embed fonts in Web pages for viewing in both Netscape and Explorer. However, in my tests, it didn't look so great in Explorer for Windows (and it doesn't work at all in Explorer for Mac). See *http://www.bitstream.com/webfont/* for more details.
- Again, quotation marks are not required around font names, although they may help some browsers understand font names that contain spaces or weird punctuation.

Creating Italics

There are two ways to apply italic formatting. Either choose Garamond Italic or Palatino Italic (or whatever) for the font *(see page 210)*, or first choose the font (Garamond or Palatino) and then choose Italics. If all of your text in a given font should be in italics, the first method is simpler. But if you want to use the font in both its Roman and italic forms, the second method, described here, will prove more flexible.

To create italics:

1. Type **font-style:**.
2. Type **oblique** for oblique text, or **italic** for italic text.

To remove italics:

1. Type **font-style:**.
2. Type **normal**.

✔ Tips

- It used to be that the italic version of a font was created by a font designer from scratch, while the oblique version was created by the computer, on the fly. This distinction has blurred somewhat, but generally holds.
- If you set the font style as italic and there is no italic style available, the browser should try to display the text in oblique style.
- One reason you might want to remove italics is to emphasize some text in a paragraph that has inherited italic formatting from a parent tag. For information on inherited styles, see page 179.
- Child elements inherit the `font-style` property from their parent elements.

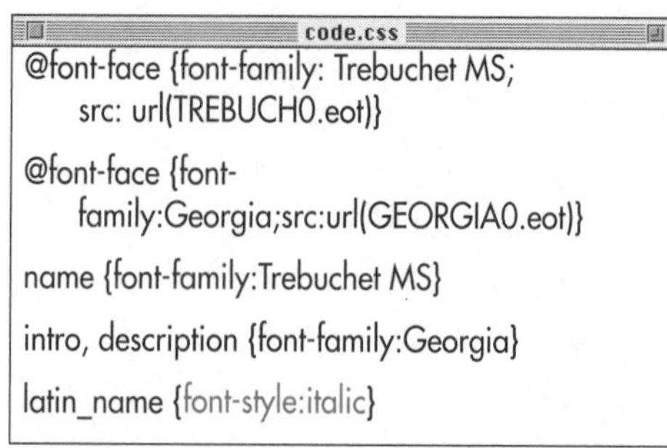

```
code.css
@font-face {font-family: Trebuchet MS;
    src: url(TREBUCHO.eot)}
@font-face {font-
    family:Georgia;src:url(GEORGIA0.eot)}
name {font-family:Trebuchet MS}
intro, description {font-family:Georgia}
latin_name {font-style:italic}
```

Figure 15.5 *I want to display all the* `latin_name` *elements in italics.*

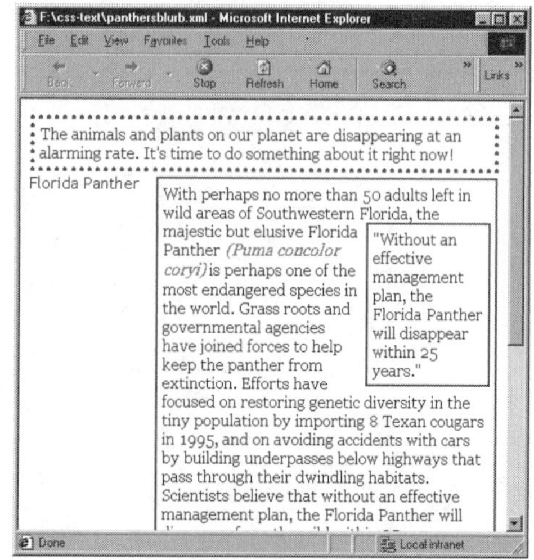

Figure 15.6 *Italics are a great way to emphasize a bit of text, especially words in foreign languages.*

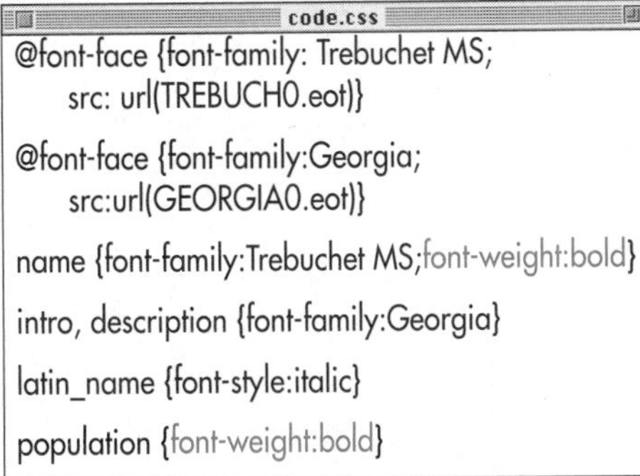

```
code.css
@font-face {font-family: Trebuchet MS;
    src: url(TREBUCH0.eot)}
@font-face {font-family:Georgia;
    src:url(GEORGIA0.eot)}
name {font-family:Trebuchet MS;font-weight:bold}
intro, description {font-family:Georgia}
latin_name {font-style:italic}
population {font-weight:bold}
```

Figure 15.7 *Another common way to emphasize text is to display it in bold face.*

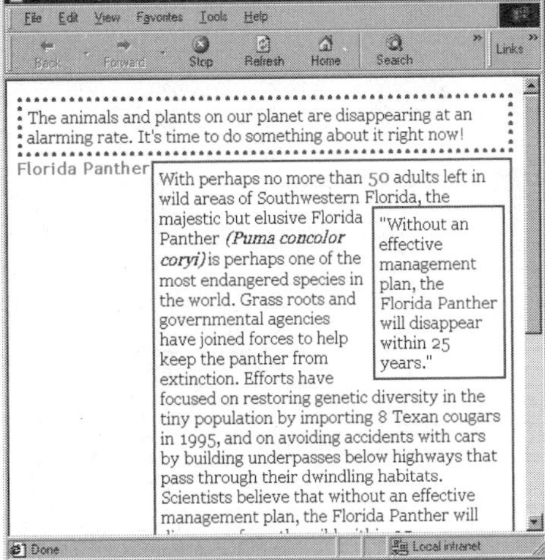

Figure 15.8 *Now the* `name` *(Florida Panther) and* `population` *(50) elements are much more prominent and thus, easier to read.*

Applying Bold Formatting

Bold formatting is probably the most common and effective way to make text stand out. Style sheets gives you a range of options with bold text, providing relative values or allowing you to get rid of it altogether.

To apply bold formatting:

1. Type **font-weight:**.
2. Type **bold** to give an average bold weight to the text.
3. Or type **bolder** or **lighter** to use a value relative to the current weight.
4. Or type a multiple of **100** between 100 and 900, where 400 represents book weight and 700 represents bold.

To remove bold formatting:

1. Type **font-weight:**.
2. Type **normal**.

✔ Tips

- Since the way weights are defined varies from font to font, the values may not be relative from font to font. They are designed to be relative *within* a given font family.
- If the font family has fewer than nine weights, or if they are concentrated on one end of the scale, it is possible that some numeric values correspond to the same font weight.
- Since child elements inherit the `font-weight` property from their parents, you may want to use **font-weight:normal** to keep children from becoming too bold, so to speak.

Setting the Font Size

You can set the font size of text marked with a particular element by specifying an exact size in points or pixels, or with descriptive words, or by specifying a relative size, with respect to a parent element.

To set the font size:

1. Type **font-size:**.
2. Type an absolute font size: **xx-small**, **x-small**, **small**, **medium**, **large**, **x-large**, or **xx-large**.

   Or type a relative font size: **larger** or **smaller**.

   Or type an exact size: say, **12pt** or **15px**.

   Or type a percentage relative to any parent style: e.g., **150%**.

✔ Tips

- There should not be any spaces between the number and the unit.
- The relative values (larger, smaller, and the percentage) are computed with respect to the size of the parent element.
- You can set the font size together with other font values *(see page 216)*.
- Child elements inherit the `font-size` property from their parent elements.

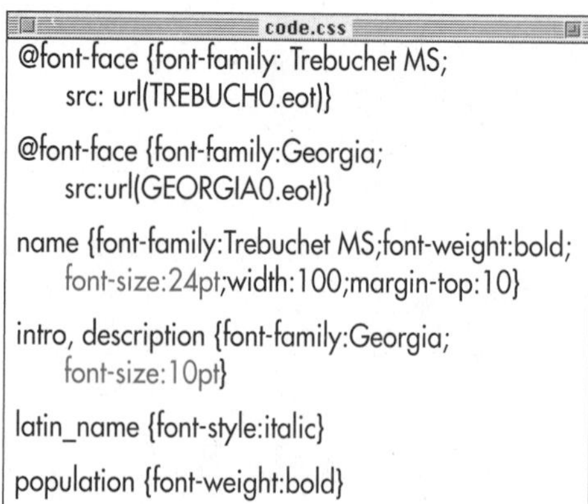

code.css

```
@font-face {font-family: Trebuchet MS;
    src: url(TREBUCHO.eot)}

@font-face {font-family:Georgia;
    src:url(GEORGIA0.eot)}

name {font-family:Trebuchet MS;font-weight:bold;
    font-size:24pt;width:100;margin-top:10}

intro, description {font-family:Georgia;
    font-size:10pt}

latin_name {font-style:italic}

population {font-weight:bold}
```

Figure 15.9 *In addition to setting the font size of the* `name`, `intro`, *and* `description` *elements, note that I also set the width and top margin of the* `name` *element (see page 194 and page 197 for details) to keep the name from overlapping the body text or bumping into the intro. It's not uncommon to have to adjust layout elements when you change the size of your text.*

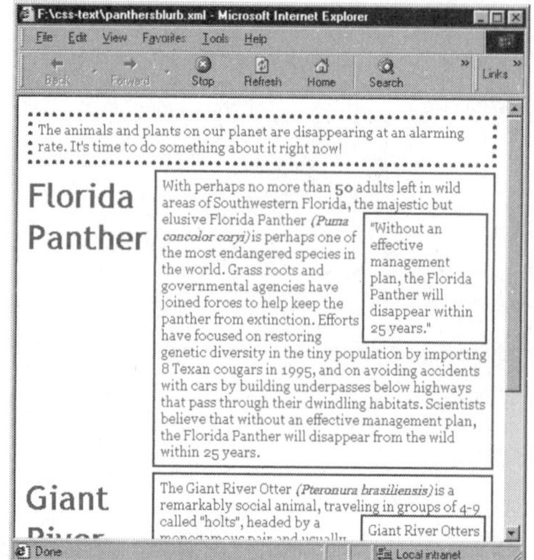

Figure 15.10 *The* `name` *element really stands out now.*

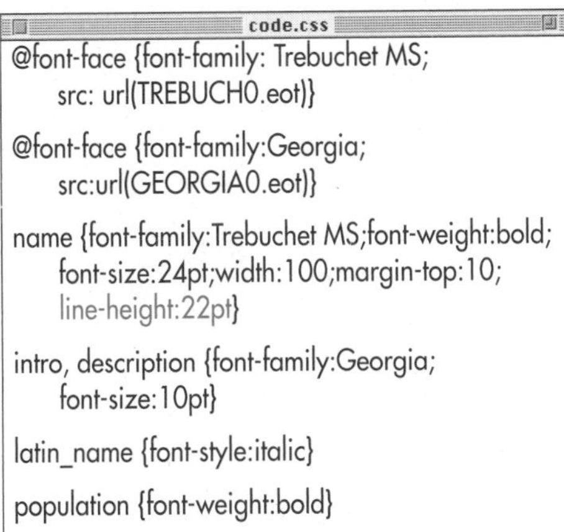

```
code.css
@font-face {font-family: Trebuchet MS;
    src: url(TREBUCH0.eot)}

@font-face {font-family:Georgia;
    src:url(GEORGIA0.eot)}

name {font-family:Trebuchet MS;font-weight:bold;
    font-size:24pt;width:100;margin-top:10;
    line-height:22pt}

intro, description {font-family:Georgia;
    font-size:10pt}

latin_name {font-style:italic}

population {font-weight:bold}
```

Figure 15.11 *The* `line-height` *property determines the amount of leading, or space between lines.*

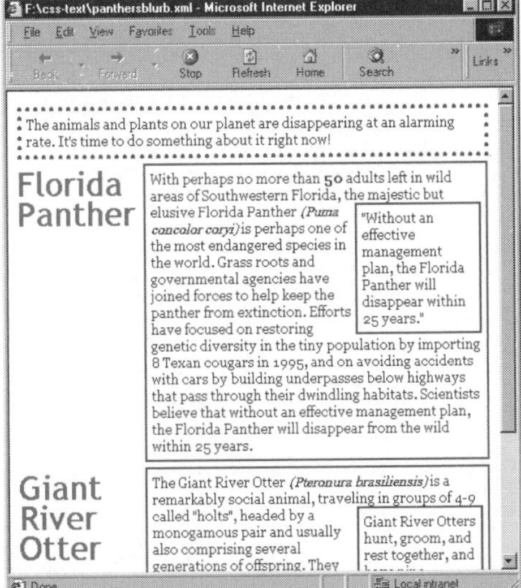

Figure 15.12 *Large sized text often looks better with a tighter line height. (Compare with Figure 15.10 on page 214.)*

Setting the Line Height

Line height refers to a paragraph's leading, that is, the amount of space between each line in a paragraph. Using a large line height can sometimes make your body text easier to read. A small line height for headers (with more than one line) often makes them look classier.

To set the line height:

1. Type **line-height:**.
2. Type **n**, where *n* is a number that will be multiplied by the font-size to obtain the desired line height.

   Or type **p%**, where *p* is a percentage of the font size.

   Or type **a**, where *a* is an absolute value in points, pixels, or whatever.

✔ Tips

- You can specify the line height together with the font family, size, weight, style, and variant, as described on page 216.
- If you use a number to determine the line height, this factor is inherited by all child items. If you use a percentage, only the resulting size is inherited, not the percentage factor.
- The `line-height` property is inherited by child elements from their parent elements.

Setting All Font Values at Once

You can set the font style, weight, variant, size, line height, and family all at once.

To set all font values at once:

1. Type **font:**.
2. If desired, type **normal**, **oblique**, or **italic** to set the font-style *(see page 212)*.
3. If desired, type **normal**, **bold**, **bolder**, **lighter**, or a multiple of **100** (up to 900) to set the font-weight *(see page 213)*.
4. If desired, type **small-caps** to use a small cap font variant *(see page 222)*.
5. Type the desired font size, using the values given in step 2 on page 214.
6. If desired, type **/line-height**, where *line-height* is expressed in the same form as the font size *(see page 215)*.
7. Type a space followed by the desired font family or families, in order of preference, separated by commas, as described on page 210.

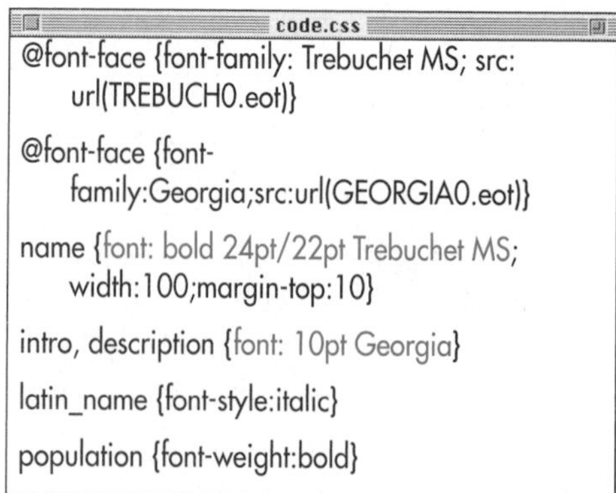

code.css

```
@font-face {font-family: Trebuchet MS; src:
    url(TREBUCH0.eot)}

@font-face {font-
    family:Georgia;src:url(GEORGIA0.eot)}

name {font: bold 24pt/22pt Trebuchet MS;
    width:100;margin-top:10}

intro, description {font: 10pt Georgia}

latin_name {font-style:italic}

population {font-weight:bold}
```

Figure 15.13 *You must always specify at least the font size and the font family in the* `font` *property. All the other property values are optional (and their defaults are assumed if they are not explicitly set).*

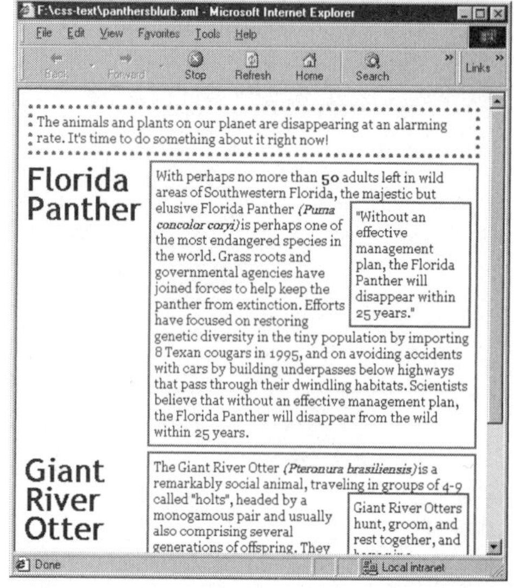

Figure 15.14 *The result is exactly the same as if you had defined each characteristic separately (cf. Figure 15.12 on page 215).*

✔ Tips

- You can also set each option separately. See the page referenced with that step.
- The order I've outlined above is required by the official specifications and by Netscape. Explorer doesn't seem to care.
- Only the size and family are required. All the other definitions may be omitted—in which case they'll be set to their default values.
- You can only set the line height with `font` if you have also set the font size.
- The `font` property is inherited by child elements from their parent elements.

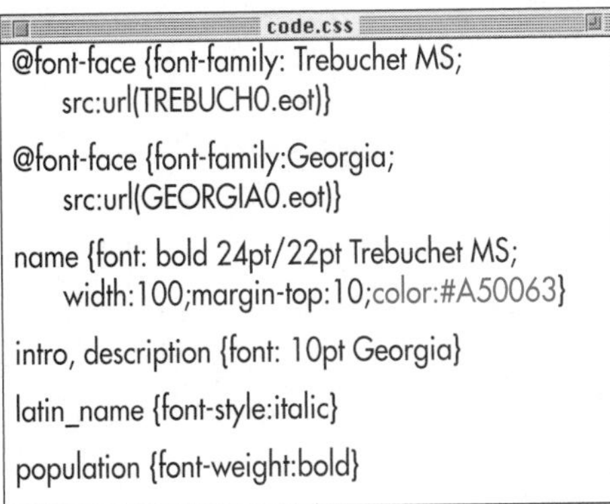

```
code.css
@font-face {font-family: Trebuchet MS;
    src:url(TREBUCH0.eot)}

@font-face {font-family:Georgia;
    src:url(GEORGIA0.eot)}

name {font: bold 24pt/22pt Trebuchet MS;
    width:100;margin-top:10;color:#A50063}

intro, description {font: 10pt Georgia}

latin_name {font-style:italic}

population {font-weight:bold}
```

Figure 15.15 *I've specified this purple color with the standard hexadecimal system.*

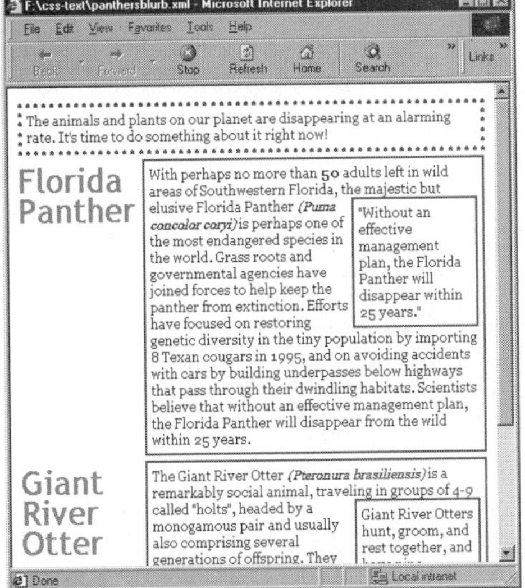

Figure 15.16 *You have to be careful when coloring text to make sure that there is enough contrast between the text color and the background (white in this case). That is, if you want your visitors to be able to read your page.*

Setting the Text Color

You can change the color of any text, whether it be a paragraph, or just a few words.

To set the text color:

1. Type **color:**.
2. Type **colorname**, where *colorname* is one of the 16 predefined colors.

   Or type **#rrggbb**, where *rrggbb* is the hexadecimal representation of the desired color.

   Or type **rgb(r, g, b)**, where *r, g,* and *b* are integers from 0–255 that specify the amount of red, green, or blue, respectively, in the desired color.

   Or type **rgb(r%, g%, b%)**, where *r, g,* and *b* specify the percentage of red, green, and blue, respectively, in the desired color.

✔ Tips

- For more on specifying colors, see Appendix D, *Colors in Hex*.
- If you type a value for r, g, or b higher than 255 it will be replaced with 255. Similarly a percentage higher than 100% will be replaced with 100%.
- You've already seen how to use the `color` property for changing the color of any element *(see page 200)*. Changing text color is no different, but it is so important that I repeat the information here.
- You can also use #rgb to set the color where the hexadecimal values are repeated digits. So you could write #FF0099 as #F09.
- The hexadecimal number should *not* be enclosed in double quotes.
- The `color` property is inherited.

Changing the Text's Background

The background refers not to the background of the entire page, but to the background of the specified tag. In other words, you can change the background of just a few paragraphs or words, by setting the background of those words to a different color.

To change the text's background:

1. Type **background:**.
2. Type **transparent** or **color**, where *color* is a color name or hex color.
3. If desired, type **url(image.gif)**, where *image.gif* is the URL of the image that you want to use for the background.

   If desired, type **repeat** to tile the image both horizontally and vertically, **repeat-x** to tile the image only horizontally, **repeat-y** to tile the image only vertically, and **no-repeat** to not tile the image.

   If desired, type **fixed** or **scroll** to determine whether the background should scroll along with the canvas.

   If desired, type **x y** to set the position of the background image, where *x* and *y* can be expressed as a percentage or an absolute distance from the top-left corner. Or use values of *top*, *center*, or *bottom* for *x* and *left*, *center*, and *right* for *y*.

✔ Tips

- You can specify both a color and a GIF image's URL for the background. The color will be used until the image is loaded—or if it can't be loaded for any reason—and will be seen through any transparent portions of the image.
- The `background` property is not inherited by child elements from their parents.

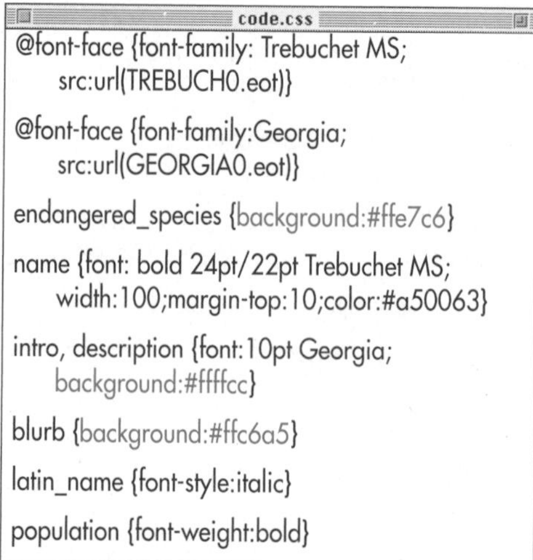

```
code.css
@font-face {font-family: Trebuchet MS;
    src:url(TREBUCH0.eot)}
@font-face {font-family:Georgia;
    src:url(GEORGIA0.eot)}
endangered_species {background:#ffe7c6}
name {font: bold 24pt/22pt Trebuchet MS;
    width:100;margin-top:10;color:#a50063}
intro, description {font:10pt Georgia;
    background:#ffffcc}
blurb {background:#ffc6a5}
latin_name {font-style:italic}
population {font-weight:bold}
```

Figure 15.17 *Now I set a background color for the root element (*`endangered_species`*), the* `intro` *and* `description` *elements, and the* `blurb`*. That might sound like a lot but they actually look rather good together.*

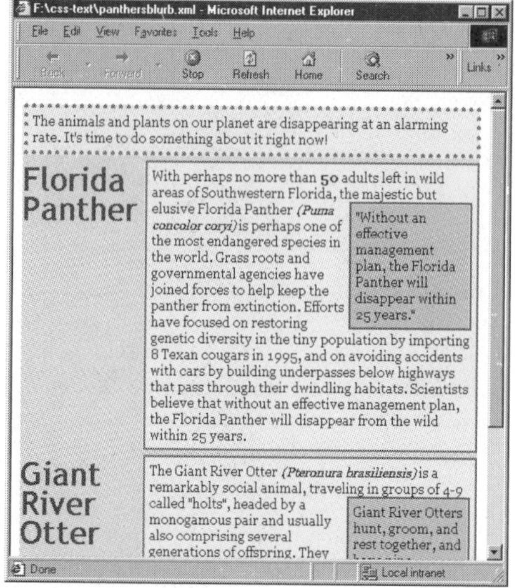

Figure 15.18 *The judicious use of color can help unify a site by guiding the eye to important, related bits of information. (This looks much better in color than it does here in this book. Check out the Web site!)*

```
code.css
@font-face {font-family: Trebuchet MS;
    src:url(TREBUCH0.eot)}

@font-face {font-family:Georgia;
    src:url(GEORGIA0.eot)}

endangered_species {background:#ffe7c6}

name {font: bold 24pt/22pt Trebuchet MS;
    width:100;margin-top:10;color:#A50063}

intro, description {font:10pt
    Georgia;background:#ffffc6}

blurb {background:#ffc6a5;letter-spacing:.1em;
    text-indent:15pt}

latin_name {font-style:italic}

population {font-weight:bold}
```

Figure 15.19 *Now I'm going to widen the spacing between letters in the* `blurb` *element by .1 em, and also add an indent of 15 points.*

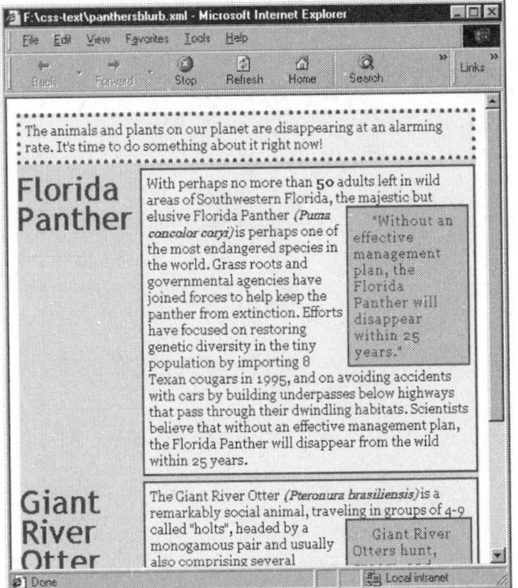

Figure 15.20 *Explorer currently supports text indents and letter spacing, but not word spacing. Netscape only supports text-indent.*

Controlling Spacing

You can add or reduce space between words (tracking) or between letters (kerning). You can also add a chunk of space, or an indent, before particular paragraphs.

To specify tracking:

1. Type **word-spacing:**.
2. Type **length**, where *length* is a numerical value in pixels, points, ems, etc.

To specify kerning:

1. Type **letter-spacing:**.
2. Type **length**, where *length* is a numerical value in pixels, points, ems, etc.

To add indents:

1. Type **text-indent:**.
2. Type a value for the text indent, either as an absolute value (either positive or negative) or as a percentage.

✓ Tips

- You may use negative values for word and letter spacing, although the actual display always depends on the browser's capabilities.
- Word and letter spacing values may also be affected by your choice of alignment.
- Use a value of `normal` to set the letter and word spacing to their defaults.
- To avoid gaping holes in justified text, use a value of 0 for letter spacing.
- Currently, Netscape only supports `text-indent`.
- All three spacing properties are inherited.

Aligning Text

You can set up certain HTML tags to always be aligned to the right, left, center, or justified, as desired.

To align text:

1. Type **text-align:**.
2. Type **left** to align the text to the left.

   Or type **right** to align the text to the right.

   Or type **center** to center the text in the middle of the screen.

   Or type **justify** to align the text on both the right and left.

✔ Tips

- If you choose to justify the text, be aware that the word spacing and letter spacing may be adversely affected. For more information, consult *Controlling Spacing* on page 219.
- Child elements inherit the `text-align` property from their parent elements.

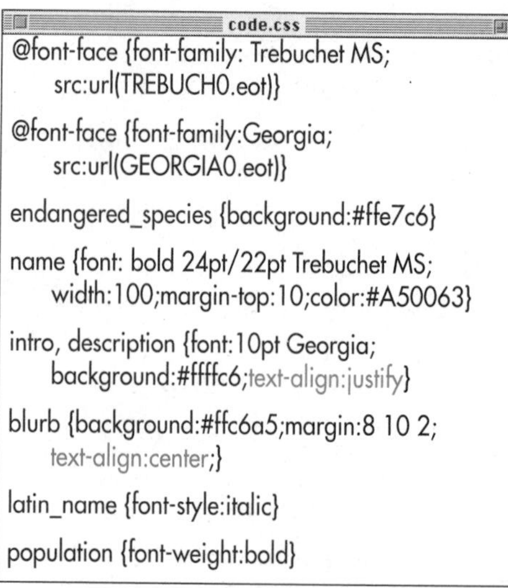

```
code.css
@font-face {font-family: Trebuchet MS;
    src:url(TREBUCHO.eot)}

@font-face {font-family:Georgia;
    src:url(GEORGIA0.eot)}

endangered_species {background:#ffe7c6}

name {font: bold 24pt/22pt Trebuchet MS;
    width:100;margin-top:10;color:#A50063}

intro, description {font:10pt Georgia;
    background:#ffffc6;text-align:justify}

blurb {background:#ffc6a5;margin:8 10 2;
    text-align:center;}

latin_name {font-style:italic}

population {font-weight:bold}
```

Figure 15.21 *I've justified the* `intro` *and* `description` *text, but then I override what would otherwise be inherited in* `blurb` *by centering the* `blurb` *text. (I also need to adjust the margins of the* `blurb` *so that it fits nicely within the justified text—see page 197 for details.)*

Figure 15.22 *The justified text in the description (along with the margin adjustments) makes the blurb stand out, and centering the blurb makes it look more elegant.*

```
code.css
@font-face {font-family: Trebuchet MS;
    src:url(TREBUCH0.eot)}
@font-face {font-family:Georgia;
    src:url(GEORGIA0.eot)}
endangered_species {background:#ffe7c6}
name {font: bold 24pt/22pt Trebuchet MS;
    width:100;margin-top:10;color:#A50063}
intro, description {font:10pt Georgia;
    background:#ffffc6;text-align:justify}
blurb {background:#ffc6a5;margin:8 10 2;
    text-align:center;}
latin_name {font-style:italic}
population {font-weight:bold}
more_info {text-decoration:underline}
```

Figure 15.23 *The* `more_info` *element is designed to be a link (once XLink and XPointer are implemented in browsers—page 223). To follow the Web standard, I format the element with an underline.*

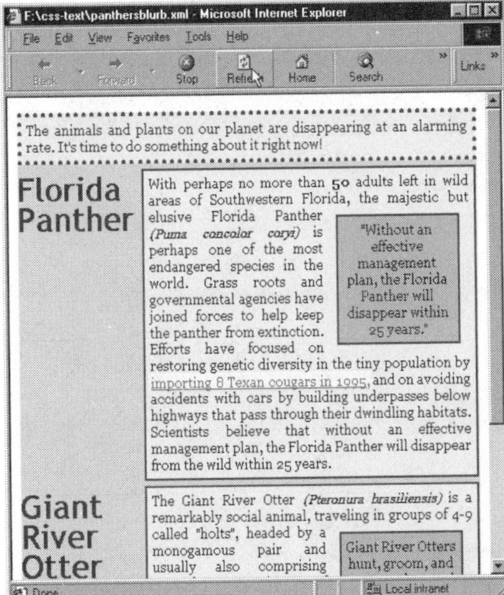

Figure 15.24 *Remember that just underlining an element doesn't make it a link. You can't click on that text and go anywhere. (It lacks XLink and XPointer—see page 225.) And while you can apply underlining to anything (even things that aren't links), you may confuse your visitors if you do so.*

Underlining Text

You can add lines under, over, and even through text (perhaps to show changes in a document).

To underline text:

1. Type **text-decoration:**.
2. To underline text, type **underline**.

   Or, for a line above the text, type **overline**.

   Or, to strike out the text, type **line-through**.

To get rid of underlining, overlining, or strike through text:

1. Type **text-decoration:**.
2. Type **none**.

✓ Tips

- You can eliminate the lines from tags that normally have them (like `u`, `strike`, `del`, `ins`, or especially `a` in HTML).
- Most graphic designers hate underlining and consider it a relic from the typewriter age. Such designers might want to use the *none* option for text decoration of links. However, the links will have to be marked in some other way or nobody will know to click on them.
- Child elements do not inherit the `text-decoration` properties from their parents.

Changing the Text Case

You can define the text case for your style by using the `text-transform` property. In this way, you can display the text either with initial capital letters, in all capital letters, in all small letters, or as it was typed.

To change the text case:

1. Type **text-transform:**.
2. Type **capitalize** to put the first character of each word in uppercase.

   Or type **uppercase** to change all the letters to uppercase.

   Or type **lowercase** to change all the letters to lowercase.

   Or type **none** to leave the text as is (possibly canceling out an inherited value).

Many fonts have a corresponding small caps variant that includes uppercase versions of the letters proportionately reduced to small caps size. You can call up the small caps variant with the `font-variant` property.

To use a small caps font:

1. Type **font-variant:**.
2. Type **small-caps**.

✔ Tips

- To stop using the small caps variant for a dependent style, use **font-variant: none**.
- I've had trouble using `text-transform` in combination with a variety of font values *(see page 216)*. If you plan to use `text-transform`, I advise specifying the font values separately.
- Both the `text-transform` and `font-variant` properties are inherited.

```
code.css
@font-face {font-family: Trebuchet MS;
    src:url(TREBUCH0.eot)}
@font-face {font-family:Georgia;
    src:url(GEORGIA0.eot)}
endangered_species {background:#ffe7c6}
name {font: bold 24pt/22pt Trebuchet MS;
    width:100;margin-top:10;color:#A50063}
intro, description {font:10pt Georgia;
    background:#ffffc6;text-align:justify}
blurb {background:#ffc6a5;margin:8 10 2; text-
    align:center}
latin_name {font-style:italic;
    text-transform:uppercase}
population {font-weight:bold}
more_info {text-decoration:underline}
```

Figure 15.25 *Here, I've decided I need my* `latin_name` *elements to be displayed in all uppercase letters. The* `text-transform` *property saves me from having to retype all the* `latin_name` *element contents.*

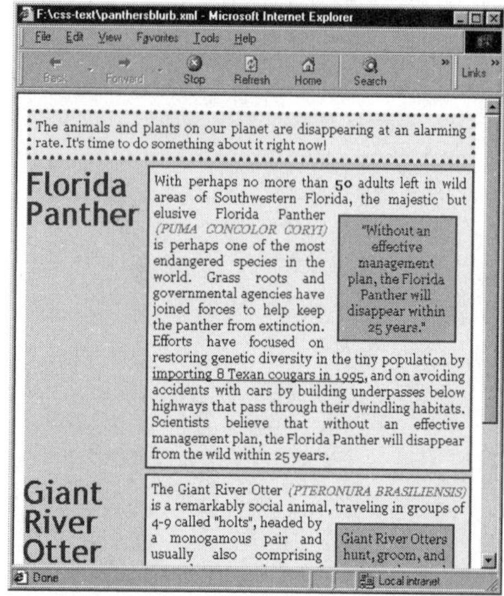

Figure 15.26 *Now the* `latin_name` *elements appear in all uppercase letters.*

PART 6: XLINK AND XPOINTER

16

LINKS AND IMAGES: XLINK AND XPOINTER

The popularity of HTML is certainly due to two things: hyperlinks and images. The former let you connect the information on your pages with information on all the other Web pages in the world, the latter give your pages visual interest.

But the designers of XML were not satisfied with HTML's basic system. Instead they opted for creating a more robust method that lets you create multi-directional links, control how and when links are acted upon, and more. This system relies on two languages: XLink and XPointer, which are described in detail in this chapter.

There's only one problem. Neither XLink nor XPointer is supported yet by any major browser. That means that you can't serve XML pages that have functioning links or embedded images. Well, you can serve them, but nobody will see the links or images. This is a huge, huge impediment. Until XLink and XPointer are integrated into the browsers, it will continue to be necessary to convert final files into HTML in order for regular folks to see links and images with their browsers.

It also means that the descriptions in this book, while based on the final specifications for both XLink *(http://www.w3.org/TR/xlink/)* and XPointer *(http://www.w3.org/TR/xptr/)* are mainly hypothetical. While I can guess how browsers will eventually treat links, there was no way to test anything or see how the specs come out when faced with the real world. So, you can use this chapter to get a taste of XLink and XPointer, but we'll all have to wait a bit to see how it really turns out.

Creating a Simple Link

In HTML, we think of links and images as quite different beasts, but really they're quite similar. You have an element with a reference to an external file. If the external file is another Web page, clicking the link often makes that other Web page replace the current contents of the window. If the external file is a supported file format, like JPEG or GIF, then the external file is often viewed right in the page itself. In XML you create both kinds of reference with the same mechanism, regardless of what the external file is.

To create a simple link:

1. In the root element of your document, (or in the element in which you're creating the link if you prefer), declare the XLink namespace by typing **xmlns:xlink="http://www.w3.org/1999/xlink"**. For more details, see Chapter 8, *Using Namespaces in XML.*

2. Within the opening tag of the link that you want to connect with another, type **xlink:type="simple"**.

3. Next type **xlink:href="URL"**, where *URL* is the location of the file that you want to reference. If you want to reference a particular section or point in the file, you'll need to append an XPointer *(see page 233)*.

4. If desired, type **xlink:role="use"**, where *use* describes—to a machine that might read the information—what the reference is for.

5. If desired, type **xlink:title="description"**, where *description* might be used by a parser to give visitors an idea where the link leads (perhaps like a tooltip).

```
code.xml
<endangered_species xmlns:xlink=
    "http://www.w3.org/1999/xlink">
```

Figure 16.1 *Before using any of the XLink attributes or elements, you must declare the XLink namespace in the root element of your document (or, if you prefer, in the individual element in which you're going to use the XLink attributes and elements).*

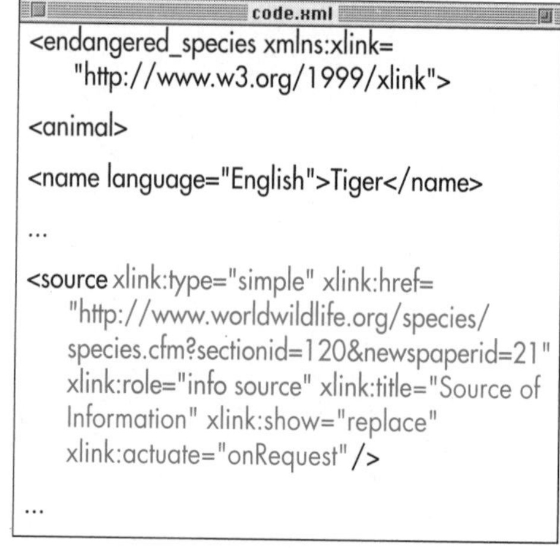

```
code.xml
<endangered_species xmlns:xlink=
    "http://www.w3.org/1999/xlink">
<animal>
<name language="English">Tiger</name>
...
<source xlink:type="simple" xlink:href=
    "http://www.worldwildlife.org/species/
    species.cfm?sectionid=120&newspaperid=21"
    xlink:role="info source" xlink:title="Source of
    Information" xlink:show="replace"
    xlink:actuate="onRequest"/>
...
```

Figure 16.2 *The* source *element in my XML document now contains a link to an external file that will* replace *the contents of the current document in the browser if and when such action* is requested.

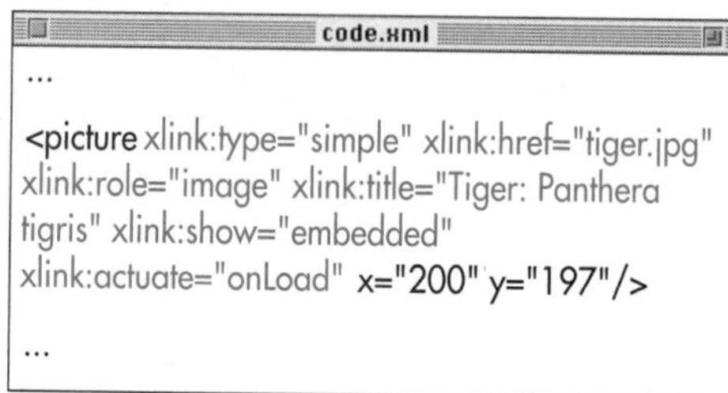

```
code.xml
...
<picture xlink:type="simple" xlink:href="tiger.jpg"
xlink:role="image" xlink:title="Tiger: Panthera
tigris" xlink:show="embedded"
xlink:actuate="onLoad" x="200" y="197"/>
...
```

Figure 16.3 *In this excerpt from the same document as in Figure 16.2, the* picture *element now contains a reference to an external file called* tiger.jpg *which will be* embedded *in the document as it is* loaded. *Notice that the* picture *element continues to contain some attributes that have nothing to do with XLink, namely* x *and* y.

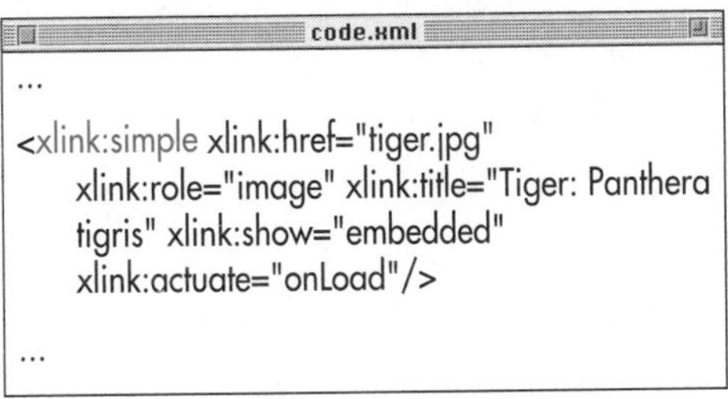

Figure 16.4 *Instead of creating a link from an existing element, you can also create a "free-standing" XLink element to contain the reference. The* `xlink:type="simple"` *attribute becomes the name of the element (*`xlink:simple`*) and the rest of the attributes remain the same.*

6. Next, type **xlink:show=** to determine *where* the external file should appear.

   Then type **"replace"** for a standard HTML-style link that replaces the entire current document in the browser.

   Or type **"embedded"** for a standard HTML-style image that is shown right in the current document.

   Or type **"new"** to open a new window for the referenced file.

7. Finally, type **xlink:actuate=** to determine *when* the external file will be called.

   Then type **"onRequest"** so that the end user has to do something (like click) to get the referenced file to appear (typical for hyperlinks).

   Or type **"onLoad"** to have the referenced file appear automatically when the link is loaded (typical for embedded images).

✔ Tips

- The method I describe here is comprised of adding XLink attributes to the element in your XML document that you would like to connect with another file. You can also create an entirely new XLink element **(Figure 16.4)**. The **xlink:type="simple"** is absorbed in the name of the element and all the other attributes remain the same: **<xlink:simple xlink:href="URL" ...>**. It doesn't matter which method you use.

- Any XLink attributes (or elements, per the previous tip) that you add to your document should also be defined in your DTD for the document to be valid. For more information about DTDs, see Chapter 2, *Creating a DTD*.

Creating a Linkset

A linkset lets you connect a whole series of files or individual points in a file, or both, at once. You create a central element that contains all the information about the files that will be connected and then define the connections between them. The result is a *linkset.*

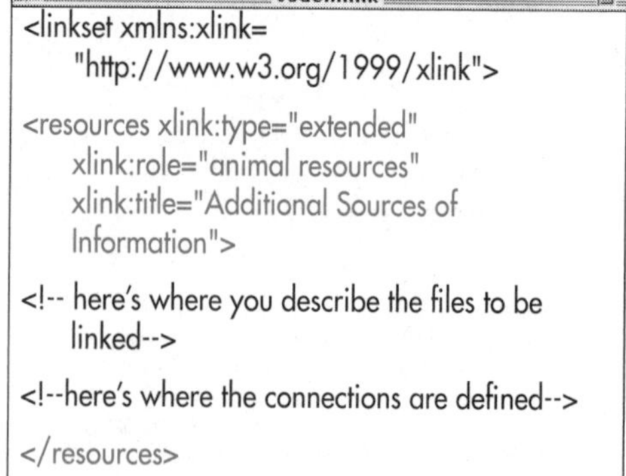

```
<linkset xmlns:xlink=
    "http://www.w3.org/1999/xlink">

<resources xlink:type="extended"
    xlink:role="animal resources"
    xlink:title="Additional Sources of
    Information">

<!-- here's where you describe the files to be
    linked-->

<!--here's where the connections are defined-->

</resources>
```

Figure 16.5 *A linkset begins with an element that contains* `xlink:type="extended"`.

To create a linkset:

1. In the root element of your document, (or in the element in which you're creating the link if you prefer), declare the XLink namespace by typing **xmlns:xlink= "http://www.w3.org/1999/xlink"**. For more details, see Chapter 8, *Using Namespaces in XML.*
2. In the element that will contain the link information, type **xlink:type="extended"**.
3. If desired, create the **xlink:role** and **xlink:title** elements as described in steps 4–5 on page 226.
4. Define the files or points that will be linked as described on page 229.
5. Define the connections between those files as described on page 230.

✔ Tips

- The definition of a linkset may be located within one of the files whose connections are defined, or it may be in an independent, external file.
- In the same way as was described earlier on page 227, you can use the **<xlink:extended...>** element instead of **<your_element xlink:type="extended"...>**. It's the same difference.
- A linkset is also referred to as an *extended link* (in contrast with a simple link, as described on page 226).

```
code.xlink
<linkset xmlns:xlink=
    "http://www.w3.org/1999/xlink">
<resources xlink:type="extended
    xlink:role="animal resources"
    xlink:title="Additional Sources of
    Information">
<animal_info xlink:type="locator"
    xlink:href="tiger.xml" xlink:role="tiger"
    xlink:title="Tiger"/>
<animal_info xlink:type="locator"
    xlink:href="panther.xml" xlink:role="panther"
    xlink:title="Florida Panther"/>
<animal_info xlink:type="locator"
    xlink:href="rhino.xml" xlink:role="rhino"
    xlink:title="Black Rhino"/>
<animal_info xlink:type="locator"
    xlink:href="otter.xml" xlink:role="otter"
    xlink:title="Great River Otter"/>
<!--here's where the connections are defined-->
</resources>
```

Figure 16.6 *Each reference point in the linkset identifies a particular file (or piece thereof) which will serve either as the beginning or the end of a link.*

Defining Reference Points

A link starts and ends with a *reference point*. If the reference point is within the file that contains the link information, it is called a *resource*. If it is in some other file, it's called a *locator*. The reference point might refer to an entire file or to a chunk of one (with XPointer, which we'll get to shortly).

To define reference points:

1. Create the first reference to a file (or point in a file) that will be linked. Type **<ref_element**, where *ref_element* is the name of the element in your XML document that will contain the information about the reference point.
2. Then type **xlink:type="locator"** to indicate that the referenced point is outside of the file that contains this set of links.

   Or type **xlink:type="resource"** to indicate that the reference point is within the file that contains this set of links.
3. Then type **xlink:href="URL"**, where *URL* is the location of the external point to be referenced. If you want to point to a particular part or point in a file, you'll have to append an XPointer *(see page 233)*.
4. Type **xlink:role="id"**, where *id* identifies the given reference point. You'll use this later when connecting one point to the next.
5. If desired, you may add **xlink:title** as well.
6. Add any other attributes or content as necessary.
7. Close the tag as usual.
8. Repeat steps 1–6 for each reference point that you want to link to or from.

Defining Connections

Now comes the good part. Once you've defined the possible link points, you get to connect the dots.

To define connections:

1. Define the connection from one point to the next by typing **<connection_element**, where *connection_element* is the name of the tag that will contain the connection information.
2. Then type **xlink:type="arc"** to indicate that you're going to define a connection.
3. Type **xlink:from="id"**, where *id* matches the value of `xlink:role` that you specified for the reference point (in step 4 on page 229) *where the link should begin.*
4. Then type **xlink:to="id"**, where *id* matches the value of `xlink:role` that you specified for the reference point (in step 4 on page 229) *where the link should point to.*
5. Next type **xlink:show="where"**, where *where* describes where and how the referenced data will appear. The choices are **replace**, **embedded**, and **new**, and are described in detail in step 6 on page 227.
6. Next type **xlink:show="when"**, where *when* describes whether the referenced data should be loaded with the page (**onLoad**) or after some user action (**onRequest**). See step 7 on page 227 for more details.
7. Add other attributes as desired and close the *connection_element* that you began in step 1.
8. Repeat steps 1–7 for each connection you want to define.

```
code.xlink
<linkset xmlns:xlink=
    "http://www.w3.org/1999/xlink">

<resources xlink:type="extended
    xlink:role="animal resources"
    xlink:title="Additional Sources of
    Information">

<animal_info xlink:type="locator"
xlink:href="tiger.xml" xlink:role="tiger"
xlink:title="Tiger"/>

<animal_info xlink:type="locator"
xlink:href="panther.xml" xlink:role="panther"
xlink:title="Florida Panther"/>

<animal_info xlink:type="locator"
xlink:href="rhino.xml" xlink:role="rhino"
xlink:title="Rhino"/>

<animal_info xlink:type="locator"
xlink:href="otter.xml" xlink:role="otter"
xlink:title="Great River Otter"/>

<connection xlink:type="arc" xlink:from="otter"
    xlink:to="panther" xlink:show="replace"
    xlink:actuate="onRequest"/>

<connection xlink:type="arc" xlink:from="panther"
    xlink:to="rhino" xlink:show="replace"
    xlink:actuate="onRequest"/>

<connection xlink:type="arc" xlink:from="rhino"
    xlink:to="tiger" xlink:show="replace"
    xlink:actuate="onRequest"/>

</resources>
```

Figure 16.7 *Here are three simple arcs that link the otter page to the panther page, the panther page to the rhino page and the rhino page to the tiger page.*

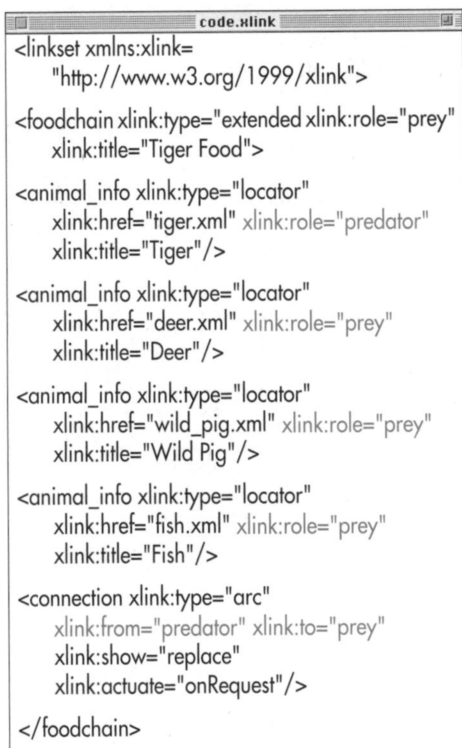

code.xlink

```
<linkset xmlns:xlink=
    "http://www.w3.org/1999/xlink">
<foodchain xlink:type="extended xlink:role="prey"
    xlink:title="Tiger Food">
<animal_info xlink:type="locator"
    xlink:href="tiger.xml" xlink:role="predator"
    xlink:title="Tiger"/>
<animal_info xlink:type="locator"
    xlink:href="deer.xml" xlink:role="prey"
    xlink:title="Deer"/>
<animal_info xlink:type="locator"
    xlink:href="wild_pig.xml" xlink:role="prey"
    xlink:title="Wild Pig"/>
<animal_info xlink:type="locator"
    xlink:href="fish.xml" xlink:role="prey"
    xlink:title="Fish"/>
<connection xlink:type="arc"
    xlink:from="predator" xlink:to="prey"
    xlink:show="replace"
    xlink:actuate="onRequest"/>
</foodchain>
```

Figure 16.8 *Here's another example of a linkset, but this time, I want to link the* tiger.xml *file with each of the three "prey" files. I only need to define one connection between all the predators (just one in this case) and all three prey.*

✔ Tip

- You can connect multiple reference points with one another in a single step by giving the same `xlink:role` value to each of the desired reference points. Then, when you use `xlink:from` or `xlink:to`, *all* of the reference points with the given role will be connected **(Figure 16.8)**.

Using a Linkset

A collection of extended links defined in a separate, independent file (and not within one of the files that contains one of the reference points) is called a *linkset*. In order for a file to use the linkset, you have to tell it that the linkset exists.

To use a linkset:

1. In the root element of your document, (or in the element in which you're creating the link if you prefer), declare the XLink namespace by typing **xmlns:xlink="http://www.w3.org/1999/xlink"**. For more details, see Chapter 8, *Using Namespaces in XML*.
2. In the XML document, type **<element**, where *element* is the name of the element that will contain the information about the linkset.
3. Type **xlink:type="extended"**.
4. Then type **xlink:role="external-linkset"** to indicate the existence of an external linkset.
5. Type **>**.
6. Type **<xlink:locator="URL"**, where *URL* indicates the location of the linkset.
7. Type **</element>** to close the element you began in step 2.

✓ Tip

- Who knows how this will actually be implemented in the browser!?

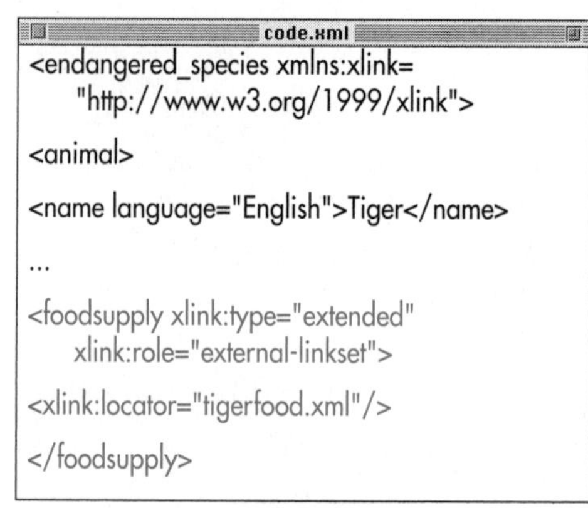

```
code.xml
<endangered_species xmlns:xlink=
    "http://www.w3.org/1999/xlink">
<animal>
<name language="English">Tiger</name>
...
<foodsupply xlink:type="extended"
    xlink:role="external-linkset">
<xlink:locator="tigerfood.xml"/>
</foodsupply>
```

Figure 16.9 *Supposing I call the file created in Figure 16.8 on page 231* tigerfood.xml. *To use those links in the Endangered Species XML document, I need to call the external linkset as shown here.*

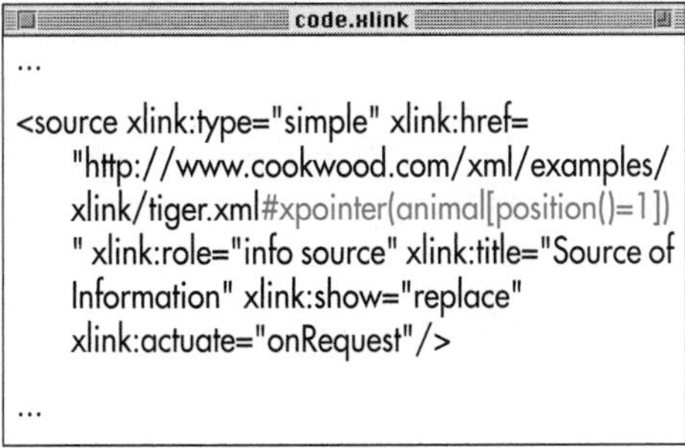

```
code.xlink
...

<source xlink:type="simple" xlink:href=
    "http://www.cookwood.com/xml/examples/
    xlink/tiger.xml#xpointer(animal[position()=1])
    " xlink:role="info source" xlink:title="Source of
    Information" xlink:show="replace"
    xlink:actuate="onRequest"/>

...
```

Figure 16.10 *This XPointer points to the first* `animal` *element in the* tiger.xml *document.*

Linking to Part of a File

Instead of linking to an entire file, you might want to link to a specific element, or range of elements. You can do just that with XPointer, which uses XPath to identify specific parts of a file and then lets you link to those parts.

To link to part of a file:

When typing the value of the `xlink:href` attribute as in step 3 on page 226 or step 3 on page 229, type **#xpointer(expression)**, after or instead of the URL, where *expression* is an XPath phrase that identifies the specific part of the file you want to connect to.

✓ Tips

- If you omit the URL, the XPointer points to something in the current file (the one that contains the link).
- For more information about XPath expressions and how to use them to identify a part of an XML document, consult Chapter 11, *XPath: Patterns and Expressions.*
- Any single parentheses in an XPointer expression must be escaped by preceding it with a ^. Matched pairs of parentheses do not need to be escaped. The ^ must also be escaped (with an additional ^, as in ^^.)
- The < also needs to be escaped if it's part of an XPointer that appears in the value of an attribute. Instead use **<**.
- XPointer includes a few extra functions not available in XPath. We'll cover a couple of those in the following pages.
- I am only going to give you a small taste of XPointer here. Until I can test it in real-world situations, I'm wary of giving you just what's available in the specifications.

Creating the Simplest XPointer

XPointers are designed to identify ID type attributes easily. If you want to link to an element that contains an ID attribute, the XPointer consists simply of the value of that attribute.

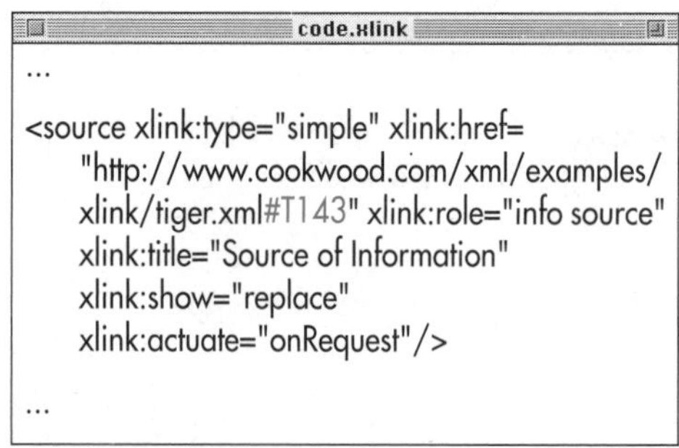

Figure 16.11 *This XPointer points to an element that contains an ID type attribute whose value is* T143.

To create the simplest XPointer:

1. Type **#** to begin the XPointer.
2. Type **id**, where *id* matches the value of the ID attribute for the element you want to connect to *(see page 52)*.

✔ Tips

- Notice that the word *xpointer* and the parentheses are completely omitted.
- Don't confuse an ID type attribute (as described in detail on page 52) with an attribute whose *name* is ID (or id). In the latter case, the XPointer would be **xpointer(//*[@id="value"])**.

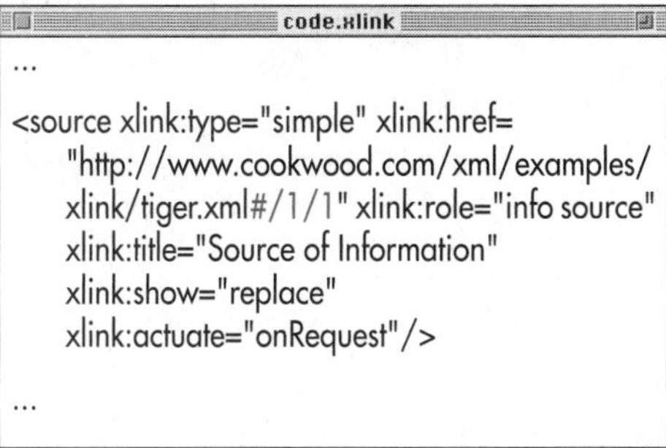

code.xlink

```
...

<source xlink:type="simple" xlink:href=
    "http://www.cookwood.com/xml/examples/
    xlink/tiger.xml#/1/1" xlink:role="info source"
    xlink:title="Source of Information"
    xlink:show="replace"
    xlink:actuate="onRequest"/>

...
```

Figure 16.12 *The first child of the root in the tiger.xml document is* `endangered_species`. *The first child of* `endangered_species` *is* `animal`. *So the highlighted XPointer in this example points to that first* `animal` *element, which is the first child of the first child of the root.*

Creating Walking XPointers

The next easiest kind of XPointer is one that literally walks down the XML document until it gets to the desired element. This kind of XPointer is officially called a *child sequence*.

To create a walking XPointer:

1. Type **#** to begin the XPointer.
2. Type **/n**, where *n* denotes the *n*th child of the root element of the document.
3. Type **/m**, where *m* denotes the *m*th child of the child found in step 2.
4. Repeat step 3 for as many levels down as you need to go.

✔ Tip

- You can combine this technique with the ID technique discussed on page 234. For example, you could use #T143/3/1 to find the first child of the third child of the element that has an ID type attribute with a value of T143.

Creating an XPointer Range

If you would like to link to a range between two given points in a document, you can use XPointer's `range-to` function.

To create an XPointer range:

1. Type **#xpointer(** to begin the XPointer.
2. Type **(start_expression)**, where *start_expression* is the XPath expression that indicates the beginning of the desired range.
3. Type **/range-to** to note that you want a range.
4. Type **(end_expression)**, where *end_expression* is the XPath expression that indicates the end of the desired range.
5. Finally type **)** to complete the XPointer.

✔ Tips

- Be careful with all of those parentheses!
- You can get more information about creating XPath expressions in Chapter 11, *XPath: Patterns and Expressions.*

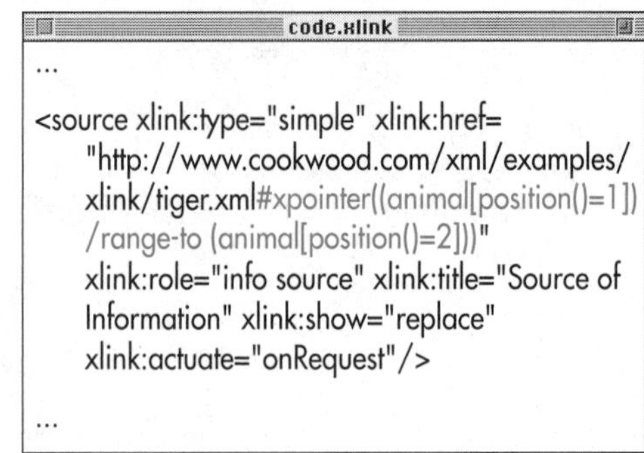

code.xlink

```
...
<source xlink:type="simple" xlink:href=
    "http://www.cookwood.com/xml/examples/
    xlink/tiger.xml#xpointer((animal[position()=1])
    /range-to (animal[position()=2]))"
    xlink:role="info source" xlink:title="Source of
    Information" xlink:show="replace"
    xlink:actuate="onRequest"/>
...
```

Figure 16.13 *This XPointer identifies the range between the first and second* `animal` *elements in the tiger.xml file.*

APPENDICES

A

XHTML

As I discussed in the Introduction and as you've probably seen throughout this book, XML doesn't quite live up to the hype that surrounds it—at least not yet. Many browsers don't support XML and the ones that do don't fully support the auxiliary technologies, like XSLT, XPath, XLink, and XPointer. That makes serving XML pages directly to your visitors' browsers very risky.

The W3C has developed an intermediary language to help people make the transition from HTML to XML. This "new" language is called XHTML. On the surface, it is nothing more than HTML's tags written with XML's strict syntactic rules *(http://www.w3.org/MarkUp/)*.

XHTML is useful for combining HTML and XML. In fact, you've already used XHTML in Chapter 10, *XSLT.* HTML code (with all lowercase tags) embedded in an XML document must meet XML's strict requirements, and thus is actually XHTML.

I have to admit to a certain bias against using XHTML independently of XML. Since XHTML has the annoying strictness of XML without the power of labeling information that XML affords, you do a lot of work for little gain.

No browser manufacturer who's doing its duty by its stockholders is going to stop supporting HTML and the billions of Web pages based on it any time soon. Until there are browsers that can actually display useful XML pages, it makes more sense to me to use XML to store and manage information and then convert it to HTML for display in a browser. And if that happens to be XHTML, fine.

How Does a Browser Know?

XHTML and HTML do not look very different. The tag names are identical and the syntax is very close. So, how does a browser know whether you're feeding it XHTML or HTML? The answer lies in the file's extension.

If you save a file with the .htm or .html extension, the browser will treat it as if it were HTML. If you use the .xml or extension for that same file, the browser will treat it as if it were XML. (There is no supported .xhtml extension.)

And since currently there is no Web browser that can view an XML page properly, especially one with links and images, that means you'll probably be serving XHTML pages as HTML, despite the care you've taken with the syntax.

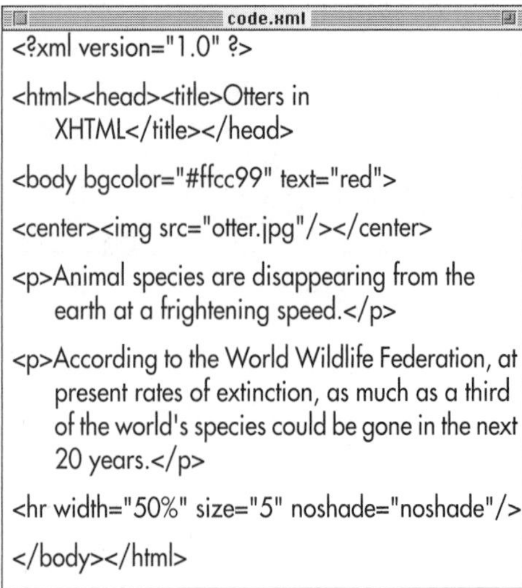

code.xml

```
<?xml version="1.0" ?>
<html><head><title>Otters in
   XHTML</title></head>
<body bgcolor="#ffcc99" text="red">
<center><img src="otter.jpg"/></center>
<p>Animal species are disappearing from the
   earth at a frightening speed.</p>
<p>According to the World Wildlife Federation, at
   present rates of extinction, as much as a third
   of the world's species could be gone in the next
   20 years.</p>
<hr width="50%" size="5" noshade="noshade"/>
</body></html>
```

Figure A.1 *Here is an example of an XHTML document. Notice that it could easily be mistaken for HTML, but is written rather more strictly.*

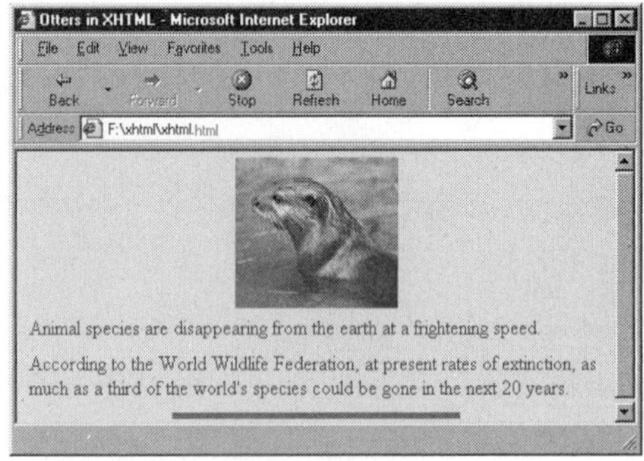

Figure A.2 *If you give the document the .htm or .html extension, it looks beautiful.*

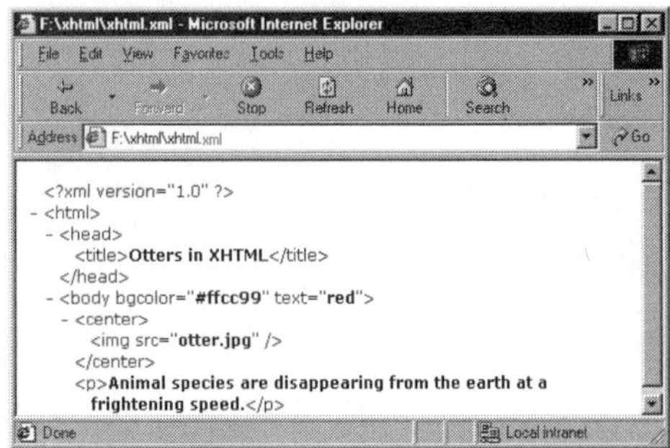

Figure A.3 *With the .xml extension (and no style sheet or other additions), the identical code is displayed in hierarchical form. Yuck!*

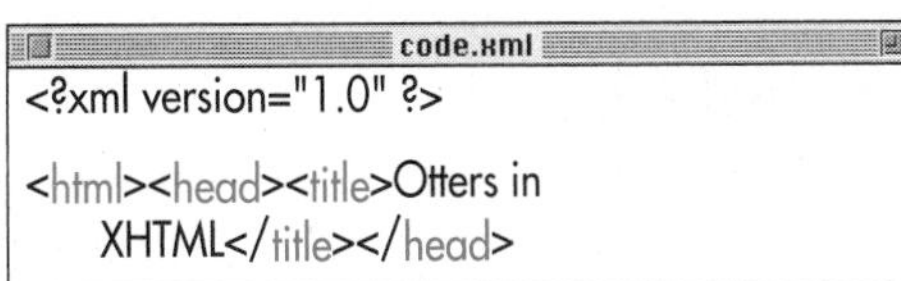

```
<?xml version="1.0" ?>

<html><head><title>Otters in
    XHTML</title></head>
```

Figure A.4 *These are all the same HTML tags that you know and love: just write them in lowercase letters. Attributes and values too!*

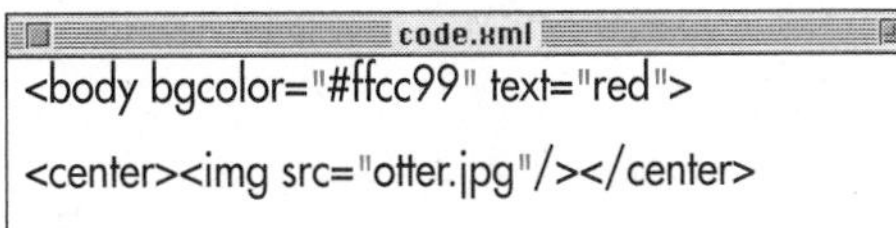

```
<body bgcolor="#ffcc99" text="red">

<center><img src="otter.jpg"/></center>
```

Figure A.5 *Enclose all attribute values in quotation marks.*

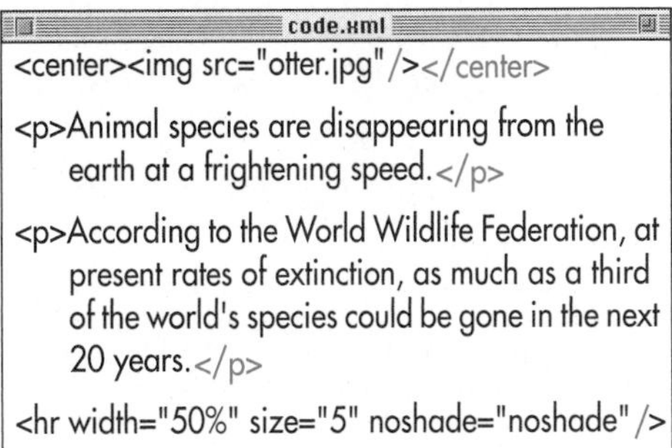

```
<center><img src="otter.jpg" /></center>

<p>Animal species are disappearing from the
    earth at a frightening speed.</p>

<p>According to the World Wildlife Federation, at
    present rates of extinction, as much as a third
    of the world's species could be gone in the next
    20 years.</p>

<hr width="50%" size="5" noshade="noshade" />
```

Figure A.6 *Make sure all elements are properly closed—either with a separate closing tag as with* `center` *and* `p` *above, or with an incorporated slash at the end of an empty element, as in* `img` *and* `hr`.

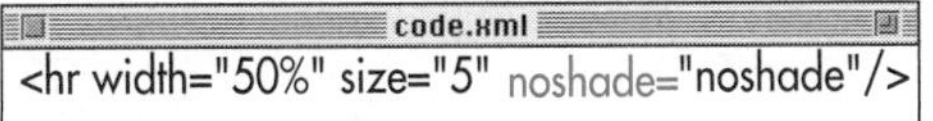

```
<hr width="50%" size="5" noshade="noshade"/>
```

Figure A.7 *Use explicit attribute names. (Note that in HTML, you could use the value* `noshade` *without an attribute name.)*

Writing XHTML

XHTML looks a lot like HTML 4. If you already know HTML 4, you only have to learn a few extra rules in order to write XHTML.

To write XHTML:

1. Use the same names for elements and attributes as in HTML 4, but always write them in exclusively lowercase letters.
2. Follow the rules for writing XML as described in this book, especially those for well-formedness on page 23. (In brief, make sure elements—even empty ones—have closing tags and that they are nested properly. And enclose all attribute values in quotation marks and make all attribute names explicit.)
3. Make sure to enclose scripts and styles in CDATA sections, as described in *Displaying Elements as Text* on page 32 and *Using Internal Style Sheets* on page 187.
4. Instead of using the name attribute for the `a`, `applet`, `form`, `frame`, `iframe`, `img`, and `map` elements, create an ID-type attribute called `id` to contain that value.

✔ Tips

- As with all XML documents, you may begin an XHTML document with the XML declaration *(see page 24)*.
- If you want to validate your XHTML document against a DTD, you should specify which DTD is appropriate. For more details, consult *Declaring a DTD for XHTML* on page 242.
- For help with the (X)HTML tags themselves, you might consult my bestselling *HTML 4 for the World Wide Web, Fourth Edition: Visual QuickStart Guide*, also published by Peachpit Press. For details, see *http://www.cookwood.com/html4_4e*.

Declaring a DTD for XHTML

Just as there are three kinds of HTML, there are also three kinds of XHTML: strict, transitional, and frameset. Each type has its own DTD that describes which elements and attributes are allowed or required in documents written with that type. If you want to validate your document to make sure it follows the rules in a particular type of XHTML, you have to declare the corresponding DTD.

To declare a DTD for XHTML:

1. At the top of the XHTML document, after the XML declaration, type **<!DOCTYPE html PUBLIC "-//W3C//DTD XHTML 1.0**.
2. Type a space and then **Strict**, **Transitional**, or **Frameset**, depending on the type of XTHML you want to validate your document against.
3. Without any additional spaces, type **//EN" SYSTEM "http://www.w3.org/TR/xhtml1/ DTD/xhtml1-**
4. Type (with no extra spaces) **strict**, **transitional**, or **frameset** again (in lowercase).
5. Finally, type **.dtd">** to complete the DTD declaration (with no extra spaces).

✔ Tips

- Use the Strict DTD if you want your XHTML to be free of all deprecated tags and framesets. Deprecated tags are those marked by the W3C for future—but *not* immediate—elimination.
- Use the Transitional DTD if your XHTML includes some of these deprecated tags.
- Use the Frameset DTD if your XHTML contains framesets (with or without deprecated tags).
- For more on DTDs, see page 35.

```
code.xml
<?xml version="1.0" ?>
<!DOCTYPE html PUBLIC "-//W3C//DTD XHTML
    1.0 Transitional//EN" SYSTEM
    "http://www.w3.org/TR/xhtml1/DTD/xhtml1
    -transitional.dtd">
<html><head><title>Otters in
    XHTML</title></head>
<body bgcolor="#ffcc99" text="red">
<center><img src="otter.jpg"/></center>
<p>Animal species are disappearing from the
    earth at a frightening speed.</p>
<p>According to the World Wildlife Federation, at
    present rates of extinction, as much as a third
    of the world's species could be gone in the next
    20 years.</p>
<hr width="50%" size="5" noshade="noshade"/>
</body></html>
```

Figure A.8 *Once you've specified a DTD for your XHTML document, you can use a validator to see if it follows all of the rules laid out in that particular DTD.*

B

XML Tools

While you can write XML with a simple text editor, like Notepad for Windows or SimpleText for Macintosh and then view it with Explorer (at least in its raw state), you'll need other tools for validating and transforming your XML files.

Now, before you start writing me to tell me that you can't find one of these tools, or can't figure out how they work, or that they don't work on your platform, realize that these are just examples. I want you to see the processes and how they are carried out. But there are many, many tools that are up to the task, and you can probably find one that is best for your circumstances. It might be the tool that I discuss, and it might not. In short, this chapter is designed to give you an idea of what should happen, not a step-by-step for each of these particular tools.

Instead of listing a bunch of URLs here in this book that will be out of date the day after the book is printed, I am going to keep a permanently updated list of pointers to useful XML tools on my Web site *(see page 18)*.

Validating XML Files against a DTD

Every XML parser is required to return an error if you feed it XML data that is not well-formed. However, if you want to test whether or not an XML document is valid, according to the rules in a particular DTD, you'll need a validator. While there are several available online, I recommend Brown University's Scholarly Technology Group's XML Validator.

To validate XML files against a DTD:

1. Make sure you've declared the DTD in your document. For more details, consult *Declaring an Internal DTD* on page 36, *Declaring a Personal External DTD* on page 39, or *Declaring a Public External DTD* on page 40.

2. With your browser, go to *http://www.stg.brown.edu/service/xmlvalid/* **(Figure B.1)**.

3. Either type in the URL of your publicly accessible XML file (that is, it must be published on a server somewhere) or copy the XML document to the Text box.

4. Click Validate. XML Validator gives you a useful report of any errors it may find **(Figure B.2)**.

✓ Tips

- If you use an external DTD, it must be publicly available as well—otherwise XML Validator can't get to it.

- Often one error causes everything below it to be misunderstood. I often correct the first thing in the list and then go back and validate again to see if those additional errors were real or just dependent on the original error (and thus solved when it was solved).

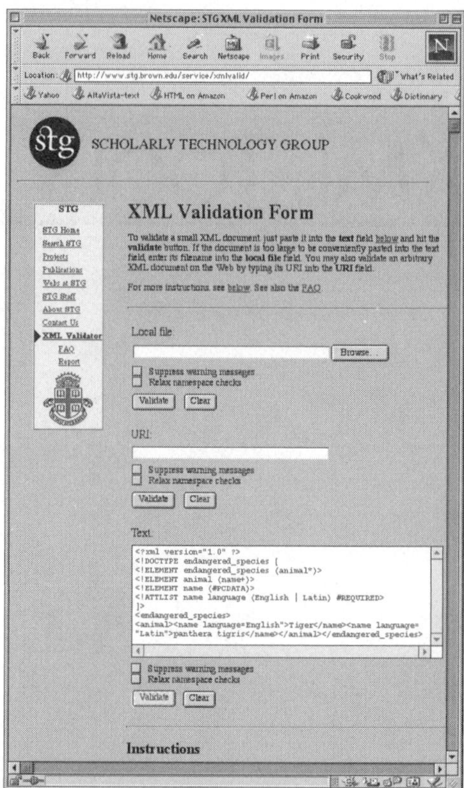

Figure B.1 *Especially when you're doing a lot of testing, it's often just easier to copy and paste your XML file into the Text box. (Can you see the error?)*

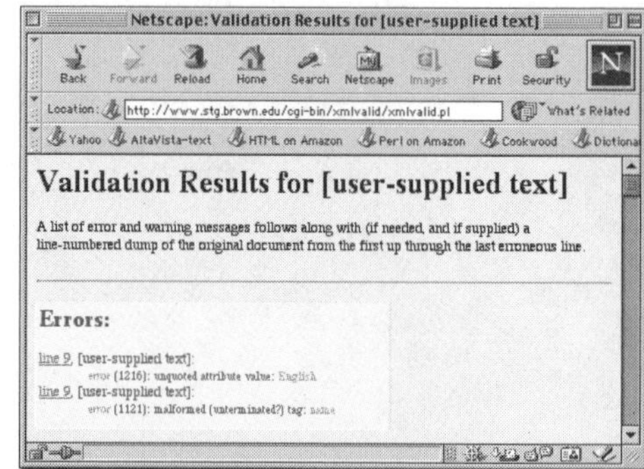

Figure B.2 *The Validator tells me that I've forgotten the opening quotation mark before the attribute value "English" (something I'm wont to do...). Also notice that this problem caused additional "ghost" errors that will disappear once I add that quotation mark.*

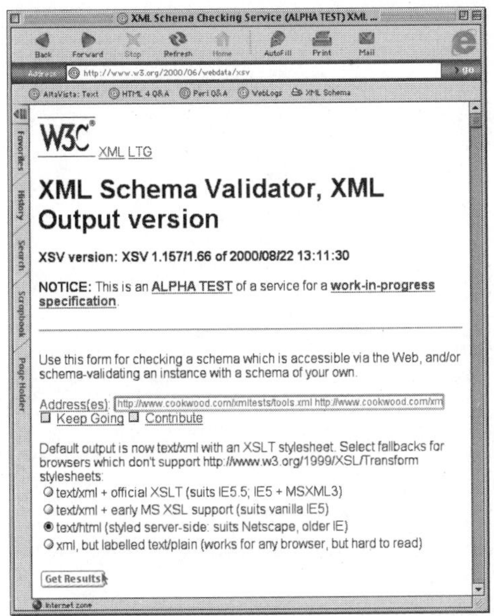

Figure B.3 *With the XML Schema Validator (XSV), you type in the URLs of the XML file and Schema file respectively, unless the XML file already references the schema file (and it's available publicly), in which case, just the XML file will suffice. (The files being tested here are* tools.xml *and* tools.xsd, *and are at* http://www.cookwood.com/xmltests. *Feel free to check them out.*

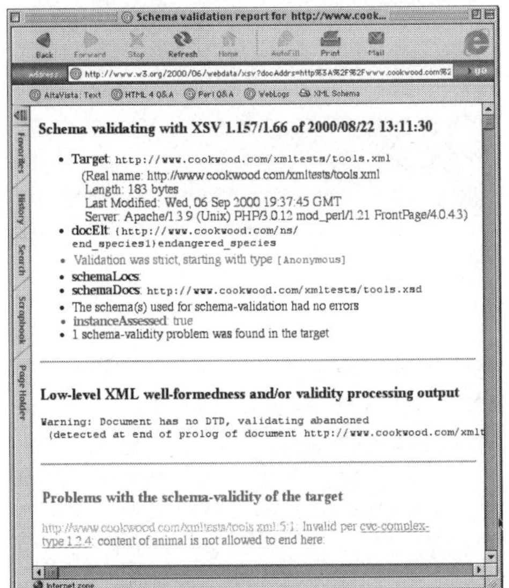

Figure B.4 *This time, I only put one* `name` *element in my XML file (while requiring at least two in my schema). Consequently, the XSV says my* `animal` *element ends too soon.*

Validating XML with a Schema

The World Wide Web Consortium offers an online XML Schema Validator (XSV) for comparing an XML file with the corresponding schema.

To validate XML with a schema:

1. Upload your XML and schema files to your server.
2. Point your browser to *http://www.w3.org/2000/06/webdata/xsv* **(Figure B.3)**.
3. Type the URL for the XML file first in the Addresses box.
4. If you do not give the location of the schema file in the XML file (as described in *Indicating a Simple Schema's Location* on page 73 or *Indicating Where a Schema Is* on page 130), type a space and then the URL for the corresponding schema right after the XML file's URL.
5. Choose an output format. (I've had the best luck with text/html.)
6. Click Get Results at the bottom of the page. XSV gives you a report of any problems it may find **(Figure B.4)**.

✓ Tip

- In the report, it should say that the "Validation was strict" and give a value of "true" for instanceAccessed **(Figure B.4)**. At that point you can begin to trust the errors it reports in the third to last and the last lines.

Transforming XML with an XSLT Processor

The simplest and best XSLT processor I've found is called Instant SAXON, and was written by Michael Kay (who is also the author of the definitive work on XSLT: *XSLT Programmers Reference*, published by Wrox Press). Its major drawback: it is only available for Windows. As soon as I find a good one for other platforms (especially Macintosh), I will post a link to it on my Web site.

To transform XML with SAXON:

1. Download and unzip Instant SAXON *(http://users.iclway.co.uk/mhkay/saxon/instant.html).*
2. Open a DOS window and change to the directory in which you installed Saxon.
3. Type **saxon**.
4. If desired, type **-o result.url**, where *result* is the name of the output file and *url* determines the default output method.
5. Then type **file.xml**, where *file.xml* is the XML file that you want to transform.
6. Type **style.xsl**, where *style.xsl* is the XSLT stylesheet that you want to use in the transformation.
7. Then hit Return. Unless you have specified a filename in step 4, the resulting file is sent to standard output.

✓ Tips

- There is more detailed information about Saxon in accompanying documentation.
- You can run Saxon in combination with a souped up text editor like UltraEdit (choose Advanced > DOS Command). It makes it a lot easier.

code.xslt

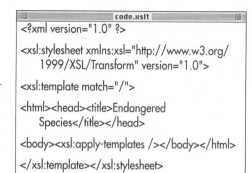

```
<?xml version="1.0" ?>
<xsl:stylesheet xmlns:xsl="http://www.w3.org/
    1999/XSL/Transform" version="1.0">
<xsl:template match="/">
<html><head><title>Endangered
    Species</title></head>
<body><xsl:apply-templates /></body></html>
</xsl:template></xsl:stylesheet>
```

Figure B.5 *Here's the sample XSLT stylesheet.*

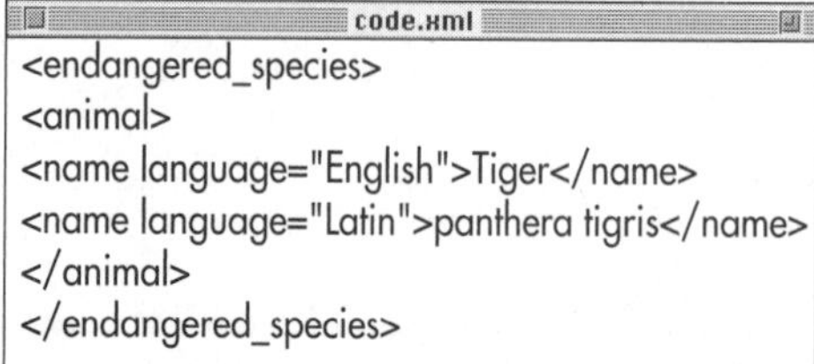

code.xml

```
<endangered_species>
<animal>
<name language="English">Tiger</name>
<name language="Latin">panthera tigris</name>
</animal>
</endangered_species>
```

Figure B.6 *The XML file consists of the first now very familiar elements.*

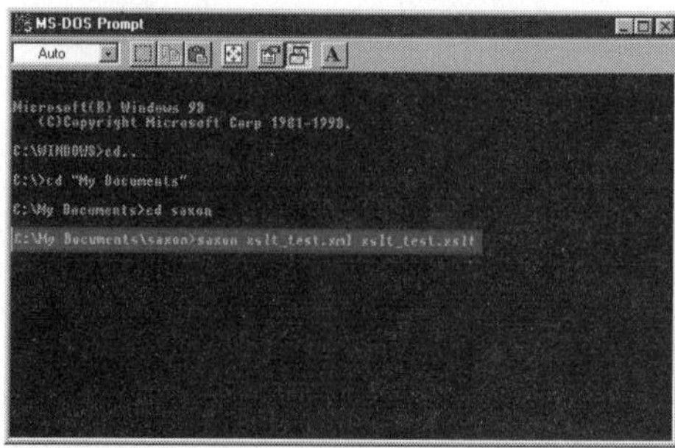

Figure B.7 *You can run Saxon at the command line, as shown here, or from within a text editor like UltraEdit.*

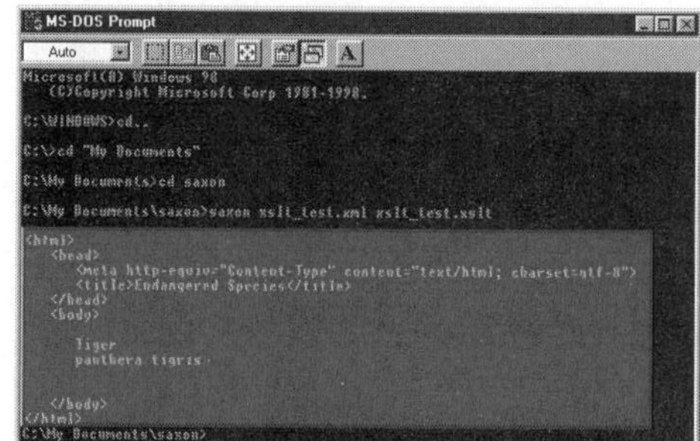

Figure B.8 *If you don't specify an output file, the resulting transformation is sent to standard output.*

Special Symbols

You can type any letter of the English alphabet or any number into your XML document and be confident that every other computer system will interpret it correctly. However, if your document contains any accents, foreign characters, or special symbols, you may have to use a special code to make sure they appear correctly on the page.

The Unicode character set is the standard for XML documents. It assigns a number to each character, number, or symbol in the set.

Unfortunately, few text editors (or the operating systems they run on) fully support Unicode. There are two simple solutions. One is to write your document as usual and then convert it to Unicode. The second, particularly useful for individual foreign characters, is to use a character reference to refer to those characters.

You are not required to use a character reference for the following symbols (although their numbers are included in the charts for your information): exclamation point (!), hash (#), dollar sign ($), percent (%), left and right parentheses "( )", asterisk (*), plus (+), minus (-), period (.), comma (,), forward slash (/), colon (:), semicolon (;), equals (=), question mark (?), carat (^), underscore (_), right and left curly brackets ({}), vertical bar (|), tilde—by itself (~).

Using Character References

Unicode shares its first 127 characters with ASCII, the standard system for most text editors and operating systems. That means, that any ASCII character, including all of the letters in the English alphabet, all the numbers, and many common symbols, can be typed directly from the keyboard of any system. Any Unicode character beyond 128 can be inserted in a document using a character reference.

To use a character reference:

1. Type **&#**.
2. *Either* type **n**, where *n* is the number that corresponds to the desired symbol,

   Or type **xn**, where *n* is the hexadecimal code that corresponds to the desired symbol (don't forget the *x*!)
3. Type **;**.

✓ Tips

- Consult the table on page 249 for the corresponding numbers for the accented characters common to Western European languages.
- The table on page 250 includes the corresponding numbers for some common symbols.
- To find the hexadecimal code for other characters, see *http://charts.unicode.org/*.
- Without the proper operating system or fonts installed, a browser probably won't be able to display every single Unicode character.
- If you want to use entity references like **à** or **ó**, which are commonly used in HTML, these must first be declared in the DTD *(see page 56)*.

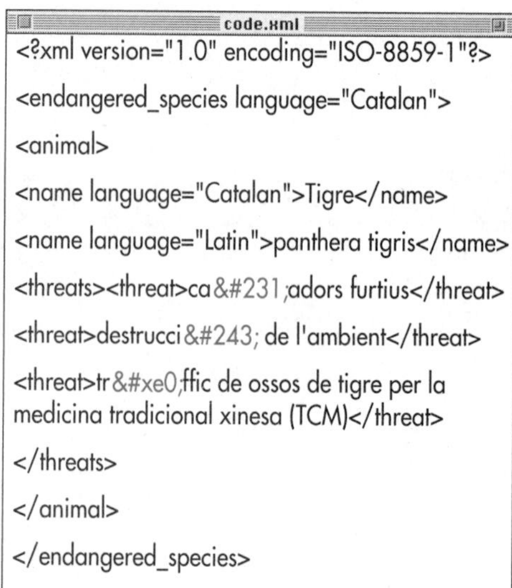

```
<?xml version="1.0" encoding="ISO-8859-1"?>
<endangered_species language="Catalan">
<animal>
<name language="Catalan">Tigre</name>
<name language="Latin">panthera tigris</name>
<threats><threat>ca&#231;adors furtius</threat>
<threat>destrucci&#243; de l'ambient</threat>
<threat>tr&#xe0;ffic de ossos de tigre per la
medicina tradicional xinesa (TCM)</threat>
</threats>
</animal>
</endangered_species>
```

Figure C.1 *In this bit of XML, the three accented characters are represented with three character references. Note that the first two are numerical while the second uses the hexadecimal code. Both systems are equivalent.*

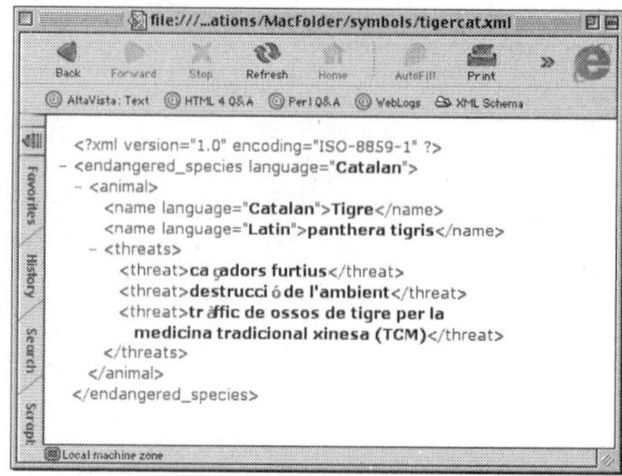

Figure C.2 *When viewed in the browser, the character reference is replaced by the proper accented character (or special symbol).*

Table I: Characters

To get this...	...type this...	...or this.
à	à	à
á	á	á
â	â	â
ã	ã	ã
ä	ä	ä
å	å	å
æ	æ	æ
À	À	À
Á	Á	Á
Â	Â	Â
Ã	Ã	Ã
Ä	Ä	Ä
Å	Å	Å
Æ	Æ	Æ
è	è	è
é	é	é
ê	ê	ê
ë	ë	ë
È	È	È
É	É	É
Ê	Ê	Ê
Ë	Ë	Ë
ì	ì	ì
í	í	í
î	î	î
ï	ï	ï
Ì	Ì	Ì
Í	Í	Í
Î	Î	Î
Ï	Ï	Ï

To get this...	...type this...	...or this.
ò	ò	ò
ó	ó	ó
ô	ô	ô
õ	õ	õ
ö	ö	ö
ø	ø	ø
œ	œ	œ
Ò	Ò	Ò
Ó	Ó	Ó
Ô	Ô	Ô
Õ	Õ	Õ
Ö	Ö	Ö
Ø	Ø	Ø
Œ	Œ	Œ
ù	ù	ù
ú	ú	ú
û	û	û
ü	ü	ü
Ù	Ù	Ù
Ú	Ú	Ú
Û	Û	Û
Ü	Ü	Ü
ÿ	ÿ	ÿ
Ÿ	Ÿ	Ÿ
ç	ç	ç
Ç	Ç	Ç
ñ	ñ	ñ
Ñ	Ñ	Ñ
ß	ß	ß

Table II: Symbols

To get	...type this...	...or this.
HTML, XML and Web		
&	&	&
#	#	#
/	/	/
~	~	~
@	@	@
_	_	_
<	<	<
>	>	>
(	(	(
)	)	)
[	[	[
]	]	]
|				
\	\	\
Other punctuation		
,	,	,
.	.	.
:	:	:
;	;	;
!	!	!
¡	¡	¡
?	?	?
¿	¿	¿
'	'	'
"	"	"
“	“	“
”	”	”
‘	‘	‘
’	’	’
«	«	«
»	»	»
{	{	{
}	}	}

To get	...type this...	...or this.
Math and Science		
=	=	=
+	+	+
-	-	-
x	×	×
÷	÷	÷
±	±	±
¬	¬	¬
%	%	%
‰	‰	‰
°	&176;	°
µ	µ	µ
Currency		
¢	¢	¢
$	$	$
£	£	£
¥	¥	¥
Legal		
™	™	™
©	©	©
®	®	®
Typographical		
*	*	*
†	†	†
¶	¶	¶
§	§	§
º	º	º
ª	ª	ª
•	·	·
Soft hyphen		
Non-breaking space		

COLORS IN HEX

You can choose the color for the background of your page as well as for the text and links. Both Netscape and Internet Explorer understand sixteen predefined color names: Silver, Gray, White, Black, Maroon, Red, Green, Lime, Purple, Fuchsia, Olive, Yellow, Navy, Blue, Teal, and Aqua. Some browsers also recognize Magenta (same as Fuchsia) and Cyan (same as Aqua).

You can also specify any color by giving its red, green, and blue components—in the form of a number between 0 and 255. To make things really complicated, you must specify these components with the hexadecimal equivalent of that number. The table on page 253 gives the corresponding hexadecimal number for each possible value of red, green, or blue.

Check my Web site for several tables of colors, together with their hexadecimal codes: *http://www.cookwood.com/html4_4e/colors.* It was originally designed for my HTML 4 book, but you can use the same system in XML documents.

Finding a Color's RGB Components—in Hex

You can use Photoshop (or another image editing program) to display the red, green, and blue components of the colors you want to use on your page. Then consult the table on page 253 for the hexadecimal equivalents of those components.

To find a color's RGB components:

1. In Photoshop, click one of the color boxes in the toolbox **(Figure D.1)**.
2. In the Color Picker dialog box that appears, choose the desired color.
3. Write down the numbers that appear in the R, G, and B text boxes. These numbers represent the R, G, and B components of the color **(Figure D.2)**.
4. Use the table on the next page to find the hexadecimal equivalents for the numbers found in step 3.
5. Assemble the hexadecimal numbers in the form *#rrggbb*, where *rr* is the hexadecimal equivalent for the red component, *gg* is the hexadecimal equivalent for the green component, and *bb* is the hexadecimal equivalent for the blue component.

Figure D.1 *In Photoshop, click on one of the color boxes in the toolbox to make the Color Picker dialog box appear.*

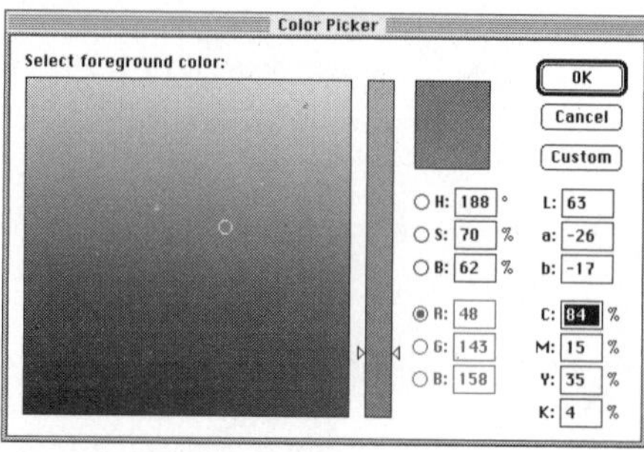

Figure D.2 *Choose the desired color and then jot down the values shown in the R, G, and B text boxes. This color, a teal blue, has an R of 48 (hex=30), a G of 143 (hex=8F), and a B of 158 (hex=9E). Therefore, the hexadecimal equivalent of this color would be #308F9E.*

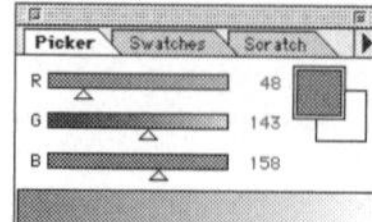

Figure D.3 *You can also use the Picker palette to choose colors and see their RGB components.*

✔ Tip

- You can find instructions for specifying the background color on page 201 and for specifying the text color on pages 217 and 218.

Hexadecimal Equivalents

#	Hex.	#	Hex.	#	Hex.	#	Hex.	#	Hex.	#	Hex.	#	Hex.	#	Hex.
0	00	32	20	64	40	96	60	128	80	160	A0	192	C0	224	E0
1	01	33	21	65	41	97	61	129	81	161	A1	193	C1	225	E1
2	02	34	22	66	42	98	62	130	82	162	A2	194	C2	226	E2
3	03	35	23	67	43	99	63	131	83	163	A3	195	C3	227	E3
4	04	36	24	68	44	100	64	132	84	164	A4	196	C4	228	E4
5	05	37	25	69	45	101	65	133	85	165	A5	197	C5	229	E5
6	06	38	26	70	46	102	66	134	86	166	A6	198	C6	230	E6
7	07	39	27	71	47	103	67	135	87	167	A7	199	C7	231	E7
8	08	40	28	72	48	104	68	136	88	168	A8	200	C8	232	E8
9	09	41	29	73	49	105	69	137	89	169	A9	201	C9	233	E9
10	0A	42	2A	74	4A	106	6A	138	8A	170	AA	202	CA	234	EA
11	0B	43	2B	75	4B	107	6B	139	8B	171	AB	203	CB	235	EB
12	0C	44	2C	76	4C	108	6C	140	8C	172	AC	204	CC	236	EC
13	0D	45	2D	77	4D	109	6D	141	8D	173	AD	205	CD	237	ED
14	0E	46	2E	78	4E	110	6E	142	8E	174	AE	206	CE	238	EE
15	0F	47	2F	79	4F	111	6F	143	8F	175	AF	207	CF	239	EF
16	10	48	30	80	50	112	70	144	90	176	B0	208	D0	240	F0
17	11	49	31	81	51	113	71	145	91	177	B1	209	D1	241	F1
18	12	50	32	82	52	114	72	146	92	178	B2	210	D2	242	F2
19	13	51	33	83	53	115	73	147	93	179	B3	211	D3	243	F3
20	14	52	34	84	54	116	74	148	94	180	B4	212	D4	244	F4
21	15	53	35	85	55	117	75	149	95	181	B5	213	D5	245	F5
22	16	54	36	86	56	118	76	150	96	182	B6	214	D6	246	F6
23	17	55	37	87	57	119	77	151	97	183	B7	215	D7	247	F7
24	18	56	38	88	58	120	78	152	98	184	B8	216	D8	248	F8
25	19	57	39	89	59	121	79	153	99	185	B9	217	D9	249	F9
26	1A	58	3A	90	5A	122	7A	154	9A	186	BA	218	DA	250	FA
27	1B	59	3B	91	5B	123	7B	155	9B	187	BB	219	DB	251	FB
28	1C	60	3C	92	5C	124	7C	156	9C	188	BC	220	DC	252	FC
29	1D	61	3D	93	5D	125	7D	157	9D	189	BD	221	DD	253	FD
30	1E	62	3E	94	5E	126	7E	158	9E	190	BE	222	DE	254	FE
31	1F	63	3F	95	5F	127	7F	159	9F	191	BF	223	DF	255	FF

The Hexadecimal System

"Regular" numbers are based on the base 10 system, that is, there are ten symbols (what we call numbers): 0, 1, 2, 3, 4, 5, 6, 7, 8, and 9. To represent numbers greater than 9, we use a combination of these symbols where the first digit specifies how many *ones*, the second digit (to the left) specifies how many *tens*, and so on.

In the hexadecimal system, which is base 16, there are sixteen symbols: 0, 1, 2, 3, 4, 5, 6, 7, 8, 9, a, b, c, d, e, and f. To represent numbers greater than *f* (which in base 10 we understand as *15*), we again use a combination of symbols. This time the first digit specifies how many ones, but the second digit (again, to the left) specifies how many sixteens. Thus, 10 is one *sixteen* and no *ones*, or simply *16* (as represented in base 10).

In addition to colors, you can use hexadecimal numbers to represent special symbols as shown in the tables on pages 249–250.

INDEX

This has been a bit of a tricky index to create because while everything in the book relates to XML, it's really about six separate topics: XML, DTDs, XML Schema, XSLT, CSS, and XLink and XPointer. I have added context where necessary so that you can tell which part of the book each entry comes from.

All of the elements and some of the attributes defined in XML Schema, XSLT, and XLink and XPointer, as well as the components of DTDs and CSS style sheets, are listed alphabetically for easy reference. I have chosen to leave off the prefix (*xsl:*, *xsd:*, or *xlink:*) so that the elements can be found alphabetized under the main word in their name. For example, you'll find the `xsl:apply-templates` element under the letter *A*, listed as `apply-templates`. Since it is not unheard of to declare a default namespace and then omit the prefixes in documents of each type *(see page 128)*, I hope you won't find this system too confusing.

I think the index is one of the most important parts of a technical book. If you find that an entry is missing, please let me know *(xml@cookwood.com)*. I'll be sure to add it in future printings or editions. You can also find a copy of this index at my Web site *(see page 18)*.

Symbols

Index

Index

M

N

V

W

X

Index

Colophon

I wrote and laid out this book entirely in Adobe FrameMaker 5.5. I could never have done all of the cross references, figure numbering, and especially the index without it. If you're curious about Frame (or indexing), drop me a line. I'm geeky enough to like to talk about it.

I took screen captures with Paint Shop Pro (Windows) and Flash-It (Macintosh) and then cleaned them up with Adobe Photoshop 5.5. I used Adobe Illustrator (version 6!) to create the line drawings. The font faces in this book are various weights of Garamond and Futura.

The photographs used in the examples in this book come from the Adobe Image Library (Animal Life).

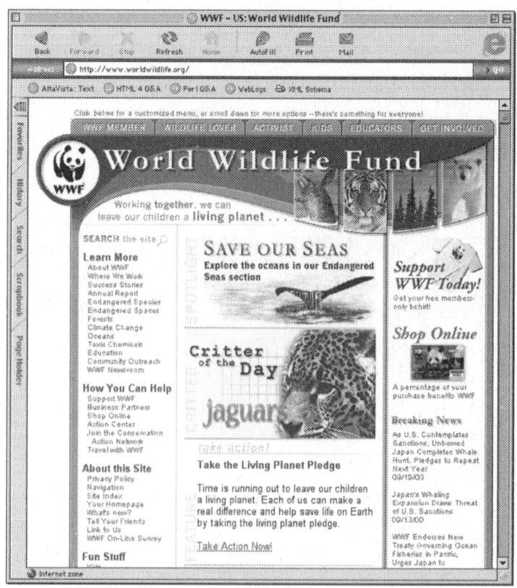

Figure x.1 *The World Wildlife Fund is one of the leading conservation organizations in the fight to save the tiger. You can find their Web site, with more information, at http://www.worldwildlife.org.*

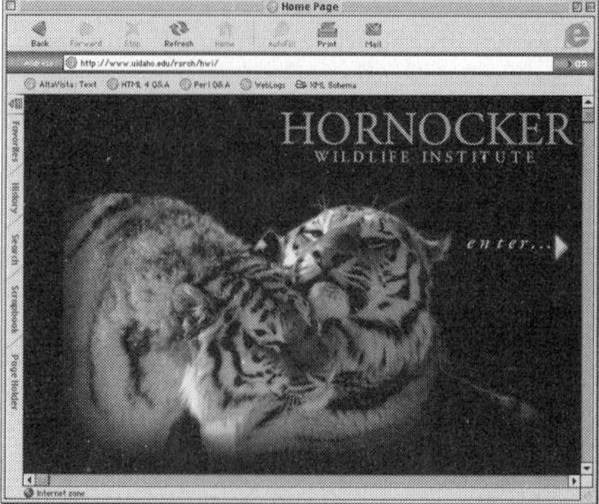

Figure x.2 *You can find more information about the Hornocker Wildlife Institute at their Web site: http://www.uidaho.edu/rsrch/hwi.*

A Note About Tigers

The examples in this book are based on real data, most of which comes from the World Wildlife Fund Web site (with their permission): *http://www.worldwildlife.org*. I also recommend reading *Tigers in the Snow*, written by Peter Matthiessen with photographs by Maurice Hornocker.

The impending extinction of the tiger makes me incredibly sad. It is an extreme example of how we are mistreating the world in which we live. It is up to all of us, conservationists or not, to take care of our planet, any way we can. I urge you to join me in supporting the World Wildlife Fund, the Hornocker Wildlife Institute *(http://www.uidaho.edu/rsrch/hwi/)*, or any other organization that is working to protect the earth and the amazing diversity of creatures who call it home.

There are only 5000 tigers left!

6047